Children's Active Transportation

Children's Active Transportation

Edited by

Richard Larouche

University of Lethbridge
Lethbridge, AB, Canada

ELSEVIER

Elsevier
Radarweg 29, PO Box 211, 1000 AE Amsterdam, Netherlands
The Boulevard, Langford Lane, Kidlington, Oxford OX5 1GB, United Kingdom
50 Hampshire Street, 5th Floor, Cambridge, MA 02139, United States

Notices
Knowledge and best practice in this field are constantly changing. As new research and experience broaden our understanding, changes in research methods, professional practices, or medical treatment may become necessary.

Practitioners and researchers must always rely on their own experience and knowledge in evaluating and using any information, methods, compounds, or experiments described herein. In using such information or methods they should be mindful of their own safety and the safety of others, including parties for whom they have a professional responsibility.

To the fullest extent of the law, neither the Publisher nor the authors, contributors, or editors, assume any liability for any injury and/or damage to persons or property as a matter of products liability, negligence or otherwise, or from any use or operation of any methods, products, instructions, or ideas contained in the material herein.

Library of Congress Cataloging-in-Publication Data
A catalog record for this book is available from the Library of Congress

British Library Cataloguing-in-Publication Data
A catalogue record for this book is available from the British Library

ISBN: 978-0-12-811931-0

Publisher: Jonathan Simpson
Acquisition Editor: Brian Romer
Editorial Project Manager: Charlotte Rowley
Production Project Manager: Anusha Sambamoorthy
Cover Designer: Matthew Limbert

Typeset by TNQ Technologies

Contents

About the Editor

Dr Richard Larouche is an Assistant Professor in the Faculty of Health Sciences at the University of Lethbridge. His research focuses primarily on the benefits and the factors associated with active transportation and physical activity among children and youth. Four years after completing his PhD at the University of Ottawa, he has published over 40 articles in academic journals. He is also regularly involved in knowledge translation projects that aim to make research findings more accessible to practitioners, policy-makers, and the public.

About the Authors

Victoria Egli is a researcher based at the Human Potential Centre, Auckland University of Technology Millennium in Auckland, New Zealand. Victoria comes from a background in public health and community engagement in health and well-being interventions. Her research centres on the obesogenic environment and its impact on children's physical activity and nutrition.

Dr Guy Faulkner is a professor in the School of Kinesiology at the University of British Columbia (since July 2015) and a Canadian Institutes of Health Research–Public Health Agency of Canada (CIHR-PHAC) Chair in Applied Public Health. Broadly, his research has focused on two interrelated themes: the development and evaluation of physical activity interventions, and physical activity and mental health. One focus has been on active school travel and independent mobility among children.

Dr Ariane Ghekiere completed a PhD at the Department of Public Health at Ghent University, Belgium. Her PhD focused on the socioecological correlates of children's cycling for transportation in Flanders. Currently she is a volunteer scientist at Ghent University and works for the Flemish Government on projects aiming to measure and improve the quality of healthcare organizations with the use of quality indicators.

Dr Cameron Gordon holds a PhD in economics and works in the areas of transport project finance, public–private partnerships, urban public transport, health and social impacts of transport policy and investment, and evaluation methods of economic and noneconomic impacts of transport. Dr Gordon holds concurrent appointments as a principal investigator with the Social Policy Simulation Center of the City University of New York and as Adjunct Associate Professor of Economics with the University of Canberra, Centre for Research and Action in Public Health. Dr Gordon has also worked for the US Congress Joint Committee on Taxation, the US Department of Defense–US Army Corps of Engineers, the US Advisory Commission on Intergovernmental Relations, the US National Academy of Sciences–Board of Infrastructure and the Constructed Environment, and the New York City Department of Environmental Protection, Bureau of Water Supply and Municipal Water Finance Authority.

Dr Erica Hinckson is currently the Head of School of Sport and Recreation at Auckland University of Technology, Auckland, New Zealand. She is focused on understanding the associations, patterns, and causes and effects of physical activity and sedentary behaviour on health across the lifespan. She studies these relationships within the context of the physical environment. She has been involved in large national and regional projects (e.g., School Travel Plan Programme, Healthy Eating–Healthy Action) and international projects (e.g., International Physical Activity and Environment Network–Adolescents, IPEN). She is the chair of the International Council of Environment and Physical Activity and inaugural member of Citizen Science Global Network.

Dr Andy Hong is currently a Postdoctoral Research and Teaching Fellow at the University of British Columbia. Andy completed his PhD at the University of Southern California and his graduate and undergraduate studies at the University of Washington. His research interests lie at the nexus of data science, geography and public health, particularly in the development of planetary-scale urban health and burden of disease metrics, leveraging big data and spatial cloud computing.

Erika Ikeda began her academic research journey at Auckland University of Technology in New Zealand. She has a passion for research on children's physical activity and active travel. She is currently pursuing a PhD on associations between environmental attributes and children's active travel to school in relation to the Neighbourhoods for Active Kids project.

Dr Jason A. Mendoza is Associate Professor of Pediatrics at the University of Washington, Investigator at the Seattle Children's Research Institute and Associate Director for Minority Health and Health Disparities at the Fred Hutch/University of Washington Cancer Consortium. His research seeks to eliminate inequities in childhood physical activity and nutrition outcomes among racial/ethnic minorities and socioeconomically disadvantaged populations through innovative behavioural interventions and policies in schools, communities and clinical settings. His recent projects focus on Safe Routes to School, wearable physical activity trackers (e.g., Fitbit), food insecurity (hunger) and managing screen time/television viewing.

Dr Lieze Mertens is a postdoctoral researcher funded by the Research Foundation Flanders in the Department of Movement and Sports Sciences at Ghent University, Belgium. She has expertise in the association between the physical environment and active transportation. Currently, she is working on a project aiming to identify critical environmental street characteristics influencing the safety and appeal for active transportation by manipulations of virtual reality three-dimensional images.

Dr Adewale L. Oyeyemi is a physiotherapist and a senior lecturer at the College of Medical Sciences, University of Maiduguri, Nigeria. Adewale's research interests are focused on understanding the social and environmental correlates and determinants of health, active living and the prevention of chronic noncommunicable diseases in low- and middle-income countries. He has published many peer review articles on active living and was part of the writing group and author on the second Lancet Series on physical activity in 2016.

Negin A. Riazi is a doctoral student in the School of Kinesiology, University of British Columbia. Her research on children's physical activity has two main foci: children's independent mobility and population-level physical activity initiatives and policy-level interventions. She has been a collaborator in several research projects focused on children's independent mobility, active transportation and outdoor play and in the knowledge translation of the Canadian 24-Hour Movement Guidelines for Children and Youth (5–17) and the Early Years (0–4 years).

Dr Shannon Sahlqvist is a senior lecturer in the Institute for Physical Activity and Nutrition (IPAN), School of Exercise and Nutrition Sciences, Deakin University, Geelong, Australia. Dr Sahlqvist's program of work focuses on population approaches to physical activity promotion. She has specific expertise in promoting walking and cycling for transport and has been involved in several large scale projects, both in the United Kingdom and Australia, to understand how best to encourage active travel among children and adults. Dr Sahlqvist has published over 30 peer-reviewed articles.

Dr Karl Saidla completed a PhD at the University of Ottawa (Human Kinetics) concerning politics and public policy related to the promotion of walking, cycling and public transit use in Helsinki, Finland, and Ottawa, Canada. Previously, he served as a public policy analyst with the Heart and Stroke Foundation of Canada, where his work focussed on public policies related to active transportation, physical activity, healthy community design and healthy living. He serves in several capacities as a volunteer and advocate in support of active transportation, particularly at the local level in Chelsea, Quebec.

Dr Olga L. Sarmiento is a professor in the School of Medicine at Universidad de los Andes (Bogota, Colombia). Her research interests include urban health, healthy behaviours and the built environment among children and adults in Latin America. Dr Sarmiento is involved in multiple international studies including the Urban Health in Latin America project (SALURBAL), the International Physical Activity and Environment Network (IPEN), The International Study of Childhood Obesity, Lifestyle and the Environment (ISCOLE) the Stanford–Colombia Collaboratory on Chronic Disease (S-C3). Dr Sarmiento received the Honorary Distinction from The National Institute of Sports in Colombia (Coldeportes Nacional) for her academic work towards promoting healthy behaviours in Colombia, and she coordinates the physical activity component of the National Nutrition Survey of Colombia (ENSIN).

Dr Melody Smith is Associate Professor and Sir Charles Hercus Research Fellow at the University of Auckland. Her research involves understanding relationships between environments and health, with a particular focus on physical activity and active travel. Aspirations for neighbourhoods where children can be independently mobile, where people can get around safely by walking and cycling and where social and physical well-being is prioritized and facilitated are key drivers of Melody's work. Her research can be found at https://www.researchgate.net/profile/Melody_Oliver.

Dr Orion T. Stewart is a program evaluator at the University of California Davis Institute for Population Health Improvement. His work focuses on assessing the built environment's impact on health-related behaviours, such as physical activity and diet. He uses this knowledge to help design and study interventions aimed at promoting and supporting healthy behaviours, including Safe Routes to School. Orion holds a Master of Urban Planning and a PhD in Epidemiology from the University of Washington.

Dr Tom Stewart is a research fellow at the Human Potential Centre, located at Auckland University of Technology, New Zealand. His research is broadly based around physical activity epidemiology, understanding the environmental determinants of health and finding preventative solutions for reducing the prevalence of obesity and other chronic diseases. His recent interests include the application of machine learning to improve the measurement of 24-h movement behaviours.

Dr Anna Timperio is an Alfred Deakin Professor in the Institute for Physical Activity and Nutrition (IPAN), School of Exercise and Nutrition Sciences at Deakin University. Her research focuses on understanding contextual influences on physical activity and sedentary behaviour among children and youth, including the built environment. She has particular interests in active transportation, measurement of physical activity and understanding changes in behaviour over key transition periods. She has published over 170 peer-reviewed articles and 6 book chapters in these and related areas.

Dr Paul Tranter is a geographer at UNSW Canberra (the Australian Defence Force Academy), where his research focuses on two critical and related issues for modern cities: children's well-being and the dominance of speed and mobility in urban planning and society. In 2011, Paul co-authored Children and their Urban Environment: Changing Worlds, with Claire Freeman, placing children's well-being within the context of global concerns about health and well-being for all citizens. The book argues that child-centred adaptations to cities need to be made if the world is to have a sustainable future. Paul's research demonstrates that child-friendly modes (walking, cycling and public transport) are also the modes that (paradoxically) reduce time pressure for urban residents. He is currently working, with Dr Rodney Tolley, on a new book to be published by Elsevier in 2019 with the working title of Slowing City Transportation: Creating healthier places to live, work and play.

Dr Jenny Veitch is a senior research fellow, supported by a National Heart Foundation of Australia Future Leader Fellowship, in the Institute for Physical Activity and Nutrition (IPAN), School of Exercise and Nutrition Sciences, Deakin University, Melbourne, Australia. Her research aims to better understand how aspects of the neighbourhood built and social environment may influence physical activity across the lifespan. Dr Veitch has a particular research focus on understanding how parks and public open spaces can be designed to encourage people of all ages to engage in physical activity.

Dr Christine Voss is a researcher at BC Children's Hospital and the University of British Columbia. Her research is focused on physical activity and health in children, with a particular focus on measuring this complex behaviour using state-of-the-art technologies. She has published over 47 peer-reviewed articles and contributed to over 80 conference presentations.

Preface

Richard Larouche

> *With only a handbrake and a handful of birthdays between the passenger's seat and the driver's seat, it may be unrealistic to expect the chauffeured children of today to become the ambulant adults of tomorrow.*
>
> **Dr Ian Roberts**[1]

Behaviours that have the potential to benefit public health, the environment and the economy are scarce. This book makes the case that active transportation—that is, *the use of non-motorized travel modes such as walking and cycling*—is one such behaviour. Active transportation can yield a myriad of health benefits, including reduced risk of cardiovascular and lung diseases and premature death.[2] It is also a good way for children to spend time outside, discover their neighbourhood, meet friends and interact with nature along the way.[3] Furthermore, it may help reduce stress and enhance happiness and well-being.[4]

Worldwide, the transportation sector accounts for about 23% of greenhouse gas emissions and is therefore one of the greatest contributors to climate change.[5] Conversely, replacing car trips by active transportation can help minimize transportation-related emissions.[6] A greater uptake of active transportation could also yield important economic benefits such as reduced traffic congestion and healthcare expenditures to name only a few. What's more, these benefits may be interrelated, and this may create a virtuous cycle.

Yet, few adults wake up in the morning and wonder how they will get to their workplace. This is normal because travel behaviours are habitual in nature.[7,8] When someone uses a given travel mode to get to a given destination, it becomes a routine that is followed almost automatically. In other words, one does not have to engage in a deliberate decision-making process, weighting the pros and cons of different alternatives. In general, the stronger the habit, the harder it is to change. As emphasized by the quote at the beginning of this chapter, it is reasonable to expect that children who are driven around everywhere will develop the habit of driving later in life. As such, it is critical to encourage children to develop a habit of engaging in active transportation.

Unfortunately, as highlighted in Chapter 4, more and more children travel to school by car. Using nationally representative surveys, many authors have reported a decline in the percentage of children who engage in active transportation to and from school over the last few decades. For example, data from the US National Household Travel Survey indicate that the proportion of children walking or cycling to school decreased from 47.7% in 1969 to 12.7% in 2009![9] Declines in active transportation have been observed in many other high-income countries as well as in some developing countries.

If active transportation has decreased over time, this is clearly not because children prefer to be driven. When asked how they would like to travel to and from school, the majority of children express a preference for active modes such as walking and cycling.[10–12] For example, in a survey of about 1000 children in the city of Toronto, we found that only 2%–3% of children cycled to or from school, but about 40% would prefer to do so if they were given the choice.[10] Unlike many adults, children do not merely see active transportation as a way to get from point A to point B. Children may also enjoy the opportunity to spend time outside with their parents and friends and even the opportunity '*to say hello to a kitty or a pup and sing along with the birds*', as a child interviewed in a previous study emphasized.[13]

Paradoxically, parental concerns about road traffic and 'stranger danger' can lead parents to drive their child to and from school and other places, and this results in increased traffic exposure for those children who walk or bike, creating a vicious circle. Instead of walking, cycling and playing in local streets, children are increasingly chauffeured to distant locations across the city to attend school, sport and other activities organized by adults.[14,15] Parents are spending an increasing amount of time playing the role of taxi drivers, and many children primarily experiment their neighbourhood as car passengers and may be deprived of their right to play although it is emphasized in the United Nations' Convention on the Rights of the Child.[16]

In parallel, today's children are granted less independent mobility than their parents or grandparents had at the same age. Independent mobility refers to *children's freedom to move around in public space without adult supervision*. In their seminal study on this topic, Hillman et al.[17] reported that the percentage of 7- and 8-year-old British children who were allowed to go to school without adult supervision decreased from 80% to 9% between 1971 and 1990. This is unfortunate because children who have greater independent mobility are more likely to engage in active transportation, and they are more physically active. Moreover, independent mobility contributes to children's resilience and cognitive development.

For all these reasons, this book focuses on children's travel behaviour. The book is divided into three main sections focusing on the following questions: (1) what are the benefits of active transportation?; (2) why are some children engaging in active transportation and other not?; and (3) how can we encourage more children to engage in active transportation? The final section summarizes the strengths and limitations of many interventions that have been implemented to promote active transportation in different jurisdictions. It also provides clear recommendations for policy-makers, practitioners and researchers.

Ensuring that many neighbourhood destinations are safely and conveniently accessible by walking and cycling may benefit children and adults alike. It is particularly important for older adults and those who have a disability. As Enrique Peñalosa, mayor of Bogotá (Colombia), famously said: '*If we can build a successful city for children we will have a successful city for all people*'.[18]

This book is written for a broad audience, including, among others, policy-makers, public health practitioners, land use and transportation planners, advocates, students and researchers. As such, chapter authors have made great effort to write in a simple style while nevertheless staying true to the science. In particular, Chapter 6 may be particularly useful for readers who have less experience in research who may benefit the most from a clear explanation of the theoretical model that underpins Section 2 of the book and from an accessible description of the type of studies that informed our work. Furthermore, definitions for technical terms are available in the glossary of terms at the end of the book and links to open access publications are provided in the reference list of each chapter.

This book is the fruit of a collaborative effort of researchers from Australia, Belgium, Canada, Colombia, New Zealand, Nigeria and the United States. Chapter authors have expertise in diverse fields of research, including economics, environmental sciences, geography, kinesiology, political science, public health and urban planning. I am grateful for this collaboration between scholars from different disciplines which, I believe, has enhanced the quality of the book. I hope that this book will help stimulate additional efforts to create more child-friendly cities where children can reap the benefits of active transportation, and society as a whole can benefit from healthier and more sustainable lifestyles.

References

1. Roberts I. Walking to school has future benefits. *BMJ* 1995;**312**:1229.
2. Larouche R. The environmental and population health benefits of active transport: a review. In: Liu G, editor. *Greenhouse gases—emissions, measurement and management*. Rijeka, Croatia: InTech; 2012. p. 413–40. Available from: http://cdn.intechopen.com/pdfs/32358/InTech-The_environmental_and_population_health_benefits_of_active_transport_a_review.pdf.
3. Fusco C, Moola F, Faulkner G, Buliung R, Richichi V. Toward an understanding of children's perceptions of their transport geographies: (non)active school travel and visual representations of the built environment. *J Transp Geogr* 2012;**20**(1):62–70.
4. Ramanathan S, O'Brien C, Faulkner G, Stone M. Happiness in motion: emotions, well-being and active school travel. *J Sch Health* 2014;**84**(8):516–23.
5. International Transport Forum. *Reducing transport greenhouse gas emissions: trends and data 2010*. Leipzig, Germany: International Transport Forum; 2010. Available from: http://www.internationaltransportforum.org/Pub/pdf/10GHGTrends.pdf.
6. Marshall JD, Wilson RD, Meyer KL, et al. Vehicle emissions during children's school commuting: impacts of education policy. *Environ Sci Technol* 2010;**44**(5):1537–43.
7. Aarts H, Verplanken B, van Knippenberg A. Predicting behavior from actions in the past: repeated decision making or a matter of habit? *J Appl Soc Psychol* 1998;**28**(15):1355–74.
8. Gardner B, Abraham C. Psychological correlates of car use: a meta-analysis. *Transp Res Part F* 2008;**11**(4):300–11.
9. McDonald NC, Brown AL, Marchetti LM, Pedroso MS. U.S. school travel, 2009: an assessment of trends. *Am J Prev Med* 2011;**41**(2):146–51.
10. Larouche R, Stone M, Buliung RN, Faulkner G. "I'd rather bike to school!": profiling children who would prefer to cycle to school. *J Transp Health* 2016;**3**(3):377–85.
11. Lorenc T, Brunton G, Oliver S, Oliver K, Oakley A. Attitudes to walking and cycling among children, young people and parents: a systematic review. *J Epidemiol Community Health* 2008;**62**:852–7.

12. Shaw B, Bicket M, Elliot B, Fagan-Watson B, Mocca E, Hillman M. *Children's independent mobility: an international comparison and recommendations for action*. London, UK: Policy Studies Institute; 2015. Available from: http://www.psi.org.uk/docs/7350_PSI_Report_CIM_final.pdf.
13. O'Brien C. Sustainable happiness and the trip to school. *World Transp Pol Pract* 2008;**14**(1):15–26.
14. Fotel T, Thomsen TU. The surveillance of children's mobility. *Surveill Soc* 2004;**1**(4):535–54. Available from: https://ojs.library.queensu.ca/index.php/surveillance-and-society/article/view/3335/3297.
15. Hjorthol R, Fyhri A. Do organized leisure activities for children encourage car-use? *Transp Res Part A* 2009;**43**(2):209–18.
16. United Nations. *Convention on the rights of the child*. New York, NY: United Nations; 1989. Available from: http://www.ohchr.org/EN/ProfessionalInterest/Pages/CRC.aspx.
17. Hillman M, Adams J, Whitelegg J. *One false move: a study of children's independent mobility*. London, UK: PSI Publishing; 1990. Available from: http://john-adams.co.uk/wp-content/uploads/2007/11/one%20false%20move.pdf.
18. Peñalosa E, Ives S. *The politics of happiness*. Bainbridge Island, WA: YES! Magazine; 2004. Available from: http://www.yesmagazine.org/issues/finding-courage/the-politics-of-happiness.

Public Health Benefits of Active Transportation

1

Christine Voss
Department of Pediatrics, University of British Columbia, Vancouver, BC, Canada

Walking is man's best medicine.

Hippocrates

Chapter Outline

1.1 Introduction

Ironically, the early landmark research studies from the 1950s that first alerted us to the critical importance of physical activity (PA) for health centred around active transportation (AT); one study identified a lower incidence of heart disease in men who used AT as part of their occupation compared with their more sedentary counterparts, such as bus conductors versus bus drivers and mail carriers versus telephonist.[1] Since then, AT has been largely ignored as a public health priority. Only in recent years has the scientific evidence on the link between AT and health become so overwhelmingly compelling that AT (walking and cycling, specifically) is now frequently featured in advocacy reports as a strategy to combat the significant global chronic disease burden.[2,3]

Children's Active Transportation. https://doi.org/10.1016/B978-0-12-811931-0.00001-6

This chapter will review the scientific evidence on the link between AT and health in children and adolescents, with particular emphasis on its meaningful contribution to PA levels. Direct links between AT and physical health outcomes, such as cardiorespiratory fitness, weight status and cardiometabolic risk factors, will also be reviewed. The chapter will conclude with recommendations for policy and practice implementation and future research in this important public health area.

1.2 Active Transportation and Physical Activity

PA is recognized as one of the most important health behaviours; in children and adolescents, the benefits of regular PA include cardiovascular and metabolic health, healthy bone and muscle development, maintenance of healthy body weight, and mental well-being.[4] In order to optimize these health outcomes, the World Health Organization recommends that children and adolescents aged 5–17 years engage in at least 60 min of moderate-to-vigorous PA (MVPA) every day.[5] In this context, it is important to note that the technical definition of PA is 'any bodily movement produced by skeletal muscles that results in energy expenditure'.[6] Guidelines typically call for activities of moderate intensity or higher, which refers to any activities that slightly increase the heart rate and breathing, such as brisk walking. This is regardless of the purpose of the activity, meaning that leisure activities and exercise contribute to daily activity goals, as do occupational labour and AT. Despite our understanding of the importance of PA for health, we are currently experiencing a global physical inactivity crisis with estimates suggesting that fewer than 1 in 5 children worldwide achieve guidelines.[7]

In light of the alarmingly low PA levels in children, AT in children and adolescents has been studied extensively over the last 2 decades. Several comprehensive review articles that vary in scope have critically evaluated and summarized the numerous original research articles on this topic.[8–13] Original research articles varied widely in terms of study design[a] (predominantly cross-sectional, few longitudinal or experimental), study setting (predominantly North America, Europe and Australia, few others), measures of PA (predominantly objective such as accelerometers and pedometers, fewer self-report), sample size and age group. Regardless of these differences, approximately 3 out of 4 studies reported that children and/or adolescents who used AT were significantly more active than those using passive transportation,[14–65] with the remainder of articles finding no association.[66–80] No study reported that children who used AT were less active. A positive association was slightly more common when objective measures of PA were used compared with self-report tools. This is not surprising because of the known recall error in younger children and the limitations of self-report tools to adequately capture dose and volume of PA, especially of non-organized activities such as walking.

[a] Different types of study designs are described in greater detail in Chapter 6.

1.2.1 How Active Transportation Causes Greater Physical Activity Levels

Walking, cycling and other types of 'rolling' (i.e., scooter) for transportation meets the technical definition of PA—namely, 'any bodily movement produced by skeletal muscles that results in energy expenditure'[6]—and can therefore be viewed as direct sources of PA. This concept is corroborated by several original research articles whose research methodologies allowed researchers to specifically assess travel-related PA. Objective devices timestamp PA data, which allows researchers to describe PA patterns at specific times of the day. In these studies, the PA levels were consistently higher during school travel windows in active travellers compared with passive travellers[19,23,26,43,47,51,52,54,63,76] (Fig. 1.1).

Some of these studies quantified how many minutes of MVPA were achieved directly from walking to and from school.[20,22,23,34,37,43,47,48,51,52,54,76] These results were summarized in a meta-analysis, which found that walking to school provided approximately 17 minutes of MVPA per day in elementary school students and 14 minutes in high school students; this equated to approximately 23% and 36% of the total daily PA in elementary and high school students, respectively.[13] The findings from this meta-analysis are important as they highlight the increasing importance of AT as a source of PA in adolescents, whose overall PA levels drop drastically during adolescence.[81] The availability of global positioning system trackers has further enabled researchers in recent years to more accurately quantify PA levels from school travel, yielding similar and consistent results.[22,34,82,83]

Further evidence for AT being a direct source of PA is provided by several studies that have reported a 'dose–response relationship'. Some studies found that the further the children travelled between home and school, the more the PA was accrued.[36,47,48,63,82] Similarly, other studies reported positive associations between the number of active trips and PA.[14,24,30,31]

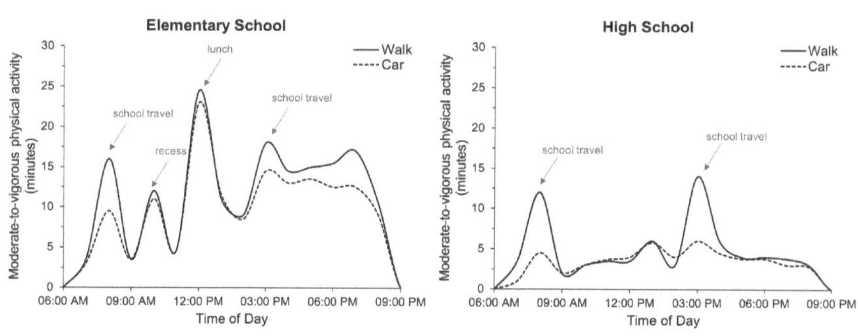

Figure 1.1 Schematic of hourly patterns of moderate-to-vigorous physical activity (PA) in elementary and high school students according to school travel mode. Note the between-mode difference in PA during school travel windows (8–9 a.m. and 3–4 p.m.), particularly in high school students, and the higher overall PA in elementary students, including at recess and after school. Figures are based on published accelerometry data,[19,23] adapted for illustration purposes.

Even more compellingly, a handful of studies have assessed whether participation in an AT intervention would directly cause significantly higher PA levels. This included several US studies that evaluated 'walking school bus' programs (see Chapter 15 for more details). Although these studies varied in terms of study designs, follow-up duration and sample size, all found increased PA in those who participated in the program.[30,35,44,55] Another school-based intervention that included both educational lessons and goal-setting techniques in Scotland was not effective, but may have at least attenuated expected seasonal declines in PA levels in the intervention group compared with the control group.[76]

In summary, there are strong objective data on (1) increased PA during school travel windows in those travelling by active modes, (2) dose–response relationships between volume of AT and PA and (3) positive effects of AT interventions on PA levels. Collectively, the current evidence base undoubtedly cements the assertion that AT is a direct and important source of PA in children and adolescents.

1.2.2 Is It All About School Travel?

The overwhelming majority of original research studies have focused solely on school travel. This is unsurprising, given that the school trip is one of the most consistent and routine transportation behaviours that children and adolescents partake in. Incidentally, these characteristics also make school transportation a relatively easy and therefore attractive construct to measure in research because even young children can reliably recall consistent and routine behaviours.

However, from the body of evidence on school travel evolved another theory that AT to school also facilitates greater PA outside of the school trip. Positive associations between AT to school and PA in the afternoon and the evening have been reported.[15,19,38,56,84] Findings regarding weekend PA are more conflicting, with some[16,20,47,56] but not all[14,19,54,63] studies reporting such associations. Studies that included self-report methods to assess type of PA participation found that those who reported active school transportation were more likely to participate in sport[45] or structured activities.[36] On the contrary, PA levels while at school (i.e., during lunch or recess) tended to be no different between those using active versus passive transportation.[19,38,54] Furthermore, some studies have suggested that children who use AT to school are also more likely to use AT to get to other destinations.[56,80,85]

While several studies have reported on associations between PA and any AT (i.e., school and other combined),[16,53,65,84,86] very few studies have focussed specifically on destinations other than school, such as a friend's house or the park, and all of these studies reported greater levels of PA in those using AT.[28,56,87] Travel to nonschool destinations is often studied in the context of 'independent mobility'—a concept that refers to the ability of children and adolescents to move around their neighbourhood without adult accompaniment.[88] Independent mobility is associated with PA, where children with greater independent mobility tend to spend more time playing outside[12] and are more likely to engage in AT—a notion that is discussed in greater detail in Chapter 5.

1.2.3 Who Benefits the Most?

Significant associations between AT and PA levels are more commonly found in adolescents compared with younger children. Although few studies failed to document an association between active school travel and objectively measured PA, most studies that did so were conducted in children of elementary school age.[66,70,73,74,77] Some studies that included a wider age range found that positive associations between AT to school and PA were stronger in older versus younger study participants.[14,16,25]

There are a number of possible explanations for this; first, elementary school children usually live closer to school than high school students, and it is possible that the short school trip distance is insufficient to generate meaningful levels of PA for many children. Next, younger children tend to be substantially more physically active overall compared with their older counterparts.[81] Therefore, any PA from the school trip may be relatively trivial compared with the larger volumes of PA that are accrued over the course of the day in younger children. This is supported by findings from a recent meta-analysis that quantified PA from school travel and in relation to total daily PA; although PA from travel was higher in younger children compared with high school students (17 vs. 14 minutes), when expressed relative to total PA, the proportion was notably lower in younger than in older students (23% vs. 36%).[13] Associations with sex are less consistent, with some studies reporting that associations between AT to school and PA are stronger in females,[14,16,24] whereas other studies reported the opposite.[18,84] These inconsistent findings are likely explained by differences in study settings and design. As females are generally less active than males,[7] AT could theoretically account for a greater proportion of their total PA. Yet, girls are typically granted less independent mobility (see Chapter 5), which could deprive them of an important opportunity to be active.

In summary, AT to school is a source of PA in all children, but it is of increasing importance in those at risk of low PA levels, namely adolescents, potentially females and all those who generally spend much of their free time in sedentary pursuits.

1.2.4 Are All Trips Equal?

Undoubtedly, active trips of longer distance and duration provide proportionately more PA.[36,47,48,63,82] Elementary schools usually have smaller catchment areas and thus shorter average distances between home and school, which is how some explain that associations between AT to school and PA tend to be weaker in younger children. Nevertheless, given the linear nature of the dose–response between distance and PA (i.e., some is better than none) and coupled with the possibility that AT may have an important role to play in enhancing independent mobility in children, no active trip should be deemed trivial or too short.

Discerning whether AT mode matters in relation to PA is difficult because of the low prevalence of cycling in most countries. In addition, accelerometers and pedometers are limited in their ability to accurately quantify PA from riding a bicycle, which further complicates estimating differences in PA between walking and cycling. Interestingly, a small number of studies that used objective measures of PA identified that using public transit to school can yield meaningful PA, and at comparable rates to walking.[47,82,89] Not all studies, however, registered such convincing results for public transit/bus use,[31,63] highlighting that the walking distance as part of such a trip plays an important role in this association.

1.3 Active Transportation and Physical Health

Physical health refers to a measurable health status or health outcome. The current chapter will mainly focus on physical health outcomes that have been identified as public health priorities due to their well-documented associations with long-term health, including cardiorespiratory fitness and weight status. While children and adolescents do not typically present with endpoints such as heart disease and stroke, the prevalence of young individuals with cardiovascular risk factors is alarming,[90] and these individuals are likely to maintain their poor physical health status as adults.[91] It is of note in this context that PA itself is related to physical health,[4] and any associations that are reported between AT and physical health are likely, at least in part, attributable to greater PA levels that arise from AT.

1.3.1 Cardiorespiratory Fitness

Cardiorespiratory fitness is an indication of how well the heart, lungs and muscles work together to produce prolonged physical effort. Although cardiorespiratory fitness is partially predetermined by our genes, it is also the product of our health behaviours. In children, there is strong evidence that better cardiorespiratory fitness is linked to better cardiovascular and metabolic health, more favourable body composition and better mental well-being,[4,92] making it a public health priority.

A number of studies have assessed cardiorespiratory fitness in relation to AT, which are also summarized in two review articles.[11,93] Although much less research exists on this topic compared with PA, cross-sectional studies consistently describe that those who used AT to school also had significantly greater levels of cardiorespiratory fitness.[18,21,64,67,94–97] Longitudinal studies found that adolescents who started to cycle to school over a 6-year follow-up period had significantly greater cardiorespiratory fitness compared with noncyclists.[68,70,98] In one study, participants who started cycling to school as a result of a 12-week intervention were significantly fitter than those who did not start to cycle,[99] whereas another 6-month intervention study found no beneficial effects on cardiorespiratory fitness.[100] These discrepant findings may be due to differences in intervention design and implementation, with the more effective study providing a more intense 'dose' (biweekly vs. monthly sessions over 3 months vs. 6 months). Regardless, all reviewed studies used a variety of methods to assess cardiorespiratory fitness, including both running tests[64,94–97,100,101] and cycle ergometers,[18,21,67,68,70,99] meaning it is unlikely that the assessment method may have influenced the findings.

However, on closer inspection of these studies, it is clear that the beneficial associations with cardiorespiratory fitness are evident only for cycling to school; only few studies were able to analyse walkers and cyclists separately, but almost all found that only the cyclists had better fitness compared with passive transport users,[18,21,67,70] with only one study finding the same for walkers.[64]

In order to stimulate the cardiorespiratory system to bring about improvements, a certain PA intensity is required; riding a bicycle for commuting is thought to be of adequate intensity even in young individuals,[102] which would explain the findings on cycling to school. There is only very sparse information on the role of sex on the association between AT and cardiorespiratory fitness, with a handful of studies reporting that associations were stronger in females than in males who cycle to school.[64,96] Although more scientific data are needed to confirm this theory, it is plausible that females benefit more from cycling to school given the fact that they tend to have lower PA and cardiorespiratory fitness than males[103]; thus, routine cycling trips may have a greater relative contribution to health in adolescent females.

1.3.2 Body Weight and Composition

Obesity, or excess adiposity (fat tissue), is linked to a whole host of physical and mental health issues during childhood,[104] and an increased risk of morbidity and mortality in adulthood.[105] Troublingly, rates of obesity in children and adolescents have risen substantially worldwide in recent decades,[106] making it a top public health priority.

Expectedly, body weight is commonly studied in relation to AT in children and adolescents, and nearly all review articles on AT included it as an outcome.[8–12,93] Results are however conflicting, with approximately half of the original research studies finding that AT use was associated with a more favourable body weight than passive commuting,[29,30,36,38,43,49,71,73,86,107–121] while the other half of studies found no such association.[19,21,26,27,35,51,52,54,61,64,66,68,69,74,77,95,96,98,99,122–128] It is unclear why the studies yielded such conflicting results, with varying results found across study populations and study designs, including superior longitudinal[29,49,51,66,68,74,98,109,115,118,122,128] and experimental study designs.[30,35,99]

The vast majority of studies utilized body mass index (BMI) or BMI-derived weight status classifications as the measure of body weight. This is a relatively crude proxy for body composition which is prone to misclassify muscular individuals as overweight or obese, although this may be less of a concern in children compared with adults. Waist circumference measurements can offer more relevant insight into abdominal body fat distribution and is considered a cardiometabolic risk factor in its own right, but studies that used this outcome yielded equally conflicting results.[43,68,86,96,98,113,116,119] A number of studies measured skinfold thickness to estimate percent body fat,[21,30,36,43,49,68,77,86,98,120,126] again with mixed results. The only two studies that used a direct imaging modality to objectively measure body composition (dual energy X-ray absorptiometry (DXA)) found no association between AT and body composition.[66,74]

Travel mode also appeared to bear small relevance with regard to body weight, with conflicting results also found in studies that assessed cycling,[21,64,68,86,96,98,99,117,127] suggesting that the greater exercise intensity of cycling compared with walking may not be sufficient in itself to provide protective effects for a healthy body weight.

In summary, while a number of studies found that AT is linked with more favourable body weight, others did not. As such, it is advisable to continue measuring body weight and composition in relation to AT in children and adolescents, but it should not be used as a primary health outcome based on which the efficacy of AT initiatives are judged.

1.3.3 Cardiometabolic Risk Factors

Cardiometabolic risk factors is a term that refers to markers that are related to the health status of the cardiovascular system or metabolism, such as blood pressure, abdominal adiposity or blood levels of glucose, cholesterol and triglycerides. When several of these factors are in an abnormal state, this is often referred to as cardiovascular risk factor clustering or metabolic syndrome. In adults, abnormal cardiometabolic risk profiles are linked with an increased risk for type 2 diabetes and cardiovascular disease[129]; in children, abnormal risk profiles during childhood track into adulthood,[91] thereby increasing the risk for chronic diseases in the future.[130] PA is related to better cardiometabolic risk profiles in children and adolescents,[131] but relatively few studies have assessed this in direct relation to AT.

Large-scale cross-sectional studies in younger children (≤12 years of age) yielded conflicting results; one study found that individuals who regularly walked to school had better cholesterol profiles than passive commuters, but no such patterns were found for triglycerides, glucose or blood pressure.[119] Other studies found no associations between AT and a composite cardiometabolic risk score[124] or with blood pressure.[120] Another study even reported higher blood pressure in active commuters, although it is of note that passive travellers in this study also reported to spend nearly double the amount of time in sports, which could have influenced the results.[126]

Cross-sectional studies in adolescents are more promising; one large study of a sample of nearly 3000 adolescents in whom cycling to school was common (25%) found that females were less likely to have metabolic syndrome if they regularly cycled to and from school compared with those that did not cycle; however, the same pattern was not observed in males.[96] A study of over 1000 adolescents identified that those who walked more than 5 hours/week or biked more than 1 hour/week had better blood lipid profiles than those who walked or biked less.[86]

There are currently very few longitudinal and intervention studies which allow for some insight into the potential causal relationship between AT and cardiometabolic health. One analysis found that individuals who had switched from passive travel to cycling to school at a 6-year follow-up time point had better blood lipid profiles, better blood glucose metabolism and a better composite cardiometabolic risk score.[68] In contrast, another study using similar methodologies reported no such findings over time.[98] In one small randomized controlled trial of children who participated in an 8-week cycling-to-school intervention, children in the intervention group significantly improved their composite cardiometabolic risk score compared with the control group.[117]

In summary, there is still relatively scarce but promising evidence that AT may be related to better cardiometabolic risk factor profiles in children and adolescents. Although some studies have shown some associations with walking, it appears that the greatest gains for improved cardiometabolic health are likely made by the greater exercise intensity that is brought about by cycling. More longitudinal and intervention studies are warranted to confirm this postulate.

1.3.4 Other Physical Health Outcomes

The growing years are a critical period for bone mass and strength, with weight-bearing PA being of critical importance during this time.[132] In the context of AT, however, this topic has been scarcely studied. There are only two studies that assessed whether AT to school was related to bone health in children, and although both used a longitudinal study design and objective imaging modalities (DXA), neither study found a significant association.[66,74] This may suggest that AT—and in particular cycling as a non–weight-bearing activity—plays a relatively trivial role in bone development compared with other weight-bearing activities that children engage in.

Muscular fitness is a collective term that refers to strength, power and endurance produced by a muscle or muscle group. There is compelling evidence that greater muscular fitness in children and adolescents is strongly related to more favourable adiposity, cardiometabolic risk factor profiles, bone health, self-esteem and sport competence.[133] Yet, few studies have investigated muscular fitness in relation to AT. One study found that cyclists performed significantly better in some but not all tests of muscular fitness (sit-ups, back strength, and sit and reach) compared with those who walked or used passive modes of travel.[67] Another study reported greater vertical jump height in active travellers compared with passive travellers, and greater handgrip scores in cyclists only.[134] Yet another study found greater handgrip scores only in adolescents walking more than 5 hours/week when compared with those who walked less.[86] Another study found mixed results for a range of muscular fitness tests between cyclists and noncyclists.[96] In summary, all of the relatively few studies found some positive association between AT and at least some aspect of muscular fitness. However, a range of factors complicates our ability to definitely comment on any potentially beneficial role of AT for muscular fitness, which include differences in how travel mode groups were defined (cycling vs. all active modes combined), a wide range of performance test used and the cross-sectional nature of these studies. Intervention studies are needed to address these issues, but to our knowledge, only one study of a 6-month AT-to-school intervention included muscular fitness outcomes, which found significant difference between intervention and control groups. However, it is of note that the intervention comprised only monthly educational sessions regarding AT, resulting in only very modest shifts in cycling rates in boys.[100] More research is needed to inform us whether AT has beneficial effects on muscular fitness.

1.4 Active Transportation and Psychosocial Health

Regular PA is related to better mental health and well-being in children and adolescents,[135] but whether AT has such beneficial effects has been scarcely studied. One very large study of over 20,000 children and adolescents found that walking and biking to school was associated with lower odds of having depressive symptoms compared with those using passive transport.[136] Another large study identified that adolescents who spent at least 15 minutes per day actively commuting to school reported higher levels of happiness, psychological well-being and lower levels of psychological distress.[137]

While it is plausible to suggest that any improvements in mental health and well-being from AT would be a direct consequence of additional PA, another important consideration in this context is that AT,[138,139] including public transit travel,[140] can provide an opportunity for socialisation with friends and peers, which in itself may have beneficial effects on mental health and well-being. Evidently, research on this important topic is lacking, and the few cross-sectional studies that do exist preclude us from commenting on whether AT may cause improvements in mental health and well-being, or whether individuals with better mental health are more likely to choose AT; longitudinal and intervention studies are clearly needed to improve our understanding in this area.

1.5 Conclusions

AT is an important source of PA and is of particular importance in individuals who are at risk of low PA levels, especially adolescents and females. While evidence regarding AT and weight status is mixed, AT is meaningfully related to cardiorespiratory fitness—although this is largely limited to cycling due to its greater exercise intensity. Promising findings have also been reported regarding AT and cardiometabolic health, muscular fitness and psychosocial health, but more research is needed, particularly in the form of longitudinal and interventional studies, to clarify the potential role of AT to improve these health outcomes.

1.6 Recommendations for Policy and Practice

1. Scientific evidence regarding the health benefits of AT in children and adolescents is so compelling that AT should be prioritized as a key strategy to improve health in children and adolescents.
2. Practitioners should work in multidisciplinary teams to identify and address barriers to AT.
3. More support from policymakers for AT interventions are needed. In particular, policymakers should aim to increase the percentage of children who live within a walkable distance to school and other destinations.

1.7 Recommendations for Future Research

1. More prospective and intervention studies are needed to improve the quality of evidence and further ascertain the extent of causal and dose–response relationships between AT and health.
2. More research on AT and psychosocial health is needed.

3. Long-term follow-up regarding AT during childhood and its effects on health and AT in adulthood are lacking to inform whether there are additional long-term benefits in terms of habit and attitude formation.
4. Mixed findings regarding school-based AT interventions are partly due to the inherently difficult task of standardizing or controlling individual factors that are critical to intervention success, such as route characteristics and length; evaluation of future programs should carefully consider what the feasible outcome expectations are in the localized context in order to avoid unjust null trials.

References

1. Morris JN, Heady JA, Raffle PAB, Roberts CG, Parks JW. Coronary heart-disease and physical activity of work. *Lancet* 1953;**262**(6796):1111–20. https://doi.org/10.1016/S0140-6736(53)91495-0.
2. British Medical Association. *Healthy transport = healthy lives*. London, UK: BMA Science and Education department and the Board of Science; 2012.
3. U.S. Department of Health and Human Services. *Step it up! The surgeon general's call to action to promote walking and walkable communities*. Washington, DC: U.S. Dept of Health and Human Services, Office of the Surgeon General; 2015. https://www.surgeongeneral.gov/library/calls/walking-and-walkable-communities/call-to-action-walking-and-walkable-communites.pdf.
4. Janssen I, LeBlanc AG. Systematic review of the health benefits of physical activity and fitness in school-aged children and youth. *Int J Behav Nutr Phys Act* 2010;**7**(1):40. https://doi.org/10.1186/1479-5868-7-40.
5. World Health Organization. *Global recommendations on physical activity for health*. Geneva: World Health Organization Press; 2010.
6. Caspersen CJ, Powell KE, Christenson GM. Physical activity, exercise, and physical fitness: definitions and distinctions for health-related research. *Public Health Rep* 1985;**100**(2):126–31. https://doi.org/10.2307/20056429.
7. Hallal PC, Andersen LB, Bull FC, et al. Global physical activity levels: surveillance progress, pitfalls, and prospects. *Lancet* 2012;**380**(9838):247–57. https://doi.org/10.1016/S0140-6736(12)60646-1.
8. Davison KK, Werder JL, Lawson CT. Children's active commuting to school: current knowledge and future directions. *Prev Chronic Dis* 2008;**5**(3):A100.
9. Lee MC, Orenstein MR, Richardson MJ. Systematic review of active commuting to school and childrens physical activity and weight. *J Phys Act Health* 2008;**5**(6):930–49. https://doi.org/10.1123/jpah.5.6.930.
10. Faulkner GEJJ, Buliung RN, Flora PK, Fusco C. Active school transport, physical activity levels and body weight of children and youth: a systematic review. *Prev Med* 2009;**48**(1):3–8. https://doi.org/10.1016/j.ypmed.2008.10.017.
11. Larouche R, Saunders TJ, Faulkner GEJ, Colley R, Tremblay M. Associations between active school transport and physical activity, body composition, and cardiovascular fitness: a systematic review of 68 studies. *J Phys Act Heal* 2014;**11**(1):206–27. https://doi.org/10.1123/jpah.2011-0345.
12. Schoeppe S, Duncan MJ, Badland H, Oliver M, Curtis C. Associations of children's independent mobility and active travel with physical activity, sedentary behaviour and weight status: a systematic review. *J Sci Med Sport* 2013;**16**(4):312–9. https://dx.doi.org/10.1016/j.jsams.2012.11.001.

13. Martin A, Kelly P, Boyle J, Corlett F, Reilly JJ. Contribution of walking to school to individual and population moderate-vigorous intensity physical activity: systematic review and meta-analysis. *Pediatr Exerc Sci* 2016;**28**(3):353–63. https://doi.org/10.1123/pes.2015-0207.
14. Abbott R, Macdonald D, Nambiar S, Davies PSW. The association between walking to school, daily step counts and meeting step targets in 5- to 17-year-old Australian children. *Pediatr Exerc Sci* 2009;**21**(4):520–32.
15. Alexander LM, Inchley J, Todd J, Currie D, Cooper AR, Currie C. The broader impact of walking to school among adolescents: seven day accelerometry based study. *BMJ* 2008;**2005**(331):1061–2. https://doi.org/10.1136/bmj.38567.382731.AE.
16. Carver A, Timperio AF, Hesketh KD, Ridgers ND, Salmon JL, Crawford DA. How is active transport associated with children's and adolescents' physical activity over time? *Int J Behav Nutr Phys Act* 2011;**8**:126. https://doi.org/10.1186/1479-5868-8-126.
17. Chillon P, Evenson KR, Vaughn A, Ward DS. A systematic review of interventions for promoting active transportation to school. *Int J Behav Nutr Phys Act* 2011;**8**:10. https://dx.doi.org/10.1186/1479-5868-8-10.
18. Chillón P, Ortega FB, Ruiz JR, et al. Active commuting to school in children and adolescents: an opportunity to increase physical activity and fitness. *Scand J Soc Med* 2010;**38**(8):873–9. https://doi.org/10.1177/1403494810384427.
19. Cooper AR, Page AS, Foster LJ, Qahwaji D. Commuting to school: are children who walk more physically active? *Am J Prev Med* 2003;**25**(4):273–6. https://doi.org/10.1016/S0749-3797(03)00205-8.
20. Cooper AR, Andersen LB, Wedderkopp N, Page AS, Froberg K. Physical activity levels of children who walk, cycle, or are driven to school. *Am J Prev Med* 2005;**29**(3):179–84. https://doi.org/10.1016/j.amepre.2005.05.009.
21. Cooper AR, Wedderkopp N, Wang H, Andersen LB, Froberg K, Page AS. Active travel to school and cardiovascular fitness in Danish children and adolescents. *Med Sci Sports Exerc* 2006;**38**(10):1724–31. https://doi.org/10.1249/01.mss.0000229570.02037.1d.
22. Cooper AR, Page AS, Wheeler BW, et al. Mapping the walk to school using accelerometry combined with a global positioning system. *Am J Prev Med* 2010;**38**(2):178–83. https://doi.org/10.1016/j.amepre.2009.10.036.
23. Cooper AR, Jago R, Southward EF, Page AS. Active travel and physical activity across the school transition: the PEACH project. *Med Sci Sports Exerc* 2012;**44**(10):1890–7. https://doi.org/10.1249/MSS.0b013e31825a3a1e.
24. Daly-Smith AJ, McKenna J, Radley D, Long J. The impact of additional weekdays of active commuting to school on children achieving a criterion of 300+ minutes of moderate-to-vigorous physical activity. *Health Educ J* 2011;**70**(4):428–34. https://doi.org/10.1177/0017896910379367.
25. Duncan EK, Scott Duncan J, Schofield G. Pedometer-determined physical activity and active transport in girls. *Int J Behav Nutr Phys Act* 2008;**5**(2). https://doi.org/10.1186/1479-5868-5-2.
26. Ford P, Bailey R, Coleman D, Woolf-May K, Swaine I. Activity levels, dietary energy intake, and body composition in children who walk to school. *Pediatr Exerc Sci* 2007;**19**(4):393–407. https://doi.org/10.1123/pes.19.4.393.
27. Fulton JE, Shisler JL, Yore MM, Caspersen CJ. Active transportation to school. *Res Q Exerc Sport* April 2005;**76**:352–7. https://doi.org/10.1080/02701367.2005.10599306.
28. Goodman A, Mackett RL, Paskins J. Activity compensation and activity synergy in British 8-13year olds. *Prev Med* 2011;**53**(4–5):293–8. https://doi.org/10.1016/j.ypmed.2011.07.019.

29. Heelan KA, Donnelly JE, Jacobsen DJ, Mayo MS, Washburn R, Greene L. Active commuting to and from school and BMI in elementary school children - preliminary data. *Child Care Health Dev* 2005;**31**(3):341–9. https://doi.org/10.1111/j.1365-2214.2005.00513.x.
30. Heelan KA, Abbey BM, Donnelly JE, Mayo MS, Welk GJ. Evaluation of a walking school bus for promoting physical activity in youth. *J Phys Act Health* 2009;**6**(5):560–7. http://journals.humankinetics.com/doi/pdf/10.1123/jpah.6.5.560.
31. Hohepa M, Schofield G, Kolt GS, Scragg R, Garrett N. Pedometer-determined physical activity levels of adolescents: differences by age, sex, time of week, and transportation mode to school. *J Phys Act Health* 2008;**5**(Suppl. 1):S140–52. http://www.ncbi.nlm.nih.gov/pubmed/18364518.
32. Johnson TG, Brusseau TA, Darst PW, Kulinna PH, White-Taylor J. Step counts of non-white minority children and youth by gender, grade level, race/ethnicity, and mode of school transportation. *J Phys Act Health* 2010;**7**(6):730–6. http://www.ncbi.nlm.nih.gov/pubmed/21088303.
33. King AC, Parkinson KN, Adamson AJ, et al. Correlates of objectively measured physical activity and sedentary behaviour in English children. *Eur J Public Health* 2011;**21**(4):424–31. https://doi.org/10.1093/eurpub/ckq104.
34. Klinker CD, Schipperijn J, Christian H, Kerr J, Ersbøll AK, Troelsen J. Using accelerometers and global positioning system devices to assess gender and age differences in children's school, transport, leisure and home based physical activity. *Int J Behav Nutr Phys Act* 2014;**11**(1):8. https://doi.org/10.1186/1479-5868-11-8.
35. Kong AS, Burks N, Conklin C, et al. A pilot walking school bus program to prevent obesity in Hispanic elementary school children: role of physician involvement with the school community. *Clin Pediatr* 2010;**49**(10):989–91. https://doi.org/10.1177/0009922810370364.
36. Landsberg B, Plachta-Danielzik S, Much D, Johannsen M, Lange D, Müller MJ. Associations between active commuting to school, fat mass and lifestyle factors in adolescents: the Kiel Obesity Prevention Study (KOPS). *Eur J Clin Nutr* 2008;**62**(6):739–47. https://doi.org/10.1038/sj.ejcn.1602781.
37. Lee C, Li L. Demographic, physical activity, and route characteristics related to school transportation: an exploratory study. *Am J Heal Promot* 2014;**28**(Suppl. 3):S77–88. https://doi.org/10.4278/ajhp.130430-QUAN-211.
38. Loucaides CA, Jago R. Differences in physical activity by gender, weight status and travel mode to school in Cypriot children. *Prev Med* 2008;**47**(1):107–11. https://doi.org/10.1016/j.ypmed.2008.01.025.
39. Loucaides CA, Plotnikoff RC, Bercovitz K. Differences in the correlates of physical activity between urban and rural Canadian youth. *J Sch Health* 2007;**77**(4):164–70. https://doi.org/10.1111/j.1746-1561.2007.00187.x.
40. Mackett RL, Lucas L, Paskins J, Turbin J. The therapeutic value of children's everyday travel. *Transp Res Part A Policy Pract* 2005;**39**(2–3):205–19. https://doi.org/10.1016/j.tra.2004.09.003.
41. McCormack GR, Giles-Corti B, Timperio A, Wood G, Villanueva K. A cross-sectional study of the individual, social, and built environmental correlates of pedometer-based physical activity among elementary school children. *Int J Behav Nutr Phys Act* 2011;**8**:30. https://doi.org/10.1186/1479-5868-8-30.
42. Mendoza JA, Watson K, Baranowski T, et al. Ethnic minority Children's active commuting to school and association with physical activity and pedestrian safety behaviors. *J Appl Res Child* 2010;**1**(1):1–23. http://www.pubmedcentral.nih.gov/articlerender.fcgi?artid=3160673&tool=pmcentrez&rendertype=abstract.

43. Mendoza JA, Watson K, Nguyen N, Cerin E, Baranowski T, Nicklas TA. Active commuting to school and association with physical activity and adiposity among US youth. *J Phys Act Health* 2011;**8**(4):488–95. https://doi.org/10.1123/jpah.8.4.488.
44. Mendoza JA, Watson K, Baranowski T, Nicklas TA, Uscanga DK, Hanfling MJ. The walking school bus and Children's physical activity: a pilot cluster randomized controlled trial. *Pediatrics* 2011. https://doi.org/10.1542/peds.2010-3486.
45. Michaud-Tomson L, Davidson M, Cuddihy TF. Walk to school - does it make a difference in children's physical activity levels? *ACHPER Heal Lifestyles J* 2003;**50**(3–4): 16–24. http://search.ebscohost.com/login.aspx?direct=true&db=sph&AN=SPHS-928817&site=ehost-live.
46. Murtagh EM, Murphy MH. Active travel to school and physical activity levels of Irish primary schoolchildren. *Pediatr Exerc Sci* 2011;**23**(2):230–6. https://doi.org/10.1123/pes.23.2.230.
47. Owen CG, Nightingale CM, Rudnicka AR, et al. Travel to school and physical activity levels in 9-10 year-old UK children of different ethnic origin; child heart and health study in England (CHASE). *PLoS One* 2012;**7**(2). https://doi.org/10.1371/journal.pone.0030932.
48. Panter J, Jones A, Van Sluijs E, Griffin S. The influence of distance to school on the associations between active commuting and physical activity. *Pediatr Exerc Sci* 2011;**23**(1):72–86. https://doi.org/10.1123/pes.23.1.72.
49. Rosenberg DE, Sallis JF, Conway TL, Cain KL, McKenzie TL. Active transportation to school over 2 years in relation to weight status and physical activity. *Obesity* 2006;**14**(10):1771–6. https://doi.org/10.1038/oby.2006.204.
50. Roth MA, Millett CJ, Mindell JS. The contribution of active travel (walking and cycling) in children to overall physical activity levels: a national cross sectional study. *Prev Med* 2012;**54**(2):134–9. https://doi.org/10.1016/j.ypmed.2011.12.004.
51. Saksvig BI, Webber LS, Elder JP, et al. A cross-sectional and longitudinal study of travel by walking before and after school among eighth-grade girls. *J Adolesc Heal* 2012;**51**(6):608–14. https://doi.org/10.1016/j.jadohealth.2012.03.003.
52. Saksvig BI, Catellier DJ, Pfeiffer K, et al. Travel by walking before and after school and physical activity among adolescent girls. *Arch Pediatr Adolesc Med* 2007;**161**(2):153–8. https://doi.org/10.1001/archpedi.161.2.153.
53. Schofield L, Mummery K. Active transportation: an important part of adolescent physical activity. *Youth Stud* 2005;**24**(1):43–7. https://search.informit.com.au/documentSummary;dn=903536502219014;res=IELHSS.
54. Sirard JR, Riner WF, McIver KL, Pate RR. Physical activity and active commuting to elementary school. *Med Sci Sports Exerc* 2005;**37**(12):2062–9. https://doi.org/10.1249/01.mss.0000179102.17183.6b.
55. Sirard JR, Alhassan S, Spencer TR, Robinson TN. Changes in physical activity from walking to school. *J Nutr Educ Behav* 2008;**40**(5):324–6. https://doi.org/10.1016/j.jneb.2007.12.002.
56. Smith L, Sahlqvist S, Ogilvie D, Jones A, Griffin SJ, van Sluijs E. Is active travel to non-school destinations associated with physical activity in primary school children? *Prev Med* 2012;**54**(3–4):224–8. https://doi.org/10.1016/j.ypmed.2012.01.006.
57. Spinks A, Macpherson A, Bain C, McClure R. Determinants of sufficient daily activity in Australian primary school children. *J Paediatr Child Health* 2006;**42**(11):674–9. https://doi.org/10.1111/j.1440-1754.2006.00950.x.
58. Trang NHHD, Hong TK, Dibley MJ, Sibbritt DW. Factors associated with physical inactivity in adolescents in Ho Chi Minh city, Vietnam. *Med Sci Sports Exerc* 2009;**41**(7):1374–83. https://doi.org/10.1249/MSS.0b013e31819c0dd3.

59. Tudor-Locke C, Neff LJ, Ainsworth BE, Addy CL, Popkin BM. Omission of active commuting to school and the prevalence of children's health-related physical activity levels: the Russian longitudinal monitoring study. *Child Care Health Dev* 2002;**28**(6):507–12. https://doi.org/10.1046/j.1365-2214.2002.00295.x.
60. Tudor-Locke C, Ainsworth BE, Adair LS, Popkin BM. Physical activity in Filipino youth: the Cebu longitudinal health and nutrition survey. *Int J Obes Relat Metab Disord* 2003;**27**:181–90. https://doi.org/10.1038/sj.ijo.802207.
61. Tudor-Locke C, Ainsworth BE, Adair LS, Popkin BM. Objective physical activity of Filipino youth stratified for commuting mode to school. *Med Sci Sports Exerc* 2003;**35**(3):465–71. https://doi.org/10.1249/01.MSS.0000053701.30307.A6.
62. Van Dyck D, De Bourdeaudhuij I, Cardon G, Deforche B. Criterion distances and correlates of active transportation to school in Belgian older adolescents. *Int J Behav Nutr Phys Act* 2010;**7**:87. https://doi.org/10.1186/1479-5868-7-87.
63. van Sluijs EMF, Fearne VA, Mattocks C, Riddoch C, Griffin SJ, Ness A. The contribution of active travel to children's physical activity levels: cross-sectional results from the ALSPAC study. *Prev Med* 2009;**48**(6):519–24. https://doi.org/10.1016/j.ypmed.2009.03.002.
64. Voss C, Sandercock G. Aerobic fitness and mode of travel to school in English schoolchildren. *Med Sci Sports Exerc* 2010;**42**(2):281–7. https://doi.org/10.1249/MSS.0b013e3181b11bdc.
65. Wen LM, Kite J, Merom D, Rissel C. Time spent playing outdoors after school and its relationship with independent mobility: a cross-sectional survey of children aged 10-12 years in Sydney, Australia. *Int J Behav Nutr Phys Act* 2009;**6–13**(6):15. https://doi.org/10.1186/1479-5868-6-15.
66. Alwis G, Linden C, Dencker M, Stenevi-Lundgren S, Gardsell P, Karlsson MK. Bone mineral accrual and gain in skeletal width in pre-pubertal school children is independent of the mode of school transportation–one-year data from the prospective observational pediatric osteoporosis prevention (POP) study. *BMC Musculoskelet Disord* 2007;**8**:66. https://doi.org/10.1186/1471-2474-8-66.
67. Andersen LB, Lawlor DA, Cooper AR, Froberg K, Anderssen SA. Physical fitness in relation to transport to school in adolescents: the Danish youth and sports study. *Scand J Med Sci Sport* 2009;**19**(3):406–11. https://doi.org/10.1111/j.1600-0838.2008.00803.x.
68. Andersen LB, Wedderkopp N, Kristensen P, Moller NC, Froberg K, Cooper AR. Cycling to school and cardiovascular risk factors: a longitudinal study. *J Phys Act Health* 2011;**8**(8):1025–33. https://doi.org/10.1123/jpah.8.8.1025.
69. Baig F, Hameed MA, Li M, Shorthouse G, Roalfe AK, Daley A. Association between active commuting to school, weight and physical activity status in ethnically diverse adolescents predominately living in deprived communities. *Publ Health* 2009;**123**(1):39–41. https://doi.org/10.1016/j.puhe.2008.08.004.
70. Cooper AR, Wedderkopp N, Jago R, et al. Longitudinal associations of cycling to school with adolescent fitness. *Prev Med* 2008;**47**(3):324–8. https://doi.org/10.1016/j.ypmed.2008.06.009.
71. Evenson KR, Huston SL, McMillen BJ, Bors P, Ward DS. Statewide prevalence and correlates of walking and bicycling to school. *Arch Pediatr Adolesc Med* 2003;**157**:887–92. https://doi.org/10.1001/archpedi.157.9.887.
72. Kremers SPJ, De Bruijn G-J, Schaalma H, Brug J. Clustering of energy balance-related behaviours and their intrapersonal determinants. *Psychol Health* 2004;**19**(5):595–606. https://doi.org/10.1080/08870440412331279630.

73. Larouche R, Lloyd M, Knight E, Tremblay MS. Relationship between active school transport and body mass index in grades 4-to-6 children. *Pediatr Exerc Sci* 2011;**23**(3):322–30. http://www.ncbi.nlm.nih.gov/pubmed/21881153.
74. Löfgren B, Stenevi-Lundgren S, Dencker M, Karlsson MK. The mode of school transportation in pre-pubertal children does not influence the accrual of bone mineral or the gain in bone size–two year prospective data from the paediatric osteoporosis preventive (POP) study. *BMC Musculoskelet Disord* 2010;**11**(1):25. https://doi.org/10.1186/1471-2474-11-25.
75. Martin SL, Lee SM, Lowry R. National prevalence and correlates of walking and bicycling to school. *Am J Prev Med* 2007;**33**(2):98–105. https://doi.org/10.1016/j.amepre.2007.04.024.
76. McMinn D, Rowe DA, Murtagh S, Nelson NM. The effect of a school-based active commuting intervention on children's commuting physical activity and daily physical activity. *Prev Med* 2012;**54**(5):316–8. https://doi.org/10.1016/j.ypmed.2012.02.013.
77. Metcalf B, Voss L, Jeffery A, Perkins J, Wilkin T. Physical activity cost of the school run: impact on schoolchildren of being driven to school (EarlyBird 22). *Br Med J* 2004;**329**(7470):832–3. https://doi.org/10.1136/bmj.38169.688102.F71.
78. Nilsson A, Andersen LB, Ommundsen Y, et al. Correlates of objectively assessed physical activity and sedentary time in children: a cross-sectional study (The European Youth Heart Study). *BMC Publ Health* 2009;**9**:322. https://doi.org/10.1186/1471-2458-9-322.
79. Santos MP, Gomes H, Mota J. Physical activity and sedentary behaviors in adolescents. *Ann Behav Med* 2005;**30**(1):21–4. https://doi.org/10.1207/s15324796abm3001_3.
80. Sjolie AN, Thuen F. School journeys and leisure activities in rural and urban adolescents in Norway. *Health Promot Int* 2002;**17**(1):21–30. https://doi.org/10.1093/heapro/17.1.21.
81. Nader PR, Bradley RH, Houts RM, McRitchie SL, O'Brien M. Moderate-to-Vigorous physical activity from ages 9 to 15 years. *J Am Med Assoc* 2008;**300**(3):295. https://doi.org/10.1001/jama.300.3.295.
82. Voss C, Winters M, Frazer A, McKay H. School-travel by public transit: rethinking active transportation. *Prev Med Rep* 2015;**2**:65–70. https://doi.org/10.1016/j.pmedr.2015.01.004.
83. Southward EF, Page AS, Wheeler BW, Cooper AR. Contribution of the school journey to daily physical activity in children aged 11-12 years. *Am J Prev Med* 2012;**43**(2):201–4. https://doi.org/10.1016/j.amepre.2012.04.015.
84. Chillón P, Ortega FB, Ruiz JR, et al. Active commuting and physical activity in adolescents from Europe: results from the HELENA study. *Pediatr Exerc Sci* 2011;**23**(2):207–17. https://doi.org/10.1123/pes.23.2.207.
85. Dollman J, Lewis NR. Active transport to school as part of a broader habit of walking and cycling among South Australian youth. *Pediatr Exerc Sci* 2007;**19**(4):436–43. https://doi.org/10.1123/pes.19.4.436.
86. Larouche R, Faulkner GEJ, Fortier M, Tremblay MS. Active transportation and adolescents' health: the Canadian Health Measures Survey. *Am J Prev Med* 2014;**46**(5):507–15. https://doi.org/10.1016/j.amepre.2013.12.009.
87. Smith L, Aggio D, Hamer M. Active travel to non-school destinations but not to school is associated with higher physical activity levels in an ethnically diverse sample of inner-city schoolchildren. *BMC Publ Health* 2017;**17**(1):13. https://doi.org/10.1186/s12889-016-3920-1.
88. Hillman A, Adams J, Whitelegg J. *One false move...: a study of children's independent mobility*. 1990. London, UK.
89. Pabayo R, Maximova K, Spence JC, Ploeg KV, Wu B, Veugelers PJ. The importance of active transportation to and from school for daily physical activity among children. *Prev Med* 2012;**55**(3):196–200. https://doi.org/10.1016/j.ypmed.2012.06.008.

90. McCrindle BW, Manlhiot C, Millar K, et al. Population trends toward increasing cardiovascular risk factors in canadian adolescents. *J Pediatr* 2010;**157**(5):837–43. https://doi.org/10.1016/J.JPEDS.
91. Bao W, Srinivasan SR, Wattigney WA, Berenson GS. Persistence of multiple cardiovascular risk clustering related to syndrome X from childhood to young adulthood. *Arch Intern Med* 1994;**154**(16):1842. https://doi.org/10.1001/archinte.1994.00420160079011.
92. Ortega FB, Ruiz JR, Castillo MJ, Sjöström M. Physical fitness in childhood and adolescence: a powerful marker of health. *Int J Obes* 2008;**32**(1):1–11. https://doi.org/10.1038/sj.ijo.0803774.
93. Lubans DR, Boreham CA, Kelly P, Foster CE. The relationship between active travel to school and health-related fitness in children and adolescents: a systematic review. *Int J Behav Nutr Phys Act* 2011;**8**(1):5. https://dx.doi.org/10.1186/1479-5868-8-5.
94. Aires L, Pratt M, Lobelo F, Santos RM, Santos MP, Mota J. Associations of cardiorespiratory fitness in children and adolescents with physical activity, active commuting to school, and screen time. *J Phys Act Health* 2011;**8**(Suppl. 2):S198–205. https://doi.org/10.1123/jpah.8.s2.s198.
95. Meron D, Rissel C, Reinten-Reynolds T, Hardy LL. Changes in active travel of school children from 2004 to 2010 in New South Wales, Australia. *Prev Med* 2011;**53**(6):408–10. https://doi.org/10.1016/j.ypmed.2011.09.017.
96. Ramirez-Velez R, Garcia-Hermoso A, Agostinis-Sobrinho C, et al. Cycling to school and body composition, physical fitness, and metabolic syndrome in children and adolescents. *J Pediatr* 2017;**188**:1–7. https://doi.org/10.1016/j.jpeds.2017.05.065.
97. Silva KS, Vasques DG, Martins CDO, Williams LA, Lopes AS. Active commuting: prevalence, barriers, and associated variables. *J Phys Act Health* 2011;**8**(6):750–7. http://www.ncbi.nlm.nih.gov/pubmed/21832289.
98. Chillón P, Ortega FB, Ruiz JR, et al. Bicycling to school is associated with improvements in physical fitness over a 6-year follow-up period in Swedish children. *Prev Med* 2012;**55**(2):108–12. https://doi.org/10.1016/j.ypmed.2012.05.019.
99. Børrestad LAB, Østergaard L, Andersen LB, Bere E. Experiences from a randomised, controlled trial on cycling to school: does cycling increase cardiorespiratory fitness? *Scand J Soc Med* 2012;**40**(3):245–52. https://doi.org/10.1177/1403494812443606.
100. Villa-González E, Ruiz JR, Mendoza JA, Chillón P. Effects of a school-based intervention on active commuting to school and health-related fitness. *BMC Publ Health* 2017;**17**(1):20. https://doi.org/10.1186/s12889-016-3934-8.
101. Madsen KA, Gosliner W, Woodward-Lopez G, Crawford PB. Physical activity opportunities associated with fitness and weight status among adolescents in low-income communities. *Arch Pediatr Adolesc Med* 2009;**163**(11):939–46. https://doi.org/10.1001/archpediatrics.2009.181.
102. Shephard RJ. Is active commuting the answer to population health? *Sport Med* 2008;**38**(9):751–8. https://doi.org/10.2165/00007256-200838090-00004.
103. Malina RM, Bouchard C, Bar-Or O. *Growth, maturation and physical activity*. 2nd ed. Champaign, IL: Human Kinetics; 2004.
104. Reilly JJ, Methven E, McDowell ZC, et al. Health consequences of obesity. *Arch Dis Child* 2003;**88**(9):748–52. https://doi.org/10.1136/ADC.88.9.748.
105. Biro FM, Wien M. Childhood obesity and adult morbidities. *Am J Clin Nutr* 2010;**91**(5):1499S–505S. https://doi.org/10.3945/ajcn.2010.28701B.
106. Lobstein T, Jackson-Leach R, Moodie ML, et al. Child and adolescent obesity: part of a bigger picture. *Lancet* 2015;**385**(9986):2510–20. https://doi.org/10.1016/S0140-6736(14)61746-3.

107. Andegiorgish AK, Wang J, Zhang X, Liu X, Zhu H. Prevalence of overweight, obesity, and associated risk factors among school children and adolescents in Tianjin, China. *Eur J Pediatr* 2012;**171**(4):697–703. https://doi.org/10.1007/s00431-011-1636-x.
108. Arango CM, Parra DC, Eyler A, et al. Walking or bicycling to school and weight status among adolescents from Montería, Colombia. *J Phys Act Health* 2011;**8**(Suppl. 2):S171–7. https://doi.org/10.1123/jpah.8.s2.s171.
109. Bere E, Oenema A, Prins RG, Seiler S, Brug J. Longitudinal associations between cycling to school and weight status. *Int J Pediatr Obes* 2011;**6**(3–4):182–7. https://doi.org/10.3109/17477166.2011.583656.
110. Bere E, Seiler S, Eikemo TA, Oenema A, Brug J. The association between cycling to school and being overweight in Rotterdam (The Netherlands) and Kristiansand (Norway). *Scand J Med Sci Sport* 2011;**21**(1):48–53. https://doi.org/10.1111/j.1600-0838.2009.01004.x.
111. De Bourdeaudhuij I, Lefevre J, Deforche B, Wijndaele K, Matton L, Philippaerts R. Physical activity and psychosocial correlates in normal weight and overweight 11 to 19 year olds. *Obes Res* 2005;**13**(6):1097–105. https://doi.org/10.1038/oby.2005.128.
112. Duncan S, Duncan EK, Fernandes RA, et al. Modifiable risk factors for overweight and obesity in children and adolescents from São Paulo, Brazil. *BMC Publ Health* 2011;**11**(1):585. https://doi.org/10.1186/1471-2458-11-585.
113. Klein-Platat C, Oujaa M, Wagner A, et al. Physical activity is inversely related to waist circumference in 12-y-old French adolescents. *Int J Obes* 2005;**29**(1):9–14. https://doi.org/10.1038/sj.ijo.0802740.
114. Li Y, Zhai F, Yang X, et al. Determinants of childhood overweight and obesity in China. *Br J Nutr* 2007;**97**(1):210. https://doi.org/10.1017/S0007114507280559.
115. Mendoza JA, Liu Y. Active commuting to elementary school and adiposity: an observational study. *Child Obes* 2014;**10**(1):34–41. https://doi.org/10.1089/chi.2013.0133.
116. Ortega FB, Ruiz JR, Sjostrom M. Physical activity, overweight and central adiposity in Swedish children and adolescents: the European Youth Heart Study. *Int J Behav Nutr Phys Act* 2007;**4**(2):61–71. https://doi.org/10.1186/1479-Received.
117. Ostergaard L, Børrestad LAB, Tarp J, Andersen LB. Bicycling to school improves the cardiometabolic risk factor profile: a randomised controlled trial. *BMJ Open* 2012;**2**(6):e001307. https://doi.org/10.1136/bmjopen-2012-001307.
118. Pabayo R, Gauvin L, Barnett TA, Nikima B, Sguin L. Sustained active transportation is associated with a favorable body mass index trajectory across the early school years: findings from the Quebec Longitudinal Study of Child Development birth cohort. *Prev Med* 2010;**50**(Suppl.):S59–64. https://doi.org/10.1016/j.ypmed.2009.08.014.
119. Pizarro AN, Ribeiro JC, Marques EA, Mota J, Santos MP. Is walking to school associated with improved metabolic health? *Int J Behav Nutr Phys Act* 2013;**10**(1):12. https://doi.org/10.1186/1479-5868-10-12.
120. Silva KS, Lopes AS. Excess weight, arterial pressure and physical activity in commuting to school: correlations. *Arq Bras Cardiol* 2008;**91**(2):84–91. http://ovidsp.ovid.com/ovidweb.cgi?T=JS&PAGE=reference&D=medl&NEWS=N&AN=18709259.
121. Wen LM, Merom D, Rissel C, Simpson JM. Weight status, modes of travel to school and screen time: a cross-sectional survey of children aged 10-13 years in Sydney. *Heal Promot J Aust* 2010;**21**(1):57–63. http://search.informit.com.au/documentSummary;dn=014385635425351;res=IELHEA.
122. Aires L, Mendona D, Silva G, et al. A 3-year longitudinal analysis of changes in body mass index. *Int J Sports Med* 2010;**31**(2):133–7. https://doi.org/10.1055/s-0029-1243255.
123. Collins AE, Pakiz B, Rock CL. Factors associated with obesity in Indonesian adolescents. *Int J Pediatr Obes* 2008;**3**(1):58–64. https://doi.org/10.1080/17477160701520132.

124. Gutiérrez-Zornoza M, Sánchez-López M, García-Hermoso A, González-García A, Chillón P, Martínez-Vizcaíno V. Active commuting to school, weight status, and cardiometabolic risk in children from rural areas. *Heal Educ Behav* 2015;**42**(2):231–9. https://doi.org/10.1177/1090198114549373.
125. Jansen W, Mackenbach JP, van Zwanenburg EJ, Brug J. Weight status, energy-balance behaviours and intentions in 9-12-year-old inner-city children. *J Hum Nutr Diet* 2010;**23**(1):85–96. https://doi.org/10.1111/j.1365-277X.2009.01027.x.
126. Machado-Rodrigues AM, Santana A, Gama A, et al. Active commuting and its associations with blood pressure and adiposity markers in children. *Prev Med* 2014;**69**:132–4. https://doi.org/10.1016/j.ypmed.2014.09.001.
127. Mota J, Gomes H, Almeida M, Ribeiro JC, Carvalho J, Santos MP. Active versus passive transportation to school-differences in screen time, socio-economic position and perceived environmental characteristics in adolescent girls. *Ann Hum Biol* 2007;**34**(3):273–82. https://doi.org/10.1080/03014460701308615.
128. Wijga AH, Scholtens S, Bemelmans WJE, et al. Diet, screen time, physical activity, and childhood overweight in the general population and in high risk subgroups: prospective analyses in the PIAMA birth cohort. *J Obes* 2010:2010. https://doi.org/10.1155/2010/423296.
129. Wilson PWF, D'Agostino RB, Parise H, Sullivan L, Meigs JB. Metabolic syndrome as a precursor of cardiovascular disease and type 2 diabetes mellitus. *Circulation* 2005;**112**(20):3066–72. https://doi.org/10.1161/circulationaha.105.539528.
130. Koskinen J, Magnussen CG, Sinaiko A, et al. Childhood age and associations between childhood metabolic syndrome and adult risk for metabolic syndrome, type 2 diabetes mellitus and carotid intima media thickness: the international childhood cardiovascular cohort consortium. *J Am Heart Assoc* 2017;**6**(8):e005632. https://doi.org/10.1161/JAHA.117.005632.
131. Poitras VJ, Gray CE, Borghese MM, et al. Systematic review of the relationships between objectively measured physical activity and health indicators in school-aged children and youth. *Appl Physiol Nutr Metab* 2016;**41**(6 (Suppl. 3)):S197–239. https://doi.org/10.1139/apnm-2015-0663.
132. Tan VP, Macdonald HM, Kim S, et al. Influence of physical activity on bone strength in children and adolescents: a systematic review and narrative synthesis. *J Bone Miner Res* 2014;**29**(10):2161–81. https://doi.org/10.1002/jbmr.2254.
133. Smith JJ, Eather N, Morgan PJ, Plotnikoff RC, Faigenbaum AD, Lubans DR. The health benefits of muscular fitness for children and adolescents:. *A Systematic Review and Meta-Analysis* 2014. https://link.springer.com/content/pdf/10.1007%2Fs40279-014-0196-4.pdf.
134. Cohen D, Ogunleye AA, Taylor M, Voss C, Micklewright D, Sandercock GRH. Association between habitual school travel and muscular fitness in youth. *Prev Med* 2014;**67**:216–20. https://doi.org/10.1016/j.ypmed.2014.07.036.
135. Biddle SJH, Asare M. Physical activity and mental health in children and adolescents: a review of reviews. *Br J Sports Med* 2011;**45**(11):886–95. https://doi.org/10.1136/bjsports-2011-090185.
136. Sun Y, Liu Y, Tao F-B. Associations between active commuting to school, body fat, and mental well-being: population-based, cross-sectional study in China. *J Adolesc Heal* 2015;**57**(6):679–85. https://doi.org/10.1016/J.jadohealth.2015.09.002.
137. Ruiz-Ariza A, de la Torre-Cruz MJ, Redecillas-Peiró MT, Martínez-López EJ. Influencia del desplazamiento activo sobre la felicidad, el bienestar, la angustia psicológica y la imagen corporal en adolescentes. *Gac Sanit* 2015;**29**(6):454–7. https://doi.org/10.1016/J.gaceta.2015.06.002.

138. Silva KS, Pizarro AN, Garcia LMT, Mota J, Santos MP. Which social support and psychological factors are associated to active commuting to school? *Prev Med* 2014;**63**:20–3. https://doi.org/10.1016/j.ypmed.2014.02.019.
139. Simons D, Clarys P, De Bourdeaudhuij I, de Geus B, Vandelanotte C, Deforche B. Factors influencing mode of transport in older adolescents: a qualitative study. *BMC Publ Health* 2013;**13**(1):323. https://doi.org/10.1186/1471-2458-13-323.
140. Jones A, Steinbach R, Roberts H, Goodman A, Green J. Rethinking passive transport: bus fare exemptions and young people's wellbeing. *Health Place* 2012;**18**(3):605–12. https://doi.org/10.1016/J.HEALTHPLACE.

Environmental Benefits of Active Transportation

2

Andy Hong
School of Population and Public Health, University of British Columbia, Vancouver, BC, Canada

Try to leave the Earth a better place than when you arrived.

Sidney Sheldon

Chapter Outline

Children's Active Transportation. https://doi.org/10.1016/B978-0-12-811931-0.00002-8

2.1 Introduction

While active transportation provides health benefits to children by increasing physical activity, it also offers secondary benefits for the environment. Walking has little or no environmental impacts, and biking produces no emissions. Public transit can also play a role in mitigating human impacts on the environment because it can move people with less energy and emissions per passenger kilometre. Some people may argue that meat-eating cyclists will generate more greenhouse gas (GHG) emissions than gasoline-powered vehicles.[1] However, the amount of carbon emissions generated by driving gasoline- or diesel-powered passenger vehicles is generally far greater than the amount generated by walking, biking or taking public transit.

Compared to the physical activity benefits of active transportation, the environmental impacts of active transportation are broader and more complex. In addition to reducing not only GHG emissions, active transportation can also minimize harmful pollution in our environment, such as air, water and soil. Also, the environmental benefits of active transportation can extend far beyond the individual to their families and neighbourhoods. Active transportation can potentially replace short trips that are made by cars. However, other social and cultural factors come into play. For example, parents' mode choice decision to workplace not only affects their behaviours but also their children's behaviours.[2] One parent's behaviour has a ripple effect on other parents and the communities to which they belong (see Chapter 9). Given this complexity, the following sections will examine the current condition and future trends in GHG emissions and discuss some of the environmental impacts of active transportation.

2.2 Climate Change and Future Trends in Greenhouse Gases

In 2015, the worldwide GHG emissions were estimated to be approximately 50 billion metric tons.[3] According to the latest estimates by the International Panel on Climate Change (IPCC), the GHG emissions will likely increase by 40% by the year 2040 under the business-as-usual scenario.[4] This will result in increasing the global temperature by 3.3–3.8°C by 2100. Under the new Paris agreement, however, over 174 countries have made a pledge to reduce GHG emissions and to keep the global temperature rise below 2°C. Containing the growth of GHG emissions will be challenging because the Paris agreement holds no legal obligation. Some big players, such as the United States, have already made a decision to withdraw from the Paris climate agreement, undermining the international efforts to reverse climate change. However, many countries are taking drastic measures to cut GHG emissions from the transportation sector. In 2017, the UK, France and India have announced ambitious plans to ban gasoline and diesel cars by 2040,[5] and other countries under the Paris agreement are following suit.

According the IPCC,[4] the transportation sector accounts for 14% of GHG emissions worldwide (Fig. 2.1). In Canada, it is the second largest source of GHG emissions, accounting for 24% of the total national emissions in 2015.[6] Over the 25-year period from 1990 to 2015, GHG emissions from the transportation sector increased

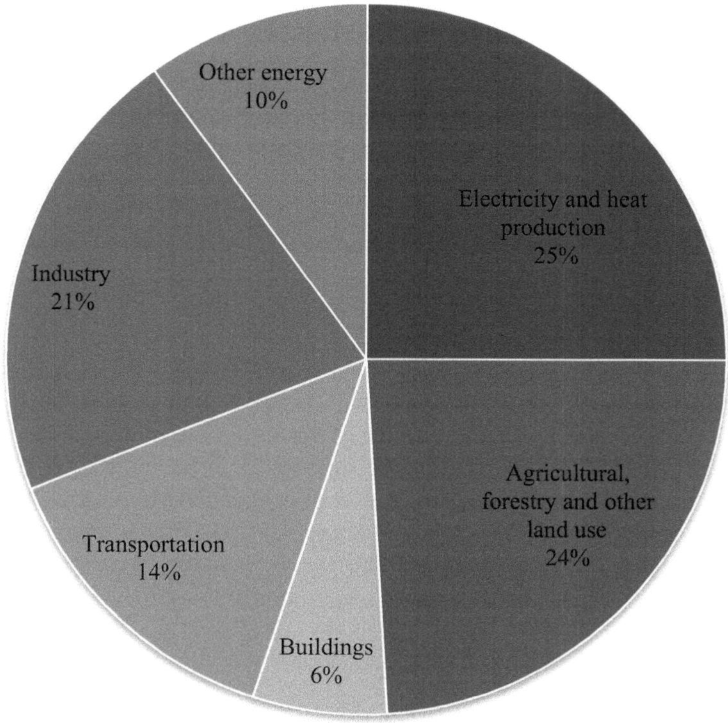

Figure 2.1 Global greenhouse gas emissions by the economic sector.[4]

by 42% in Canada.[6] Passenger travel increased by 17%, and much of this increase was due to the growing number of light trucks, including trucks, vans and sport utility vehicles (SUVs).[6]

When it comes to GHG emissions from passenger travel, the market share of less energy efficient light trucks has increased substantially. In the United States, 20% of all new passenger vehicles sold were light trucks in 1980, but the percentage rose to 65% in 2017, and the sales of light trucks are continuing to increase.[7] Recent statistics in Canada indicated that light trucks, including pickups, minivans and SUVs, have surpassed the sales of passenger cars, with 1.2 million light trucks sold compared to 563 million passenger cars, accounting for over 70% of new vehicle sales in 2017.[8]

The growing market shares of light trucks (pickups, minivans and SUVs) suggest that many households have a preference for larger vehicles. Because households with children are more likely to purchase larger vehicles,[9] children do play an important role in a family's car-buying habits and travel behaviours. If children attend schools far away from their home, parents will most likely drive their kids to and from school, unless they are eligible for taking the school bus. However, if the children can bike or walk to school, parents will have more options for their commute mode, rather than relying on their cars to drive their kids around. This suggests that household-level GHG emissions can be affected by household composition and travel behaviour dynamics within that household.

2.3 Key Mechanisms

Active transportation has a reputation for being healthy as it can promote physical activity (Chapter 1). Some of its environmental impacts, however, may be less known among the public. Active transportation can play an important role as a policy lever to reduce GHG emissions and air pollution. To understand the environmental dimensions, it is useful to begin with some of the key mechanisms through which active transportation can be beneficial to the environment.

2.3.1 *First Mechanism: "Small Form Factor"*

Compared to automobiles, active transportation modes require very small physical space. Walking requires very little space, simply because there is no need for additional power—only two legs suffice. Other modes of human-powered transport, such as bicycles or skateboards, also require minimal space. Public transit, which involves some active transportation to and from transit stops, generally requires less space per passenger kilometre than automobiles. The geometric dimension of transit vehicles varies substantially; however, a single public transit vehicle can typically carry more passengers per unit than a single car, making it a lot more efficient in terms of land consumption. Taken together, active transportation modes consume less land than automobiles and therefore impose little burden on the environment.

2.3.2 *Second Mechanism: "Clean Transportation"*

Active transportation modes are generally cleaner than passenger vehicles. Compared to cars, walking and biking require no gasoline or diesel fuel, thus generating no carbon emissions and pollutants. Public transportation requires more energy and can generate substantial carbon emissions and pollutants. Diesel-powered buses and commuter rails are particularly problematic because diesel particles, such as black carbon or elemental carbon, have significant contribution to GHG emissions and adverse impact on human health. Despite some negative environmental impacts of diesel-based public transit systems, only a small fraction of public transit fleets are diesel based, and many jurisdictions have adopted policies to retrofit old diesel fleets with cleaner vehicles powered by electricity or compressed natural gas. Therefore, active transportation modes and public transit are much more favourable based on per-capita measure of carbon emission and air pollution.

2.3.3 *Third Mechanism: "Fewer Wastes and Resources"*

Active transportation modes produce less waste and require fewer resources. There are virtually no waste or disposal problems associated with walking. Similarly, the life cycle cost of producing, using and disposing one bicycle is far less than that of a passenger vehicle. Bicycles are made up of a smaller number of parts and less complicated components than an automobile; therefore, they are more likely to be recycled and repurposed for other uses. Although the production cost of a public transit vehicle can be substantially higher than manufacturing a car, public transit vehicles can serve more passengers and can last longer than cars, making it more cost effective in terms of operating costs.

These three key mechanisms help us understand some of the environmental dimensions of active transportation. Beyond the requirements in terms of space, resources and the emissions and waste generated by different transportation modes, their impact on other environmental issues, such as water and soil contamination, should not be ignored. In the rest of the chapter, we will discuss the ecological impacts of transportation in various environmental dimensions that pertain to the aforementioned key mechanisms.

2.4 Environmental Dimensions

2.4.1 Land Consumption and Impervious Surface

The most straightforward method to assess the environmental impact of various transport modes is to measure its land consumption, primarily roadway and parking spaces.

2.4.1.1 Road Space

Fig. 2.2 shows a powerful illustration of space required to transport the same number of passengers by car, bus and bicycle. Compared to bus and bicycle, cars consume and require substantially larger space to move passengers.

Pedestrians and bicyclists take up considerably less roadway space than automobiles. In fact, sidewalks and bike lanes are usually built with the minimum width standard of 1.2 m (4 ft) based on an average adult's physical dimension.[10,11] In fact, this standard width adopted in typical sidewalk design practices should even suffice for two

Figure 2.2 Amount of space required to transport and same number of passengers by car, bus or bicycle.

pedestrians side by side. For an automobile, however, the minimum width standard is three times (3.7 m or 12 ft) that for a sidewalk or a bike lane.[12] Cars are designed to carry multiple passengers; therefore, it makes sense to have a wider geometric dimension than that for pedestrians or bicyclists. However, an overwhelming number of people drive their cars alone,[13] resulting in unnecessary waste of space and energy. Public transportation generally requires less space per passenger kilometre than automobiles. The geometric dimension of transit vehicles vary widely, from relatively small size (vanpool) to a substantially large size (commuter rail). Public transit ridership fluctuates depending on time and place, thus it is difficult to estimate the exact number of passengers on board. However, a single public transit vehicle can typically carry more passengers per unit than a single car, making it more efficient in terms of space in dense urban environments.

2.4.1.2 Parking Space

The above illustration only considers roadway space, so the actual space needed for parking each individual car can add up significantly. For example, typical suburban shopping malls in North America and other high-income countries often have large parking lots to accommodate many shoppers and visitors during weekends. However, most of these spaces are left empty during the day (Fig. 2.3). Taken together, more land demand for roadway and parking spaces means less land supply for environmentally beneficial land uses, such as parks, green space, water reservoir and land reserves.

2.4.2 Energy Consumption, Emission and Pollution

2.4.2.1 Energy Consumption

Active transportation modes have lower energy consumption compared to other modes (Fig. 2.4). Walking and biking consume less energy than cars. Public transportation modes also consume less energy per unit because they can carry significantly more

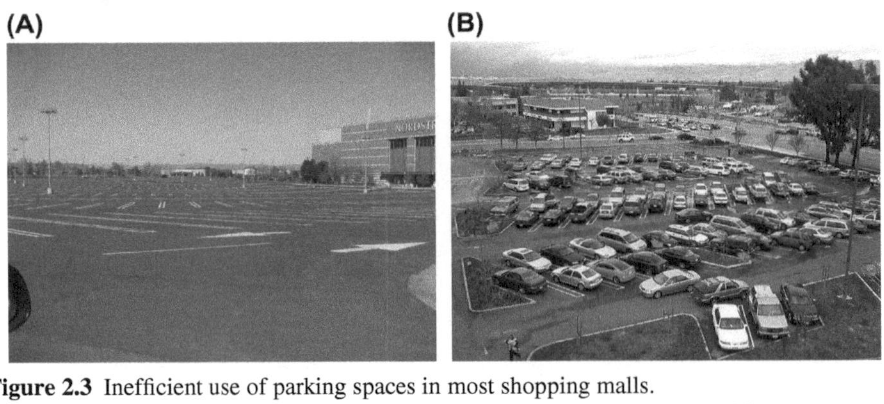

Figure 2.3 Inefficient use of parking spaces in most shopping malls.
Sources: (A) Empty parking lot of a large shopping mall. Photograph by Paul Swansen, https://www.flickr.com/photos/pswansen/5704173856. (B) Photograph by Elf, distributed under CC-BY-SA-3.0 license, https://en.wikipedia.org/wiki/Parking_lot#/media/File:P3030027ParkingLot_wb.jpg.

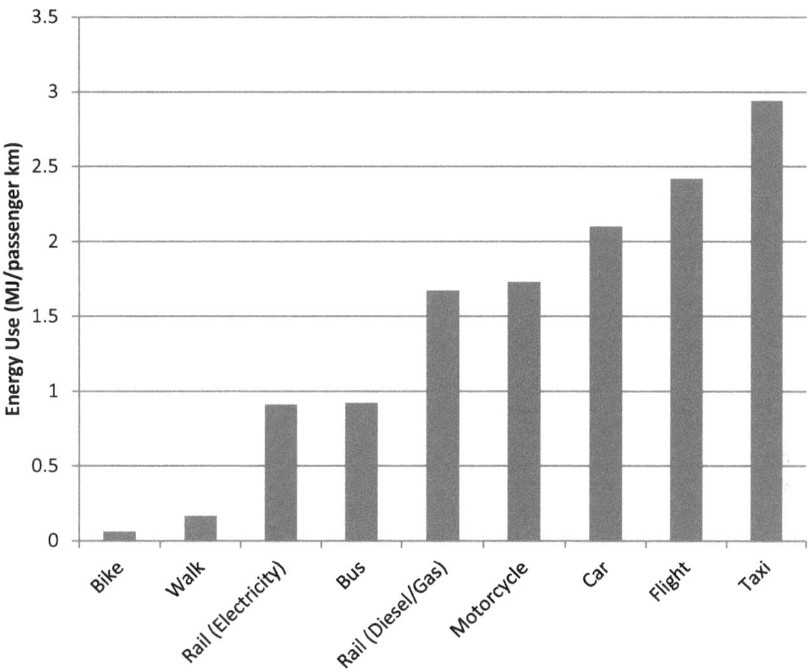

Figure 2.4 Primary energy consumption by mode.[15]

passengers per trip than private cars. Bus fleets can also be retrofitted to natural gas, which can increase fuel economy. Energy consumption is the highest for taxis simply because taxis need to keep driving to search for potential customers. Ride-hailing services, such as Lyft and Uber, may actually be more efficient than typical taxis because they rely on mobile phone technology to match passengers and drivers in real time and thus can reduce unnecessary trips to search for customers.[14] However, they still consume substantially more energy than active transportation modes because they are constantly moving on the road. Airplanes also consume a lot of energy because they rely on energy-intensive engines, which require large volumes of fuel for operation.

2.4.2.2 Greenhouse Gas Emissions and Air Pollution

Active transportation modes also generate less emissions and pollution (Fig. 2.5). Apart from the manufacturing and recycling processes, walking and biking virtually emit little or no pollution. Rail, if run on electricity, is also a very clean mode, although gasoline- or diesel-based rail transportation generates more pollution.

Automobiles may produce even more pollution than what's shown in Fig. 2.5. This is because vehicles contribute disproportionately to emissions due to cold starts and hot soaks (Fig. 2.6). Cold start refers to the phenomenon whereby higher emissions are generated during the first minutes of engine operation due to incomplete combustion than once ordinary operating temperature is reached. Hot soak refers to the time when the vehicle is off but continues to evaporate emissions due to hot engine. Taken together, automobiles may generate greater emissions than what can be estimated only by distance driven.

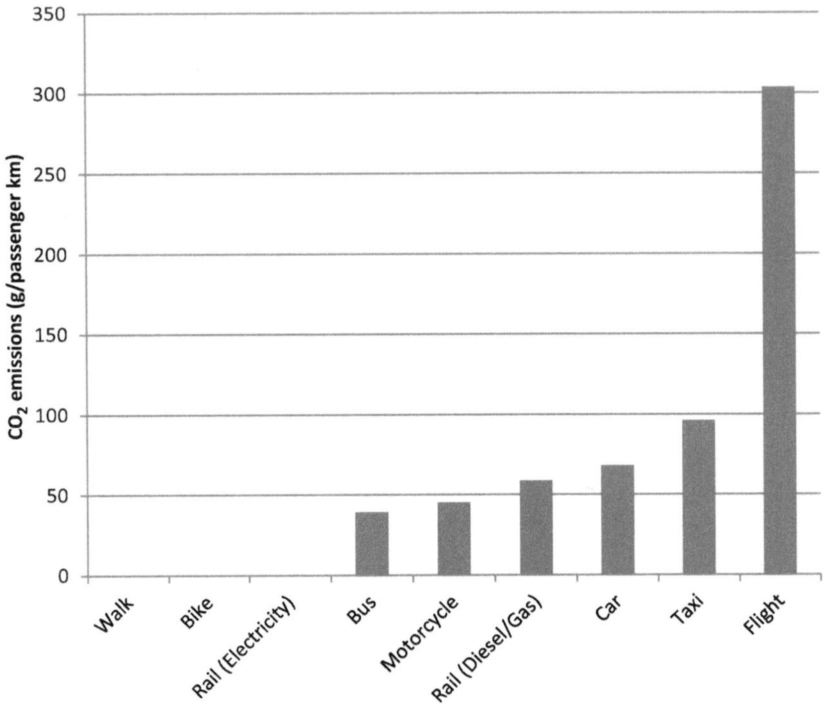

Figure 2.5 Tailpipe carbon emissions by mode.[16]

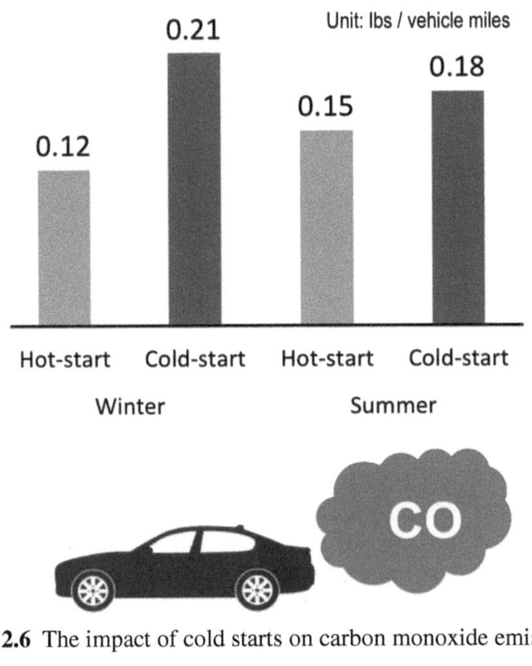

Figure 2.6 The impact of cold starts on carbon monoxide emissions.[17]

2.4.2.3 Potential for Replacing Short Auto Trips

In particular, shorter auto trips or frequent stop-and-go movements that typically occur during congested urban traffic conditions are problematic because of cold starts and hot soaks. According to the 2009 US National Household Travel Survey, 28% of all vehicle trips were less than 1 mile. More than two-thirds of all the trips were less than 5 miles, suggesting that there is a potential to achieve greater reduction in emissions by targeting short-distance car trips for air pollution mitigation.

Notably, replacing short-distance car trips by active transportation modes could have significant environmental benefits. A US-based study has developed a simulation model to estimate the potential for replacing auto trips by active transportation modes.[18] Focusing on the short trips ranging between 0.5 and 3 miles from the 1995 US National Personal Transportation Survey, the study made an assumption that 35%–70% of short noncommute trips and 15%–45% of short commute trips by automobiles can be replaced by walking and biking. The study concluded that a conversion of short auto trips to active transportation modes can reduce daily emissions of volatile organic compounds and carbon monoxides (CO) by at least 30 and 400 tons, respectively.

However, the potential for replacing short car trips with active transportation modes may be lower than what can be estimated from a simulation. A recent study conducted in Australia reported that 7%–14% of short car trips (1.6–2.0 km for a single trip; 3.4–4.7 km for a trip-chain) could be potentially replaced by walking.[19] Another study from Belgium indicated that about 9.5% of short-distance trips less than 8 km were replaceable by walking or biking, after taking into account various factors that limit active transportation.[20]

The lower percentage of short car trips that can be replaced by active transportation is not surprising because there are other factors that affect mode choice than travel distance. For example, transporting heavy goods is commonly perceived as a barrier to active transportation.[21] Other factors, such as the perceived need to transport children to various places, and the use of trip chains as a strategy to save time may also encourage driving for short-distance trips.[19] Furthermore, the percentage of car trips that can be replaced by active transportation would likely differ based on various characteristics such as urban form,[21] social norms,[22] weather[19] and perceived convenience of driving[23] and policies[24] that may encourage or deter active transportation. Given the larger impact of short car trips on emissions, however, targeting short-distance auto trips could still be a promising strategy to reduce traffic-related air pollution and GHG emissions.

2.4.3 Life Cycle and Ecological Impacts

2.4.3.1 Life Cycle Impact

Life cycle analysis refers to the analytical technique used to examine the cost of a system over a defined period of time.[25] The time span can range from the early feasibility assessment period to the various steps of production, implementation and operation. It seeks to determine all costs throughout the life cycle of a product or a service. Life cycle analysis considers both upfront cost of production and incremental costs of operation and depreciation.

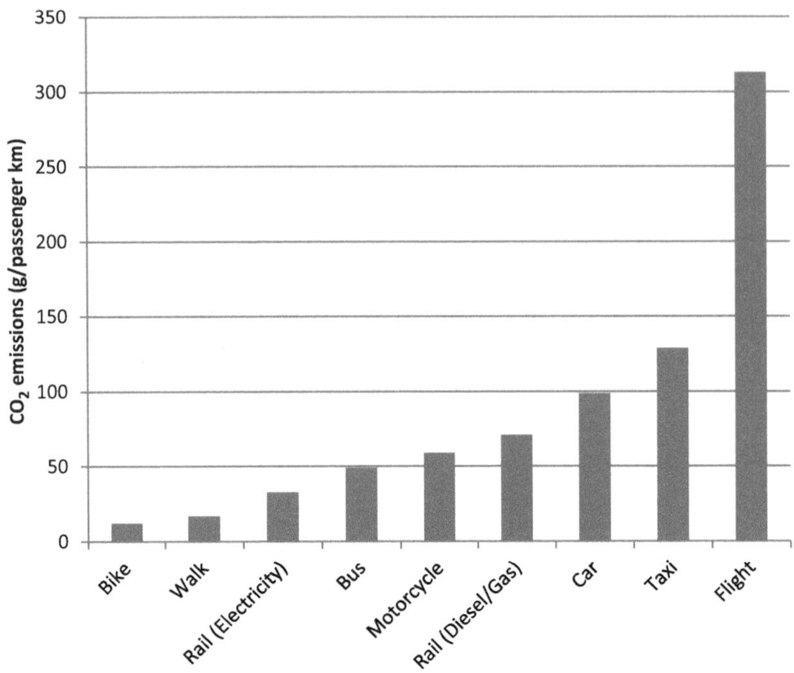

Figure 2.7 Life cycle carbon emissions by mode.[16]

When taking into account life cycle costs (Fig. 2.7), airplanes show the highest GHG emissions—three times that of cars and six times that of buses. Interestingly, cars or buses show higher GHG emissions when considering life cycle impacts than the results without the life cycle impacts. This is because the GHG impact of manufacturing and operating automobiles and buses could be greater than that of other modes. Walking does not require any tools, so its life cycle impact is minimal compared to other modes. The GHG impact of producing and maintaining bicycles is much smaller than that of automobiles or public transportation vehicles. On balance, active transportation modes produce far less emissions than other modes even after taking into account all the life cycle impacts. Life cycle analysis provides a comprehensive view of the environmental impact of transportation infrastructure due to processes involving construction, operation and maintenance.

2.4.3.2 Ecological Impact

Aside from the environmental impacts due to life cycle costs, transportation can have additional burden on the environment. In particular, the ecological impact of roads has long been discussed in the ecology literature.[26] Roads and railroads can disrupt ecological processes, increase animal mortality, and lead to fragmentation and degradation of wildlife habitat and landscape. Roads have far reaching impacts on the environment because their effects can extend beyond the roadway itself.

A study of the ecological impact of roads in the United States reported that while roads and roadsides cover only 1% of the total land, their ecological impacts are estimated to be between 19% and 22%.[27] The outer limits of the significant ecological effects of a road were thus described as a "road-effect zone," which can extend greater than 300 m for highways and major arterials carrying 50,000 vehicles per day.[28] The actual ecological impact of roadway infrastructure may depend on a variety of factors, including traffic characteristics, topography, weather, wind, slope and vegetation. The impacts may vary by different animal and plant species. Therefore, the ecological impacts of transportation should be carefully considered when planning and designing new transportation infrastructure because of its long-term impacts on the environment, especially with respect to habitat and landscape functions.

Many transportation agencies have been incorporating natural habitat protection measure as part of their environmental mitigation plan. Wildlife crossing is one measure of preventing wildlife habitat fragmentation due to highways or arterials (Fig. 2.8). Wildlife crossings include overpasses, bridges, viaducts or tunnels designed to facilitate safe movement of animals across road infrastructure. The crossings provide physical connection between habitats, which would have been separated otherwise. They can also reduce animal mortality by preventing animal–vehicle collisions, which are estimated to be about 300,000 deaths per year in the United States.[29] A review of various wildlife crossings indicates that it is difficult to measure the effectiveness of such structures because there are many factors involved, including human–animal interactions, wildlife biology and animal behaviours.[30] Future studies investigating the before-and-after effects of installation of wildlife crossing structures will help inform decision makers about the efficacy of various crossing structures.[31]

Figure 2.8 A wildlife overpass on the Trans-Canada Highway between Banff and Lake Louise, Alberta.
Source: Creative Commons, https://commons.wikimedia.org/wiki/File:Wildlife_overpass_Trans-Canada_Hwy_between_Banff_and_LakeLouise_Alberta.jpg.

2.4.4 Urban Water Runoff and Soil Contamination

2.4.4.1 Urban Runoff

Transportation infrastructures, such as roads, bridges and parking lots, are artificial structures that have very little ecological value. They usually consist of impenetrable materials such as cement, concrete or asphalt, which are also known as "impervious surfaces."[33] Evidently, impervious surfaces have an adverse impact on the environment. Compared to natural landscapes, urban built-up areas tend to trap more heat without releasing it back to the atmosphere, which exacerbates urban heat island effect.[34] Impervious surfaces also block rainwater from entering the soil, producing stormwater runoff that can be highly toxic and detrimental to aquatic wildlife and fish (Fig. 2.9). Stormwater runoff from parking lots, bridges and roads contain a number of chemical, metal and toxic substances from brake, tire and pavement wears.[35] Urban runoff mixed with vehicle exhausts and resuspended road dust can potentially contaminate drinking water supplies, posing a serious public health threat.[36]

2.4.4.2 Soil Contamination

Stormwater runoff from highways and arterial roads can also contaminate soils. Metal components in stormwater runoffs do not degrade naturally; high concentration of metals and particulate matters can accumulate in the roadside soils at levels that are toxic to humans and other organisms in the surrounding environments.[37] Road dusts and tire wear can also contaminate roadside soils. Chemical tests on soils along major highways consistently identify various toxic substances, including lead, cadmium, copper and zinc.[38–40] Gas- and diesel-powered vehicles are primarily responsible for stormwater runoffs and potential soil contamination. While some public transit vehicles rely on the same gasoline fuel as cars, natural gas fleets and electric rail systems produce little or no residues that contaminate soils. Walking and biking also produce no toxic chemicals that lead to soil contamination.

Figure 2.9 Urban stormwater runoff.
Source: Photograph by WikiPedant, distributed under CC-BY-SA-4.0 license, https://commons.wikimedia.org/wiki/File:Wildlife_overpass_Trans-Canada_Hwy_between_Banff_and_LakeLouise_Alberta.jpg

2.5 Potential Trade-offs With Regards to Human Health Impacts

Although active transportation modes offer a vast array of environmental benefits, there may be some trade-offs in terms of human health effects. A growing body of research has reported that walking and biking can actually increase personal exposure to traffic air pollution notably due to increased ventilation.[41,42] Therefore, the benefits of active transportation should be balanced against the risks associated with elevated exposure to pollutants.

2.5.1 *Risks of Increased Exposure to Air Pollution*

Although shifting to active transportation can help reduce traffic emissions in general, it can potentially increase exposure to traffic pollutants among active travellers.[43–45] In particular, bicycling in dense urban environments could disproportionately affect personal exposure to traffic-related air pollution by placing emission sources closer to travellers and increasing exposure to localized air pollution.[46] Further, higher intake fraction and increased dose of air pollutants among bicyclists can result in increased inhalation of traffic air pollution, potentially offsetting the physical activity benefits of bicycling.[47] A study from Belgium[48] measured exposure and ventilation rates of 55 persons and found that inhaled doses of air pollutants while bicycling were four to nine times higher than for car drivers on the same route. This indicates that significantly higher exposure to pollutants could occur for active transportation users than for car drivers, and the actual amount of pollutants deposited into the lungs could be greater due to higher ventilation rates of active transportation users. Such findings suggest the need for: (1) implementing policies aiming to reduce vehicle exhaust emissions and (2) raising awareness of less polluted routes that bicyclists could use to reduce their exposure to pollution. Previous studies suggest that bicyclists are willing to go out of their way to use cleaner and higher quality bicycling infrastructure.[49,50]

2.5.2 *Benefits of Increased Physical Activity*

In contrast, many studies suggest that the benefits of active transportation far outweigh the risks associated with increased exposure to pollutants.[51–53] A study from Barcelona[54] estimated that if 40% of car trips were shifted to bicycling, 76 deaths would be avoided per year, due in large part to health benefits accrued from increased physical activity. In addition, most of the health benefit–cost research has been conducted in developed countries with relatively good air quality. However, recent studies[55] included low-income countries and found that the break-even point where the risk from air pollution exposure starts to outweigh the benefits of physical activity is reached only at substantially high levels of pollution (fine particulate matter ($PM_{2.5}$) levels exceeding 100 μg/m^3) or with extended hours of walking and bicycling in those highly polluted environments. Given that the average global levels of $PM_{2.5}$ are 22 μg/m^3, this study reinforces findings from earlier studies[51] that the benefits of active transportation generally outweigh the risks associated with air pollution exposure in most cities.[56] Regardless, switching from active to motorized transport to reduce one's exposure to air pollution would only make the problem worse for everyone else! This emphasizes the need for collective rather than individualistic responses to air pollution.

2.6 Conclusions

Active transportation offers more environmental benefits than harm compared to automobiles or airplanes. Furthermore, public transit is relatively more environmentally friendly than automobiles in most cases. In the earlier part of the chapter, we introduced three key mechanisms that make active transportation more environmentally friendly: (1) small form factor, (2) clean transport and (3) fewer wastes. Under this framework, it is clear that active transportation modes outperform automobiles and airplanes in all environmental aspects. Active transportation modes occupy less land space, produce fewer emissions per passenger kilometre, create fewer wastes and have much lower life cycle impacts. Some concerns about potential risks of increased exposure to air pollution do exist; however, there is a growing consensus that the health and environmental benefits of active transportation far outweigh its risks.

2.7 Recommendations for Policy and Practice

1. Active transportation modes may not be well suited for long-distance travel. Public transit can extend travel distance, but it has limited service coverage in suburban and rural communities, making it less practical for most households. To overcome this distance barrier, policy makers should focus on improving the integration between walking, biking and public transit.
2. Policy makers should develop a broad range of strategies to replace short car trips with active transportation modes. The aim should be to make environmentally friendly choices the easy choices. Given the increasing percentage and contribution of short trips for air pollution and GHG emissions, the potential environmental impacts of curbing short-distance car trips could be substantial.
3. Policy makers should consider the life cycle costs when evaluating the environmental impacts of public transit projects. Although upfront costs of using clean fuel vehicles for public transportation may be higher, they may be more cost effective given that the benefits may be larger when considering the entire life cycle costs of operating cleaner vehicles.
4. When planning and building infrastructure for active transportation, policy makers should consider ecological impacts on wildlife habitat and ecosystem functions. Bike lanes and pedestrian facilities can be designed and built with ecological considerations, and it would be preferable and aesthetically superior to use environmentally friendly materials and to adopt design principles that seek to minimize ecological impacts.

2.8 Recommendations for Future Research

1. Alternative forms of mobility, such as electric bikes and hover boards, are getting increasingly more popular in many cities. Researchers should pay attention to the environmental impacts of these emerging hybrid forms of active transportation.
2. There is a clear need for more research on the risks and benefits of active transportation in low-income and more polluted countries. While the benefits of active transportation often outweigh the risks in high-income countries, the benefits are less clear in more polluted urban environments. Such research will inform future policies on active transportation for low-income countries that often have higher levels of air pollution.
3. Researchers should simultaneously examine the environmental and health benefits of active transportation to provide a more comprehensive analysis of economical impacts.
4. Because of the link between active transportation and environmental attitudes, it will be fruitful to conduct a study to examine whether active transportation in childhood leads to environmental attitudes and stewardship later in life. Such a study would be novel given the need for adopting climate change mitigation strategies.

References

1. Shore R. Are meat-eating cyclists worse for the planet than drivers? [Internet]. *Vanc Sun* June 10, 2016. Available from: http://vancouversun.com/news/local-news/are-meat-eating-cyclists-worse-for-the-planet-than-drivers.
2. Henne HM, Tandon PS, Frank LD, Saelens BE. Parental factors in children's active transport to school. *Publ Health* 2014;**128**(7):643–6.
3. UNFCCC. GHG data [Internet]. *United Nations Framew Convention Clim Chang* 2017. [cited 2017 Jan 1]. Available from: http://unfccc.int/ghg_data/new_reporting_requirements/items/9560.php.
4. Intergovernmental Panel on Climate Change. *Climate change 2014: mitigation of climate change [Internet]*, vol. 3. Cambridge, United Kingdom and New York, NY, USA: Cambridge University Press; 2015. Available from: http://www.ipcc.ch/report/ar5/wg3/.
5. Muoio D. These countries are banning gas-powered vehicles by 2040 [Internet]. *Bus Insid* October 23, 2017. Available from: http://www.businessinsider.com/countries-banning-gas-cars-2017-10.
6. Environment and Climate Change Canada. *Canadian environmental sustainability indicators: greenhouse gas emissions [Internet]*. Quebec: Gatineau; 2017. Available from: www.ec.gc.ca/indicateurs-indicators/default.asp?lang=En&n=FBF8455E-1.
7. U.S. Bureau of Economic Analysis. *Motor vehicle retail sales: light weight trucks [Internet]*. 2017. [cited 2017 Dec 20]. Available from: https://fred.stlouisfed.org/series/LTRUCKSA.
8. Siekierska A. Revenge of the SUV: why is this gas-loving ride once again king of the road? [Internet]. *Financ Post* November 8, 2017. Available from: http://business.financialpost.com/transportation/revenge-of-the-suv-why-is-this-gas-guzzling-ride-once-again-king-of-the-road.
9. Choo S, Mokhtarian PL. What type of vehicle do people drive? The role of attitude and lifestyle in influencing vehicle type choice. *Transp Res Part A Policy Pract* 2004;**38**(3):201–22.

10. AASHTO. *Guide for the development of bicycle facilities*. 2012. Washington, D.C.
11. AASHTO. *Guide for the planning, design, and operation of pedestrian facilities*. 2000. Washington, D.C.
12. AASHTO. *A policy on geometric design of highways and streets*. 2011. Washington, D.C.
13. McKenzie B. *Who drives to work? Commuting by automobile in the United States [Internet]*. 2013. Washington, D.C. Available from: https://www.census.gov/library/publications/2015/acs/acs-32.html.
14. Cramer J, Krueger AB. Disruptive change in the taxi business: the case of Uber. *Am Econ Rev* 2016;**106**(5):177–82.
15. Banister D. Sustainable transport and public policy. In: Kim TJ, editor. *Transportation engineering and planning*, vol. II. Oxford, UK: EOLSS Publishers/UNESCO; 2004.
16. Choppin S. Emissions by transport type [Internet]. *Guardian* 2009. [cited 2017 Oct 11]. Available from: https://www.theguardian.com/environment/datablog/2009/sep/02/carbon-emissions-per-transport-type.
17. Mcmichael WF, Sigsby JE. Automotive emissions after hot and cold starts in summer and winter [Internet]. *J Air Pollut Contr Assoc* 1966;**16**(9):474–7. Available from: https://www.tandfonline.com/doi/full/10.1080/00022470.1966.10468502.
18. de Nazelle A, Morton BJ, Jerrett M, Crawford-Brown D. Short trips: an opportunity for reducing mobile-source emissions? *Transp Res Transport Environ* 2010;**15**(8):451–7.
19. Cole R, Turrell G, Koohsari MJ, Owen N, Sugiyama T. Prevalence and correlates of walkable short car trips: a cross-sectional multilevel analysis. *J Transp Heal* 2017;**4**(December 2016):73–80.
20. Beckx C, Broekx S, Degraeuwe B, Beusen B, Int Panis L. Limits to active transport substitution of short car trips. *Transp Res Transport Environ* 2013;**22**:10–3.
21. Mackett RL. Why do people use their cars for short trips? *Transportation* 2003;**30**(3):329–49.
22. Gardner B, Abraham C. Psychological correlates of car use: a meta-analysis. *Transp Res F Traffic Psychol Behav* 2008;**11**(4):300–11.
23. Forward SE. The prediction of travel behaviour using the theory of planned behaviour. In: Rothengatter T, Huguenin RD, editors. *Traffic & Transport Psychology*. Amsterdam: Elsevier; 2004. p. 481–92.
24. Ryley TJ. The propensity for motorists to walk for short trips: evidence from West Edinburgh. *Transp Res Part A Policy Pract* 2008;**42**(4):620–8.
25. Scientific Applications International Corporation. *Life cycle assessment: principles and practice*. 2006. Washington, D.C.
26. Trombulak SC, Frissell CA. Review of ecological effects of roads on terrestrial and aquatic communities. *Conserv Biol* 2000;**14**(1):18–30.
27. Forman RTT. Estimate of the area affected ecologically by the road system in the United States. *Conserv Biol* 2000;**14**(1):31–5.
28. Forman RTT, Alexander LE. Roads and their major ecological effects. *Annu Rev Ecol Systemat* 1998;**29**(1):207–31.
29. Huijser MP, McGowen P, Fuller J, Hardy A, Kociolek A, Clevenger AP, et al. *Wildlife vehicle collision reduction study: report to congress [Internet]*. Bozeman, MT: U.S. Department of Transportation; 2008. Available from: https://www.fhwa.dot.gov/publications/research/safety/08034/08034.pdf.
30. Glista DJ, DeVault TL, DeWoody JA. A review of mitigation measures for reducing wildlife mortality on roadways. *Landsc Urban Plann* 2009;**91**(1):1–7.
31. Huijser MP, Fairbank ER, Camel-Means W, Graham J, Watson V, Basting P, et al. Effectiveness of short sections of wildlife fencing and crossing structures along highways in reducing wildlife-vehicle collisions and providing safe crossing opportunities for large mammals. *Biol Conserv* 2016;**197**:61–8.

32. Deleted in review.
33. Arnold CL, Gibbons CJ. Impervious surface coverage: the emergence of a key environmental indicator. *J Am Plann Assoc* 1996;**62**(2):243–58.
34. Oke T, Mills G, Christen A, Voogt J. Urban heat island. In: *Urban climates*. Cambridge, U.K: Cambridge University Press; 2017. p. 197–237.
35. Kayhanian M, Fruchtman BD, Gulliver JS, Montanaro C, Ranieri E, Wuertz S, et al. Review of highway runoff characteristics : comparative analysis and universal implications. *Water Res* 2012;**46**(20):6609–24.
36. Gaffield SJ, Goo RL, Richards LA, Jackson RJ. Public health effects of inadequately managed stormwater runoff. *Am J Publ Health* 2003;**93**(9):33–6.
37. Sansalone JJ, Buchberger SG. Partitioning and first flush of metals in urban roadway storm water. *J Environ Eng* 1997;**123**(2):134–43.
38. Fergusson J, Ryan D. The elemental composition of street dust from large and small urban areas related to city type, source and particle size. *Sci Total Environ* 1984;**34**(1–2):101–16.
39. Fujiwara F, Rebagliati RJ, Dawidowski L, Gómez D, Polla G, Pereyra V, et al. Spatial and chemical patterns of size fractionated road dust collected in a megacitiy. *Atmos Environ* 2011;**45**(8):1497–505.
40. Harrison RM, Laxen DPH, Wilson SJ. Chemical associations of lead, cadmium, copper, and zinc in street dusts and roadside soils. *Environ Sci Technol* 1981;**15**(11):1378–83.
41. de Nazelle AJ, Nieuwenhuijsen MJ, Antó JM, Brauer M, Briggs D, Braun-Fahrlander C, et al. Improving health through policies that promote active travel: a review of evidence to support integrated health impact assessment. *Environ Int* 2011;**37**:766–77.
42. Cepeda M, Schoufour J, Freak-Poli R, Koolhaas CM, Dhana K, Bramer WM, et al. Levels of ambient air pollution according to mode of transport: a systematic review. *Lancet Public Heal* 2017;**2**(1):e23–34.
43. Briggs DJ, de Hoogh K, Morris C, Gulliver J. Effects of travel mode on exposures to particulate air pollution. *Environ Int* 2008;**34**(1):12–22.
44. Kaur S, Nieuwenhuijsen M, Colvile R. Pedestrian exposure to air pollution along a major road in Central London, UK. *Atmos Environ* 2005;**39**(38):7307–20.
45. Adams HS, Nieuwenhuijsen MJ, Colvile RN, McMullen MAS, Khandelwal P. Fine particle ($PM_{2.5}$) personal exposure levels in transport microenvironments, London, UK. *Sci Total Environ* 2001;**279**(1–3):29–44.
46. Hertel O, Hvidberg M, Ketzel M, Storm L, Stausgaard L. A proper choice of route significantly reduces air pollution exposure–a study on bicycle and bus trips in urban streets. *Sci Total Environ* 2008;**389**(1):58–70.
47. Bigazzi AY, Figliozzi MA. Review of urban bicyclists' intake and uptake of traffic-related air pollution. *Transport Rev* 2014;**34**(2):221–45.
48. Int Panis L, de Geus B, Vandenbulcke G, Willems H, Degraeuwe B, Bleux N, et al. Exposure to particulate matter in traffic: a comparison of cyclists and car passengers. *Atmos Environ* 2010;**44**(19):2263–70.
49. Broach J, Dill J, Gliebe J. Where do cyclists ride? A route choice model developed with revealed preference GPS data. *Trans Res Part A* 2012;**46**(10):1730–40.
50. Winters M, Teschke K. Route preferences among adults in the near market for bicycling : findings of the cycling in cities study. *Am J Health Promot* 2010:40–8.
51. de Hartog JJ, Boogaard H, Nijland H, Hoek G. Do the health benefits of cycling outweigh the risks? *Environ Health Perspect* 2010;**118**(8):1109–16.
52. Rabl A, de Nazelle AJ. Benefits of shift from car to active transport. *Transport Pol* 2012;**19**(1):121–31.
53. Rojas-Rueda D, de Nazelle AJ, Tainio M, Nieuwenhuijsen MJ. The health risks and benefits of cycling in urban environments compared with car use: health impact assessment study. *BMJ* 2011;**343**:d4521.

54. Rojas-Rueda D, de Nazelle AJ, Teixidó O, Nieuwenhuijsen MJ. Replacing car trips by increasing bike and public transport in the greater Barcelona metropolitan area: a health impact assessment study. *Environ Int* 2012;**49**:100–9.
55. Tainio M, de Nazelle AJ, Götschi T, Kahlmeier S, Rojas-Rueda D, Nieuwenhuijsen MJ, et al. Can air pollution negate the health benefits of cycling and walking? *Prev Med* 2016;**87**:233–6.
56. Mueller N, Rojas-Rueda D, Cole-Hunter T, de Nazelle A, Dons E, Gerike R, et al. Health impact assessment of active transportation: a systematic review. *Prev Med* 2015;**76**:103–14.

Economic Benefits of Active Transportation

3

Cameron Gordon[1,2]
[1]Centre for Research and Action in Public Health (CeRAPH), University of Canberra, Canberra, ACT, Australia; [2]Social Policy Simulation Center, City University of New York, New York, NY, United States

> *The roots of inactivity go deep into the cultural and socioeconomic logic of post-industrial societies .... Think about it this way—nobody is in the market for a labour-creating device. Sit-on mowers, leaf blowers, self-opening doors and automatic car windows, robot vacuum cleaners, sensor lighting, dishwashers and microwaves all yield daily microsavings in energy expenditure that add up to hundreds of kilojoules.*[1]

Chapter Outline

Children's Active Transportation. https://doi.org/10.1016/B978-0-12-811931-0.00003-X

3.1 Introduction

The policy implication of this striking statement by Olds[1] is that increasing activity levels have positive health impacts, which in turn lower economic costs and increase economic benefit. Encouraging activity, especially through active school travel, i.e., walking and cycling to school, can be powerful. To take but one example, a study of school districts in Ontario, Canada, estimated that on average $371.74 per enrolled student was spent on school busing, an expenditure that could be substantially reduced if more students walked or cycled.[2] Removal of a portion of buses and automobiles in this way would, in turn, reduce overall road congestion and its associated costs of traffic and pollution.[3] This is only the tip of a very large active travel economic benefit iceberg, as will be discussed in more detail below.

Economic benefits (and reduced costs) garnered by active transportation are generally defined and evaluated using two standard approaches: (1) cost–benefit analysis (CBA) and (2) cost-effectiveness analysis.

3.1.1 *Cost–Benefit Analysis*

CBA is designed to measure whether a proposed policy intervention yields a net gain in societal welfare. If not, the project should be rejected (on economic grounds, at least); if so, the project should be accepted.

The theory behind CBA contains a number of simplifying assumptions. There are individual agents ('individuals') who are posited to want as much 'satisfaction' ('utility' to use economic parlance) as possible, where satisfaction is gained through consumption of material goods and services chosen to meet individual preferences. Society is simply the sum of all individuals. Thus if individuals obtain the most individual satisfaction possible, then 'social welfare' (the total of individual 'utilities') is also maximized. Net benefit therefore equals the total of individual utility benefits (economic benefits) minus the total of individual utility losses (economic costs), valued in market (i.e., monetary) terms. The appropriate valuation standard is said to be derived from individual willingness to pay (WTP) for the goods and services.[4,5] Fig. 3.1 provides a simplified conceptual depiction of a CBA process.

3.1.2 *Cost-Effectiveness Analysis*

A related but somewhat simpler economic evaluation method is cost-effectiveness analysis. Here, one is not trying to estimate an overall societal gain or loss but only the cost of achieving a particular gain in a desired objective as delivered by different interventions. For example, one might compare the cost of saving an individual life according to different road safety interventions, e.g., a traffic signal versus a roundabout. In this case, the lowest cost intervention per life would be preferred. Cost-effectiveness analysis requires less data than CBA but is also cruder because all outcomes are standardized in unit cost terms, in effect treating all outcomes equally.[6]

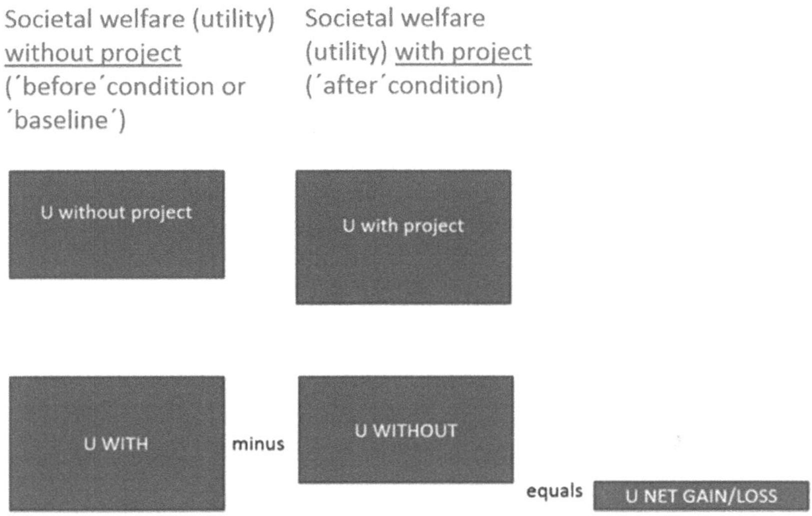

Figure 3.1 Cost–benefit analysis decision rule using a baseline.

3.2 Active Transportation Economic Benefits

3.2.1 The Co-benefit Concept

The phrase co-benefit has a somewhat variable definition depending upon the context, but a standard usage distinguishes co-benefits as the intended positive side effects of a policy, as opposed to ancillary benefits or unintended positive side effects.[7] Giles-Corti et al.[8] remarked that 'when benefits across multiple policy areas are considered concurrently, the term co-benefits is used' and provided an example in how the 'City of London's congestion tax not only reduced traffic by 30%, and CO_2, NO_x and large particulate emissions by 16%–20%, it also increased walking and cycling.'

Most active transportation interventions have immediate objectives that are not ends in themselves but a means to an end of particular health outcomes. Thus building of cycling and walking paths (hopefully) produces a mode shift from motorized to nonmotorized travel. The 'cause' in this example would be the installation of paths; the 'effect' or ancillary benefit would be mode shift to active travel; and the health co-benefits would include reduced mortality and morbidity from the human energy expenditure and exercise delivered by cycling and walking that otherwise would not occur. Reynolds et al.[9] claim that in practice co-benefit assessment in economic analysis is 'embryonic'.

Thus the core task of an economic evaluation is to estimate relevant health co-benefits and then to estimate the economic benefits flowing out of those co-benefits. The economic 'bottom-line' is whether the intervention delivers a positive net benefit to society (for CBA) or whether it is the most cost-effective way of delivering a particular goal (for cost-effectiveness analysis) considering all benefits and co-benefits. To do this, benefits and co-benefits need to be 'monetized' in some way to allow for adding apples and oranges and to provide an actual estimate of economic benefit.

3.2.2 Categories of Health Co-benefits of Active Transportation

The literature identifies a number of types of co-benefits accruing to population health from active transportation. Major categories of co-benefits are indicated in Table 3.1.

The literature, overall, does indicate substantial health co-benefit from increased rates of physical activity. There is, moreover, an advantage at the population level of obtaining such activity from active transportation rather than leisure activity. It is harder to put off a commute to work and travel to school than it is to skip a visit to the gym or engage in a sports activity. Active travel is also more equitably distributed than leisure activities which require time and money that some groups may not have.[13,16]

Cycling, in particular, delivers more aerobic benefit than walking, but different population groups benefit differently from active transportation. For example, walking offers greater benefits for unfit and older people because it is a more intense form of physical activity than it is for children and young adults.[16] Finally, as individuals become more active, the incremental benefit they may receive from additional active transportation declines.

3.2.3 Categories of Economic Benefits of Active Transportation

There are three major types of economic impact that potentially arise from active transportation interventions.

1. The flow-through of health co-benefits through the wider economy, especially reduced costs or mortality and morbidity. Cavill et al.[17] did a meta-review of active transportation economic evaluations and noted that most studies considered value of and costs savings from population mortality reductions, but few considered morbidity reductions. Some issues that crop up regularly include:
   - **a.** Simplistic assumptions about changes in overall level of physical activity due to better active transportation facilities. For example, rather than using patterns drawn from data (often sketchy in any case), a typical 'conservative' approach is to reduce linear extrapolation by 50%, or use some other approximation;
   - **b.** Focus on journey to work solely or primarily (in this case, obviously applying only to adults not children) rather than nonwork journeys;
   - **c.** Opacity about data or assumptions, e.g., drawing conclusions from incompletely described data sets or models;
   - **d.** Incomplete specification of the set of possible health outcomes, with chronic disease often left out.
   - **e.** A relative dearth of information about child populations more generally, especially their travel patterns.

   These findings, on both gains to general health and limitations of most analyses, have been confirmed by other sources.[18–21]
2. Nonhealth impacts that may arise from an intervention, e.g., reduced air pollution from reduced automobile trips due to mode shift away from car to cycling and walking. Such benefits are not health co-benefits but are other effects of any means which deliver increased active transportation. Mode shift is often the largest provider of such benefits. It should be noted that some of these nonhealth benefits do have health co-benefits, e.g., reduced auto emissions, which deliver both climate change improvements and potential reductions in the millions who currently die worldwide due to air pollution.[22]

Table 3.1 Major categories of active transportation co-benefits

Category	Comments	References
Physical health: • Healthy weight • Aerobic fitness • Healthy child development (e.g., bone and muscle health) • Bone, joint and muscle health generally • Reduced mortality/morbidity from disease associated with sedentary lifestyle (osteoporosis, high blood pressure, cardiopulmonary disease, adult-onset diabetes)	Current research suggests no effect on bone health in children. Presumably, walking could delay the loss of bone mass in adulthood but cycling would likely not because ground impact is insufficient. Evidence is quite inconsistent regarding a relationship between active transportation and body weight, and the literature suggests that aerobic fitness benefits are more important for cyclists than for walkers.	Litman,[10,11] Frank et al.,[12] Garrard,[13] Wang et al.[14]
Mental health: • Emotional well-being • Lowered stress and anxiety • Reduced incidence of mental health ailments (e.g., depression)	Emotional and mental health benefits tend to be secondary (but important) gains from increased physical activity. Separating out the various causes of such gains is quite difficult and thus these benefits tend to be left out of most active travel analyses (even though they may be quite important).	Garrard,[13] Winters et al.[15]
Intellectual and developmental health • IQ and educational attainment	The literature finds strong associations between general physical fitness and health and academic performance and performance on standardized intelligence tests. Active travel is only one of the many ways to achieve fitness.	Garrard[13]
Social well-being: • Increased community and neighbourhood cohesion • Greater social interaction	Causality is two ways, i.e., social well-being encourages physical activity and physical activity can encourage social well-being. Active travel may be especially beneficial here as more social connections may occur during it (as opposed to other activity such as going to the gym). A "safety in numbers" effect has been noted, where past a critical mass point, density of cyclists and walkers can improve overall safety for such active travellers.	Litman,[11] Giles-Corti,[8] Winters et al.[15]

Note that the above refer to population benefits. Obviously, individuals will garner these benefits unevenly.

Some of the major categories of economic benefits include:

a. motorized vehicle operating cost reductions
b. roadway congestion reduction (due to reduced number of automobiles on the roads)
c. roadway cost savings (reduced wear and tear on infrastructure)
d. parking cost savings
e. road safety impacts (reduced accidents from less vehicle traffic)
f. energy conservation (due to fewer vehicle-kilometres travelled)
g. vehicular pollution reduction (e.g., lowered auto exhaust emissions and noise)
h. climate change benefits (from lowered greenhouse gas emissions, etc.)
i. increased personal security—perceived and actual
j. amenity benefits (user appreciation and enjoyment from walking and cycling)
k. increased accessibility (the range of locations and activities expands)
l. mobility increases (the ability to move around is expanded).[19,23–25]

Elvik[26] conducts a hypothetical CBA for separate cycling tracks in Norwegian localities and finds that increases in walking and cycling lead to: a reduced need for public school bus transport; improvements in health resulting in reduced work absences; reduction in number and severity of road accidents; changes in auto traffic volume; changes in health state; and changes in perceptions of safety, amongst others.

The amenity benefits of subjective experience of travel by walking or cycling is interesting. Litman[11] poses the provocative question of what people would say when offered the choice of losing their ability to walk or losing their ability to drive. This question points to the fact that walking, in particular, is somehow fundamental to being human and that transport powered by walking can be satisfying in ways that other modes are not. Even car travel requires short bouts of walking.

By conventional measures, active transportation generally is slower than motorized transport, and these increases in travel time are typically modelled as a major cost of active travel interventions that reduce travel by faster modes. Amenity benefit is sometimes offset against this, e.g., travel may take longer—a cost, but it also may be more pleasant—a benefit. There are also some,[27] for example, who question the whole premise of travel time savings by automobiles, and, indeed, if one looks at an overall travel time budget, active travel might reduce travel time in other areas, e.g., if you get sufficient activity through active transportation, you don't need to drive to the gym to get your exercise. As of yet, mainstream evaluation practice does not consider such things, though, obviously, they should be examined further.

In particular instances, active travel actually can be faster than auto travel, especially for trip 'chains' in which there are multiple stops between a given origin and destination (e.g., dropping off the laundry on the way to work). In conducting a detailed analysis in Sydney, Ellison and Greaves[28] found that cycling was equally competitive with automobile trips for trip chains shorter than 10 km. Findings parallel to this were reported by the Roads and Traffic Authority[29] for New South Wales. Time savings advantage to active travel may also occur in instances for trips during rush hours and trips in urban areas where automobile speed limits are lower and cycling routes may be more direct (e.g., fewer intersections).

3. Potential wider 'productivity' effects driven by improved health. For example, healthier workers may produce more per work-hour than less healthy ones. Even after measuring intervention health co-benefits, monetized direct and indirect cost savings, and nonhealth benefits, there may still be additional effects on overall economic productivity, e.g., the labour productivity increases mentioned above, and more hours on the job due to reduced sick leave. This is a separate and additional benefit on top of any reduced costs from sickness and disability. It is not widely used in most current evaluations.[25]

3.2.4 Valuing Health Co-benefits

What is the 'economic' value of health, i.e., the mortality and morbidity implications of transport? Economists use WTP as the value metric. Blomquist[30] notes that consumer 'choice' of risk prevention activities can be used to derive WTP, e.g., if people choose not to wear seatbelts, this indicates that people value their life a certain amount, trading off the time and effort of wearing a seatbelt against the risk of injury or death in an accident. WTP is implicitly the basis of the Value of a Statistical Life and other measures used for calculating the economic value of morbidity and mortality improvements.[31–33]

There are issues in using the WTP metric because of its philosophical stance of subjectivity, e.g., the implication that life-years saved later in life and by sicker people should be worth less than those for younger and healthier people.[34] A standard methodological alternative is to value statistical life in terms of lost earnings; if a person can be expected to earn $100,000 per year (in present value terms) on average during a working life, then 3 lost life-years would be valued at $300,000. This standard has the advantage of being based on measurable evidence but has some of the same methodological limitations (e.g., lower income people's years lost are worth less than higher income ones). But valuation of mortality and morbidity is a necessity for any economic evaluation that hopes to come up with a bottom-line number.

3.3 Types of Active Transportation Interventions

Scheepers et al.[35] in a meta-review of active transportation studies indicated that interventions are quite heterogeneous and concluded that 'the included studies support the notion that a combination of different intervention tools is more effective than using only one tool' for 'stimulating active transportation (278).'

3.3.1 Infrastructure-Based Interventions

These refer to provision of physical facilities designed to enhance active travel choice and experience. Such changes include:

- building dedicated cycling or walking tracks, or adding lanes to existing streets and roads
- providing cycling facilities such as secure parking, showers, repair stations, etc.
- cycle-sharing facilities, docking stations, either commercial or free
- improved signage and enhanced signalling, e.g., cycle and/or pedestrian-dedicated traffic lights, improved way finding and directional guidance on walking/cycling paths, etc.
- vehicular traffic calming (e.g., roundabouts, speed bumps, etc.

These changes can be done singly or in tandem, and their scale can vary from small (e.g., the addition of one cycle parking area) to large (e.g., cycling 'highways'). Location can be varied according to target group and desired effects. For example, bike-sharing might be located at transit stations to increase both active travel and the uptake of transit generally. If the goal is to make more commuters walk or cycle to work, cycle facilities might be sited in major employment areas. Similarly, dedicated paths might be built around schools to increase active travel to school.

3.3.2 Built Environment, Transport System and Land-Use/ Planning Changes

A related type of intervention is to adjust the use of the built environment in some way. Examples include:

- car-free zones or automobile-restricted areas
- shared pedestrian/cycle/car areas with low speed (e.g., 'Complete Streets' which refers to fully integrated design of the actual street)
- conversion of roads to pedestrian malls
- on-street automobile parking restrictions (e.g., banning parking in central commercial zones)
- zoning restrictions, e.g., encouraging targeted housing and employment density to reduce auto dependency
- development policies encouraging active travel (e.g., requirements to provide footpaths on both sides of the street or a certain amount of green space for new housing complexes)
- integrated transit/road/active network planning (i.e., considering all three modes together when making system investment and management decisions, and resource allocations; this transport service and infrastructure provision should be coordinated with 'Complete Streets' and other design elements)
- free transit provision (e.g., free city bus loops).

The time required for these interventions to have an impact will obviously vary. Zoning restrictions, for example, are more medium-term or long-term in their potential impacts, though their ultimate effect may be more profound. Specific infrastructure may be required to implement these measures effectively, though these can be relatively low-scale, e.g., movable traffic barriers to close off a commercial street to automobiles during shopping hours.

This particular suite of policies is often only indirectly related to active travel. Several reports illustrate that, in addition to interventions supporting walking and cycling, measures that restrict car use are needed because perceived convenience is a key factor underlying decisions to drive.[20,24,36] Sometimes other outcomes, such as greenhouse gas reduction, may be the primary concern, with active travel a secondary outcome.

3.3.3 Economic and Other Incentives

Imposition of financial penalties and rewards, direct and indirect, is another method of fostering active transportation uptake. This includes mechanisms such as:

- subsidies for cycling or walking, e.g., provision of discounts on cycles and equipment
- lessening automobile subsidies, e.g., 'cashing out' of employer-paid parking in which employees are offered a monetary equivalent of the value of their provided parking space
- transit fare subsidies
- road pricing (e.g., the London and Stockholm congestion charge schemes).

These tend to be the least common interventions, perhaps because of expense, political challenges and difficulties in targeting effectively.

3.3.4 Behaviour Change Programmes

In a broad sense, any intervention is about changing behaviour, but this category directly aims to change the individual choice towards active transportation. Examples include:

- public information and awareness campaigns (e.g., brochures informing people of the benefits of active travel)
- one-off events to inform and encourage people to walk or cycle (e.g., Walk to Work or School days, active transportation fairs, etc.)
- self-help materials, such as activity-monitoring diaries or personalized active travel plans
- walking or cycling skills training classes
- social marketing campaigns and apps.

3.3.5 An Intervention Portfolio

There is, of course, much overlap between these various types of interventions. In general, they should be applied as part of a suite of measures because, when implemented in combination, they could result in larger mode shifts[12,37] . This has both analytical and project design implications. Younger et al.[38] argue that the tendency in policy and project analysis has been to focus on technology change, such as fuel efficiency, rather than influencing personal choice through built environment redesign. Such a narrow approach may limit the effectiveness of interventions.

3.4 Focus on Children: Active Transportation Interventions and Outcomes

There is no one-size-fit-all active transportation intervention that works for all population groups. Children are a special case given that they are not fully autonomous, so interventions must attend to both carer (usually parent) as well as child.

3.4.1 Travel to School Programmes

Most child active transportation interventions are focused on journeys to and from school. These programmes focus on encouraging children to cycle or walk to school and convincing their parents of the safety and benefit of doing so. There are relatively few robust evaluations here, and those that exist provide limited evidence of effectiveness. Some major examples include:

- *Walking school buses.* These programmes described in Chapter 15 involve groups of children led by adult volunteers in walking to and from school. Major efforts have been undertaken in the UK and the Australian state of Victoria for example.

- *School travel plans/Safe Routes to School (SRTS)* (see Chapters 13 and 14). These are active travel plans identifying barriers and opportunities for active travel to school. These plans are typically supported at the programme level by a dedicated staff member, possibly supported by individual teachers as part of normal classes or special events. The US SRTS programme is an example of a multimillion dollar effort.
- *Active transportation curricula.* Schools provide a natural opportunity for carrying the message of the benefits of walking and cycling and providing skills training to do so. These efforts can be in dedicated curricula and/or integrated into other courses. TravelSMART is an example of a national effort undertaken in Australia (though no longer currently active).[39]

3.4.2 Interventions for Active Transportation in General

There is less attention paid to children's travel outside of school, other than it being captured by more general active travel interventions focused on the larger population. But they do exist and include programmes such as:

- *Cycling/walking promotion programmes.* These are largely public information campaigns that have children and parents as their intended audience.
- *Independent mobility programmes.* These are essentially travel plans for children to go places without adult supervision other than school. They can be similarly structured to school programmes, including having community action groups to identify active travel barriers and local champions to coordinate and disseminate materials. The Streets Ahead programme in the Australian state of Victoria is an example of a major programme undertaken in 2008–11.[40]
- *Cycling and walking skills programmes.* These can be both offered within and outside of schools.

3.4.3 Economic Efficacy of Childhood Interventions

There have been numerous analyses of these types of programmes. The general findings on health co-benefits are positive: child walking and cycling do increase as a result of these interventions, and these have the expected morbidity and mortality improvements. The lifecycle impacts of these may in fact be greater for children than for adults, since the habit of active transportation may carry over into adult life.[41–43] Some interventions have shown little change in active transportation,[44,45] but, generally, these are due to identifiable intervention shortcomings, such as lack of funding, etc.

While there is a fairly large body of academic literature on economic evaluation of cycling and walking programmes, in general, there appears to be very little such literature on programmes that deal with children. Moodie et al.[44] conducted a cost-effectiveness analysis of the Walking School Bus programme in Victoria and found it mostly cost-inefficient, i.e., its health outcomes were not generally worth as much as the expenditure on the intervention. However, the health co-benefit measure was very narrow: energy expenditure and body mass index (BMI) reduction. A cost-effectiveness evaluation of the TravelSMART programme[45] was similarly negative. But again, the approach (conducted by the same study team) was limited to the BMI, even though this was not a stated objective of the programme. A broader measure of co-benefits would presumably have yielded better results, though that does not mean that the intervention would have been considered cost-effective.

A study of the cost-effectiveness of the New York City SRTS programme was more positive. Various simulations indicated that the programme was highly cost-effective, even though it was limited to just road safety rather than health outcomes: 'SRTS was associated with an overall net societal benefit of $230 million and 2055 quality-adjusted life years gained in New York City.'[46] The benefits would likely have been even larger had the researchers considered the effects of increased physical activity. Korber,[47] conducting a meta-review of interventions of economic evaluations of health promotion programmes for children and adolescents (and which includes interventions other than active transportation), found relatively few studies done and all those suffering from limitations such as short time horizons or very narrow ranges of health outcomes. In general, there appears to be much more economic evaluation work to be done in this area.

3.5 Conclusions

The literature on active transportation shows that it is overall an effective way to claw back some of those energy 'microsavings' mentioned at the beginning of this chapter and that the health co-benefits are positive. The actual economic value of these effects are more contested, and contestable, and in the area of child health, very sketchy. More analysis needs to be done, but it also needs to be done better and with greater clarity. The same can be said for intervention design.

3.6 Recommendations for Policy and Practice

1. Economic evaluations should assess packages of interventions rather than narrowly focusing on individual interventions. For example, there is clear evidence that neighbourhood design attributes are associated with increased physical activity through walking and that this, in turn, is associated with reduced weight and improved morbidity and mortality outcomes.[48] Thus rather than looking at different 'projects' in isolation, evaluations should consider different co-intervention bundles (complementary strategies), e.g., cycle investment joined with a traffic-calming project, etc.
2. Intervention design should interact more with intervention evaluation. Right now, the two tend to be done independently. Yet, interventions should be seen as portfolios of actions with multicausal outcomes, and it would be helpful to know more about those outcomes before designing interventions, especially with respect to economic benefits. Thus not only the analysis might need to change, so might the project, with interaction between project design and evaluation at the earliest stages.
3. Valuation should be examined in a more interdisciplinary way. The economic approach has merits and is widely used, but WTP and risk assessment may be too narrow for some purposes and problematic for others.

3.7 Recommendations for Future Research

1. Our understanding of the economic impacts of childhood active travel interventions is currently very limited. There simply are not many economic evaluations, and the existing ones are too limited in scope. More evaluations need to be conducted.
2. Greater effort is needed to more robustly examine health aspects of active transportation interventions, especially those involving active transportation, both with data collection and analytics. For example, travel surveys generally focus on journeys to work and ignore short trips, nonwork travel, travel by children, recreational travel and nonmotorized links all of which militate against active travel in particular.[10,11] Walking is generally at least a part of most trips, but most surveys and data categories ignore this. This is true, to a lesser extent, for cycling too, with Yi et al.[21] noting that 'the development of cycling choice models is still nascent (p. 4).'
3. Chain mobility, links between subtrips across a larger trip, is especially difficult when considering active mode shifts. Ellison and Greaves[28] say: '[Almost] all trips are made as a sequence of trips that together make up a trip chain or trip tour ... many chains consist of trips to multiple destinations, which may have different purposes (p. 16).' We need a better understanding of these issues. Thus, for example, the interventions aimed at parent-supervised child travel to school should not just focus on such trips in isolation but consider how they might fit into overall chains. A well-designed trip chain may yield more time savings and active travel than a tweaked single journey considered separately.

References

1. Olds T. Australia vying to be world champion of inactivity. *Conversation* September 21, 2014.
2. Green Communities Canada. *Saving money and time with active school travel.* 2010. http://www.playbrucegrey.com/public_docs/documents/Saving_Money_and_Time_with_AT.pdf.
3. McDonald N, Brown A, Marchetti L, Pedroso M. U.S. School travel, 2009: an assessment of trends. *Am J Prev Med* 2011;**41**(2):146–51.
4. European Commission: SafetyNet. *Cost-benefit analysis.* 2009. http://ec.europa.eu/transport/road_safety/specialist/knowledge/pdf/cost_benefit_analysis.pdf.
5. Mishan EJ, Quah E. *Cost-benefit analysis.* Routledge; 2007.
6. Chapter 3, cost-effectiveness analysis. In: Jamison DT, Breman JG, Measham AR, et al., editors. *Priorities in health.* Washington (DC): The International Bank for Reconstruction and Development/The World Bank; 2006. Available from: https://www.ncbi.nlm.nih.gov/books/NBK10253/.
7. Miyatsuka A, Zusman E. *Fact sheet no. 1, what are co-benefits? ACP Asian co-benefits partnership.* 2010.
8. Giles-Corti B, Foster S, Shilton T, Falconer R. The co-benefits for health of investing in active transportation. *New South Wales Public Health Bull* 2010;**21**(6):122–7.
9. Reynolds CC, Harris MA, Teschke K, Cripton PA, Winters M. The impact of transportation infrastructure on bicycling injuries and crashes: a review of the literature. *Environmental Health* 2009;**8**(47).
10. Litman T. Bicycling and transportation demand management. *Transportation research record 1441.* Transportation Research Board; 1994. p. 134–40.
11. Litman T. Economic value of walkability. *World Transport Pol Pract* 2004;**10**(1).

12. Frank LD, Sallis JF, Conway TL, Chapman JE, Saelens BE, Bachman W. Many pathways from land use to health: associations between neighborhood walkability and active transportation, body mass index, and air quality. *J Am Plann Assoc* 2006;**72**(1):75–87.
13. Garrard J. *Active travel to school: literature review*. ACT Government; 2011.
14. Wang G, Macera CA, Scudder-Soucie B, Schmid T, Pratt M, Buchner D. Cost effectiveness of a bicycle/pedestrian trail development in health promotion. *Prev Med* 2004;**38**(2):237–42.
15. Winters M, Ries F, Gouge B. *Active transportation in urban areas: exploring health benefits and risks*. National Collaborating Centre for Environmental Health; 2010.
16. Shephard RJ. Is active commuting the answer to population health? *Sports Med* September 1, 2008;**38**(9):751–8.
17. Cavill N, Kahlmeier S, Rutter H, Racioppi F, Oja P. Economic analyses of transport infrastructure and policies including health effects related to cycling and walking: a systematic review. *Transport Policy* 2008;**15**(5):291–304.
18. Krizec KJ. Estimating the economic benefits of bicycling and bicycle facilities: an interpretive review and proposed methods. In: *Essays on transport economics*. Physica-Verlag HD; 2007. p. 219–48.
19. Ministry of Infrastructure and Environment (Netherlands). *Social costs and benefits of cycling – Summary*. [Prepared by Decisio]. 2012.
20. Sælensminde K. Cost–benefit analyses of walking and cycling track networks taking into account insecurity, health effects and external costs of motorized traffic. *Transport Res Pol Pract* 2004;**38**(8):593–606.
21. Yi M, Feeney K, Adams D, Garcia C, Chandra P. Valuing cycling – evaluating the economic benefits of providing dedicated cycle ways at a strategic network level. In: *Australasian transport research forum 2011 proceedings 28–30 September 2011, Adelaide, Australia*. 2011. Publication website: http://www.patrec.org/atrf.aspx.
22. World Health Organization. *WHO releases country estimates on air pollution exposure and health impact*. September 27, 2016. http://www.who.int/mediacentre/news/releases/2016/air-pollution-estimates/en/.
23. Götschi T, Hintermann B. Valuation of public investment to support bicycling. *Swiss Soc Econom Stat* 2014;**150**(4):297–329.
24. Krag T. *Cost benefit analysis of cycling–Denmark*. Stockholm, Norway: CBA of Cycling, Nordic Council of Ministers; 2005.
25. Litman T. *Evaluating active transport benefits and costs*. Victoria Transport Policy Institute; 2015.
26. Elvik R. Which are the relevant costs and benefits of road safety measures designed for pedestrians and cyclists? *Accid Anal Prev* 2000;**32**(1):37–45.
27. Tranter PJ. Speed kills: the complex links between transport, lack of time and urban health. *J Urban Health* March 1, 2010;**87**(2):155–66.
28. Ellison R, Greaves S. Travel time competitiveness of cycling in Sydney, Australia. *Transport Res Rec J Transport Res Board* 2011;**2247**:99–108.
29. Roads, Traffic Authority of NSW and the Department of Environment and Climate Change. *Evaluation of the costs and benefits to the community of financial investment in cycling programs and projects in New South Wales: final Report*. 2009. http://www.pcal.nsw.gov.au/__data/assets/pdf_file/0008/90899/Evaluation_of_NSW_cycling_study.pdf.
30. Blomquist GC. Self-protection and averting behavior, values of statistical lives, and benefit cost analysis of environmental policy. *Rev Econ Househ* 2004;**2**(1):89–110.
31. De Blaeij A, Florax RJ, Rietveld P, Verhoef E. The value of statistical life in road safety: a meta-analysis. *Accid Anal Prev* 2003;**35**(6):973–86.
32. Graham JD, Vaupel JW. The value of a life: what difference does it make?. In: *Risk/benefit analysis in water resources planning and management*. US: Springer; 1981. p. 233–43.

33. Viscusi WK, Aldy JE. The value of a statistical life: a critical review of market estimates throughout the world. *J Risk Uncertain* 2003;**27**(1):5–76.
34. Alberini A, Cropper M, Krupnick A, Simon NB. Does the value of a statistical life vary with age and health status? Evidence from the US and Canada. *J Environ Econ Manag* 2004;**48**(1):769–92.
35. Scheepers CE, Wendel-Vos GCW, den Broeder JM, van Kempen EEMM, van Wesemael PJV, Schuit AJ. Shifting from car to active transport: a systematic review of the effectiveness of interventions. *Transport Res Part A Pol Pract* 2014;**70**:264–80.
36. National Cooperative Highway Research Program (NCHRP). *Guidelines for analysis of investments in bicycle facilities. NCHRP report 552*. Washington (DC): Transportation Research Board; 2006.
37. Piatowski D, Marshall W, Krizek K. Assessing intervention effectiveness and implementation carrots versus sticks: challenges for active transport. *J Plann Educ Res* June 21, 2017. Online first.
38. Younger M, Morrow-Almeida HR, Vindigni SM, Dannenberg AL. The built environment, climate change, and health: opportunities for co-benefits. *Am J Prev Med* 2008;**35**(5):517–26.
39. Australian Government. *About TravelSMART*. 2011. http://www.travelsmart.gov.au/about.html.
40. Victorian Government. *About streets ahead*. 2011. https://www.vichealth.vic.gov.au/programs-and-projects/streets-ahead2.
41. Chillón P, Evenson KR, Vaughn A, Ward DS. A systematic review of interventions for promoting active transportation to school. *Int J Behav Nutr Phys Activ* February 14, 2011;**8**(1):10.
42. Faulkner GE, Buliung RN, Flora PK, Fusco C. Active school transport, physical activity levels and body weight of children and youth: a systematic review. *Prev Med* January 31, 2009;**48**(1):3–8.
43. McDonald NC. Critical factors for active transportation to school among low-income and minority students: evidence from the 2001 National Household Travel Survey. *Am J Prev Med* 2008;**34**(4):341–4.
44. Moodie M, Haby M, Galvin L, Swinburn B, Carter R. Cost-effectiveness of active transport for primary school children - walking school bus program. *Int J Behav Nutr Phys Act* 2009;**6**:63. https://doi.org/10.1186/1479-5868-6-63.
45. Moodie M, Haby MM, Swinburn B, Carter R. Assessing cost-effectiveness in obesity: active transport program for primary school children–TravelSMART schools curriculum program. *J Phys Act Health* 2011;**8**(4):503–15.
46. Muennig PA, Epstein M, Li G, DiMaggio C. The cost-effectiveness of New York City's safe routes to school program. *Am J Pub Health* July 2014;**104**(7):1294–9.
47. Korber K. Quality assessment of economic evaluations of health promotion programs for children and adolescents—a systematic review using the example of physical activity. *Health Econom Rev* 2015;**5**:35. https://doi.org/10.1186/s13561-015-0071-5.
48. Berrigan D, Pickle LW, Dill J. Associations between street connectivity and active transportation. *Int J Health Geogr* 2010;**9**(1).

Further Reading

1. Sallis JF, Frank LD, Saelens BE, Kraft MK. Active transportation and physical activity: opportunities for collaboration on transportation and public health research. *Transport Res Pol Pract* 2004;**38**(4):249–68.

Last Child Walking?—Prevalence and Trends in Active Transportation

4

Richard Larouche
Faculty of Health Sciences, University of Lethbridge, Lethbridge, AB, Canada

When I was your age, I used to walk 5 miles. Uphill. Both ways. In the snow!
Unknown author

Chapter Outline

4.1 Introduction

When I explain to middle-aged and older adults that I do research on active transportation, they often respond by discussing about when they travelled to school in the "good old days" as a child. While adults sometimes romanticize how they travelled to school, this chapter clearly shows that time has changed—and arguably not for the better. Compared to their parents or grandparents at the same age, today's children are

Children's Active Transportation. https://doi.org/10.1016/B978-0-12-811931-0.00004-1

much less likely to walk or cycle to school, and this pattern has been observed in many countries. As I explain later on, there are many factors that may explain the decline in active transportation over the last few decades. Before discussing the extent to which active transportation declined over time and the potential reasons why, let us explore the prevalence of active transportation among today's children and how much it varies between countries. Because very few studies have examined travel to/from other places such as parks, shops, and friends' and relatives' houses, I focus specifically on children's travel to/from school in this chapter.

4.2 Prevalence of Active Transportation to and From School

When comparing the prevalence of active transportation across studies, it is important to bear in mind that studies have used different methods to assess children's travel mode. For example, some report children's *usual* school travel mode while others report the proportion of children undertaking at least one active trip to or from school per week. The prevalence of active transportation may be markedly higher when using the latter approach. For example, synthesizing data from different sources, Australian researchers noted that 45%–47% of Australian children engaged in active transportation *at least once per week*, whereas only 25%–32% reported that they *usually* walked or biked to/from school.[1] Such discrepancies make it difficult to compare results from studies that have used different measures of travel behaviours. Moving forward, this limitation could be minimized by using a standard protocol to assess children's school travel.

As a strategy to avoid comparing apples and oranges, I first compare data from studies and governmental reports that have examined children's *usual* school travel mode, which is the mode that they use most of the time. In Table 4.1, I present the findings of several population-based studies (or reports) about the prevalence of active transportation in many countries around the world. Studies are considered to be population-based when the researchers have selected a sample of participants who are representative of the target population of a country (or region). Such studies provide more reliable estimates of the prevalence of active transportation. To be included in this comparison, studies had to meet the following criteria:

1. clearly indicate that the sample is representative of the target population;
2. report children's usual mode of transportation—not how they travelled on a particular day or if they undertook at least one active trip over a week;
3. provide data on school-aged children and youth specifically;
4. have been published in the 10 years prior to the review (since January 2008).

The latter inclusion criterion is important given that many studies have observed declines over time in active transportation (see Section 4.2), so older estimates of the prevalence of active transportation to school may be somewhat misleading.

Table 4.1 shows large variations in children's usual school travel mode between countries and regions. For example, McDonald et al.[11] reported that only 12.7% of Americans aged 5 to 14 years engaged in active transportation in 2009. Other predominantly English-speaking countries, including Canada,[5] Ireland[12] and New

Table 4.1 **Findings of population-based studies on the prevalence of children's active transportation to school in many countries around the world**

Lead author, year and country	Data source, participants and region	Active transportation (%)	Walking (%)	Biking (%)	Motorized transportation (%)	Car (%)	Bus/public transit (%)	Other (%)[a]
Agence française de sécurité sanitaire des aliments (2009), France[2]	Étude Individuelle Nationale des Consommations Alimentaires 2 (2006–07); 455 French children aged 11–14 years	31	27	4	69	30	39	N/A
Amornsriwatanakul (2017), Thailand[3]	National survey of 13,255 children aged 6–17 years (2015)	51.9	N/A	N/A	48.1	N/A	N/A	N/A
Department for Transport (2013), England[4]	2012–13 National Travel Survey; 4670 children aged 5–16 years	43	41	2	57	35	19	2
Gray (2014), Canada[5]	2010 Physical Activity Monitor; 1797 children aged 5–17 years across Canada	24	N/A	N/A	62	N/A	N/A	14[b]

Continued

Table 4.1 Findings of population-based studies on the prevalence of children's active transportation to school in many countries around the world—cont'd

Lead author, year and country	Data source, participants and region	Active transportation (%)	Walking (%)	Biking (%)	Motorized transportation (%)	Car (%)	Bus/public transit (%)	Other (%)[a]
Grize (2010), Switzerland[6]	2005 Swiss Microcensus on Travel Behaviour; 1753 children aged 6–14 years	71.4	54.5	16.9	28.6	13.8	14.8	0.0
Jáuregui (2015), Mexico[7]	2012 Mexican National Health and Nutrition Survey; 2952 youths aged 10–14 years	70.8	68.8	2.0	29.2	13.3	14.6	1.3
Johansson (2011), Sweden[8]	2005–06 Health Behaviour in School-aged Children survey; 4415 youth aged 11–15 years	62.9	N/A	N/A	37.1	N/A	N/A	N/A
Mandic (2015), New Zealand[9]	2009–2011 Otago School Students Lifestyle Survey; 2108 youths aged 13–19 years in the province of Otago	37	34	3	63	39	24	N/A
Martínez-Gómez (2013), Spain[10]	2007–08 AFINOS study; 2029 adolescents aged 13–17 years; City of Madrid	56.8	N/A	N/A	43.2	N/A	N/A	N/A

McDonald (2011), the United States[11]	2009 National Household Travel Survey; 19,671 students aged 5–14 years	12.7	11.7	1.0	84.7	45.3	39.4	2.6
Murtagh (2016), Ireland[12]	Growing Up in Ireland Study; 7479 13-year-olds in 2011–12	19.8	17.8	2.0	80.2	49.7	30.5	N/A
Netherlands Ministry of Transport, Public Works and Water Management (2009), the Netherlands[13]	2009 Cycling in the Netherlands [report]. Limited data were provided about the study sample	86	37	49	14	14	0	0
Østergaard (2012), Denmark[14]	All 12- to 16-year-olds in the City of Odense were invited to participate in this 2009 study (n = 3847)	83.7	21.7	62.0	16.4	N/A	N/A	N/A
Pavelka (2017), Czech Republic[15]	Czech arm of the 2014 Health Behaviour in School-aged Children survey; 4288 youth aged 11–15 years	53.4	N/A	N/A	46.6	N/A	N/A	N/A

Continued

Table 4.1 Findings of population-based studies on the prevalence of children's active transportation to school in many countries around the world—cont'd

Lead author, year and country	Data source, participants and region	Active transportation (%)	Walking (%)	Biking (%)	Motorized transportation (%)	Car (%)	Bus/public transit (%)	Other (%)[a]
Reimers (2013), Germany[16]	2003–06 Motorik Modul and German Health Interview and Examination Survey for Children and Adolescents; 1828 youths aged 11–17 years across Germany	41.6	19.4	22.2	58.3	5.2	45.5	6.7
Welsh Government Social Research (2015), Wales[17]	2013–14 Welsh arm of the Health Behaviour in School-aged Children survey; 8754 youth aged 11–16 years	33	32	1	67	25	42	1
Yang (2017), China[18]	2011 China Health and Nutrition Survey; 1506 children aged 6–18 years in 9 Chinese provinces	69.3	57.0	12.3	30.7	N/A	N/A	N/A

Percentages may not add up to 100% because some studies included other travel modes. N/A is shown when no data are available for a given category.
[a]Other modes may include active or motorized modes.
[b]14% of participants used a combination of active and motorized modes.
When data were reported for boys and girls separately, a weighted average was calculated for this table.

Zealand,[9] tend to have a low prevalence of active transportation. In contrast, rates of active transportation above 70% have been reported in countries such as Mexico,[7] the Netherlands[13] and Switzerland.[6]

Consistent with studies of adults,[19] the studies presented in Table 4.1 show a very low prevalence of cycling in most countries except in Central and Northern Europe. Nationally representative surveys in Germany, Sweden and Switzerland all indicate a prevalence of cycling above 15%.[6,8,16] Moreover, almost half of Dutch children cycle to school.[13] In the city of Odense (Denmark), many studies have revealed that up to two-thirds of adolescents usually cycle to/from school.[14,20,21] It is interesting to note that Odense is thought to be the birthplace of Safe Routes to School interventions which aim to encourage more children to engage in active transportation by making school neighbourhoods safer (see Chapter 13 for more details).

Even among children using motorized travel modes, there are striking differences between countries. For example, van der Ploeg et al.[22] noted that two-thirds of 5- to 9-year-olds and 47.8% of 10- to 14-year-olds in New South Wales (Australia) were driven by car. In contrast, although the majority of German youths used motorized travel modes, only about 5% travelled by car.[16] Children using public transit may accumulate a fair amount of physical activity by walking to/from transit stops.[23] In contrast, car travel involves almost no activity and usually contributes to air pollution and congestion to a greater extent than other motorized travel modes.

4.2.1 Limitations of Comparisons Between Studies

There are some important challenges to comparing data between studies. In addition to the different assessment methods, it is noteworthy that some of the studies listed in Table 4.1 have been conducted in entire countries while others have focussed on a single city or region. The prevalence of active transportation may differ markedly from one region to another. For example, Fig. 4.1 shows that in Canada, the prevalence of active transportation is much higher in Western compared to Eastern provinces according to data from the 2010 Physical Activity Monitor study.[6,24]

In addition, some studies have asked children to report how they travel to school while others have asked parents. Thankfully, studies that have compared children and parent reports have generally indicated good agreement.[25] This means that children are generally capable of reporting their usual mode of transportation accurately. However, the studies presented in Table 4.1 have also categorized participants' responses differently. For example, some merely reported the overall prevalence of active versus motorized transportation while others reported the prevalence of a greater range of travel modes.

4.2.2 International Study of Childhood Obesity, Lifestyle and the Environment

While international comparisons are complicated by methodological differences across studies, the International Study of Childhood Obesity, Lifestyle and the Environment provides comparable estimates of the prevalence of active transportation in 12 sites within 12 countries representing all inhabited continents.[26] These included

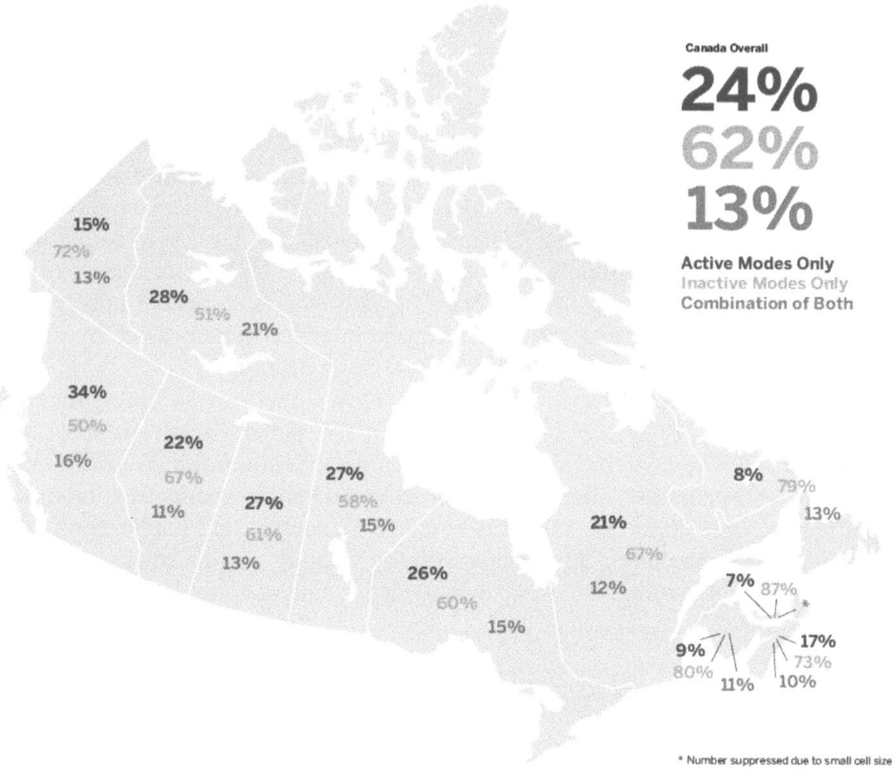

Figure 4.1 Prevalence of active transportation to school by province or territory in Canada. Note: data from the 2010 Physical Activity Monitor study (Ref. 24).
Reproduced with permission from ParticipACTION.

Australia (Adelaide), Brazil (São Paulo), Canada (Ottawa), China (Tianjin), Colombia (Bogotá), Finland (Helsinki, Espoo and Vantaa), India (Bangalore), Kenya (Nairobi), Portugal (Porto), South Africa (Cape Town), the United Kingdom (Bath and North East Somerset) and the United States (Baton Rouge). In each site, a sample of approximately 500 nine- to eleven-year-olds were recruited in urban and suburban areas that differed in wealth. Data were collected from September 2011 through December 2013, and study staffs were thoroughly trained and used the same methods in each country.

Fig. 4.2 shows that there were large differences in school travel modes between sites. The highest prevalence of active transportation was observed in the Helsinki region (79.4%), and Bogotá was a close second (73.8%). In Bogotá, walking represented the overwhelming majority of active trips (71.6%), whereas Helsinki had the highest rate of cycling (24.4%). In contrast, the lowest prevalence of active transportation was observed in Bangalore (5.2%), which also had the highest proportion of trips made by bus/train/van (61.8%). Finally, the highest percentage of trips made by car was observed in Adelaide (63.8%).

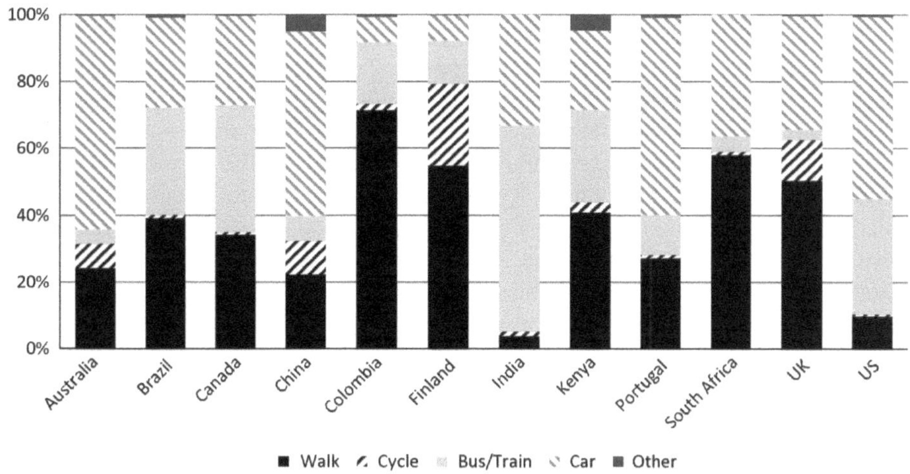

Figure 4.2 School travel mode in the International Study of Childhood Obesity, Lifestyle and the Environment, 2011–13.
Reproduced from Larouche R, Sarmiento OL, Broyles ST, Denstel KD, Katzmarzyk PT, Church TS, et al. For the ISCOLE Research Group. Are the correlates of active school transport context-specific? *Int J Obes Suppl* 2015;**5**:S89–99, as published in the *International Journal of Obesity Supplements* with permission from Springer Nature.

Two caveats of this study are worth mentioning. First, the prevalence of active transportation within a city or region may not reflect the situation of a country as a whole. For example, the prevalence of active transportation in Bangalore might be much lower than elsewhere in India, as suggested by another study in Hyderabad.[27] Second, rural areas were not included in the study. Children living in rural areas in developing countries such as Kenya and India, where access to motorized vehicles is very limited, may be much more likely to engage in active transportation, even if that entails walking very long distances (see Chapter 12 for a more detailed discussion of active transportation in developing countries). In contrast, children living in rural areas in the United States, where car ownership is extremely high, would be much less likely to engage in active transportation than their urban counterparts who likely live much closer to their school on average.

4.3 Time Trends in Active Transportation

While the prevalence of active transportation varies markedly across countries, it is of greater concern that it has decreased steeply over the last few decades in many countries. In this section, I present data from population-based studies examining trends over time in children's usual mode of transportation.

4.3.1 Time Trends in Active Transportation at the Country Level

Studies conducted in Canada,[5] Czech Republic,[15] England,[4,28,29] Switzerland[6] and the United States[11] report time trends in children's usual school travel mode based on nationally representative data. As shown in Fig. 4.3, all of these studies reveal a decline in the prevalence of active transportation over time. The period of time represented by the studies ranges from 8 years in the Czech Republic to 40 years in the United States. To compare the rate of decline between countries, it is thus necessary to use a comparable measure of time. As in a previous review of children's physical activity, I express the observed declines in percentage points per decade.[30] Using this metric, the declines in active transportation per decade in percentage points were 4% in Canada, 6%–7% in England and Switzerland, 9% in the United States and 26% in the Czech Republic.

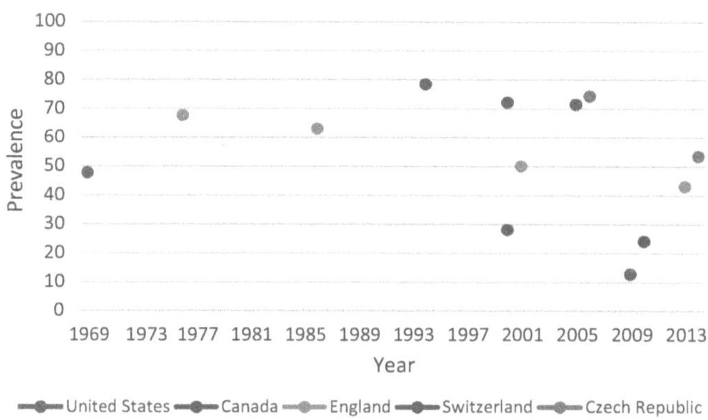

Figure 4.3 Time trends in the prevalence of active transportation to school in five countries. Note: data are reported as the percentage of children engaging in active transportation for the year corresponding to each survey cycle.
Data were collated from Department for Transport. *Table NTS9908 Trips to and from school by main mode—region and area type: Great Britain, 2012/13* [database online]. London (England): Department for Transport; 2013. Available from: https://www.gov.uk/government/statistical-data-sets/nts99-travel-by-region-and-area-type-of-residence. Gray C, Larouche R, Barnes JD, Colley RC, Tremblay MS, Cowie Bonne J, et al. Are we driving our kids to unhealthy habits? Results from the active healthy kids Canada 2013 report card on physical activity for children and youth. *Int J Environ Res Public Health* 2014;**11**(6):6009–20. Available from: https://www.ncbi.nlm.nih.gov/pmc/articles/PMC4078562/. Grize L, Bringolf-Isler B, Martin E, Braun-Fahrländer C. Trend in active transportation to school among Swiss school children and its associated factors: three cross-sectional surveys 1994, 2000 and 2005. *Int J Behav Nutr Phys Act* 2010;**7**:28. Available from: https://ijbnpa.biomedcentral.com/articles/10.1186/1479-5868-7-28. McDonald NC, Brown AL, Marchetti LM, Pedroso MS. U.S. school travel, 2009: an assessment of trends. *Am J Prev Med* 2011;**41**(2):146–51. Pavelka J, Sigmundová D, Hamřik Z, et al. Trends in active commuting to school among Czech schoolchildren from 2006 to 2014. *Cent Eur J Public Health* 2017;**25**(Suppl. 1):S21–5. Department of Transport. *1979 National travel survey: 1975/6 report*. London: Department for Transport; 1979. Department of Transport. *2001 National travel survey: 1999/2001 update*. London: Department for Transport; 2001.

In Canada, the prevalence of active transportation among school-aged children decreased from 28% to 24% between 2000 and 2010, but this decline was not statistically significant.[6] Conversely, the prevalence of motorized travel increased from 51% to 62%, whereas the percentage of students using a combination of active and motorized modes (for example, walking part of the way and then taking the city bus) decreased from 21% to 14%. Both of these changes were significant.

The decline in active transportation was much steeper in the Czech Republic.[15] From 2006 to 2014, the proportion of children engaging in active transportation to school declined from 74.3% to 53.4%. Furthermore, a study using census data from 6236 adolescents in the cities of Olomouc and Hradec Králové observed that, within a single decade, the prevalence of active transportation decreased almost by half, from 49.1% to 26.0%![31] The researchers matched the census data with objective measures of neighbourhood walkability obtained with geographic information systems. The concept of neighbourhood walkability is described in more detail in Chapter 10, but essentially, a walkable area is one where it is easy to walk to/from places (e.g., workplaces, schools, shops, restaurants, sport centres, etc.). The decline in active transportation was much steeper in areas that initially had low walkability (from 37.4% to 14.6%) compared to those that had high walkability (from 51.7% to 32.2%). The authors also noted a substantial increase in car ownership in the Czech Republic during the study period.[31]

In England, comparable data on school travel mode covering a period of 37 years have been published by the Department for Transport.[5,28,29] The proportion of 5- to 16-year-olds driven to/from school by car has more than tripled, whereas the prevalence of walking declined from 63.3% to 41.0%. Cycling accounted for less than 5% of trips at all time points. From 1975 to 2001, the average distance between home and school has increased from 1.6 to 2.3 km for 5- to 10-year-olds and from 3.9 to 4.7 km for 11- to 16-year-olds. Data from the 1985–86 and 1999–2001 surveys also indicate that the percentage of 5- to 10-year-olds travelling to/from school without adult accompaniment has decreased from 21% to 10%.[32]

In Switzerland, Grize et al.[6] reported changes in children's school travel mode using data from the 1994, 2000 and 2005 Swiss Microcensus on Travel Behaviour. The prevalence of active transportation decreased from 78.4% to 71.4% over 11 years, although the distance between home and school did not change significantly over time. However, the average number of cars per household increased while the opposite trend was observed for bicycle ownership. In turn, children whose family owned at least 2 cars were more likely to be driven to school whereas children who had more limited access to a bicycle were less likely to cycle to/from school.

In the United States, the proportion of children in kindergarten to grade 8 who engaged in active transportation decreased by nearly 4 times (from 47.7% to 12.7%) between 1969 and 2009.[11] Even among children living within a quarter mile (~400 m) from school, more than 40% were driven to school in 2009! The decline in active transportation was mirrored by an increase in car travel (from 12.2% to 45.3%), while school bus use did not change over time. In a similar study using a different data set, McDonald[33] reported that the percentage of children who engaged in active transportation on the day of the survey declined from 40.7% to 12.9% between 1969 and 2001, with the steepest decline occurring between 1969 and 1977.

4.3.2 Regional Surveys of Time Trends in Active Transportation

Many studies report on time trends in children's school travel mode among representative samples of children and youth living in a specific city, region or province. While it is unclear if similar trends would have been observed across the entire country where the study took place, these studies contribute to our understanding of the changes in active transportation. Consistent with the nationally representative studies discussed above, the majority of regional studies observed significant declines in active transportation, although Denmark is a noteworthy exception.

4.3.2.1 Belgium

Marique et al.[34] described the changes in school travel mode among children in Walloon using data from the 1991 and 2001 censuses. Over 10 years, the prevalence of active transportation decreased from 28.9% to 17.0%, and most of this decline was compensated by an increase in car travel.

4.3.2.2 Brazil

Silva et al.[35] examined time trends in school travel mode between 2001 and 2011 in a large sample of adolescents living in the state of Santa Catarina. The proportion of children who travelled by car or motorcycle almost doubled (from 6.4% to 12.6%), primarily at the expense of active transportation which declined from 56.3% to 51.3%.

4.3.2.3 China

Yang et al.[18] studied changes in school transportation between 1997 and 2011 among 6- to 18-year-olds living in urban and rural areas within 9 Chinese provinces. There was a sevenfold increase in the proportion of participants travelling by motor vehicle within only 14 years (from 4.2% to 30.7%). Distance was identified as a key correlate of active transportation. Compared to children living at least 2 miles (3.2 km) away from school, those who lived less than 0.5 miles (800 m) away were 41 times more likely to engage in active transportation. From 1997 to 2011, the percentage of children living within 0.5 miles away from school decreased from 22% to 13%, whereas the percentage of those who lived at least 2 miles away rose from 27% to 44%. The percentage of households who owned private motorized vehicles also tripled during that time. In a previous analysis that included data from 1997 to 2006, a decline in bicycle ownership (from about 80% to 60%) was also noted.[36]

4.3.2.4 Denmark

Notwithstanding the fact that data were gathered from different surveys, Denmark may be one of few countries where active transportation has not declined significantly over the last few decades. Indeed, Table 4.2 compiles data on school travel mode among adolescents who participated in population-based studies conducted in 1983, 2003 and 2009. In all three studies, 60%–70% of boys and girls reported that cycling was their main mode of transportation.[14,20,21] In the two most recent

Table 4.2 Time trends in school travel mode among Danish adolescents

Lead author (year)	Survey characteristics	Cycling (%)	Walking (%)	Motorized travel (%)
Andersen (2009)	Danish Youth and Sports Study (1983). 1249 adolescents aged 15–19 years across Denmark	Boys: 61.1 Girls: 64.6	Boys: 10.6 Girls: 14.8	Boys: 28.3 Girls: 20.6
Andersen (2011)	334 adolescents participating in the 2003 follow-up of the Danish arm of the European Youth Heart Study at the age of 15 years in the city of Odense	Boys: 61.2 Girls: 68.3	Boys: 20.4 Girls: 18.8	Boys: 18.4 Girls: 13.0
Østergaard (2012)	Survey of Grade 7–9 students in all schools in the city of Odense in 2009 (3847 adolescents; mean age = 14.8 years)	Boys: 62.5 Girls: 61.4	Boys: 21.5 Girls: 21.9	Boys: 16.1 Girls: 16.7

surveys conducted in the city of Odense, over 80% of children engaged in active transportation. Therefore, these data suggest that the decline in active transportation is not inevitable.

4.3.2.5 Spain

Chillón et al.[37] compared the prevalence of active transportation between two population-based studies conducted in the city of Madrid in 2001–02 and 2006–07. Both studies involved 13- to 17-year-olds and used similar questions about adolescents' usual school travel mode. Interestingly, they observed a nonsignificant increase in the prevalence of active transportation among boys (from 44.4% to 49.0%). However, active transportation decreased steeply in girls, from 61% to 48% over 5 years.

4.4 What's Driving the Decline in Active Transportation?

Given that many studies have reported substantial declines in active transportation over the last few decades, it is important to consider the reasons that may explain why today's children are much less likely to walk or bike to school than their parents and grandparents were at the same age. These may include an increase in the average distance between home and school (potentially exacerbated by a decline in the distance that individuals are willing to walk or bike); a decrease in children's independent mobility combined with the perceived convenience of driving children to school; and parental concerns about their child's safety from traffic and crime (which may have increased over time). Importantly, these factors may be interrelated. For example, to reduce safety concerns, a mother might decide to drive her child to school on the way to work, thus increasing traffic in the neighbourhood.

4.4.1 Distance

Distance between home and school is known to be a major determinant of travel mode choices.[11,18,38,39] Therefore, it is reasonable to hypothesize that increasing distance might have contributed to the decline in active transportation over the last few decades. Indeed, McDonald[33] estimated that as much as half of the decrease in active transportation in the United States could be explained by increasing distance! Longer distance appears to be partly responsible for the rapid increase in motorized travel among Chinese children.[18] Distance is a complex issue because it is the result of decisions taken at many levels, from children's and parents' school preferences to political choices.[40,41] Table 4.3 illustrates some of the key interrelated

Table 4.3 Factors associated with a greater distance between home and school

Factor	Level	Implications
Child school preference	Personal	If a child prefers to go to a minority language school, or to one that offers a special programme (sports, arts, etc.), then the distance will likely be greater.
Parent school preference	Interpersonal	Same as above.
Urban sprawl	Policy/built environment	Urban planning policies and practices that favour sprawl result in greater distances between locations.
School choice policies	Policy	If these policies are liberal, then it's likely that the average child will travel a greater distance to and from school. In many jurisdictions, these policies have become more liberal during the last few decades.
School siting guidelines	Policy	These guidelines determine where new schools are being built. New schools are commonly built in the outskirts of cities where land is cheaper, but this leads to larger trip distance for the average child.
Small school closure	Policy	Over the last few decades, many small schools have been closed (particularly in rural areas) to save money. Thus, instead of attending a school in their neighbourhood, many children are bussed over long distances.

factors that determine the distance between home and school. For example, liberal school choice policies allow families to register their child in a more distant school rather than to a neighbourhood school.[41,42] Many studies have found that children attending minority language schools or schools that offer special programmes are less likely to engage in active transportation.[43,44] Urban planning policies and practices that favour urban sprawl also result in increased distances between locations, thereby deterring active transportation.[45] Sprawling areas are typically characterized by lower neighbourhood walkability, so it is not surprising that Dygrýn et al.[31] observed a steeper decline in active transportation in low walkability areas relative to high walkability areas.

Furthermore, decisions about where to build new schools also affect the distance between home and school. The Council of Educational Facility Planners International[46] recommended that schools be built on lots covering a minimal area of one acre of land (about 4000 square metres) for every 100 students plus an additional 10 acres for elementary schools, 20 for middle schools and 30 for high schools. Following these guidelines, new schools were typically built in the outskirts of cities where land is cheaper and plentiful.[41,47] These guidelines were revised in 2004 to remove minimal size standards and encourage urban planners to incorporate smart growth principles.[48] In contrast with urban sprawl, smart growth favours development in compact and walkable urban centres. Furthermore, new guidelines developed in Canada explicitly recommend that the potential for children to walk or bike to school be taken into consideration when deciding where to build new schools.[49]

While distance may explain the lion's share of the decrease in active transportation, other factors are certainly at play. For example, Grize et al.[6] reported no change in distance over time among Swiss children. The increase in average distance between home and school reported in England over the last two generations was relatively modest.[32] Moreover, McDonald[33] also noted that the percentage of American children living within 1 mile (1.6 km) from school, who engaged in active transportation, decreased from 85.9% to 49.9% between 1969 and 2001. In other words, even among children who lived within a walkable distance, there has been a substantial decline in active transportation suggesting that the distance that people are willing to travel actively has decreased over time.[33] While a 5-mile (8-km) journey by bike may have been totally acceptable a few generations ago, it may not be the case today. Nevertheless, children living in more bike-friendly countries such as Denmark and Finland may be more willing to walk or bike over longer distances,[30,50] suggesting that the answer to the question "how far is too far?" is equivocal, and likely depends on cultural factors.

In many jurisdictions, schools buses are provided for children living further than a set distance (often 1 mile or 1.6 km). Even children living closer are often offered to ride the bus if their route to school involves a "hazard". For example, crossing a major road with a high speed limit might be considered a hazard. However, hazards are often perceived, and not objectively determined, and therefore their definition is quite subjective and may vary markedly between school boards. While children who are eligible for bussing are not necessarily obligated to take the bus, doing so is convenient for parents who may save time by not having to escort their child to/from school. Similarly, parents who drive their children to school may believe that, in doing so, they are acting as "good parents", doing what they think their friends or other parents would do. Psychologists refer to the latter concept as a "social norm"[51–53] and believe that this can have a substantial impact on individuals' behaviour.

4.4.2 Children's Independent Mobility

The next chapter will explain in detail how independent mobility has shrunken over time, with fewer children allowed to travel to/from school without adult supervision. Hence, a growing number of children are accompanied by parents (or other adults) on the way to school. Parents typically choose the mode of transportation that they believe is most convenient to them, and the car is often seen as "quickest and easiest" compared to other travel modes.[54,55] It is therefore not surprising that children who are escorted to school by their parents are less likely to engage in active transportation than children who travel alone or with friends.[56] Data from Pooley et al.[32] show that active transportation and independent mobility declined concurrently in England.

4.4.3 Safety From Crime and Traffic

Many studies have shown that parental concerns about safety from crime and road traffic are major deterrents of active transportation.[38,57] Many authors believe that parents have become more worried about their child's safety over time and this may, in turn, restrict opportunities for children to engage in active transportation and play outside unsupervised by adults.[58,59]

Stranger danger refers to the potential danger to children posed by strangers who may approach them.[60] This unpredictable threat has grown as adults are becoming less prone to trust each other, and arguably with the neoliberal reforms favouring individual—rather than collective—responsibility, thereby putting more pressure on parents to ensure their child's well-being.[60,61] In an Australian study, 81% of parents of 10- to 12-year-olds reported that they worried about strangers.[62] This fear is linked with the emergence of so-called "helicopter parents" who constantly monitor their ("bubble-wrapped") children's activities.[58] Yet, recent studies suggest that helicopter parenting may do more harm than good, notably, by depriving children of opportunities to develop their independence and by limiting their physical activity.[59,63]

The concept of stranger danger may be somewhat misleading because cases of child abduction by total strangers are extremely rare. For example, only 1 case of child abduction by a total stranger was confirmed by the Royal Canadian Mounted Police over a period of 2 years across Canada.[64] In the large majority of cases of violence against children, the perpetrators are actually parents, relatives and other known persons.[60] Yet, child safety campaigns typically put much emphasis on stranger danger.

While children and parents may have had concerns about "bogeymen" and "wicked witches" for generations, ubiquitous media coverage has likely played an important role in amplifying fear of strangers.[60,61,65] In addition, the way in which child murders are portrayed by the media may have changed over time. According to Gill, such events were portrayed as "isolated atrocities committed by evil individuals" in the early 20th century, but they are now considered the result of a society in decline.[66]

Sensationalistic media reports focusing extensively on the bereaved families' perspective may exacerbate feelings of fear and anxiety among the public. Furthermore, media stories about parents accused of child neglect for letting their child play in the park or walk alone[67,68] may discourage parents to let their kids walk to school on their own.

Parental concerns about road safety are another major deterrent of active transportation.[38,57] Road injury is the ninth leading cause of death globally.[66] While the number of fatalities has plateaued since 2007, road traffic injuries kill approximately 1.25 million people per year, of which 26% are pedestrians and cyclists. Most deaths occur in developing countries, with the African region having by far the highest fatality rate.[69] Yet, road injury is among the leading causes of deaths for young people in high-income countries too. For instance, it is the leading cause of death resulting from injuries among Canadians aged 1–24 years.[70] Nevertheless, the risks associated with active transportation should not be viewed in isolation of the benefits of walking and cycling, as described in Chapter 1.

Many initiatives have been implemented to minimize the risk of road injury, such as Safe Routes to School, walking school buses, traffic calming devices (e.g., speed bumps and narrower intersections) and reduced speed limits. These interventions are covered in greater detail in the third section of the book. Nevertheless, at the end of the day—and irrespective of the reasons why—when parents start to drive their children to/from school, this increases exposure to traffic for walkers and cyclists, putting them at an increased risk of injury. When a critical number of children in the neighbourhood are driven, parents who did not drive their child may start doing so in order to be viewed as "good parents". This vicious circle may lead to "social traps" where driving begets driving as described by Tranter.[71] Later in life, it is unlikely that children who have constantly been driven will become active travellers in adulthood.[72]

4.5 Black Clouds and Silver Lining?

While the overwhelming majority of studies described in this chapter show significant declines in active transportation over time, there may be some light at the end of the tunnel. In recent years, some reports have shown decreases in driver license ownership and car ownership among so-called "millennials" (individuals born between 1980 and 1999) in some high-income countries of North America, Europe and Oceania.[73–76] For example, Kuhminhof et al.[76] observed declines in car travel in 16- to 34-year-olds in France, Germany, Great Britain, Japan, Norway and the United States since 2000, particularly among males.

Different theories have been proposed to explain the recent decrease in licensure and car use in the scientific literature. Hypothesized reasons include: longer education, decreasing employment rates, delaying marriage and parenthood, increased costs associated with car ownership (e.g., license, gas, insurance, etc.), the global recession of 2008, reduced travel demand, stricter licensing requirements (e.g., graduated license schemes), changes in attitudes towards driving, increase in virtual communication/shopping, etc.[74] According to many authors, it is unrealistic to believe that there is a unique cause for these changes.[74,77,78]

It remains unclear whether the decrease in licensure and vehicle miles travelled among millennials will persist over time as they get older and wealthier,[77,78] so there is a clear need for studies to continue monitoring millennials' travel behaviour. Furthermore, declines in licensure and car travel are far from universal. Increases in licensure among young people have been noted in other high-income countries over the last 15–30 years.[74] To my knowledge, decreases in licensure and car travel have only been reported in high-income countries. In developing countries, car travel is increasing rapidly.[18,78]

4.6 Conclusions

Collectively, the studies reviewed in this chapter highlight large differences between countries in the prevalence of active transportation to/from school, but consistently indicate a substantial decline in active transportation over the last few decades in many countries. Increasing distance appears to be a key contributor to this decline, but other factors such as decreasing independent mobility, unfavourable social norms and parental safety concerns may also play important roles. Recent declines in licensure and car travel among young people in some high-income countries may be encouraging, but it is unclear if this trend will persist over time, and large increases in car ownership in developing countries are forecasted.[78]

4.7 Recommendations for Policy and Practice

1. Given the important role of distance in influencing travel mode decisions, policymakers should consider children's transportation when deciding where to build new schools. Of particular interest, the Canadian Child- and Youth-Friendly Land-Use and Transport Planning Guidelines[49] provide useful strategies on how to ensure that children's needs are duly taken into account. Other jurisdictions may develop similar guidelines.
2. Policymakers should encourage parents to register their children in a neighbourhood school because liberal school choice policies are associated with a reduced prevalence of active transportation, and higher traffic congestion and exhaust gas emissions.[42,79,80]
3. Policymakers and practitioners should develop and implement interventions and launch social marketing campaigns to promote active transportation. These may include walking school buses, bike trains, school travel plans (i.e., comprehensive plans to address barriers to active transportation), educational programmes, cycling skill classes as well as traffic calming (i.e., implementation of speed bumps, narrower roadways, etc.) and reduction of speed limits.
4. Urban planners and policymakers should draw lessons from countries such as Denmark—a rich country that has maintained a large prevalence of active transportation (particularly cycling) over time, despite a relatively high rate of car ownership.

4.8 Recommendations for Future Research

1. This chapter focused on the trip to/from school because, to my knowledge, no data are available about changes in active transportation to/from other places. This is a key research gap that should be addressed.

2. There is a need to develop a standardized protocol for measuring active transportation which would facilitate comparisons between jurisdictions and the study of trends over time.
3. To help prevent further declines in active transportation, a better understanding of the factors associated with changes in travel modes over time is needed. As such, population-based studies should monitor factors such as distance, perceived convenience of different travel modes, perceived traffic and safety from crime, etc.
4. Similarly, more research is needed to investigate the reasons why, in some high-income countries, there has been a decline in licensure among young people. This may inform future interventions aiming to minimize car use and encourage active transportation.

References

1. Active Healthy Kids Australia. *The road less travelled: 2015 progress report card on active Transport for children and young people*. Adelaide (South Australia): Active Healthy Kids Australia; 2015. Available from: http://www.activehealthykidsaustralia.com.au/siteassets/documents/ahka_reportcard_2015_web.pdf.
2. Agence française de sécurité sanitaire des aliments. *Étude Individuelle Nationale des Consommations Alimentaires 2*. Nancy (France): Agence française de sécurité sanitaire des aliments; 2009. Available from: https://www.anses.fr/fr/system/files/PASER-Ra-INCA2.pdf.
3. Amornsriwatanakul A, Lester L, Bull FC, Rosenberg M. Are Thai children and youth sufficiently active? Prevalence and correlates of physical activity from a nationally representative cross-sectional study. *Int J Behav Nutr Phys Act* 2017;**14**:72. Available from: https://ijbnpa.biomedcentral.com/articles/10.1186/s12966-017-0529-4.
4. Department for Transport. *Table NTS9908 Trips to and from school by main mode—region and area type: Great Britain, 2012/13*. [database online] London (England): Department for Transport; 2013. Available from: https://www.gov.uk/government/statistical-data-sets/nts99-travel-by-region-and-area-type-of-residence.
5. Gray C, Larouche R, Barnes JD, Colley RC, Tremblay MS, Cowie Bonne J, et al. Are we driving our kids to unhealthy habits? Results from the active healthy kids Canada 2013 report card on physical activity for children and youth. *Int J Environ Res Public Health* 2014;**11**(6):6009–20. Available from: https://www.ncbi.nlm.nih.gov/pmc/articles/PMC4078562/.
6. Grize L, Bringolf-Isler B, Martin E, Braun-Fahrländer C. Trend in active transportation to school among Swiss school children and its associated factors: three cross-sectional surveys 1994, 2000 and 2005. *Int J Behav Nutr Phys Act* 2010;**7**:28. Available from: https://ijbnpa.biomedcentral.com/articles/10.1186/1479-5868-7-28.
7. Jáuregui A, Medina C, Salvo D, Barquera S, Rivera-Dommarco JA. Active commuting to school in Mexican adolescents: evidence from the Mexican national nutrition and health survey. *J Phys Act Health* 2015;**12**(8):1088–95.
8. Johansson K, Hasselberg M, Laflamme L. Active commuting to and from school among Swedish children – a national and regional study. *Eur J Public Health* 2012;**22**(2):209–14.
9. Mandic S, de la Barra SL, Bengoechea EG, Stevens E, Flaherty C, Moore A, et al. Personal, social and environmental correlates of active transport to school among adolescents in Otago, New Zealand. *J Sci Med Sport* 2015;**18**(4):432–7.
10. Martínez-Gómez D, Veiga OL, Gomez-Martinez S, et al. Behavioural correlates of active commuting to school in Spanish adolescents: the AFINOS (physical activity as a preventive measure against overweight, obesity, infections, allergies, and cardiovascular disease risk factors in adolescents) study. *Public Health Nutr* 2011;**14**(10):1779–86.

11. McDonald NC, Brown AL, Marchetti LM, Pedroso MS. U.S. school travel, 2009: an assessment of trends. *Am J Prev Med* 2011;**41**(2):146–51.
12. Murtagh EM, Dempster M, Murphy MH. Determinants of uptake and maintenance of active commuting to school. *Health Place* 2016;**40**:9–14.
13. Netherlands Ministry of Transport, Public Works and Water Management. *2009 Cycling in The Netherlands*. The Hague (The Netherlands): Ministry of Transport, Public Works and Water Management; 2009. http://www.fietsberaad.nl/library/repository/bestanden/CyclingintheNetherlands2009.pdf.
14. Østergaard GA, Børrestad LAB, Froberg K, Gravesen M, Andersen LB. Cycling to school is associated with lower BMI and lower odds of being overweight or obese in a large population-based study of Danish adolescents. *J Phys Act Health* 2012;**9**:617–25.
15. Pavelka J, Sigmundová D, Hamřik Z, et al. Trends in active commuting to school among Czech schoolchildren from 2006 to 2014. *Cent Eur J Public Health* 2017;**25**(Suppl. 1):S21–5.
16. Reimers AK, Jekauc D, Peterhans E, Wagner MO, Woll A. Prevalence and socio-demographic correlates of active commuting to school in a nationwide representative sample of German adolescents. *Prev Med* 2013;**56**(1):64–9.
17. Welsh Government Social Research. *2013/14 Health behaviour in school-aged children (HBSC) Wales: key findings*. Cardiff (Wales): Welsh Government Social Research; 2015. Available from: http://gov.wales/docs/caecd/research/2015/151022-health-behaviour-school-children-2013-14-key-findings-en.pdf.
18. Yang Y, Hong X, Gurney JG, Wang Y. Active travel to and from school among school-aged children during 1997–2011 and associated factors in China. *J Phys Act Health* 2017;**14**:684–91.
19. Pucher J, Buehler R. Making cycling irresistible: lessons from The Netherlands, Denmark and Germany. *Transp Rev* 2008;**28**(4):495–528.
20. Andersen LB, Lawlor DA, Cooper AR, Froberg K, Anderssen SA. Physical fitness in relation to transport to school in adolescents: the Danish youth and sports study. *Scand J Med Sci Sports* 2009;**19**(3):406–11.
21. Andersen LB, Wedderkopp N, Kristensen P, Moller NC, Froberg K, Cooper AR. Cycling to school and cardiovascular risk factors: a longitudinal study. *J Phys Act Health* 2011;**8**(8):1025–33.
22. van der Ploeg HP, Merom D, Corpuz G, Bauman AE. Trends in Australian children travelling to school 1971–2003: burning petrol or carbohydrates? *Prev Med* 2008;**46**(1):60–2.
23. Voss C, Winters M, Frazer A, McKay H. School-travel by public transit: rethinking active transportation. *Prev Med Rep* 2015;**2**:65–70. Available from: http://www.sciencedirect.com/science/article/pii/S2211335515000054.
24. Active Healthy Kids Canada. *Are we driving our kids to unhealthy habits? 2013 active healthy kids Canada report card on physical activity for children and youth*. Toronto (ON): Active Healthy Kids Canada; 2013. Available from: http://dvqdas9jty7g6.cloudfront.net/reportcard2013/Active-Healthy-Kids-2013-Report-Card_en.pdf.
25. Larouche R, Oyeyemi AL, Prista A, Onywera VO, Akinroye KK, Tremblay MS. A systematic review of active transportation research in Africa and the psychometric properties of measurement tools in children and youth. *Int J Behav Nutr Phys Act* 2014;**11**(129). Available from: http://ijbnpa.biomedcentral.com/articles/10.1186/s12966-014-0129-5.
26. Larouche R, Sarmiento OL, Broyles ST, Denstel KD, Katzmarzyk PT, Church TS, For the ISCOLE Research Group, et al. Are the correlates of active school transport context-specific? *Int J Obes Suppl* 2015;**5**:S89–99.

27. Tetali S, Edwards P, Murthy GVS, Roberts I. How do children travel to school in urban India? A cross-sectional study of 5,842 children in Hyderabad. *BMC Publ Health* 2016;**16**(1099). Available from: http://bmcpublichealth.biomedcentral.com/articles/10.1186/s12889-016-3750-1.
28. Department of Transport. *1979 National travel survey: 1975/6 report*. London: Department for Transport; 1979.
29. Department of Transport. *2001 National travel survey: 1999/2001 update*. London: Department for Transport; 2001.
30. Tremblay MS, Gray CE, Akinroye K, Harrington DM, Katzmarzyk PT, Lambert EV, et al. Physical activity of children: a global matrix of grades comparing 15 countries. *J Phys Act Health* 2014;**11**:113–125.
31. Dygrýn J, Mitáš J, Gába A, Rubin L, Frömel K. Changes in active commuting to school in Czech adolescents in different types of built environment across a 10-year period. *Int J Environ Res Public Health* 2015;**12**(10):12988–98. Available from: http://www.mdpi.com/1660-4601/12/10/12988.
32. Pooley CG, Turnbull J, Adams A. The journey to school in Britain since the 1940s: continuity and change. *Area* 2005;**37**(1):43–53.
33. McDonald NC. Active transportation to school: trends among U.S. schoolchildren, 1969–2001. *Am J Prev Med* 2007;**32**(6):509–16.
34. Marique A-F, Dujardin S, Teller J, Reiter S. School commuting: the relationship between energy consumption and urban form. *J Transp Geogr* 2013;**26**:1–1.
35. Silva KS, Lopez AS, da Silva RCR, Costa FF, de Assis MAA, Nahas MV. Time spent by Brazilian students in different modes of transport going to school: changes over a decade (2001–2011). *Cad Saúde Pública* 2014;**30**(11):2472–6.
36. Cui Z, Bauman A, Dibley MJ. Temporal trends and correlates of passive commuting to and from school in children from 9 provinces in China. *Prev Med* 2011;**52**(6):423–7.
37. Chillón P, Martínez-Gómez D, Ortega FB, et al. Six-year trend in active commuting to school in Spanish adolescents: the AVENA and AFINOS studies. *Int J Behav Med* 2013;**20**(4):529–37.
38. Panter JR, Jones AP, Van Sluijs EMF. Environmental determinants of active travel in youth: a review and framework for future research. *Int J Behav Nutr Phys Act* 2008;**5**:34. Available from: https://ijbnpa.biomedcentral.com/articles/10.1186/1479-5868-5-34.
39. Wong BYM, Faulkner G, Buliung R. GIS measured environmental correlates of active school transport: a systematic review of 14 studies. *Int J Behav Nutr Phys Act* 2011;**8**:39. Available from: https://ijbnpa.biomedcentral.com/articles/10.1186/1479-5868-8-39.
40. Larouche R, Barnes J, Tremblay MS. Too far to walk or bike? *Can J Public Health* 2013;**104**(7):e487–9.
41. McDonald NC. Children's mode choice for the school trip: the role of distance and school location in walking to school. *Transportation* 2008;**35**(1):23–35.
42. Wilson EJ, Marshall J, Wilson R, Krizek KJ. By foot, bus or car: children's school travel and school choice policy. *Environ Plan A* 2010;**42**(9):2168–85.
43. Larouche R, Chaput J-P, Leduc G, Boyer C, Bélanger P, LeBlanc AG, et al. A cross-sectional examination of socio-demographic and school-level correlates of children's school travel mode in Ottawa, Canada. *BMC Publ Health* 2014;**14**:497. Available from: https://bmcpublichealth.biomedcentral.com/articles/10.1186/1471-2458-14-497.
44. Torres J, Bussière Y, Lewis P. Primary schools' territorial policy and active commuting: institutional influences in montreal and trois-rivières. *J Urban Plan Dev* 2010;**136**(4):287–93.
45. Frumkin H. Urban sprawl and public health. *Public Health Rep* 2002;**117**(3):201–17.

46. Council of Educational Facility Planners International. *Guide for planning educational facilities*. Scottsdale (AZ): Council of Educational Facility Planners International; 1991. Available from: http://eric.ed.gov/?id=ED344336.
47. Ewing R, Schroeer W, Greene W. School location and student travel analysis of factors affecting mode choice. *Transp Res Rec* 2004;**1895**:55–63.
48. Council of Educational Facility Planners, International, U.S. Environmental Protection Agency. *Schools for successful communities: an element of smart growth planning*. Scottsdale (AZ): Council of Education Facility Planners International; 2004.
49. Gilbert R, O'Brien C. *Canadian child- and youth-friendly land-use and Transport planning guidelines*. Winnipeg (MB): Centre for Sustainable Transportation; 2010. Available at: http://kidsonthemove.ca/uploads/Canadian%20Guidelines%202.pdf.
50. Christiansen LB, Toftager M, Schipperijn J, Ersbøll AK, Giles-Corti B, Troelsen J. School site walkability and active school transport – association, mediation and moderation. *J Transp Health* 2014;**34**:7–15.
51. Ajzen I. The theory of planned behavior. *Org Behav Hum Decis Process* 1991;**50**(2):179–211.
52. Bandura A. Health promotion from the perspective of social cognitive theory. *Psychol Health* 1998;**13**:623–49.
53. Triandis HC. Values, attitudes, and interpersonal behavior. *Nebr Symp Motiv Paper* 1979;**27**:195–259.
54. Faulkner GEJ, Richichi V, Buliung RN, Fusco C, Moola F. What's "quickest and easiest?": parental decision making about school travel mode. *Int J Behav Nutr Phys Act* 2010;**7**:62. Available from: http://ijbnpa.biomedcentral.com/articles/10.1186/1479-5868-7-62.
55. McDonald NC, Aalborg AE. Why parents drive children to school: implications for safe routes to school programs. *J Am Plann Assoc* 2009;**3**:331–42.
56. Mammen G, Faulkner G, Buliung RN, Lay J. Understanding the drive to escort: a cross-sectional analysis examining parental attitudes towards children's school travel and independent mobility. *BMC Publ Health* 2012;**12**:862. Available from: http://bmcpublichealth.biomedcentral.com/articles/10.1186/1471-2458-12-862.
57. Carver A, Timperio A, Crawford D. Playing it safe: the influence of neighbourhood safety on children's physical activity—a review. *Health Place* 2008;**14**(2):217–27.
58. Malone K. The bubble-wrapped generation: children growing up in walled gardens. *Environ Educ Res* 2007;**13**(4):513–27.
59. Tremblay MS, Gray CE, Babcock S, Barnes J, Bradstreet CC, Carr D, et al. Position statement on active outdoor play. *Int J Environ Res Public Health* 2015;**12**:6475–505. Available from: http://www.mdpi.com/1660-4601/12/6/6475.
60. Stokes MA. Stranger danger: child protection and parental fears in the risk society. *Amsterdam Soc Sci* 2009;**1**(3):6–24.
61. Scott S, Jackson S, Backett-Milburn K. Swings and roundabouts: risk anxiety and the everyday worlds of children. *Sociology* 1998;**32**(4):689–705.
62. Timperio A, Crawford D, Telford A, Salmon J. Perceptions of the local neighborhood and walking and cycling among children. *Prev Med* 2004;**38**:39–47.
63. Janssen I. Hyper-parenting is negatively associated with physical activity among 7–12 year olds. *Prev Med* 2015;**73**:55–9.
64. Dalley ML, Ruscoe J. *The abduction of children by strangers in Canada: nature and scope*. Ottawa: Royal Canadian Mounted Police; 2003.
65. Barr J, de Souza M, Harrison C, Hyde B, Van Vliet H, Saltmarsh S. Parenting the 'millennium child': choice, responsibility and playing it safe in uncertain times. *Global Studies of Childhood* 2012;**2**(4):302–18.

66. Aitkenhead D. *Why we need to set our kids free*. London (UK): The Guardian; November 3, 2007. Available from: https://www.theguardian.com/lifeandstyle/2007/nov/03/familyandrelationships.family5.
67. Friedersdorf C. Working mom arrested for letting her 9-year-old play alone in the park. *Atlantic* July 15, 2014. Available from: http://www.theatlantic.com/national/archive/2014/07/arrested-for-letting-a-9-year-old-play-at-the-park-alone/374436/.
68. McCarren A. *Parents in trouble again for letting kids walk alone*. Washington (DC): USA Today; April 13, 2015. Available from: http://www.usatoday.com/story/news/nation/2015/04/13/parents-investigated-letting-children-walk-alone/25700823/.
69. World Health Organization. *Global status report on road safety 2015*. Geneva: World Health Organization; 2015. Available from: http://www.who.int/violence_injury_prevention/road_safety_status/2015/en/.
70. Public Health Agency of Canada. *Injury in review, 2012 edition: spotlight on road and Transport safety*. Ottawa: Public Health Agency of Canada; 2012.
71. Tranter P. Overcoming social traps: a key to child-friendly cities. In: Gleeson B, Sipe N, editors. *Creating child friendly cities: reinstating kids in the city*. New York: Routledge; 2006. p. 121–35.
72. Roberts I. Walking to school has future benefits. *BMJ* 1995;**312**:1229.
73. Davis B, Dutzik T, Baxandall P. *Transportation and the new generation: why young people are driving less and what it means for transportation policy*. Santa Barbara (CA): Frontier Group U.S. PIRG Education Fund; 2012.
74. Delbosc A, Currie G. Causes of youth licensing decline: a synthesis of the literature. *Transp Rev* 2013;**33**(3):271–90.
75. Dargay J, Gately D, Sommer M. Vehicle ownership and income growth, worldwide: 1960–2030. *Energy J* 2007;**28**(4):143–70.
76. Kuhminhof T, Armoogum J, Buehler R, Dargay J, Denstadli JM, Yamamoto T. Men shape a downward trend in car use among young adults—evidence from six industrialized countries. *Transp Rev* 2012;**32**(6):761–79.
77. McDonald NC. Are millennials really the "Go-Nowhere" generation? *J Am Plann Assoc* 2015;**81**(2):90–103.
78. Goodwin P, Van Dender K. 'Peak car' – themes and issues. *Tranp Rev* 2013;**33**(3):243–54.
79. Marshall JD, Wilson RD, Meyer KL, Rajandam SK, McDonald NC, Wilsson EJ. Vehicle emissions during children's school commuting: impacts of education policy. *Environ Sci Technol* 2010;**44**(5):1537–43.
80. McDonald NC. School siting: contested visions of the community school. *J Am Plann Assoc* 2010;**76**(2):184–98.

Children's Independent Mobility

5

Negin A. Riazi, Guy Faulkner
School of Kinesiology, University of British Columbia, Vancouver, BC, Canada

> *There's no weight given to the long game of good parenting—allowing kids to earn independence at a younger age, so they turn into better humans later in life. Instead, constant supervision and prevention of all risk on a minute-by-minute basis is the government's gold standard for parenting*
>
> ***Adrian Crook (father; faulted for allowing his children to take the bus independently in Vancouver, British Columbia)***[1]

Chapter Outline

5.1 Background

In June 2017, public discussion in Canada centred on a father, faulted for allowing his four children (7–11 years old) to take the bus alone in Vancouver, British Columbia.[2] He would let his children take a 13-km trip from their downtown condominium to a stop directly in front of their school. He had spent 2 years training his children to take the 45-minute public transit trip and they always travelled with a cell phone, so he could track their location. However, after an anonymous complaint to the Ministry of

Children's Active Transportation. https://doi.org/10.1016/B978-0-12-811931-0.00005-3

Children and Family Development, provincial child welfare officials investigated and ruled that due to safety concerns he could not let unsupervised children under the age of 10 out in the community alone. Although he is currently considering legal options, the father or another adult must now accompany his children on the trip to and from school. This case study reflects a broader concern regarding the loss of children's independent mobility in the 21st century. What are the implications of this? What factors influence the independent mobility of children—what are the safety concerns? This chapter will provide an overview of the literature addressing these questions.

5.1.1 What Is Children's Independent Mobility?

Children's independent mobility refers to a child's freedom to travel around their neighbourhood or city by themselves without adult supervision.[3,4] It can refer to children travelling on their own, or with friends, to a variety of destinations within their neighbourhood such as school, shops, parks and playgrounds. Independent mobility may involve active (e.g., walking, cycling) and passive (e.g., public transport) modes of transportation and can encompass travel as well as outdoor play.

Children's independent mobility has been operationalized in several different ways. Independent mobility has been assessed according to 'territorial range', which shows how far children can travel from their home without adult supervision.[5] Mobility 'licenses' are another way to examine independent mobility. Six main questions have been proposed to explain the degree of freedom that children have to travel independently. Hillman et al.[3] and Shaw et al.[6] termed these core questions about children's mobility as 'licenses'. These licenses granted by parents encompass whether a child can cross main roads alone, go to places besides school alone, travel home from school alone, go out after dark alone, travel on local buses alone and cycle on main roads alone. Children's independent mobility can also be viewed in regard to their play participation (e.g., outdoor, autonomous play) or measured during a certain period of time (e.g., the after-school period, measured via travel diaries).

5.1.2 Why Is Children's Independent Mobility an Important Issue?

In Canada, only 8% of children and youth meet the recommended 60 minutes of moderate-to-vigorous physical activity.[7] This trend can be seen globally where a large proportion of children are not engaging in adequate levels of moderate-to-vigorous physical activity on a regular basis.[8,9] Independent mobility may be important for facilitating opportunities for physical activity. By having opportunities to walk to school with friends, go to a friend's place after school or travel to the park to play, children can accumulate physical activity. Research demonstrates that children with higher levels of independent mobility are typically more physically active than their counterparts with lower levels of independent mobility.[10–13] Increased levels of physical activity help children increase muscular and cardiorespiratory fitness, maintain a healthy body composition, improve bone health, reduce the risk of hypertension and several types of cancer, and enhance mental health and academic performance.[14–17]

Beyond the instrumental benefits of independent mobility as a source of physical activity, children's independent mobility may also be important for social, cognitive and personal development. The opportunity to travel independently and interact with the environment helps children develop better spatial awareness and way-finding skills.[4,5,18] Independent mobility also gives children the opportunity to improve problem-solving skills; to interact with adults, peers and places in the neighbourhood; and to acquire social competence.[19] It may be beneficial in helping children build friendships[19] as well as a sense of community.[20] Additionally, children develop better decision-making skills, traffic safety, self-confidence and competence to safely navigate their neighbourhood environment.[4,5,12,21,22]

5.1.3 Review of Trends in Children's Independent Mobility

Children's independent mobility, however, has declined since the early 1900s. One early study examined trends over the course of three generations and found a decline in the *number* and *variety* of places where children could independently visit along with increased adult-led outdoor play.[23] In a well-known study by Hillman et al.,[3] researchers examined the differences in children's independent mobility in England from the 1970s to the 1990s where a steep decline in independent mobility was noted. For example, the proportion of children travelling to school on their own declined from 80% in 1971 to 9% in 1990.

Similarly, the age at which children are granted independent mobility has risen in comparison to previous generations (e.g., parents' age of independent mobility). This trend is seen in a number of countries including Australia, Brazil, England, Finland, Germany, Ireland, Italy and Sweden, pointing towards a global decline in independent mobility over the course of generations.[3,6,24,25] Even in Scandinavian countries (e.g., Denmark, Finland, Norway), where children are often granted higher independence, a downward trend can be seen.[25,26] This decline is partly associated with car use and increasing distances to school. Car ownership, use and dependency have increased globally over the past few decades[25–27] (refer to Chapter 4 for further information).

5.1.4 Are We 'Bubble-Wrapping' Children Today?

In September 2017, a Northern Ontario elementary school decided to ban cartwheels given the potential for '...concussions, and neck and wrist injuries'.[28] These kinds of events have prompted discussion regarding 'how young is too young' for children to be independent[29] and raises questions about risk. In an effort to keep children safe, are we, as a society, 'bubble-wrapping' children to prevent *any* exposure to risk, relying on automobile-based commuting and little unstructured outdoor play? As some have argued, children today may be living in a 'risk averse' society. Activities that children have enjoyed for many generations, such as climbing trees or doing cartwheels, are now deemed dangerous and risky.[30]

In the 1970s, English children as young as 7 or 8 years travelled to schools and shops with friends or by themselves. However by 1990, this freedom of independent travel was withheld until the age of 10.[3] Similar trends are seen across the world in the United States[23] and Denmark.[27] In one study, parents asked about their childhood experiences reported they played much more than their children do now.[31] Research suggests restricted mobility during childhood could actually have adverse consequences for motor and social development.[32]

5.2 Examining Independent Mobility: A Socioecological Approach

To fully consider the factors influencing children's independent mobility, a socioecological framework encompassing multiple levels of influence (refer to Chapter 6) should be adopted.

5.2.1 Individual Correlates

Individual factors are crucial in the negotiation of children's freedom to move and travel independently. These individual factors encompass factors such as a child's gender, age and confidence in their abilities, parents' age, gender, physical activity levels and socioeconomic status.

One distinct difference is the degree of independent mobility granted to boys versus girls. A majority of studies examining children's independent mobility have found that boys tend to have higher levels of independent mobility in comparison to girls.[19,33–46] The social construction of girls' identities as 'weaker', 'endangered', or in need of more protection may limit girls' independence and their freedom to travel around their neighbourhood or city.[47] Views of children's competencies (e.g., competency to travel in the neighbourhood safely) are evolving and sometimes conflicting but highly gendered. Hart[48] and Tindal[49] found that parents were less strict with boys' spatial ranges compared with girls, on the basis that 'boys will be boys' and will engage in more rambunctious behaviour and girls were more vulnerable to social dangers.[48] On the other hand, Valentine and McKendrick[31] found that parents worried equally for sons and daughters. Unlike some previous studies, girls were described as 'sensible, logical and therefore responsible enough to manage their own safety', whereas boys were commonly described as 'easily led, irrational, slow to mature and consequently as less capable of negotiating their own safety'[33(p. 71)]. The social construction of gendered identities may influence the degree of independent mobility granted to children. A gendered approach to raising children may affect parental and child perceptions of risk as well as confidence of each in a child's abilities. For example, imparting more warnings to girls compared to boys may affect how girls perceive and travel in their neighbourhood.[50]

Children's competency plays an important role in affecting children's independent mobility. This competency can stem from a number of moderators such as a child's age. Many studies have shown that older children typically have higher levels of independent mobility. As children get older, they gain more experience, develop social and physical competencies, improve their ability to deal with traffic and gain more independence.[38,51] Additionally, children's confidence in their own abilities,[45,52] as well as their parents' confidence in their child's abilities[53] are positively associated with children having independent mobility. As children gain more experience and become more competent, they gain more confidence in their abilities.[54]

5.2.2 *Interpersonal Correlates*

Although a child's individual traits may affect their independent mobility, it is important to remember that parents or caregivers are often the 'gatekeepers'. As 'gatekeepers', adults can either restrict or promote children's independent mobility as they see fit. As Brussoni et al. found, mothers often felt anchored in household and child-related chores while fathers were identified as the 'fun guy' in charge of recreational activities and play[55(p. 1395)]. Fathers were also described as the 'risk experts' while mothers often found themselves countering what they perceived as excessive risk allowance. The National Household Travel Survey data from 2001 indicates that mothers are five times more likely to transport children in comparison to fathers.[56] Mothers also tend to limit children's travel range more than fathers[57] and are often more concerned about safety and vocalize this concern to their children, especially daughters.[50,55]

Parents are in an ideal position to provide children with a positive example of healthy, active behaviours. A study by McMillan et al.[47] found that parent or caregiver activity levels moderated the influence of gender on the child's travel to school. Having a more active caregiver increased the chances of girls walking or biking to school. More active caregivers can be role models of a healthy lifestyle; consequently, they may have more familiarity with the neighbourhood and may be more likely to grant children independent mobility in comparison to inactive caregivers.

There have been contrasting findings in regard to family socioeconomic status and its influence on children's independent mobility. A few studies have found that a higher proportion of children from lower socioeconomic areas have higher levels of independent mobility[41] and travel to more destinations independently.[58] Children from lower socioeconomic backgrounds may have less access to motorized modes of transport. In one large study examining children's independent mobility across 16 countries, Shaw et al.[25] noted that when a household owned a car, the child was less likely to travel independently to school. Other studies found that as the number of cars in a household increased, the likelihood of independent mobility for the child decreased.[33,38,40,59–61]

5.2.3 *Social Environment*

The social environment is composed of perceptions of the neighbourhood, safety, crime, traffic, as well as social cohesion, social norms and car use. Neighbourhood perceptions can influence both children and parents. When children perceived neighbourhoods with lots of children playing, people walking, talking and doing outdoor activities, they tended to have higher levels of independent mobility.[41,45,52] These elements may affect the overall atmosphere or *social climate* of the neighbourhood. Positive parental perceptions of social climate have been found to be positively associated with children's independent mobility.

When parents perceive a friendly neighbourhood, children appear to have greater independent mobility. A 'friendly' neighbourhood can involve a number of factors, including other children in the neighbourhood walking and biking to school, neighbours and other adults looking out for children (i.e., informal social control) and a higher satisfaction with the neighbourhood environment.[38,52,53] Additionally, social cohesion, which describes the ties that bind residents of a neighbourhood together (e.g., shared values, beliefs), helps increase the likelihood of children's independent mobility.[46] As the sense of trust and community increases, parents are more likely to grant children the license to roam. Mothers' perceptions of a strong neighbourhood community and relationships were found to be especially significant in promoting their children's independent mobility.[19,62]

Conversely, children's independent mobility lessens when parents perceive an unsupportive social norm for children's independent travel.[34] One social norm may involve the notion of 'bad parenting'. If children travel to destinations independently, this is often equated to bad parenting (e.g., the Vancouver father whose children took the bus by themselves). Not surprisingly, higher parental confidence in their child's ability to travel independently increases the level of independent mobility granted to the child.[63] Referring back to the situation in Vancouver, the father in question may have felt his children were capable and mature enough to be able to take public transit independently. Other social factors that decrease the likelihood of independent mobility include a low sense of community, high perception of social danger and low confidence in a child's traffic and safety skills.[39,62,63]

Parental perceptions of a safe neighbourhood are highly associated with the levels of children's independent mobility. When parents felt that a neighbourhood was safe, including safety from traffic, safe streets and sidewalks, and their child was safe, there was a higher chance of children being independently mobile.[39,41,46,53,64–66] Conversely, when parents were concerned about strangers, crime, bullying, traffic and an unsafe environment, children were less likely to be granted independent mobility.[33,34,37,40,41,61,63]

Parental perceived risks of the social environment influence children's independent mobility and should not be dismissed. The meaning of 'risk' has shifted from simply referring to 'a probability of an event occurring' to meaning 'dangerous' or 'harmful'. Many activities that were deemed appropriate (e.g., climbing trees) a few generations ago are now considered 'too risky'. For children, risk taking helps test their physical limits, develops risk identification and management, and helps them recognize their abilities and limitations.[67]

Heightened parental fears of traffic and 'stranger danger', as a consequence of societal influences, contribute to diminishing outdoor play opportunities for children.[68] Parental fear perceptions can be disproportionate to actual statistics on injury rates, which are shown to be declining.[69,70] This disproportionate fear can influence parenting styles, such as 'helicopter parenting' (e.g., parents who strive to solve all their children's problems and protect them from all dangers), which can consequently affect children's independent mobility.[71] The urge to protect children from *all* risks somewhat undermines safety initiatives (e.g., road, traffic safety) as children are not allowed to develop the skills needed to safely navigate their environment.[30,72]

5.2.4 Built and Physical Environment

The fourth layer of the socioecological model focuses on the built and physical environment, which encompasses a number of factors including distance to destination, density (e.g., population, residential), diversity (e.g., land use mix), walkability of the neighbourhood and urbanization (e.g., rural, suburban and urban). Distance is one of the most measured environmental factors with regard to independent mobility. As distance to a destination (e.g., school, parks) increases, the likelihood of children's independent mobility decreases.[19,34,38,52,53,59–61,63] Distances under 1 km are considered ideal for children's independent travel, but as distances to school, leisure activities and parks increase above 1 km, independent mobility becomes less likely.[38,59–61] Families that live closer to their child's school, ideally under 1 km away, are more likely to grant children travel independence to school. Living in proximity of retail shops and recreation centres (<800 m) also favours boys' independent mobility.[52]

Density is another factor that influences the degree of children's independent mobility. Density can encompass population density (e.g., population within a distinct buffer), residential density (e.g., the number of housing units per hectare within a buffer) and street density. Overall, it appears that increased density results in a higher likelihood of children's independent mobility. For example, higher residential (or housing) and population densities mean more homes and people within a distinct area. A higher perception of social cohesion, children playing outside and individuals out and about in the neighbourhood may contribute to a sense of a friendly, safe neighbourhood.

Neighbourhood design and density influence children's independent mobility. Street density and walkability go hand in hand and are positively associated with children's freedom to travel independently.[45,52] Walkability is characterized by high street density, land use mix and street connectivity, making it easier to travel from one destination to another. High walkability can make the journey easier and more enjoyable for children and can potentially ease parental fears. Land use mix, characterized by the diversity of destinations within a buffer (e.g., proportion of commercial, residential, office and institutional land use), also influences independent mobility.[33,36] For example, the number and presence of primary and secondary schools, along with the number and proportion of green spaces (e.g., parks), the presence of religious institutions (e.g., churches, synagogues), small food stores, fast food joints, shops and restaurants all add to the diversity of the neighbourhood and increase the number of destinations that a child can visit.[34,41,52,73,74] The availability of walking and cycling infrastructures also has positive effects on independent mobility.[33,36]

There are no definitive conclusions regarding the influence of urbanization (e.g., rural, suburban, urban) on children's independent mobility. While suburban areas have been associated with higher levels of children's independent mobility, rural areas are typically associated with reduced independent mobility.[40,63] Suburban areas may have higher walkability and greater land use mix in comparison to rural areas where distances to destinations may be further. Conversely, other studies have indicated that low-density or rural areas lend themselves to higher levels of independent mobility.[75,76] Rural areas may lessen parental fears of traffic and 'stranger danger', which may outweigh the issue of longer distances to destinations. Despite their higher density and accessibility to destinations, urban areas have been associated with reduced independent mobility.[75] These counterintuitive findings may reflect that urban areas involve greater exposure to traffic and strangers.

Natural environment features include seasonality, weather, air quality and temperature. Children's independent mobility can be influenced by the time of year.[38] For example, inclement weather and less-than-ideal temperatures (e.g., rain, snow, ice) can affect travel plans and may prompt parents to drive children to destinations.[38] In the case of poor air quality, whether from potential forest fires in the summer, smog, vehicular exhaust or factory pollution, children may be forced to curb their active outdoor activities.

5.2.5 Policy Environment

The policy environment can play a crucial role in either promoting or restricting children's independent mobility. As Shaw et al.[25] demonstrated in their review of 16 countries, there was variation in road traffic rules and legislation to promote walking and cycling between countries. The majority of countries with the highest levels of children's independent mobility had legislation in place to promote walking or cycling. These child-centred policies and child-friendly urban planning and development may be steps in the right direction. The United Nations International Children's Emergency Fund (UNICEF) and UN-Habitat launched their Child-Friendly Cities Initiative in 1996,[77] which identified nine fundamental building blocks in designing child-friendly cities, including child participation (e.g., active involvement by the child in the issues that affect them), a child-friendly legal framework (e.g., ensuring legislation that promote and protect the rights of all children), a children's rights strategy (e.g., a comprehensive plan for building a child-friendly city), a coordinating mechanism/agency for children (e.g., permanent structures in the local government to ensure consideration of children's perspective), assessment of policy/programme impact on children (e.g., assessment of law, policy and practice to maintain quality and effectiveness), a budget and resources for children (e.g., adequate resources dedicated for children), a regular report on the state of children in the city (e.g., a report on state of children based on monitoring and data collection), awareness-raising and capacity building on child rights (e.g., ensuring awareness of children's rights) and independent advocacy for children (e.g., UNICEF). Cities like Vancouver, Canada and Rotterdam, the Netherlands, have designed public spaces that welcome a variety of transport modes and child-friendly streets, housing and spaces.[25,78–81] Creating child-friendly cities promotes accessibility, diversity of locations and ultimately benefits everyone, not just children.

5.3 Addressing 'Fears'

As stories in Vancouver, British Columbia, and Northern Ontario demonstrated, 'risk' is still a controversial issue in society. These types of stories raise the questions, 'how much risk is too much?' and 'how young is too young for children to travel independently'? Children's independent mobility is declining over time, so what can be done to diminish this downward trend? Parents are the 'gatekeepers' to children's independent travel, and therefore, it is important to assuage their concerns and fears. 'Traffic danger' and 'stranger danger' are two of the most commonly cited barriers to granting independent mobility.[3,6] Addressing these barriers should start upstream with city and urban planning. Child-friendly cities and spaces are important in helping enable independent mobility. For example, the 'Living First' strategy was developed in Vancouver, Canada, in the late 1980s and early 1990s. This concept focused around building and redeveloping parts of the inner city to allow for child-use; simply put, 'if it works for kids, it works for everybody'.[25,79] Accessible destinations (e.g., greenspaces, commercial areas), traffic-calmed areas, shorter distances to destinations, and walking and cycling infrastructure come to fruition at the planning stage. It takes the combined effort of researchers, urban planners, city designers and policy makers to design spaces that are inviting, are child-friendly, and enable children's independent mobility.

Another barrier to granting independent mobility is the parents' fear of being judged for 'poor' parenting.[82] For instance, social norms may indicate that supervising children constantly is considered 'good' parenting while allowing a child to walk on its own to a friend's house may be deemed as 'poor' parenting. However, as discussed earlier, independent mobility helps children grow in terms of cognitive and social development and helps them engage in physical activity as well. Instead of judgement, the focus should be on shifting neighbourhood and community beliefs to encompass independent travel as important and valuable while encouraging higher community relations, social cohesion and informal social control.

At an individual level, educational initiatives could be developed that adopt a risk-reframing approach. Ungar[83] has noted that statistics indicating their communities are safe may not be sufficient to convince parents to be less overprotective. Rather, parents may be more persuaded by the case that their 'protective' actions place their child at a developmental disadvantage. In the context of outdoor play, such a risk-reframing approach has been implemented[84] and shown to be effective in changing parent attitudes towards outdoor play.[85] In Canada, the development of an online platform (https://outsideplay.ca/)[86] has enabled a scalable version of these education workshops that could be applied in facilitating parental reflection on the advantages of independent mobility and challenging perceptions of potential risk. Future research examining the impact of risk reframing is warranted.

5.4 Conclusion

Children's independent mobility is characterized by children's travel and play in the neighbourhood, unsupervised by parents. Independent mobility may be an important facilitator of active transportation and physical activity, with a number of benefits for health, cognitive and social development. A decline in independent mobility is a result of a complex interplay of factors including the individual, social and environmental. Age and gender are the most influential individual factors while parental perceptions of neighbourhood safety, stranger danger and traffic safety are important social determinants. Distance, density (e.g., residential, population, land use mix) and design of neighbourhoods all influence children's freedom to travel on their own. In line with an ecological approach, increasing levels of independent mobility will require a multilevel approach that includes policies and environmental modifications that support independent mobility and interventions that address the social and individual barriers to independent mobility. In particular, these approaches will need to tackle parental safety concerns more explicitly.

5.5 Recommendations for Policy and Practice

1. A multilevel approach is recommended for increasing children's independent mobility. Policies and environmental modifications are needed at local, provincial and national levels that support independent mobility and promote safety, accessible locations and child-friendly cities. Policies that directly or indirectly alleviate parental safety concerns need consideration to support children's independent mobility.
2. The physical and built environment is crucial to children's independent mobility, and developing safe neighbourhoods, sidewalks and streets are important steps to encouraging independent travel. Making a variety of locations, including green (e.g., parks), commercial (e.g., shops) and educational (e.g., school) spaces, accessible and providing cycling and walking infrastructure, traffic-calmed streets and housing quality help support children's independent mobility.
3. Interventions should focus on the individual and social barriers to children's independent mobility. Parent and caregivers' concerns and urge to 'overprotect' may lead to increased restrictions of independent mobility. Educational initiatives that reframe risk should be developed and evaluated in addressing parental fears of the risks of active transportation and independent mobility. It is also essential to shift social norms, so that parents are not judged negatively for allowing their children to be independently mobile.

5.6 Recommendations for Future Research

1. The majority of studies examining children's independent mobility are cross-sectional in design. Longitudinal studies may help researchers better understand the evolution of children's independent mobility and how it changes over time. How this evolution is moderated by factors such as gender, socioeconomic status, level of urbanization (urban, suburban, rural) or ethnicity warrants closer examination. In turn, such research could inform future interventions to promote independent mobility.
2. Much research has focused on the individual, interpersonal and environmental factors that influence independent mobility. Future research should examine how the policy environment interacts with commonly examined correlates of independent mobility.
3. Age is one of the most consistent predictors of children's independent mobility, and as children age, they gain a greater amount of independent mobility. Do we allow children to naturally gain more independence or will delaying independent mobility have long-term effects on children's development? There is a need to better understand long-term effects of early versus delayed independent mobility.

References

1. Cook A. *Very superstitious: how fact-free parenting policies rob our kids of independence | 5 kids 1 condo [internet]*; 2017. Available from: https://5kids1condo.com/very-superstitious-how-fact-free-parenting-policies-rob-our-kids-of-independence/.
2. *Here are the rules about putting kids on a bus alone: there aren't any [internet]*. CBC News; 2017. Available from: http://www.cbc.ca/news/canada/british-columbia/5-children-ride-bus-alone-debate-vancouver-adrian-crook-free-range-helicopter-parenting-1.4280001.
3. Hillman M, Adams J, Whitelegg J. *One false move: A study of children's independent mobility*. London: Policy Studies Institute; 1990. Available from: http://www.psi.org.uk/site/publication_detail/904.
4. Tranter P, Whitelegg J. Children's travel behaviours in Canberra: car-dependent lifestyles in a low-density city. *J Transport Geogr* 1994;**2**(4):265–73.
5. Rissotto A, Tonucci F. Freedom of movement and environmental knowledge in elementary school children. *J Environ Psychol* 2002;**22**(1):65–77.
6. Shaw B, Watson B, Frauendienst B, Redecker A, Jones T, Hillman M. *Children's independent mobility: a comparative study in England and Germany*. 1971–2010. London: Policy Studies Institute; 2013. Available from: http://www.psi.org.uk/site/publication_detail/852.
7. *The daily — Canadian health measures Survey: activity monitor data [internet]*. 2017. Available from: http://www.statcan.gc.ca/daily-quotidien/170419/dq170419e-eng.htm.
8. Janssen I, Katzmarzyk PT, Boyce WF, Vereecken C, Mulvihill C, Roberts C, Currie C, Pickett W. Comparison of overweight and obesity prevalence in school-aged youth from 34 countries and their relationships with physical activity and dietary patterns. *Obes Rev* 2005;**6**(2):123–32.
9. Hallal PC, Andersen LB, Bull FC, Guthold R, Haskell W, Ekelund U. Lancet Physical Activity Series Working Group. Global physical activity levels: surveillance progress, pitfalls, and prospects. *Lancet* 2012;**380**(9838):247–57.
10. Schoeppe S, Duncan MJ, Badland H, Oliver M, Curtis C. Associations of children's independent mobility and active travel with physical activity, sedentary behaviour and weight status: a systematic review. *J Sci Med Sport* 2013;**16**(4):312–9.
11. Page AS, Cooper AR, Davis L, Hillsdon M, Griew P. Independent mobility in relation to weekday and weekend physical activity in children aged 10–11 years: the PEACH Project. *Int J Behav Nutr Phys Activ* 2009;**6**(1):2.
12. Mackett R, Brown B, Gong Y, Kitazawa K, Paskins J. Children's independent movement in the local environment. *Built Environ* 2007;**33**(4):454–68.
13. Pearce M, Page AS, Griffin TP, Cooper AR. Who children spend time with after school: associations with objectively recorded indoor and outdoor physical activity. *Int J Behav Nutr Phys Activ* 2014;**11**(1):45.
14. Biddle SJ, Gorely T, Stensel DJ. Health-enhancing physical activity and sedentary behaviour in children and adolescents. *J Sports Sci* 2004;**22**(8):679–701.
15. *Physical activity and young people [internet] global strategy on diet, physical activity and health*. 2017. Available from: http://www.who.int/dietphysicalactivity/factsheet_young_people/en/.
16. Singh A, Uijtdewilligen L, Twisk JW, Van Mechelen W, Chinapaw MJ. Physical activity and performance at school: a systematic review of the literature including a methodological quality assessment. *Arch Pediatr Adolesc Med* 2012;**166**(1):49–55.
17. Strong WB, Malina RM, Blimkie CJ, Daniels SR, Dishman RK, Gutin B, Hergenroeder AC, Must A, Nixon PA, Pivarnik JM, Rowland T. Evidence based physical activity for school-age youth. *J Pediatr* 2005;**146**(6):732–7.

18. Cohen SL, Cohen R. The role of activity in spatial. *Dev Spatial Cogn* 2013:199.
19. Prezza M, Pilloni S, Morabito C, Sersante C, Alparone FR, Giuliani MV. The influence of psychosocial and environmental factors on children's independent mobility and relationship to peer frequentation. *J Community Appl Soc Psychol* 2001;**11**(6):435–50.
20. Prezza M, Pacilli MG. Current fear of crime, sense of community, and loneliness in Italian adolescents: the role of autonomous mobility and play during childhood. *J Community Psychol* 2007;**35**(2):151–70.
21. Carver A, Timperio A, Crawford D. Playing it safe: the influence of neighbourhood safety on children's physical activity—a review. *Health Place* 2008;**14**(2):217–27.
22. Oliver M, Witten K, Kearns RA, Mavoa S, Badland HM, Carroll P, Drumheller C, Tavae N, Asiasiga L, Jelley S, Kaiwai H. Kids in the city study: research design and methodology. *BMC Publ Health* 2011;**11**(1):587.
23. Gaster S. Urban children's access to their neighborhood: changes over three generations. *Environ Behav* 1991;**23**(1):70–85.
24. Björklid P, Gummesson M. *Children's independent mobility in Sweden*. 2013.
25. Shaw B, Bicket M, Elliott B, Fagan-Watson B, Mocca E, Hillman M. *Children's Independent Mobility: an international comparison and recommendations for action*. 2015.
26. Fyhri A, Hjorthol R, Mackett RL, Fotel TN, Kyttä M. Children's active travel and independent mobility in four countries: development, social contributing trends and measures. *Transport Pol* 2011;**18**(5):703–10.
27. Fotel T, Thomsen TU. The surveillance of children's mobility. *Surveill Soc* 2002;**1**(4).
28. *Northern Ontario school set to ban cartwheels [internet]. Ottawa Citizen*. 2017. Available from: http://ottawacitizen.com/news/local-news/northern-ontario-school-set-to-ban-cartwheels.
29. Parents wonder how young is too young for their kids to be independent [Internet]. *Globe Mail* 2017. Available from: https://beta.theglobeandmail.com/life/parenting/parents-wonder-how-young-is-too-young-for-their-kids-to-beindependent/article36334354/?ref=http%3A%2F%2F%3ca%20href=.
30. Gill T. *No fear. Growing up in a risk averse society*. London: Calouste Gulbenkian Foundation; 2007.
31. Valentine G, McKendrck J. Children's outdoor play: exploring parental concerns about children's safety and the changing nature of childhood. *Geoforum* 1997;**28**(2):219–35.
32. Hüttenmoser M. Children and their living surroundings: empirical investigations into the significance of living surroundings for the everyday life and development of children. *Children Environ* 1995:403–13.
33. Carver A, Veitch J, Sahlqvist S, Crawford D, Hume C. Active transport, independent mobility and territorial range among children residing in disadvantaged areas. *J Trans Health* 2014;**1**(4):267–73.
34. Christian HE, Klinker CD, Villanueva K, Knuiman MW, Foster SA, Zubrick SR, Divitini M, Wood L, Giles-Corti B. The effect of the social and physical environment on children's independent mobility to neighborhood destinations. *J Phys Activ Health* 2015;**12**(s1):S84–93.
35. Christian HE, Villanueva K, Klinker CD, Knuiman MW, Divitini M, Giles-Corti B. The effect of siblings and family dog ownership on children's independent mobility to neighbourhood destinations. *Aust N Z J Publ Health* 2016;**40**(4):316–8.
36. De Meester F, Van Dyck D, De Bourdeaudhuij I, Cardon G. Parental perceived neighborhood attributes: associations with active transport and physical activity among 10–12 year old children and the mediating role of independent mobility. *BMC Public Health* 2014;**14**(1):631.
37. Foster S, Villanueva K, Wood L, Christian H, Giles-Corti B. The impact of parents' fear of strangers and perceptions of informal social control on children's independent mobility. *Health Place* 2014;**26**:60–8.

38. Fyhri A, Hjorthol R. Children's independent mobility to school, friends and leisure activities. *J Transport Geogr* 2009;**17**(5):377–84.
39. Ghekiere A, Deforche B, Carver A, Mertens L, de Geus B, Clarys P, Cardon G, De Bourdeaudhuij I, Van Cauwenberg J. Insights into children's independent mobility for transportation cycling—which socio-ecological factors matter? *J Sci Med Sport* 2017;**20**(3):267–72.
40. Kyttä M, Hirvonen J, Rudner J, Pirjola I, Laatikainen T. The last free-range children? Children's independent mobility in Finland in the 1990s and 2010s. *J Transport Geogr* 2015;**47**:1–2.
41. Mitra R, Faulkner GE, Buliung RN, Stone MR. Do parental perceptions of the neighbourhood environment influence children's independent mobility? Evidence from Toronto, Canada. *Urban Stud* 2014;**51**(16):3401–19.
42. Oliver M, Parker K, Witten K, Mavoa S, Badland HM, Donovan P, Chaudhury M, Kearns R. Children's out-of-school independently mobile trips, active travel, and physical activity: a cross-sectional examination from the kids in the City study. *J Phys Activ Health* 2016;**13**(3):318–24.
43. Pacilli MG, Giovannelli I, Prezza M, Augimeri ML. Children and the public realm: antecedents and consequences of independent mobility in a group of 11–13-year-old Italian children. *Child Geogr* 2013;**11**(4):377–93.
44. Schoeppe S, Tranter P, Duncan MJ, Curtis C, Carver A, Malone K. Australian children's independent mobility levels: secondary analyses of cross-sectional data between 1991 and 2012. *Child Geogr* 2016;**14**(4):408–21.
45. Villanueva K, Giles-Corti B, Bulsara M, Trapp G, Timperio A, McCormack G, Van Niel K. Does the walkability of neighbourhoods affect children's independent mobility, independent of parental, socio-cultural and individual factors? *Child Geogr* 2014;**12**(4):393–411.
46. Wolfe MK, McDonald NC. Association between neighborhood social environment and Children's independent mobility. *J Phys Activ Health* 2016;**13**(9):970–9.
47. McMillan T, Day K, Boarnet M, Alfonzo M, Anderson C. Johnny walks to school—does Jane? Sex differences in children's active travel to school. *Child Youth Environ* 2006;**16**(1):75–89.
48. Hart R. *Children's experience of place*. 1979. Irvington.
49. Tindal MA. *The home range of Black elementary school children: an exploratory study in the measurement and comparison of home range*. Environmental Research Group; 1971.
50. Morrongiello BA, Zdzieborski D, Normand J. Understanding gender differences in children's risk taking and injury: a comparison of mothers' and fathers' reactions to sons and daughters misbehaving in ways that lead to injury. *J Appl Dev Psychol* 2010;**31**(4):322–9.
51. Ampofo-Boateng K, Thomson JA. Children's perception of safety and danger on the road. *Br J Psychol* 1991;**82**(4):487–505.
52. Villanueva K, Giles-Corti B, Bulsara M, McCormack GR, Timperio A, Middleton N, Beesley B, Trapp G. How far do children travel from their homes? Exploring children's activity spaces in their neighborhood. *Health Place* 2012;**18**(2):263–73.
53. Veitch J, Carver A, Salmon J, Abbott G, Ball K, Crawford D, Cleland V, Timperio A. What predicts children's active transport and independent mobility in disadvantaged neighborhoods? *Health Place* 2017;**44**:103–9.
54. Corbin CB. Physical activity for everyone: what every physical educator should know about promoting lifelong physical activity. *J Teach Phys Educ* 2002;**21**(2):128–44.
55. Brussoni M, Olsen LL, Creighton G, Oliffe JL. Heterosexual gender relations in and around childhood risk and safety. *Qual Health Res* 2013;**23**(10):1388–98.
56. McDonald NC, Brown AL, Marchetti LM, Pedroso MS. US school travel, 2009: an assessment of trends. *Am J Prevent Med* 2011;**41**(2):146–51.

57. Schoeppe S, Duncan MJ, Badland HM, Rebar AL, Vandelanotte C. Too far from home? Adult attitudes on children's independent mobility range. *Child Geogr* 2016;**14**(4):482–9.
58. Veitch J, Salmon J, Ball K. Children's active free play in local neighborhoods: a behavioral mapping study. *Health Educ Res* 2007;**23**(5):870–9.
59. Cordovil R, Lopes F, Neto C. Children's (in) dependent mobility in Portugal. *J Sci Med Sport* 2015;**18**(3):299–303.
60. Lin EY, Witten K, Smith M, Carroll P, Asiasiga L, Badland H, Parker K. Social and built-environment factors related to children's independent mobility: the importance of neighbourhood cohesion and connectedness. *Health Place* 2017;**46**:107–13.
61. Mammen G, Faulkner G, Buliung R, Lay J. Understanding the drive to escort: a cross-sectional analysis examining parental attitudes towards children's school travel and independent mobility. *BMC Publ Health* 2012;**12**(1):862.
62. Alparone FR, Pacilli MG. On children's independent mobility: the interplay of demographic, environmental, and psychosocial factors. *Child Geogr* 2012;**10**(1):109–22.
63. Lopes F, Cordovil R, Neto C. Children's independent mobility in Portugal: effects of urbanization degree and motorized modes of travel. *J Transport Geogr* 2014;**41**:210–9.
64. Janssen I, Ferrao T, King N. Individual, family, and neighborhood correlates of independent mobility among 7 to 11-year-olds. *Prevent Med Rep* 2016;**3**:98–102.
65. Johansson M. Environment and parental factors as determinants of mode for children's leisure travel. *J Environ Psychol* 2006;**26**(2):156–69.
66. Santos MP, Pizarro AN, Mota J, Marques EA. Parental physical activity, safety perceptions and children's independent mobility. *BMC Publ Health* 2013;**13**(1):584.
67. Fromberg DP, Bergen D. *Play from birth to twelve and beyond: contexts, perspectives, and meanings*. Psychology Press; 1998.
68. Brussoni M, Olsen LL, Pike I, Sleet DA. Risky play and children's safety: balancing priorities for optimal child development. *Int J Environ Res Publ Health* 2012;**9**(9):3134–48.
69. Birken CS, Parkin PC, To T, Macarthur C. Trends in rates of death from unintentional injury among Canadian children in urban areas: influence of socioeconomic status. *Can Med Associat J* 2006;**175**(8). 867–.
70. Centers for Disease Control, Prevention (CDC). Vital signs: unintentional injury deaths among persons aged 0-19 years-United States, 2000–2009. *MMWR Morbid Mortal Week Rep* 2012;**61**:270.
71. Janssen I. Hyper-parenting is negatively associated with physical activity among 7–12 year olds. *Prev Med* 2015;**73**:55–9.
72. *Healthy living [internet] government of Canada*. 2017. Available from: https://www.canada.ca/en/services/health/healthy-living.html.
73. Broberg A, Kyttä M, Fagerholm N. Child-friendly urban structures: bullerby revisited. *J Environ Psychol* 2013;**35**:110–20.
74. Broberg A, Salminen S, Kyttä M. Physical environmental characteristics promoting independent and active transport to children's meaningful places. *Appl Geogr* 2013;**38**:43–52.
75. Kyttä M. Children's independent mobility in urban, small town, and rural environments. *Growing up in a changing urban landscape*. 1997. p. 41–52.
76. O'brien M, Jones D, Sloan D, Rustin M. Children's independent spatial mobility in the urban public realm. *Childhood* 2000;**7**(3):257–77.
77. *Child-friendly city building blocks [internet] UNICEF*. 2017. Available from: http://childfriendlycities.org/building-a-cfc/building-blocks/.
78. Price G, Reis R. Making kid-friendly cities: lessons from two cities. *Prev Med* 2010;**50**:S95–6.

79. *Guidelines for high-density housing for Families with children. City of Vancouver land use and development policies and guidelines [internet]. City of Vancouver.* 2017. Available at: former.vancouver.ca/commsvcs/guidelines/H004.pdf.
80. Rotterdam G. *Vrije tijd [Internet]. Gemeente Rotterdam.* 2017. Available from: https://www.rotterdam.nl/vrije-tijd/.
81. *Urbanism awards: Rotterdam takes top prize [internet].* Academy of Urbanism; 2017. Available from: www.academyofurbanism.org.uk/urbanism-awards-rotterdam-takes-top-prize/.
82. Dowling R. Cultures of mothering and car use in suburban Sydney: a preliminary investigation. *Geoforum* 2000;**31**(3):345–53.
83. Ungar M. *Too safe for their own good: how risk and responsibility help teens thrive.* McClelland & Stewart; 2009.
84. Bundy AC, Naughton G, Tranter P, Wyver S, Baur L, Schiller W, Bauman A, Engelen L, Ragen J, Luckett T, Niehues A. The Sydney playground project: popping the bubble wrap-unleashing the power of play: a cluster randomized controlled trial of a primary school playground-based intervention aiming to increase children's physical activity and social skills. *BMC Public Health* 2011;**11**(1):680.
85. Niehues AN, Bundy A, Broom A, Tranter P, Ragen J, Engelen L. Everyday uncertainties: reframing perceptions of risk in outdoor free play. *J Advent Educ Outdoor Learn* 2013;**13**(3):223–37.
86. *Outside play [internet]. Outsideplay.ca.* 2017. Available at: https://outsideplay.ca/.

An Ecological Model of Active Transportation

6

Richard Larouche[1], *Ariane Ghekiere*[2]
[1]Faculty of Health Sciences, University of Lethbridge, Lethbridge, AB, Canada; [2]Department of Public Health, Ghent University, Ghent, Belgium

It takes a village to raise a child.

Unknown Author

Chapter Outline

6.1 Introduction

The social–ecological approach proposed by Harvard University professor Urie Bronfenbrenner[1] in the late 1970s sheds light on the multiplicity of factors influencing human behaviour and their complex interactions. In 1986, this approach was adopted by the World Health Organization in its landmark Ottawa Charter for Health Promotion.[2] The Charter insisted on the importance of 'making the healthy choice the easy choice', notably by creating environments that make it easier for individuals to adopt healthy behaviours such as physical activity, healthy eating and so on. The social–ecological approach was then rapidly adopted by disciplines such as physical activity and health promotion in general.[3–5]

In this chapter, we explain how a **social–ecological model** can be used to investigate the factors associated with children's active transportation. A central tenet of social–ecological models is that human behaviour is influenced by multiple **levels of influence**. Typically, authors use four or five levels of influence, ranging from the most proximal (i.e., individual factors) to the most distal factors (i.e., policies). As shown in Fig. 6.1, this book considers five levels of influence.[6] Key factors that belong to each

Children's Active Transportation. https://doi.org/10.1016/B978-0-12-811931-0.00006-5

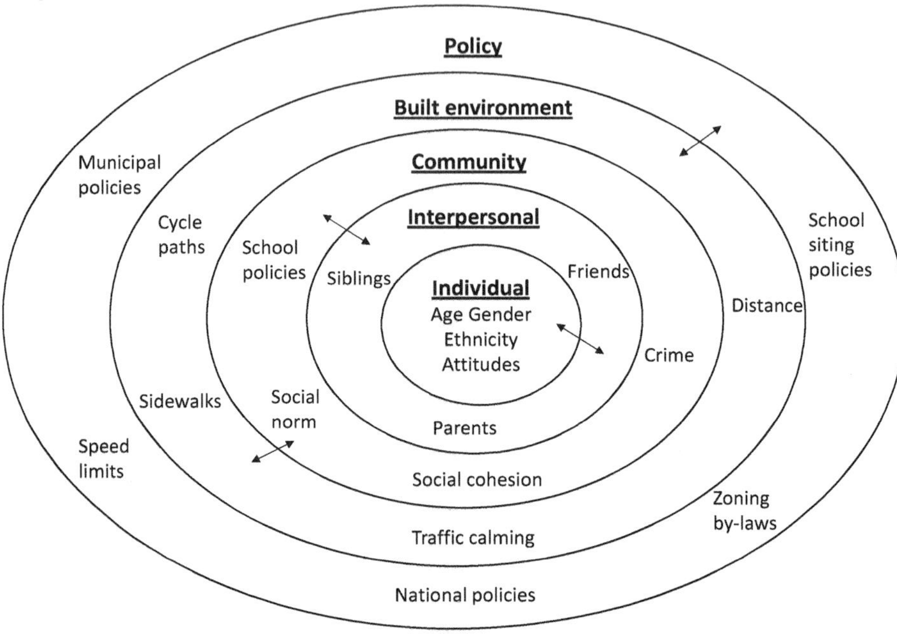

Figure 6.1 Social-ecological model of the correlates of active transportation. This model illustrates some of the key factors associated with active transportation. Other factors are discussed in chapters 7–12.

of these levels of influence are briefly summarized in the figure and are explored in more details in Chapters 7–12.

This chapter provides a roadmap of the levels of influence which are discussed individually in the next five chapters. It is crucial to keep in mind that there may be important interactions between the levels of influence. Remember that in Chapter 4, we saw that distance between home and school (which may be conceived as a **built environment** factor) is shaped by policies that govern urban sprawl and school choice, as well as by parental neighbourhood and school choice, among others. This clearly shows that the levels of influence do not exist in a vacuum.

Previous research suggests that the direct influence of individual factors on travel mode choice and physical activity may be larger than that of the more distal levels.[6,7] Yet, this is not to say that policies and the built environment are unimportant. While a change in transport policy may have limited impact on the behaviours of individuals, it can influence many individuals simultaneously over a long period of time.[8,9] In contrast, a one-on-one intervention aiming to increase children's attitudes, confidence and motivation to engage in active transportation might be a game changer for some children, but it may not work with other children living in an unfavourable environment.

Theoretically, interventions targeting both individuals (people), significant others, and the environment (places) may be most effective because they can combine the advantages of the two approaches discussed above. Ball[10] elegantly argued that we should not envision a false dichotomy between focusing on people or on places in the context of physical activity interventions. Instead, we should endeavour to focus on both aspects—without neglecting the importance of significant others (friends and parents for example).[10] Her comments would be of great relevance in the context of active transportation interventions as well.

At the end of the day, multilevel interventions have the potential to be more effective in increasing active transportation. For example, in the United States, Safe Routes to School interventions that included both educational activities and infrastructure changes resulted in greater increases in active transportation to/from school than interventions using only one of these strategies.[11,12] Safe Routes to School interventions are discussed in much details in Chapter 13. Similarly, we observed that children were much more likely to engage in active transportation to/from school if the two following features were both present than if only one was present: (1) school officials identified safe routes to school (e.g., streets where children could safely walk or bike) and (2) traffic-calming features were observed by study staff.[13] **Traffic-calming** features include speed bumps and narrower intersections, and they are discussed in greater details in Chapter 16.

Before discussing each level of influence in detail, it is important to define some of the language that is used to describe the factors associated with active transportation. Table 6.1 provides a list of key definitions.[14–16]

6.2 What Kind of Studies Provides Information About the Factors Associated With Active Transportation?

Chapters 7–11 will review the literature for each level of influence. In order to better understand the materials in these chapters, it is important to understand that there are different types of studies which have their respective strengths and limitations.[17] We describe below four broad types of studies that can provide information on the factors associated with active transportation: cross-sectional studies, longitudinal studies, intervention studies and literature reviews.

6.2.1 Cross-Sectional Studies

The majority of studies on active transportation have used a cross-sectional design. In such studies, children's travel behaviours are measured at the same time as the potential correlates of active transportation. As a result, the researchers cannot determine the direction of observed relationships between travel behaviours and the other factors that they have measured. For example, in a cross-sectional study, a researcher may observe that children who engage in active transportation are more physically active.[18] However, because both variables were measured at the same time, the researcher cannot tell whether active transportation leads to more physical activity or if physically active children are more inclined to engage in active transportation. This situation is similar to the debate on whether the egg preceded the chicken or vice versa. Cross-sectional studies are generally less expensive to conduct than longitudinal studies and

Table 6.1 Definition of key concepts related to active transportation and the social–ecological model

Concept	Definition
Correlate	A correlate is a variable that is associated with our variable of interest (i.e., active transportation in this book). The term correlate is preferred for cross-sectional studies wherein the researchers cannot determine the direction of the relationships observed between different variables.[14]
Determinant	A determinant is a variable whose fluctuation *causes* change in our variable of interest. For example, a researcher may find that an increase in distance decreases the likelihood of active transportation. The term determinant is often used interchangeably with correlate. However, this is a mistake because determinant is a much stronger term.[14]
Mediator	A mediator is an intermediate variable that is necessary to *explain* the relationship between two variables. In other words, it can be described as a *mechanism* through which a variable influences another. For example, an intervention may lead to an increase in active transportation by decreasing parental concerns about road safety. In this case, parental concerns would be a mediator.[14]
Moderator	A moderator is a variable that affects the direction and/or the strength of a relationship between two variables. For example, researchers may observe that an intervention may result in larger changes in active transportation in boys compared to girls. In this case, gender would be a moderator.[14]
Confounder	A confounder is a 'third variable' that is associated with the two variables that a researcher is truly interested in. For example, age may be related to both whether a child participates in an active transportation intervention and to a child's travel behaviour. The presence of a confounder may lead the researcher to draw misguided conclusions about the effect of an intervention. Yet, the effect of a confounder can be controlled for using appropriate statistical analyses.[14]
Social environment	The social environment can be defined as 'the immediate physical or social setting in which people live or in which something happens or develops. It includes the culture that the individual was educated or lives in, and the people and institutions with whom they interact'[15]
Built environment	Built environment is 'defined broadly to include land use patterns, the transportation system, and design features that together provide opportunities for travel and physical activity. Land use patterns refer to the spatial distribution of human activities. The transportation system refers to the physical infrastructure and services that provide the spatial links or connectivity among activities. Design refers to the aesthetic, physical, and functional qualities of the built environment, such as the design of buildings and streetscapes, and relates to both land use patterns and the transportation system.'[16]
Physical environment	Physical environment refers to 'the part of the human environment that includes purely physical factors (as soil, climate, water supply)' (Source: Merriam-Webster dictionary)

intervention studies, and they are useful in identifying factors that may be *associated* with active transportation. When such studies consistently observe that a given variable is associated with active transportation, it increases our confidence that there is indeed a relationship between these variables. For example, studies have consistently shown that children living further away from school are less likely to engage in active transportation to school as discussed in Chapter 4.

6.2.2 Longitudinal Studies

In a **longitudinal study**, the researchers follow the same participants over time. This can allow them to determine the direction of observed relationships between travel behaviours and other variables. For example, researchers conducting a longitudinal study on the correlates of active transportation observed that children who lived closer to school and whose parents reported that driving to school was inconvenient were more likely to take up active transportation in the following year.[19] There are two fundamental types of longitudinal studies. First, in a **prospective study**, the researchers follow individuals—or cohorts of individuals—over time. Some prospective studies have followed individuals for very long periods of time. For example, the Young Finns study has followed six cohorts of participants over 27 years in Finland. This study provides a unique perspective on how active transportation and physical activity evolved from childhood to adulthood.[20] In contrast, in a **retrospective study**, the researchers attempt to 'go back in time' by questioning individuals about their past. While retrospective studies are generally less expensive to conduct compared to prospective studies, researchers have to rely on participants' memory of past events which may be inaccurate. For instance, adults may romanticize their experience of walking to school during childhood, and pretend that they walked 5 miles, uphill both ways and in the snow!

6.2.3 Intervention Studies

A study wherein a variable thought to be related to active transportation is modified by the researchers is called an intervention study. The most rigorous intervention type is a **randomized controlled trial** wherein participants (or groups of participants such as schools) are randomly assigned to an experimental group that gets the intervention and a control group that does not get the intervention. This type of intervention can maximize **internal validity**.[21] Internal validity is the extent to which we can conclude that our intervention—and not something else—caused a change in our outcome of interest (say, active transportation). Internal validity is high when potential sources of bias are minimized, so that we are confident that our intervention is indeed the cause of the observed changes. Given that interventions targeting the built environment may be costly, researchers in Belgium have developed a novel experimental approach using manipulated photographs to learn more about which factors should be targeted in an intervention (see Box 6.1).[22,23] Using such an approach could help researchers and policy-makers to make the case for an intervention.

Because it is often impossible (or impractical) to randomly assign participants to different groups, many researchers conduct **quasi-experimental studies**.[24] In such

Box 6.1 An experimental study using manipulated photographs

Ghekiere et al.[22] aimed to understand which physical environment features are most important for children and their parents in order to support cycling for transport. As conducting intervention studies on site is expensive and time consuming, the authors worked with photographs. These photographs were systematically developed by manipulating seven environmental features that parents and children considered to be important for cycling.[23] These photographs were then integrated in a choice-based conjoint task, in which participants were repeatedly shown two streets where the child could cycle along. Parents and children had to indicate which street they preferred to (let their child) cycle to a friend living 15 min away from their residence. From choosing 12 times, it was possible to rank the importance of each of the included factors. Findings indicated that both parents and children preferred to cycle in streets where cycling infrastructure is present, preferably well separated from motorized traffic. Other safety elements such as traffic density, traffic speed and evenness of the cycling infrastructure were also important, followed by aesthetic features such as amount of vegetation and general maintenance of the streets. Although this study did not examine which physical factors are most important for actual cycling, it provides information on which features are preferred by parents and children.

studies, the researchers may select a control group to be compared with their experimental group. However, the absence of randomization increases the likelihood that changes observed by the researchers are attributable to something else than the intervention itself. For example, if at the beginning of study, children from the control group substantially differed from those of the experimental group in a given characteristic (e.g., age, gender, household income, etc.), then changes observed during the intervention may be influenced by this characteristic. To date, most interventions focusing on children's active transportation have used a quasi-experimental design.[25]

There also exists another type of intervention studies wherein a variable that is thought to be related to active transportation is modified by a third party rather than by the researchers themselves. This is called a '**natural experiment**'. Because interventions addressing road safety issues are often very expensive and require the collaboration of many agencies (e.g., government, public works, public health, police, etc.), large active transportation interventions are often natural experiments. A key challenge with these natural experiments is that the researchers are not in control of the implementation of the intervention, so it can be difficult to ensure that the intervention was implemented as planned and to schedule preintervention and postintervention measures at the right time.[26] Nevertheless, an important advantage of natural experiments is that they better reflect how interventions are implemented in the 'real world'. The disadvantage of natural experiments is that observed changes in active transportation levels may be due to other factors (e.g., other policies or interventions) than the intervention evaluated by the researchers.

6.2.4 Literature Reviews

Finally, literature reviews are studies where the researchers synthesize results from previous studies. The most robust type of reviews is a **systematic review** where the researchers elaborate a detailed strategy to search multiple scientific databases in order to respond to a precise research question. An example of a research question amenable to a systematic review is 'which physical environment factors are associated with active transportation among children?'[27] To answer their question, the researchers have to define strict inclusion and exclusion criteria to determine which studies should be included in their review and which ones should be excluded. They also have to determine what information to extract from the included studies and to rigorously assess the quality of included studies. The ability to synthesize results from many different studies is particularly important because it allows the researchers to determine the consistency of relationships between variables of interest.

Some systematic reviews also include a **meta-analysis** which is a statistical technique where the researchers pool data from multiple original studies. This allows the researchers to get a more precise estimate of the difference between groups of participants. For example, a meta-analysis could tell us how many additional minutes of daily physical activity are accrued on average by active travellers compared to motorized travellers.

However, it is important to mention that systematic reviews are not the only type of reviews. **Narrative reviews** are also useful when the research question is more general, to the extent that it would be hardly amenable to a single systematic review. In essence, this book aims to provide a very broad overview of current knowledge on active transportation among children and youth, using a narrative review approach.

6.3 Qualitative and Quantitative Studies

There are two general approaches to conduct the types of studies described in Section 6.2: **qualitative** and **quantitative research** methods. While a detailed description of these approaches is beyond the scope of this book, it is important to distinguish their goals, methods, and strengths and limitations. Qualitative research is particularly useful when studying a topic that is not well understood and when it is unclear how the variables of interest should be measured. Qualitative research often involves interviews, focus groups (i.e., small groups of people convened by the researchers for a focused discussion) and other methods whereby the researchers observe the participants in their natural settings (e.g., home, parks, streets, etc.). Through these methods, the researchers collect a large amount of data for each participant in the form of words, behaviours, pictures, videos, etc. A key limitation of qualitative studies is that they typically involve a small number of participants who are not representative of the target population, so it is unclear if the findings can be applied to other populations. Qualitative researchers generally use an **inductive** approach in which they categorize the data that they gathered into different themes, and from this information, they can develop concepts and hypotheses. Box 6.2 illustrates a novel example of a qualitative

Box 6.2 Qualitative study of children's perspective on active transportation

Fusco et al.[28] aimed to understand how children who engage in active transportation and those who are driven experience their trip to/from school. They recruited 41 children living in diverse neighbourhoods within the city of Toronto, Canada. They used 'photovoice', a novel approach in which children were asked to take pictures during their trip to and from school and explain why they took the picture and what it means to them. In addition, the researchers asked children to participate in an interview to learn more about their perceptions of their journeys. Both active and motorized travellers emphasized the importance of their home and school, and the role of road signs, and expressed concerns related to traffic and dangerous drivers. However, active travellers expressed a greater engagement and familiarity with their natural environment (e.g., trees, flowers, paths, forests and green spaces) and discussed more about social interactions during their journey. In contrast, many children lamented that car travel prevented them from experiencing interesting things on the way to school.

study investigating active transportation from children's perspective using 'photovoice' and interview methods.[28]

In contrast, quantitative research is concerned with quantifying and explaining a phenomenon in a more objective way. Quantitative data can be collected in a variety of ways, including direct measures, devices such as pedometers and global positioning systems, questionnaires, as well as structured interviews where questions are asked in a systematic and quantifiable way. The data collected are readily amenable to statistical analyses which can be used to validate a theory. An important advantage of quantitative research is that it can be carried in large populations or in tightly controlled conditions where the researchers can eliminate many sources of bias. However, quantitative studies restrict the ways in which participants can respond, and they may not provide such a rich understanding of the context in which a behaviour occurs compared to qualitative studies. Box 6.3 summarizes a clever quantitative study that aimed to determine what distinguishes active and motorized travellers living in the same environment and attending the same school.[29]

It is important to recognize that the qualitative and quantitative approaches are not mutually exclusive. Indeed, combining quantitative and qualitative methods can allow researchers to study active transportation from different, but complementary, perspectives. Such studies are commonly described as '**mixed-methods**' studies.[30] For example, researchers could first conduct a qualitative study exploring barriers to active transportations through in-depth interviews with children and parents. Then, using the knowledge gleaned from this study, they could develop a questionnaire that would allow them to conduct quantitative analyses

Box 6.3 Quantitative study of the factors associated with active transportation

Lee et al.[29] conducted a quantitative study to identify factors associated with children's school travel mode while controlling for the distance between home and school and the neighbourhood in which they live. To do so, they identified 601 pairs of children that included a child who walked (labelled as 'walker') and one who was driven by car (labelled as 'driver'). Children within each pair attended the same school and lived within 200 feet (about 60 m) from each other. Despite living so close from one another, 'drivers' were less likely to report that the school is close enough to walk. This suggests that the perception of proximity matters over and above the actual distance. Children were more likely to be 'walkers' if their parents reported that parks are present, that walking is convenient and that they enjoy walking with their child. In contrast, children were less likely to be 'walkers' if their parents were concerned about road crashes or 'stranger danger', perceived that driving is faster and easier and if they reported that sidewalks are not well maintained or that there is a lot of traffic.

to determine which barriers are particularly important. From a different perspective, researchers may have first evaluated an intervention which aimed to increase uptake of active transportation, only to find that the intervention did not achieve its objective. Rather than quickly dismissing the intervention as ineffective, the researchers could conduct interviews with participants and/or with the people who were responsible for implementing the intervention. Maybe they might find that the intervention was not implemented as planned or that it was not well tailored for the participants (e.g., a walking school bus intervention might work with primary but not secondary school students).

6.4 Conclusion

We presented the social–ecological model that will be used in the next chapters to provide a detailed overview of the factors associated with children's active transportation. We then emphasized the importance of focusing on multiple levels of influence in order to encourage more children to engage in active transportation. Next, we defined key terms that are routinely used in studies of the correlates of active transportation. Finally, we discussed the strengths and limitations of different types of studies that can be used to investigate children's active transportation and provided examples of innovative studies on this topic. It is our hope that this chapter will make it easier for the reader to understand the materials discussed in the next chapters.

References

1. Bronfenbrenner U. *The ecology of human development: experiments by nature and design.* Cambridge, MA: Harvard University Press; 1979.
2. World Health Organization. *Ottawa charter for health promotion.* Geneva: World Health Organization; 1986.
3. McLeroy KR, Bibeau D, Steckler A, Glanz K. An ecological perspective on health promotion programs. *Health Educ Behav* 1988;**15**(4):351–77.
4. Stokols D. Establishing and maintaining healthy environments: toward a social ecology of health promotion. *Am Psychol* 1992;**47**(1):6–22.
5. Stokols D. Translating social ecological theory into guidelines for community health promotion. *Am J Health Promot* 1996;**10**(4):282–98.
6. Giles-Corti B, Donovan RJ. The relative influence of individual, social and physical environment determinants of physical activity. *Soc Sci Med* 2002;**54**(12):1793–812.
7. Lemieux M, Godin G. How well do cognitive and environmental variables predict active commuting? *Int J Behav Nutr Phys Act* 2009;**6**:12.
8. Sallis JF, Cervero RB, Ascher W, et al. An ecological approach to creating active living communities. *Annu Rev Public Health* 2006;**27**:297–322.
9. Sallis JF, Floyd MF, Rodriguez DA, Saelens BE. Role of built environments in physical activity, obesity, and cardiovascular disease. *Circulation* 2012;**125**:729–37.
10. Ball K. People, places... and other people?: Integrating understanding of intrapersonal, social and environmental determinants of physical activity. *J Sci Med Sport* 2006;**9**(5):367–70.
11. McDonald NC, Yang Y, Abbott SM, Bullock AN. Impact of the safe routes to school program on walking and biking: Eugene, Oregon study. *Transp Policy* 2013;**29**:243–8.
12. McDonald NC, Steiner RL, Lee C, Smith TR, Zhu X, Yang Y. Impact of the safe routes to school program on walking and bicycling. *J Am Plann Assoc* 2014;**80**(2):153–67.
13. Larouche R, Chaput J-P, Leduc G, Boyer C, Bélanger P, LeBlanc AG, Borghese MM, Tremblay MS. A cross-sectional examination of socio-demographic and school-level correlates of children's school travel mode in Ottawa, Canada. *BMC Publ Health* 2014;**14**(497).
14. Bauman AE, Sallis JF, Dzewaltowski DA, Owen N. Toward a better understanding of the influences on physical activity: the role of determinants, correlates, causal variables, mediators, moderators, and confounders. *Am J Prev Med* 2002;**23**(2 Suppl. 1):5–14.
15. Barnett E, Casper M. A definition of "social environment". *Am J Public Health* 2001;**91**(3):465.
16. Transportation Research Board & Institute of Medicine. *Does the built environment influence physical activity? Examining the evidence.* Washington, DC: Transportation Research Board; 2005. Available from: http://onlinepubs.trb.org/onlinepubs/sr/sr282.pdf.
17. Thomas JR, Nelson JK, Silverman SJ. *Research methods in physical activity.* 7th ed. Champaign, IL: Human Kinetics; 2015.
18. Cooper AR, Page AS, Foster LJ, Qahwaji D. Commuting to school: are children who walk more physically active. *Am J Prev Med* 2003;**25**(4):273–6.
19. Panter J, Corder K, Griffin SJ, Jones AP, van Sluijs EMF. Individual, socio-cultural and environmental predictors of uptake and maintenance of active commuting in children: longitudinal results from the SPEEDY study. *Int J Behav Nutr Phys Act* 2013;**10**:83.
20. Yang X, Telama R, Hirvensalo M, Tammelin T, Viikari JSA, Raitakari OT. Active commuting from youth to adulthood and as a predictor of physical activity in early midlife: the Young Finns Study. *Prev Med* 2014;**59**:5–11.

21. Campbell DT. Factors relevant to the validity of experiments in social settings. *Psychol Bull* 1957;**54**(4):297–312.
22. Ghekiere A, Deforche B, Mertens L, De Bourdeaudhuij I, Clarys P, de Geus B, et al. Creating cycling-friendly environments for children: which micro-scale factors are most important? An experimental study using manipulated photographs. *PLoS One* 2015;**10**(12):e0143302.
23. Ghekiere A, Van Cauwenberg J, de Geus B, Clarys P, Cardon G, Salmon J, et al. Critical environmental factors for transportation cycling in children: a qualitative study using bike-along interviews. *PLoS One* 2014;**9**(9):e106696.
24. Cook TD, Campbell DT. *Quasi-experimentation: design & analysis issues in field settings.* Boston, MA: Houghton Mifflin; 1979.
25. Chillón P, Evenson KR, Vaughn A, Ward DS. A systematic review of interventions for promoting active transportation to school. *Int J Behav Nutr Phys Act* 2011;**8**:10.
26. Ramanathan S, Allison KR, Faulkner G, Dwyer JJM. Challenges in assessing the implementation and effectiveness of physical activity and nutrition policy interventions as natural experiments. *Health Promot Int* 2008;**23**(3):290–7.
27. D'Haese S, Vanwolleghem G, Hinckson E, de Bourdeaudhuij I, Deforche B, Van Dyck D, Cardon G. Cross-continental comparison of the association between the physical environment and active transportation in children: a systematic review. *Int J Behav Nutr Phys Act* 2015;**12**:145.
28. Fusco C, Moola F, Faulkner G, Buliung R, Richichi V. Toward an understanding of children's perceptions of their transport geographies: (non)active school travel and visual representations of the built environment. *J Transp Geogr* 2012;**20**:62–70.
29. Lee C, Zhu X, Yong J, Varni JW. Beyond distance: children's school travel mode choice. *Ann Bev Med* 2013;**45**(1):S55–67.
30. Creswell JW, Plano Clark VL. *Designing and conducting mixed methods research.* 2nd ed. Thousand Oaks, CA: Sage; 2011.

Individual Correlates of Active Transportation

7

Lieze Mertens[1], Ariane Ghekiere[2]
[1]Department of Movement & Sports Sciences, Ghent University, Ghent, Belgium;
[2]Department of Public Health, Ghent University, Ghent, Belgium

Chapter Outline

7.1 Introduction

Active transportation allows children to increase their physical activity levels and has been found to be beneficial for health. Despite the fact that the benefits of active transportation are generally well known, children's active transportation rates vary largely between countries, within countries and even between and within families. The socio-ecological model posits that children's active transportation is influenced by a range of factors including individual, social and environmental factors. The most proximal factors are hypothesized to have the largest effects on children's active transportation. This chapter aims to provide an overview of existing literature on those individual correlates of children's active transportation. Additionally, some practical implications and suggestions for future research are formulated.

7.2 Demographical Correlates: Age and Gender

As young children age, their walking and cycling levels increase until they reach adolescence[1–3] and steeply decline during adolescence and adulthood.[4,5] Most children start to ride a bicycle around the age of 5–7 years,[6] although few use it for

Children's Active Transportation. https://doi.org/10.1016/B978-0-12-811931-0.00007-7

transportation, except in Northern European countries (see Chapter 4). The transition from primary to secondary school is a key factor involved in the decline of active transportation (to school), likely because secondary schools have larger catchment areas resulting in larger average distances that need to be covered.[7] The decline in active transportation in adolescence has also been confirmed by other studies. A previous study conducted in the United States reported that active transportation to school was more frequent among children in the lower grades in comparison to children in the upper grades.[8] A longitudinal study in Canada showed that as children aged, the likelihood of using active transportation to school increased, peaked at the age of 10 years and then decreased.[9]

Most studies indicate a large difference in active transportation levels between boys and girls, with boys reporting more active transportation compared to girls.[2,10,11] A first possible explanation could be that boys are more advanced in motor competence at the age of 9 years compared to girls,[12] which might give parents more confidence to give more independent mobility to boys compared to girls. However, a recent meta-analysis indicated that only certain aspects of motor competence are better in boys compared to girls.[13] Therefore, socialization seems to be a more likely explanation of the observed differences in active transportation levels between boys and girls. Girls are being socialized differently from an early age in terms of risk taking, with parents being more protective of their daughters compared to their sons.[14] Valentine[15] also indicated that parenting practices are gendered as a consequence of the traditional views that girls are more at risk of harm in public areas compared to boys. However, some studies did not observe such a difference. For example, one study found difference in neither the likelihood of being a cyclist (i.e., cycling for transportation for at least 1 minute a week) between boys and girls nor in the amount of cycling for transportation (i.e., minutes cycling/week) among 10- to 12-year-old children in Flanders, Belgium.[16] This is in line with other studies conducted in Flanders in the same age group,[17] as well as in other European countries where cycling for transportation is more common, such as the Netherlands, Denmark and Sweden.[18–20] The lack of gender differences in these countries suggest that other elements are more important in determining children's active transportation levels. Therefore, it might be hypothesized that the 'protectiveness towards girls' is stronger in countries with lower cycling levels as the gender differences are more pronounced in these countries.

7.3 Familial Correlates

No consistent associations can be found between children's active transportation and their socioeconomic status (SES). Common indicators of SES include parental education levels, household income and/or neighbourhood income, and car ownership. For example, among a sample of Portuguese children, active transportation was lower if their father had a higher level of education in comparison to a child whose father had a lower level of education.[21] Similarly, having a lower family SES (expressed as years of education) was associated with an increased likelihood to start cycling for transportation among a sample of British children.[22] Both studies indicated that children from low SES families were more likely to engage in active transportation. However, there are also examples of studies finding no association between SES and active transportation behaviour in children.[16,17,23,24] Nevertheless, a consistent negative association was found between the number of household cars and levels of children's active transportation.[1,25,26] Furthermore, limited access to a bicycle has been shown to result in less active transportation to school in one study.[27] Although many studies have suggested that children from high SES families are more physically active,[28] no such consistent association can be found between children's active travel and SES with the exception of car ownership.

Furthermore, studies on the association between ethnicity and active transportation found mixed results. For example, two studies showed that children from ethnic minorities were more likely to engage in active transportation to school,[29,30] while another study observed that black children were more likely to be driven to school compared to their white counterparts in London.[26] It is plausible that these associations are different according to country culture and the prevalence of active transportation. For example, in countries where cycling for transportation is more common such as the Netherlands, studies indicated a higher prevalence of active transportation in Dutch (i.e., native) versus other ethnic groups (i.e., immigrant).[18] Similarly, Maki-Opas et al. found that Turkish and Moroccan adolescents are not likely to cycle for transport in the Netherlands, even if good cycling infrastructure is present.[31] Furthermore, other studies found no association between ethnicity and active transportation.[8,32,33] Other demographic characteristics such as parents' marital status and number of children in the household have been investigated in fewer studies, and no clear conclusion could be drawn, as findings are mixed.[34]

7.4 Psychosocial Correlates

Theories such as the Theory of Planned Behavior[35] and the Social Cognitive Theory[36] posit that an individual's behaviour is influenced by their own psychosocial characteristics towards that behaviour (e.g., attitudes, subjective norms, self-efficacy, intention, etc.). Limited research has explored which role these psychosocial characteristics may play in explaining children's active transportation behaviour. One can obtain insights into the psychosocial correlates of children by questioning either the child itself or one of the parents. In many studies, parents were asked to complete questions regarding their child's psychosocial characteristics, although children from the age of 10 years are capable of completing these types of questionnaires.[37]

Three studies were conducted in Flanders, Belgium,[16,24,38] to assess psychosocial factors associated with cycling for transportation among 10- to 12-year-olds. In the study by Zwerts et al.,[38] parents reported that children prefer to cycle for transportation, as it provides them possibilities to explore nature, and it allows social interaction and creates a sense of responsibility to take care for themselves. Ducheyne et al.[24] found that children had higher odds of cycling to school if parents reported positive attitudes towards their child's cycling to school. Ghekiere et al.[16,39] found that children with higher perceived barriers for cycling had lower odds of cycling for transportation, and those reporting higher self-efficacy levels (i.e., those who were more confident in their ability to cycle) had higher odds of cycling for transportation. Other studies assessing children's preferences indicated that children more often prefer cycling over walking because cycling provides them a greater sense of independence.[2,40] Finally, a study conducted in the United States indicated that children's self-efficacy was positively associated with their active transportation levels, but parental self-efficacy had an even stronger influence on children's active transportation levels.[41]

Although the Theory of Planned Behavior[35] significantly predicts children's active travel, habit strength augments the predictive validity of the model.[42] A study indicated that children's active travel (to school) is controlled by both intentional and habitual processes.[42] Habit strength is an important but often overlooked individual correlate of active transportation. Developing the habit of using active transportation at a young age has been found to be associated with a higher probability of being active in adulthood.[43] Therefore, it is important to adopt this healthy behaviour at a young age.

7.5 Motor Development Correlates

Riding a bicycle is a more complex behaviour compared to walking because it requires a combination of many skills such as steering, balancing, signalling and checking over one's shoulder. Therefore, most studies investigating the relationship between active transportation and motor competence have focused on cycling. A recent meta-analysis indicated that boys outperform girls in some types of motor competence (i.e., object control competence and motor coordination) but not in others (i.e., composite skill scores, locomotor competence and stability).[13] These gender-dependent motor skills do not necessarily correspond with cycling skills, as a study investigating children's cycling skills showed no differences between boys and girls.[44]

Furthermore, cycling skills generally improve with age, likely due to an age-related improvement in motor coordination and mental development.[45] Older children (11- to 12-year-olds) outperform younger children (6- to 7-year-olds) in cycling skills, assessed by a practical bicycle test consisting of 13 items with different points of interest.[45] For example, younger children have more difficulties with estimating distance and speed, connecting perceptual information and steering behaviour.[46] Children often miscalculate their stopping range and have difficulties to perceive and integrate visual information.[47] Since children are overrepresented in cycling accidents (e.g., in Belgium, 33% of all child fatalities happened during cycling in traffic),[48] it is very important that sufficient attention is given to develop cycling skills in children and to provide safer infrastructure for cycling such as physically separated paths and traffic-calming measures.[49]

The effectiveness of cycle training to improve children's cycling skills has already been confirmed by the literature.[50,51] For example, in the UK, a national cycle training programme, Bikeability, has been developed and successfully implemented. This programme aims to improve cycling and traffic skills in order to increase children's traffic- and bicycle-handling skills and behaviour, and it has been shown to be effective.[51] Consequently, parents, school and youth organizations should be informed that cycle training is valuable to develop or improve cycling skills. An important finding is that cycle training is equally effective among boys and girls, and it improves cycling skills in both the short and long term, and might automatize different cycling skills.[50] As a cycling course might often contain only one aspect of cycling competence (i.e., cycling skills, knowledge of the highway code, attitudes and psychomotor skills), it is important to integrate them all to maximize improvement in children's cycling competence.[52] However, offering cycling skills training more broadly might not be sufficient to increase cycling for transport among children. Previous cycle training programs appeared to be effective in improving children's skills, but no differences were found in cycling behaviour or the occurrence of cycling independently.[44,53,54] Nevertheless, good cycling skills might make parents more confident in their child's bicycle-handling skills, which may lead to increases in their independent mobility, although future research is needed to test this hypothesis.

7.6 Independent Mobility as a Key Correlate

Young pedestrians or cyclists are a vulnerable group of road users. By developing their motor competence, perceptual and cognitive abilities, children should be able to increase their independent mobility.[44,55] Independent mobility can be defined as the ability of children to walk or cycle around their neighbourhood without adult accompaniment (see Chapter 5). Parents may restrict the independent mobility of younger children for the sake of safety. This might be even more stringent for cycling in comparison to walking because this is a more complex task that requires more attention and skills of the child.[56] Consequently, the mobility range of children is lower compared to adolescents' and adults' mobility range and is commonly restricted to their own neighbourhood or even less.[57]

Many studies have shown that boys have greater independent mobility compared to girls.[16,58,59] Since cycling levels did not differ between boys and girls in European countries with higher levels of cycling for transportation, these findings might suggest that girls are more often accompanied during cycling trips compared to boys from the same age.[24,60–62]

Studies consistently show that children who are granted more independent mobility are more likely to engage in active transportation and that independent mobility increases with age.[62,63] Results from a survey conducted in 16 countries indicate that independent mobility increases markedly from 7 to 15 years of age in most countries.[65] Another study indicated that 11- and 12-year-old children were allowed to cycle up to 5.0 km from their homes without adult supervision, whereas 7- to 8-year-old children were seldom allowed to cycle on their own.[46] Furthermore, the association between independent mobility and cycling to school was stronger among the older children (11- to 12-year-olds) in comparison to younger children

(8- to 10-year-olds).[24] However, as reviewed in Chapter 5, there has been a large decline in independent mobility over the last few decades that coincided with a marked decline in active transportation.

7.7 Conclusion

It can be concluded that when aiming to increase children's active transportation, a wide range of individual correlates should be targeted. Since it is not possible to modify individual correlates such as age, gender or ethnicity, we might focus future interventions on the groups who are less likely to engage in active transportation (e.g., girls, younger children). Overall, older children will experience greater independent mobility and are consequently more likely to use active transportation until they get their drivers' license. Secondly, the important role parents play in determining their child's travel mode needs to be acknowledged. Parents act as a role model, encourage or discourage certain behaviours, and set children's independent mobility. Currently, only limited evidence suggests that children's psychosocial characteristics play a role in explaining their travel behaviour. Lastly, improving motor development of the child might support increases in children's active travel and improve safety, although more research is needed to test this hypothesis.

7.8 Recommendations for Policy and Practice

1. Children should be stimulated to develop their fundamental motor skills by engaging in sufficient physical activity at school, active transportation to school and active leisure-time activities after school. Training in cycling and traffic skills is especially important to improve the fundamental motor skills needed for cycling.
2. Children prefer active transportation modes to reach their destination, but parents often restrict them due to a variety of reasons, of which traffic safety concern is the key factor. However, children are able to discuss which travel modes they prefer. Parents should involve children in the process of decision making on travel modes and hear children's voices in order to take into account preferences of children. Parents should encourage children to use active travel modes and assist in creating positive feelings and attitudes towards active transportation modes. Additionally, children could be encouraged to not only use active travel modes to school but also to other destinations, which may be closer.
3. Schools should be encouraged to schedule cycle courses within the compulsory curriculum,[50] ideally with support from the government. Since cycle training is equally effective among boys and girls, the implementation of cycle training at school settings could be an effective way to reach all children. Furthermore, other efforts can be made by teachers, schools and policymakers to support children and their parents to travel by foot or by bicycle rather than by car, for example, by introducing car-free days involving the whole school. Parents could also be provided with advice on how to improve their child's cycling skills, or how to integrate their child's active transportation within their lives too (e.g., creating a daily routine of walking and cycling together).

7.9 Recommendations for Future Research

1. Future studies should explore to what extend psychosocial characteristics play a role in explaining children's active transportation levels. To get a better understanding of the relationships between children's cycling behaviours and children's cycling skills, it could be useful to objectively measure children's cycling behaviours by using, for example, global positioning systems attached to their bicycles. This makes it possible to know where, when and for how long the cycling occurred.
2. Future research should focus on interventions aiming to increase the prevalence of active transportation, especially for short distances, where it is most feasible. However, other initiatives are needed in order to increase active travel levels among those living in more rural areas. To reach children living too far for using active transportation to school, for example, a drop-off spot intervention might be a feasible and effective way to increase active transportation to school.[64] Drop-off spots are places in the neighbourhood of the school where parents can drop off or pick up their child before or after school hours. From these points, children can walk to and from their school. Since the effects of this intervention were rather small, the drop-off spot should be used as part of a larger multicomponent intervention.
3. Consequently, future research should focus on implementing multicomponent interventions and assess their effectiveness.
4. More research is needed on how to develop children's intrinsic motivation and the right attitudes towards active travel modes. Based on psychological theories (e.g., Ajzen[35]; Ryan and Deci),[66] these factors seem to be important, as children should be convinced about the benefits of active travel compared to motorized travel, and need to be intrinsically motivated to use active travel modes. As current evidence is rather scarce, more studies should be conducted in order to explore which methods seem effective to create positive attitudes and motivation towards active transportation.

References

1. Timperio A, Ball K, Salmon J, Roberts R, Giles-Corti B, Simmons D. Personal, family, social, and environmental correlates of active commuting to school. *Am J Prev Med* 2006;**30**:45–51.
2. Trapp GSA, Giles-Corti B, Christian HE, Bulsara M, Timperio AF, McCormack GR, Villaneuva KP. On your bike! a cross-sectional study of the individual, social and environmental correlates of cycling to school. *Int J Behav Nutr Phys Act* 2011;**8**:10.
3. De Meester F, Van Dyck D, De Bourdeaudhuij I, Deforche B, Cardon G. Changes in physical activity during the transition from primary to secondary school in Belgian children: what is the role of the school environment? *BMC Publ Health* 2014;**14**(261):1471–2458.
4. Chillón P, Ortega FB, Ruiz JR, De Bourdeaudhuij I, Martínez-Gómez D, Vicente-Rodriguez G, Widhalm K, Molnar D, Gottrand F, González-Gross M. Active commuting and physical activity in adolescents from Europe: results from the HELENA study. *Pediatr Exerc Sci* 2011;**23**(2):207.
5. European Commission. *Special Eurobarometer 422a: quality of transport*. European Commission; 2014.
6. McDonald NC. *Children and cycling. City cycling*. Cambridge (MA): MIT Press; 2012. p. 211–34.

7. Cooper AR, Jago R, Southward EF, Page AS. Active travel and physical activity across the school transition: the PEACH project. *Med Sci Sports Exerc* 2012;**44**(10):1890–7.
8. Fulton S, Shisler J, Yore M, Caspersen C. Active transportation to school: findings from a national survey. *Res Q Exerc Sport* 2005;**76**:352–7.
9. Pabayo R, Gauvin L, Barnett TA. Longitudinal changes in active transportation to school in Canadian youth aged 6 through 16 years. *An Pediatr* 2011;**128**(2):e404–13.
10. Panter JR, Jones AP, Van Sluijs EM. Environmental determinants of active travel in youth: a review and framework for future research. *Int J Behav Nutr Phys Act* 2008;**5**.
11. Biddle SJH, Atkin AJ, Cavill N, Foster C. Correlates of physical activity in youth: a review of quantitative systematic reviews. *Int Rev Sport Exerc Psychol* 2011;**4**(1):25–49.
12. McIntyre F. *A longitudinal examination of the contribution of perceived motor competence and actual motor competence to physical activity in 6 to 9 year old children*. 2009.
13. Barnett LM, Lai SK, Veldman SLC, Hardy LL, Cliff DP, Morgan PJ, Zask A, Lubans DR, Shultz SP, Ridgers ND, Rush E, Brown HL, Okely AD. Correlates of gross motor competence in children and adolescents: a systematic review and meta-analysis. *Sports Med* 2016;**46**(11):1663–88.
14. Morrongiello BA, Dawber T. Parental influences on toddlers' injury-risk behaviors: are sons and daughters socialized differently? *J Appl Dev Psychol* 1999;**20**(2):227–51.
15. Valentine G. 'My son's a bit dizzy.' 'my wife's a bit soft': gender, children, and cultures of parenting. *Gend Place Cult* 1997;**4**:37–62.
16. Ghekiere A, Van Cauwenberg J, Carver A, Mertens L, de Geus B, Clarys P, Cardon G, De Bourdeaudhuij I, Deforche B. Psychosocial factors associated with children's cycling for transport: a cross-sectional moderation study. *Prev Med* 2016.
17. D'Haese S, De Meester F, De Bourdeaudhuij I, Deforche B, Cardon G. Criterion distances and environmental correlates of active commuting to school in children. *Int J Behav Nutr Phys Act* 2011;**8**:88.
18. de Bruijn G-J, Kremers SP, Schaalma H, Van Mechelen W, Brug J. Determinants of adolescent bicycle use for transportation and snacking behavior. *Prev Med* 2005;**40**(6):658–67.
19. Cooper AR, Wedderkopp N, Wang H, Andersen LB, Froberg K, Page AS. Active travel to school and cardiovascular fitness in Danish children and adolescents. *Med Sci Sports Exerc* 2006;**38**(10):1724–31.
20. Johansson K, Laflamme L, Hasselberg M. Active commuting to and from school among Swedish children-a national and regional study. *Eur J Public Health* 2012;**22**(2):209–14.
21. Mota J, Gomes H, Almeida M, Ribeiro JC, Carvalho J, Santos MP. Active versus passive transportation to school - differences in screen time, socio-economic position and perceived environmental characteristics in adolescent girls. *Ann Hum Biol* 2007;**34**(3):273–82.
22. Panter J, Griffin S, Dalton A, Ogilvie D. Patterns and predictors of changes in active commuting over 12 months. *Prev Med* 2013;**57**:776–84.
23. De Meester F, Van Dyck D, De Bourdeaudhuij I, Deforche B, Sallis JF, Cardon G. Active living neighborhoods: is neighborhood walkability a key element for Belgian adolescents? *BMC Publ Health* 2012;**12**:7.
24. Ducheyne F, De Bourdeaudhuij I, Spittaels H, Cardon G. Individual, social and physical environmental correlates of 'never' and 'always' cycling to school among 10 to 12 year old children living within a 3.0 km distance from school. *Int J Behav Nutr Phys Act* 2012;**9**:9.
25. Tudor-Locke C, Ainsworth BE, Adair LS, Popkin BM. Objective physical activity of Filipino youth stratified for commuting mode to school. *Med Sci Sports Exerc* 2003;**35**(3):465–71.
26. DiGuiseppi C, Roberts I, Li L, Allen D. Determinants of car travel on daily journeys to school: cross sectional survey of primary school children. *BMJ* 1998;**316**(7142):1426–8.

27. Grize L, Bringolf-Isler B, Martin E, Braun-Fahrländer C. Trend in active transportation to school among Swiss school children and its associated factors: three cross-sectional surveys 1994, 2000 and 2005. *Int J Behav Nutr Phys Act* 2010;**7**(1):28.
28. Stalsberg R, Pedersen AV. Effects of socioeconomic status on the physical activity in adolescents: a systematic review of the evidence. *Scand J Med Sci Sports* 2010;**20**(3):368–83.
29. Martin S, Lee S, Lowry R. National prevalence and correlates of walking and bicycling to school. *Am J Prev Med* 2007;**33**:98–105.
30. McDonald NC. Active transportation to school: trends among U.S. schoolchildren, 1969–2001. *Am J Prev Med* 2007;**32**(6):509–16.
31. Maki-Opas T, de Munter J, Maas J, den Hertog F, Kunst AE. The association between physical environment and cycling to school among Turkish and Moroccan adolescents in Amsterdam. *Int J Public Health* 2014;**59**(4):629–36.
32. Kerr J, Rosenberg D, Sallis J, Saelens B, Frank L, Conway T. Active commuting to school: associations with environment and parental concerns. *Med Sci Sports Exerc* 2006;**38**:787–94.
33. Borrestad LA, Andersen LB, Bere E. Seasonal and socio-demographic determinants of school commuting. *Prev Med* 2011;**52**(2):133–5.
34. Pont K, Ziviani J, Wadley D, Bennett S, Abbott R. Environmental correlates of children's active transportation: a systematic literature review. *Health Place* 2009;**15**(3):827–40.
35. Ajzen I. Theory of planned behavior. *Handb Theor Soc Psychol Vol One* 2011;**1**:438.
36. Bandura A. Health promotion from the perspective of social cognitive theory. *Psycho Health* 1998;**13**(4):623–49.
37. Saunders RP, Pate RR, Felton G, Dowda M, Weinrich MC, Ward DS, Parsons MA, Baranowski T. Development of questionnaires to measure psychosocial influences on children's physical activity. *Prev Med* 1997;**26**(2):241–7.
38. Zwerts E, Allaert G, Janssens D, Wets G, Witlox F. How children view their travel behaviour: a case study from Flanders (Belgium). *J Transp Geogr* 2010;**18**(6):702–10.
39. Ghekiere A, Carver A, Veitch J, Salmon J, Deforche B, Timperio A. Does parental accompaniment when walking or cycling moderate the association between physical neighbourhood environment and active transport among 10–12 year olds? *J Sci Med Sport* 2016;**19**(2):149–53.
40. Macarthur C, Parkin P, Sidky M, Wallace W. Evaluation of a bicycle skills training program for young children: a randomized controlled trial. *Injury Prev* 1998;**4**(2):116–21.
41. Lu W, McKyer E, Lee C, Ory M, Goodson P, Wang S. Children's active commuting to school: an interplay of self-efficacy, social economic disadvantage, and environmental characteristics. *Int J Behav Nutr Phys Act* 2015;**12**(1):29.
42. Murtagh S, Rowe DA, Elliott MA, McMinn D, Nelson NM. Predicting active school travel: the role of planned behavior and habit strength. *Int J Behav Nutr Phys Act* 2012;**9**:9.
43. Craigie AM, Lake AA, Kelly SA, Adamson AJ, Mathers JC. Tracking of obesity-related behaviours from childhood to adulthood: a systematic review. *Maturitas* 2011;**70**(3):266–84.
44. Ducheyne F, De Bourdeaudhuij I, Lenoir M, Spittaels H, Cardon G. Children's cycling skills: development of a test and determination of individual and environmental correlates. *Accid Anal Prev* 2013;**50**(Suppl. C):688–97.
45. Vandorpe B. *The contribution of motor coordination to sports participation in school-aged children and to talent identification in young female gymnasts*. Ghent University; 2011.
46. Zeuwts L, Vansteenkiste P, Cardon G, Lenoir M. Development of cycling skills in 7- to 12-year-old children. *Traffic Injury Prev* 2016;**17**(7):736–42.
47. Briem V, Radeborg K, Salo I, Bengtsson H. Developmental aspects of Children's behavior and safety while cycling. *J Pediatr Psycho* 2004;**29**(5):369–77.

48. DaCota. *Children in road traffic*. 2013. [Brussels].
49. Duperrex O, Bunn F, Roberts I. Safety education of pedestrians for injury prevention: a systematic review of randomised controlled trials. *BMJ* 2002;**324**(7346):1129.
50. Ducheyne F. *Cycling to school: correlates, cycling skills and effectiveness of cycle training on cycling skills and levels of cycling to school*. Ghent University; 2013.
51. Hodgson C, Worth J. *Research into the impact of bikeability training on Children's ability to perceive and appropriately respond to hazards when cycling on the road*. ERIC; 2015.
52. *Fietsersbond vzw, Fietsen is (g)een kinderspel*. Berchem: Drukkerij De Bie; 2005.
53. Goodman A, Panter J, Sharp S, Ogilvie D. Effectiveness and equity impacts of town-wide cycling initiatives in England: a longitudinal, controlled natural experimental study. *Soc Sci Med* 2013;**97**:228–37.
54. Goodman A, van Sluijs EMF, Ogilvie D. Impact of offering cycle training in schools upon cycling behaviour: a natural experimental study. *Int J Behav Nutr Phys Act* 2016;**13**(1):1–12.
55. Whitebread D, Neilson K. The contribution of visual search strategies to the development of pedestrian skills by 4-11 year-old children. *Br J Educ Psychol* 2001;**70**(4):539–57.
56. Wierda M, Brookhuis KA. Analysis of cycling skill: a cognitive approach. *Appl Cogn Psycho* 1991;**5**(2):113–22.
57. Spilsbury JC. 'we don't really get to go out in the front yard'—children's home range and neighborhood violence. *Children Geogr* 2005;**3**(1):79–99.
58. Brockman R, Fox KR, Jago R. What is the meaning and nature of active play for today's children in the UK? *Int J Behav Nutr Phys Act* 2011;**8**:7.
59. Prezza M, Pilloni S, Morabito C, Sersante C, Alparone FR, Giuliani MV. The influence of psychosocial and environmental factors on children's independent mobility and relationship to peer frequentation. *J Commun Appl Soc Psycho* 2001;**11**(6):435–50.
60. Page AS, Cooper AR, Griew P, Jago R. Independent mobility, perceptions of the built environment and children's participation in play, active travel and structured exercise and sport: the PEACH Project. *J Commun App Soc Psychol* 2010;**7**:10.
61. Merom D, Tudor-Locke C, Bauman A, Rissel C. Active commuting to school among NSW primary school children: implications for public health. *Health Place* 2006;**12**:678–87.
62. Ghekiere A. *Insights into children's cycling for transport: a socio-ecological approach*. UGent; 2016.
63. Schoeppe S, Duncan MJ, Badland H, Oliver M, Curtis C. Associations of children's independent mobility and active travel with physical activity, sedentary behaviour and weight status: a systematic review. *J Sci Med Sport* 2013;**16**(4):312–9.
64. Vanwolleghem G, D'Haese S, Van Dyck D, De Bourdeaudhuij I, Cardon G. Feasibility and effectiveness of drop-off spots to promote walking to school. *Int J Behav Nutr Phys Act* 2014;**11**(1):136.
65. Shaw B, Bicket M, Elliott B, Fagan-Watson B, Mocca E, Hillman M. Children's independent mobility. An international comparison and recommendations for action. *Policy Studies Institute*. London; 2015.
66. Ryan RM, Deci EL. Self-determination theory and the facilitation of intrinsic motivation, social development, and well-being. *American Psychologist* 2000;**55**(1):68–78. http://dx.doi.org/10.1037/0003-066X.55.1.68.

Interpersonal Correlates of Active Transportation

8

Victoria Egli[1], *Erika Ikeda*[1], *Tom Stewart*[1], *Melody Smith*[2]
[1]Human Potential Centre, Auckland University of Technology, Auckland, New Zealand;
[2]School of Nursing, The University of Auckland, Auckland, New Zealand

Chapter Outline

8.1 Introduction

Children show a preference for active transportation,[1,2] and many contemporary parents understand how active transportation and independent mobility is beneficial for their children.[3] Children's independent mobility is discussed in detail in Chapter 5 and defined for the purposes of this chapter as the freedom to actively travel without supervision.[4,5] Despite child preference for active transportation and independent mobility, and their aforementioned benefits to health and well-being (see Chapter 1), there has been a global decline in rates of active transportation and independent mobility in recent decades,[6–8] with large variations between countries.[9,10]

Research shows parents/caregivers (hereafter 'parents') are conflicted between known benefits of physical activity accumulation and unsupervised outdoor play with modern-day practical concerns that focus on 'time scarcity', prevailing social norms

Children's Active Transportation. https://doi.org/10.1016/B978-0-12-811931-0.00008-9

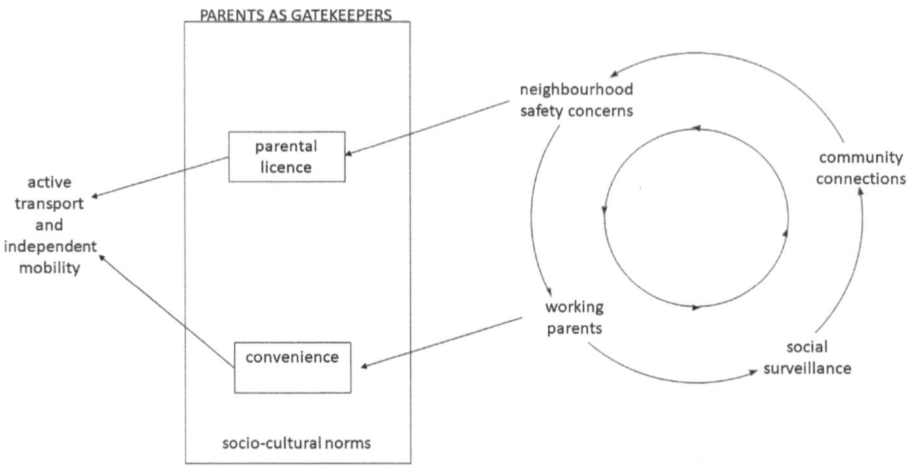

Figure 8.1 Interpersonal correlates of active transportation.

on what constitutes a 'good parent' as well as concerns regarding neighbourhood safety.[3] Even so, there is hope for the future. While debate exists for the reasons some young adults today use active transportation (for example, economic hardship and social inequality,[11–14] and/or environmental concern and awareness[15–17]), there is a possibility that this may have a trickle-down effect on individual and family motivations for active transportation and independent mobility in the future. This chapter will explore the influences underlying many of the day-to-day decisions that parents make regarding their child's active transportation.

Fig. 8.1 illustrates the interpersonal correlates of active transportation and independent mobility in children. Influenced by sociocultural norms, parents act as gatekeepers to children's active transportation and independent mobility. This is primarily expressed through parental licence and convenience. Behind this is a circular network of factors underpinning parental licence and convenience, which influence each other. Each of the factors in the diagram below is explained in detail in this chapter. We will start by working backwards through the diagram.

8.2 Parents as Gatekeepers

Parents act as 'gatekeepers' to children's active transportation and independent mobility as they govern decisions regarding travel mode. When parents act as gatekeepers to children's active transportation, this is commonly expressed as sentiments of parental licence, e.g., 'I will/won't allow my child to actively transport to school' and convenience, e.g., 'It is easier to drop my child off at school on my way to/from work'. When children are given agency and have some input into travel mode decision making, they are more likely to engage in active transportation.[2,18] In the context of this chapter, parental licence is considered the granting of permission for children to engage in active transportation, and convenience refers to the ease with which parents are able to facilitate their child getting from point A to point B.

8.3 Sociocultural Norms

Sociocultural norms form an important foundation on which an understanding of parents as gatekeepers to children's active transportation is built. This is particularly reflected in the commonly held and culturally varied perceptions of what constitutes a 'good' parent. Research shows that parents who are looking to 'provide the best' for their child often seek out before and after school sports clubs and academic tuition services.[3] Perceived to be safe and supervised, these services and activities can be highly valued by parents[3] but commonly provide little opportunity for active transportation or independent mobility. Additionally, social perceptions of a 'good mother' being one who chauffeurs their child between local destinations have led to the creation of what Dowling (2000)[3a] terms the 'backseat generation'. One downstream consequence of this phenomenon is reduced parental licence. Further influencing parental licence are misunderstandings of the varied contemporary child protection legislations that may result in parents not granting permission for active transportation and independent mobility (O'Connor and Brown[34]), in addition to perceived consequences of granting independent mobility 'too young'.[19] A recent Canadian position statement on active outdoor play was created in direct response to issues such as these.[20] This position statement highlights the benefits afforded to children who engage in outdoor activity, including risky activity, and challenges the need for constant supervision. Social norms are also influenced by urban design and the efficiency and availability of public transportation.

8.4 Parental Licence

It is interesting to note that even in contemporary times, parental licence differs by sex of the child, with boys being typically granted permission for active transportation and independent mobility earlier than girls.[21,22] In one study of Australian parents, parental licences were based on different factors for boys and girls.[23] For boys, the most important factor was parental confidence in the child's ability to travel independently, whereas for girls the more important factor was parental perceptions of neighbourhood safety.[23] Parental licence is not static throughout childhood and adolescence, and it changes with the child's age and in response to local events, perhaps intensified by media coverage.[24] As children progress through childhood into adolescence, active transportation restrictions lessen and greater permission for independent mobility is granted.[25]

8.5 Neighbourhood Safety Concerns

The notion of safety is multifaceted and complex. It includes many varied components, commonly reported as stranger danger, road safety, personal injury and bullying. As shown in Fig. 8.1, parental perceptions of neighbourhood safety directly influence parental licence for active transportation.

The perceived social quality of the neighbourhood, particularly parental concerns regarding stranger danger and neighbourhood safety, are theoretically major influences on children's active transportation and independent mobility.[22] Indeed, popular interventions to promote active transportation to school often address road and personal safety concerns through the supervision of active transportation. Notable examples are walking school buses and bike trains[26] (see also Chapter 15). Actual occurrences of stereotypical 'stranger danger' scenarios are extremely rare.[27,28] Nonetheless, news of child abductions and associated harm are regularly broadcasted by the media; subsequently, parents are overly attuned to the extreme examples of child harm.[29,30] Perceived harm from strangers is associated with greater parental restrictions for active transportation and independent mobility.[29–31]

It is interesting to note the impact of the neighbourhood built environment on parental perceptions of safety. Besides stranger danger, parents also report concerns related to pedestrian safety from traffic exposure.[30] Built environment changes such as safe routes to cross intersections, lower speed limits around schools, traffic calming and interventions that stop children running out onto roads have been implemented in many countries to specifically address parental traffic safety concerns.[32,33] Research from Australia illustrates that neighbourhood features which encourage pedestrians and minimize vehicle traffic are most conducive to parental perceptions of a safer neighbourhood regardless of the socioeconomic status.[5] It may be that the natural surveillance generated by a more walkable neighbourhood may help alleviate parents' fears about strangers, as well as reduce the fear of 'the man in the white van/truck',[34,35] in addition to minimizing the risk of road accidents. Additional neighbourhood-level safety concerns are reported to be roaming dogs,[36] the presence of gangs and a lack of pedestrian/cycling infrastructure, e.g., walking paths, sidewalks and pedestrian crossings.[37,38]

In most countries, mobile phone ownership among children does not appear to influence parental licence for active transportation and independent mobility.[1] While many parents report safety concerns as a reason to equip children with mobile phones,[1] easier access to parents as a 'transport service' by the help of mobile phones has been shown to reduce active transportation and independent mobility.[6,39] Nevertheless, qualitative work with children in New Zealand shows some indication for increased licence for independence when children are 'accompanied' by a mobile phone.[40]

8.6 Community Connections

As shown in Fig. 8.1, community connections influence neighbourhood safety concerns. There is no agreed-upon definition of community connections; however, in this chapter, the term encompasses the number, quality and strength of ties that children and parents have, to both people and places within their neighbourhood.[41] For example, the people they know and the connections they have to specific places.

The influence of community connectedness through social networks, trust and integration within the local home/school neighbourhood appear closely tied to parental perceptions of neighbourhood safety. Longitudinal studies from Australia and the United Kingdom show that parents with many neighbourhood connections have children who are more likely to engage in active transportation.[42,43] In New Zealand, parental perceptions of neighbourhood social cohesiveness and connectedness were significantly related to independent mobility of children aged 8–13 years.[44] It is supposed that increased community connections provide knowledge and understanding of the local neighbourhood, thereby reducing parents' 'fear of the unknown' and giving greater parental licence for active transportation.[3,31,43] Thus, frequent residential moves, either through economic hardship or neighbourhood self-selection, lessen community connections and may also contribute to negative parental perceptions of neighbourhood safety.[3]

8.7 Social Surveillance

Greater and more frequent community connections avail more 'eyes' to provide increased coverage and attention to social surveillance for children who are engaging in active transportation and independent mobility.[34,45] Neighbourhoods with greater foot traffic, both from adults and children, can lead to greater parental licence for active transportation and independent mobility. Indeed, qualitative studies from New Zealand, Canada and Great Britain show that greater parental licence is given when siblings or friends accompany children on active trips.[33,35,46] A Canadian study of parents whose children use active transportation to school report that their children are safer when they travel with other children.[35] The 'buddy system' and 'safety in numbers' when 'travelling in a group' were mentioned as specific strategies used to alleviate parental safety concerns.[35] In addition, dog ownership is strongly associated with independent mobility to destinations.[47]

Active transportation with other children seems conducive to greater parental licence for active transportation[48]; however, results are mixed, with some studies showing fear of bullying and arguments between siblings reduces parental licence.[33,49] Indeed, children's fear of violence and worries about bullying may reduce participation in active transportation and lead to parents chauffeuring children in cars.[33,50] Conversely, a recent North American study found more bullying is experienced by students who use the school bus compared to active travellers.[51] Research examining the role of bullying in active transportation and independent mobility across a variety of settings and sociodemographic contexts is needed, to inform future active transportation interventions, decrease parental safety concerns and support children's preference for active transportation.

8.8 Working Parents

Parents working long hours outside of home/school neighbourhood can result in reduced neighbourhood foot traffic and decreased opportunities for neighbourhood-level social surveillance.[52] The increasing prevalence of smaller families coupled with the prevalence of children attending schools outside of their local neighbourhood means that there is a reduction in the opportunity for 'safety in numbers' when children engage in active transportation and independent mobility.[3] Increasing numbers of single-parent families and families in which both parents work has led to a dependence on formal and informal before- and after-school care programmes that limit opportunities for active transportation. Likewise, as parents juggle increased work demands and increased commute times, dependence on formal and informal after-school care programmes, not previously seen in generations past, has developed.[53]

8.9 Convenience

A myriad of day-to-day decisions, made by working parents and parents faced with multiple demands on their time, combine to ultimately make perceived 'convenience' a primary determinant of children's active transportation and independent mobility. Multiple demands on parents' time, coupled with increased scheduling of after-school activities, often located outside of the local school/home neighbourhood, commonly results in 'trip chaining' in private cars. While a practical solution to the problem of 'time scarcity', 'trip chaining' in cars limits opportunities for active transportation and independent mobility.[35] 'Time scarcity' is often expressed in the sentiment 'so much to do and so little time'.[54] While this is a common sentiment, particularly among working parents, it is important to highlight that it is often a perception, as population-based surveys indicate, that despite 'time-scarcity' most adults find hours in their day to sedentarily watch television.[55] Perceived 'time scarcity' influences parental decision making around active transportation and independent mobility through its influence on convenience.

8.10 Breaking the Cycle: Looking to the Future

Fig. 8.1 shows the current state of parents as gatekeepers to children's active transportation and independent mobility. What Fig. 8.1 does not show is how the cycle of neighbourhood safety concerns→working parents→social surveillance→community connections→neighbourhood safety concerns can be broken. The key to breaking this cycle may sit with the millennial generation or tomorrow's parents.

Some studies show that among young adults today, that is, those born between 1980 and 2000, there is an increasing environmental awareness, a concern about climate change, greenhouse gas emissions and the need to reduce reliance on cars for transportation.[16,17] Commonly termed the millennial generation, or millennials, this population has received attention for their reduced car use,[17] concern over environmental sustainability[12] and 'green' consumerism.[56] One of the ways millennials are showing this concern for the environment is by using public transport and engaging in active transportation themselves.[15] Research shows that parents who use active transportation are more likely to have a child who also engages in active transportation,[43] therefore it is hypothesized that in the future, a trickle-down effect might be seen from contemporary interventions to increase and support active transportation among millennials, in conjunction with successful active transportation and independent mobility interventions targeted at children and parents.

While promising, there is an alternative rationale for the reasons millennials appear to be opting out of car ownership and 'buying a big house and moving to the suburbs' and that is one of economic hardship and social inequality.[12] Indeed, it could be that we are seeing higher rates of active transportation among young people today as in previous generations due to increased economic hardship, increased housing prices, traffic congestion and having children at a later age.[12–14] While millennials appear to be getting much of the attention for environmental awareness, there is debate over actual generational differences in environmental concern with some studies finding that older generations show greater environmental concern[57] and are more likely to volunteer in environmental clean-up programmes than millennials.[11]

There is a role for built environment practitioners, policy makers and urban planners to facilitate a move towards more compact cities. Doing so may encourage parents, regardless of economic hardship and social inequality, to work in neighbourhoods where they reside and where their children go to school. Downstream impacts of this are having more eyes to avail social surveillance, as well as a greater number, quality and strength of community connections. Ultimately, this could result in fewer neighbourhood safety concerns and therefore increased parental licence for active transportation and independent mobility. Additional discussion on transportation and land use policies specifically regarding the role that they play in breaking this cycle can be found in Chapter 11.

8.11 Conclusion

Parents generally act as gatekeepers to children's active transportation and independent mobility, and their day-to-day decisions are influenced by social norms. Behind this is a continuous cycle of factors, including neighbourhood safety concerns, community connections, social surveillance and perceived time scarcity. Although much of this may explain the declining rates of active transportation and independent mobility recently seen worldwide, future research is needed to assess the role that the millennial generation may play in breaking the cycle.

8.12 Recommendations for Policy and Practice

1. If government legislation exists permitting children's independent mobility only from a certain age, policy makers should ensure that such legislation is easily understood by parents and the wider public. This would help to prevent parental restrictions on active transportation and independent mobility out of a fear of breaking the law.
2. Facilitate and support moves towards more compact cities to enable families to reside, work and go to school in one neighbourhood.
3. Encourage activities that promote neighbourhood ties and social connection within residential communities.

8.13 Recommendations for Future Research

1. Opportunities exist for research to gain a greater understanding of the role of social relationships, specifically bullying in active transportation and independent mobility.
2. Research opportunities exist to gain a greater understanding of the millennial generation's active transportation behaviour, including an exploration into the impact (if any) on parental license for active transportation and independent mobility among tomorrow's children
3. Community-level interventions to increase social cohesion and neighbourhood ties may impact active transportation and independent mobility in children, but further investigation is required.

References

1. Shaw B, Bicket M, Elliott B, Fagan-Watson B, Mocca E, Hillman M. *Children's Independent Mobility: an international comparison and recommendations for action*. London: Policy Studies Institute; 2015. Available from: http://www.psi.org.uk/site/publication_detail/1823.
2. Hinckson E. Perceived challenges and facilitators of active travel following implementation of the School Travel-Plan programme in New Zealand children and adolescents. *J Trans Health* 2016.
3. Witten K, Kearns R, Carroll P, Asiasiga L, Tava'e N. New Zealand parents' understandings of the intergenerational decline in children's independent outdoor play and active travel. *Child Geogr* 2013;**11**(2):215–29.

3a. Dowling R, Cultures of mothering and car use in suburban sydney: A Preliminary Investigation. *Geoforum* 2000;**31**(3):345–53. https://doi:10.1016/S0016-7185(99)00048-2.

4. Hillman M, Adams J, Whitelegg J. *One false move: a study of children's independent mobility*. London: Policy Studies Institute; 1990. Available from: http://www.psi.org.uk/site/publication_detail/904.
5. Foster S, Wood L, Francis J, Knuiman M, Villanueva K, Giles-Corti B. Suspicious minds: can features of the local neighbourhood ease parents' fears about stranger danger? *J Environ Psychol* 2015;**42**:48–56.
6. Fyhri A, Hjorthol R, Mackett RL, Fotel TN, Kyttä M. Children's active travel and independent mobility in four countries: development, social contributing trends and measures. *Transport Pol* 2011;**18**(5):703–10.
7. Schoeppe S, Tranter P, Duncan MJ, Curtis C, Carver A, Malone K. Australian children's independent mobility levels: secondary analyses of cross-sectional data between 1991 and 2012. *Child Geogr* 2016;**14**(4):408–21.
8. Shaw B, Watson B, Frauendienst B, Redecker A, Jones T, Hillman M. *Children's independent mobility: a comparative study in England and Germany (1971–2010)*. London: Policy Studies Institute; 2013. Available from: http://www.psi.org.uk/site/publication_detail/852.
9. Larouche R, Sarmiento OL, Broyles ST, Denstel KD, Church TS, Barreira TV, et al. Are the correlates of active school transport context-specific? *Int J Obes Suppl* 2015;**5**:S89–99.
10. Tremblay MS, Barnes JD, González SA, Katzmarzyk PT, Onywera VO, Reilly JJ, et al. Global Matrix 2.0: report card grades on the physical activity of children and youth comparing 38 countries. *J Phys Activ Health* 2016;**13**(11 Suppl. 2):S343–66.

11. Twenge JM, Campbell WK, Freeman EC. Generational differences in young adults' life goals, concern for others, and civic orientation, 1966–2009. *J Pers Soc Psychol* 2012;**102**(5):1045.
12. Delbosc A, Ralph K. A tale of two millennials. *J Trans Land Use* 2017;**10**(1).
13. Astone NM, Martin S, Peters HE. *Millennial Childbearing and the Recession.* 2015. Available from: http://www.urban.org/sites/default/files/alfresco/publicationpdfs/2000203_Millennial_Childbearing_and_the_Recession.pdf.
14. Xu Y, Johnson C, Bartholomae S, O'Neill B, Gutter MS. Homeownership among millennials: the deferred American dream? *Fam Consum Sci Res J* 2015;**44**(2):201–12.
15. Korkala EA, Hugg TT, Jaakkola JJ. Voluntary climate change mitigation actions of young adults: a classification of mitigators through latent class analysis. *PLoS One* 2014;**9**(7):e102072. Available from: http://journals.plos.org/plosone/article?id=10.1371/journal.pone.0102072.
16. Hopkins D. Can environmental awareness explain declining preference for car-based mobility amongst generation Y? A qualitative examination of learn to drive behaviours. *Transport Res Pol Pract* 2016;**94**:149–63.
17. Delbosc A, Currie G. Causes of youth licensing decline: a synthesis of evidence. *Transport Rev* 2013;**33**:271–90.
18. Wong BY-M, Faulkner G, Buliung R, Irving H. Mode shifting in school travel mode: examining the prevalence and correlates of active school transport in Ontario, Canada. *BMC Publ Health* 2011;**11**(1):618. Available from: https://bmcpublichealth.biomedcentral.com/articles/10.1186/1471-2458-11-618.
19. Stueck W. Parents wonder how young is too young to be independent. *Globe Mail* 2017. Available from: https://www.theglobeandmail.com/life/parenting/parents-wonder-how-young-is-too-young-for-their-kids-to-beindependent/article36334354/.
20. Tremblay MS, Gray C, Babcock S, Barnes J, Bradstreet CC, Carr D, et al. Position statement on active outdoor play. *Int J Environ Res Publ Health* 2015;**12**(6):6475–6505. Available from: http://www.mdpi.com/1660-4601/12/6/6475.
21. Carver A, Panter JR, Jones AP, van Sluijs EMF. Independent mobility on the journey to school: a joint cross-sectional and prospective exploration of social and physical environmental influences. *J Trans Health* 2014;**1**(1):25–32.
22. Mitra R, Faulkner G, Buliung R, Stone M. Do parental perceptions of the neighbourhood environment influence children's independent mobility? Evidence from Toronto, Canada. *Urban Stud* 2014;**51**(16):3401–19.
23. Villanueva K, Giles-Corti B, Bulsara M, Trapp G, Timperio A, McCormack G, et al. Does the walkability of neighbourhoods affect children's independent mobility, independent of parental, socio-cultural and individual factors? *Child Geogr* 2014;**12**(4):393–411.
24. Mammen G, Faulkner G, Buliung R, Lay J. Understanding the drive to escort: a cross-sectional analysis examining parental attitudes towards children's school travel and independent mobility. *BMC Publ Health* 2012;**12**(1):862. Available from: https://bmcpublichealth.biomedcentral.com/articles/10.1186/1471-2458-12-862.
25. Carver A, Timperio A, Hesketh K, Crawford D. Are children and adolescents less active if parents restrict their physical activity and active transport due to perceived risk? *Soc Sci Med* 2010;**70**(11):1799–805.
26. Collins D, Kearns RA. Walking school buses in the Auckland region: a longitudinal assessment. *Transport Pol* 2010;**17**(1):1–8.
27. Pimentel D. Criminal child neglect and the free range kid: is overprotective parenting the new standard of care. *Utah L Rev* 2012:947.

28. Francis J, Martin K, Wood L, Foster S. 'I'll be driving you to school for the rest of your life': a qualitative study of parents' fear of stranger danger. *J Environ Psychol* 2017;**53**:112–20.
29. Foster S, Villanueva K, Wood L, Christian H, Giles-Corti B. The impact of parents' fear of strangers and perceptions of informal social control on children's independent mobility. *Health Place* 2014;**26**:60–8.
30. Sweeney SM, Von Hagen LA. Stranger danger, cell phones, traffic, and active travel to and from schools: perceptions of parents and children. *Transport Res Rec: J Transport Res Board* 2016;**2582**:1–7.
31. Prezza M, Pacilli MG. Current fear of crime, sense of community, and loneliness in Italian adolescents: the role of autonomous mobility and play during childhood. *J Community Psychol* 2007;**35**(2):151–70.
32. Schwebel DC, Barton BK, Shen J, Wells HL, Bogar A, Heath G, et al. Systematic review and meta-analysis of behavioral interventions to improve child pedestrian safety. *J Pediatr Psychol* 2014;**39**(8):826–45.
33. Lang D, Collins D, Kearns R. Understanding modal choice for the trip to school. *J Transport Geogr* 2011;**19**(4):509–14.
34. O'Connor J, Brown A. A qualitative study of 'fear' as a regulator of children's independent physical activity in the suburbs. *Health Place* 2013;**24**:157–64.
35. Faulkner GEJ, Richichi V, Buliung RN, Fusco C, Moola F. What's "quickest and easiest?": Parental decision making about school trip mode. *Int J Behav Nutr Phys Activ* 2010;**7**(62). https://doi.org/10.1186/479-5868-7-62. Available from: https://ijbnpa.biomedcentral.com/articles/10.1186/1479-5868-7-62.
36. Oliver M, Mavoa S, Badland H, Parker K, Donovan P, Kearns RA, et al. Associations between the neighbourhood built environment and out of school physical activity and active travel: an examination from the Kids in the City study. *Health Place* 2015;**36**:57–64.
37. Carver A, Timperio A, Crawford D. Playing it safe: the influence of neighbourhood safety on children's physical activity—a review. *Health Place* 2008;**14**(2):217–27.
38. Trapp GS, Giles-Corti B, Christian HE, Bulsara M, Timperio AF, McCormack GR, et al. On your bike! a cross-sectional study of the individual, social and environmental correlates of cycling to school. *Int J Behav Nutr Phys Activ* 2011;**8**(1):123. Available from: https://www.ncbi.nlm.nih.gov/pmc/articles/PMC3224764/.
39. Carver A, Timperio AF, Crawford DA. Young and free? A study of independent mobility among urban and rural dwelling Australian children. *J Sci Med Sport* 2012;**15**(6):505–10.
40. Chaudhury M, Hinckson E, Badland H, Smith M. Children's independence and affordances experienced in the context of public open spaces: a study of diverse inner-city and suburban neighbourhoods in Auckland, New Zealand. *Child Geogr* 2018:1–15.
41. Bruhn JG. *The sociology of community connections*. Springer Science & Business Media; 2011.
42. Hume C, Timperio A, Salmon J, Carver A, Giles-Corti B, Crawford D. Walking and cycling to school: predictors of increases among children and adolescents. *Am J Prev Med* 2009;**36**(3):195–200.
43. Panter JR, Jones AP, Van Sluijs EM, Griffin SJ. Attitudes, social support and environmental perceptions as predictors of active commuting behaviour in school children. *J Epidemiol Commun Health* 2010;**64**(01):41–8.
44. Lin E-Y, Witten K, Smith M, Carroll P, Asiasiga L, Badland H, et al. Social and built-environment factors related to children's independent mobility: the importance of neighbourhood cohesion and connectedness. *Health Place* 2017;**46**:107–13.
45. Jacobs J. *The death and life of great American cities*. Vintage; 1961.

46. Jago R, Thompson JL, Page AS, Brockman R, Cartwright K, Fox KR. Licence to be active: parental concerns and 10–11-year-old children's ability to be independently physically active. *J Publ Health* 2009;**31**(4):472–7.
47. Christian HE, Villanueva K, Klinker CD, Knuiman MW, Divitini M, Giles-Corti B. The effect of siblings and family dog ownership on children's independent mobility to neighbourhood destinations. *Aust N Z J Publ Health* 2016;**40**(4):316–8.
48. Veitch J, Carver A, Salmon J, Abbott G, Ball K, Crawford D, et al. What predicts children's active transport and independent mobility in disadvantaged neighborhoods? *Health Place* 2017;**44**:103–9.
49. Carver A, Timperio A, Crawford D. Parental chauffeurs: what drives their transport choice? *J Transport Geogr* 2013;**26**:72–7.
50. Cozma I, Kukaswadia A, Janssen I, Craig W, Pickett W. Active transportation and bullying in Canadian schoolchildren: a cross-sectional study. *BMC Publ Health* 2015;**15**(1):99. Available from: https://www.ncbi.nlm.nih.gov/pubmed/25885322.
51. Sampasa-Kanyinga H, Chaput J-P, Hamilton HA, Larouche R. School bus travel is associated with bullying victimization among Canadian male, but not female, middle and high school students. *Child Abuse Neglect* 2016;**58**(Suppl. C):141–8.
52. Tranter P, Pawson E. Children's access to local environments: a case-study of Christchurch, New Zealand. *Local Environ* 2001;**6**(1):27–48.
53. Black DA, Kolesnikova N, Taylor LJ. Why do so few women work in New York (and so many in Minneapolis)? Labor supply of married women across US cities. *J Urban Econ* 2014;**79**:59–71.
54. Strazdins L, Loughrey B. Too busy: why time is a health and environmental problem. *N S Wales Publ Health Bull* 2008;**18**(12):219–21.
55. Owen N, Healy GN, Matthews CE, Dunstan DW. Too much sitting: the population-health science of sedentary behavior. *Exerc Sport Sci Rev* 2010;**38**(3):105.
56. Kanchanapibul M, Lacka E, Wang X, Chan HK. An empirical investigation of green purchase behaviour among the young generation. *J Clean Prod* 2014;**66**(Suppl. C):528–36.
57. Liu X, Vedlitz A, Shi L. Examining the determinants of public environmental concern: evidence from national public surveys. *Environ Sci Pol* 2014;**39**:77–94.

Community Factors Related to Active Transportation

9

Richard Larouche
Faculty of Health Sciences, University of Lethbridge, Lethbridge, AB, Canada

Driving children to and from school may also facilitate the infantilization of children, while simultaneously instilling in them a desire to drive and be driven

Buliung et al.[1]

Chapter Outline

9.1 Introduction

As the saying goes, it takes a village to raise a child. In this chapter, I explain how the community in which a child lives can either encourage or deter active transportation. Some communities are more favourable to active transportation for a variety of reasons including more proactive school policies and practices, better social cohesion, reduced fear of crime and favourable social norms. In this chapter, I provide a detailed overview on how these community factors relate to active transportation. First, I explain more generally how school-level factors influence the likelihood that children engage in active transportation.

Many studies have reported large differences between schools in the percentage of children using active transportation.[2–4] Using data from the US 2009–2010 Health Behavior in School-aged Children study, Yang et al.[4] found that the prevalence of active transportation ranged from 0% to 92.9% among the 229 participating schools.

Children's Active Transportation. https://doi.org/10.1016/B978-0-12-811931-0.00009-0

In the majority of schools, fewer than 20% of children engaged in active transportation. Nevertheless, in 18.9% of schools more than half of the children were active travellers. Similarly, in a study that included 118 elementary schools in Toronto, the percentage of children observed walking to school range from 28% to 98%.[3]

Using data from the International Study of Childhood Obesity, Lifestyle and the Environment, Larouche et al.[2] have quantified the amount of variation in the odds of active transportation explained by school-level factors. This study included over 6000 children recruited in the following sites: Australia (Adelaide), Brazil (São Paulo), Canada (Ottawa), China (Tianjin), Colombia (Bogotá), Finland (Helsinki, Espoo and Vantaa), India (Bangalore), Kenya (Nairobi), Portugal (Porto), South Africa (Cape Town), the United Kingdom (Bath and North East Somerset) and the United States (Baton Rouge). Within each site, the amount of variation attributable to school-level factors ranged from 0% in Bangalore to 56% in Bogotá. It was at least 25% in 6 of the 12 sites. This example illustrates that school characteristics can have a substantial influence on children's travel behaviour. Furthermore, based on the social–ecological model (Chapter 6), changes in school practices and policies could theoretically affect a large number of individuals.

Understanding why some schools have a much higher prevalence of active transportation than others might provide insight for policies and interventions. Although built environment characteristics (see Chapter 10 for review) and policies at the regional, provincial/state and national levels (Chapter 11) likely explain a certain proportion of these differences, the role of schools themselves should not be overlooked.

9.2 The Importance of School Officials in the Context of Active Transportation

While schools can implement their own policies and practices to encourage more students to engage in active transportation, schools are also a key target for interventions implemented by third parties, such as Safe Routes to School programmes, school travel planning and walking school buses (Chapters 13–15). Even for the latter, school "buy in" and support is crucial to the success of interventions. In a recent systematic review, the importance of having a school "champion" was described in a number of included studies as a key contributor to the success of interventions.[5]

9.2.1 School Policies, Practices and Fears That Deter Active Transportation

Policies and practices enacted by individual schools can also discourage children from engaging in active transportation. For example, the secondary school that I attended did not allow students to walk or bike to school due to concerns about liability. Administrators were afraid that they would be sued should a child be injured while travelling to school. Due to limited resources, they feared that they would have to close the school should they lose an eventual lawsuit. Their fear was heightened by the fact that the school was located next to an interchange of the Trans-Canada highway;

yet, older students were allowed to drive to school, and it is well known that teen drivers are involved in a disproportionally large percentage of road accidents and deaths.[6]

Sadly, this is not an isolated case. A report from the US Centers for Disease Control and Prevention revealed that 6% of parents surveyed cited a policy that prohibits active transportation as a key barrier to walking or cycling to and from school.[7] Similarly, data from the Canadian Health Behavior in School-aged Children survey indicated that 4% of schools did not allow bicycles on school property, 14% did not have a sidewalk leading to school and, appallingly, 42% were located on roads with speed limits of 60 km/h or more.[8] As discussed in Chapter 16, such high speed limits increase the likelihood and severity of collisions with motor vehicles and likely deter parents for granting their child permission to walk or bike to school.

Fear of lawsuits is indeed a common barrier to interventions promoting active living in schools, including active transportation and joint-use agreements allowing students to use school facilities for play outside of school hours.[9,10] School administrations are often divided by the desire to provide opportunities for children to be active and the fear of liability. Zimmerman et al.[10] have provided insightful recommendations to alleviate this fear. First, for a school to be held responsible of a road injury, the plaintiff would have to demonstrate that the school has neglected its duty to exercise reasonable care. The plaintiff would also have to demonstrate that this negligence has caused the injury and that they have suffered damages as a direct result of the negligence.

Zimmerman et al.[10] also identify injury prevention as the key to minimizing liability when implementing programmes such as Safe Routes to School which are described in more details in Chapter 13. This can be done by identifying safety issues as part of the intervention and taking reasonable measures to address them. This might involve adding a crosswalk or traffic-calming devices or improving regulations and signage about the zone where parents can park to drop off their children at school. To this end, schools can collaborate with city staff to identify and promote the safest routes for pedestrians and cyclists. They can also advocate for increased law enforcement in an attempt to reduce the speed of vehicles and increase the likelihood that drivers follow the rules of the road. All of these measures can help demonstrate that the school followed its duty to exercise reasonable care. Of particular interest, Zimmerman et al.[10] concluded that Safe Routes to School programmes had not been implicated in a single tort law (e.g., the laws that govern personal injury) case in the United States. While such laws can vary within and between countries, a programme that proactively identifies and addresses road safety concerns as part of a strategy to promote active transportation should reasonably be given the benefit of the doubt in the event of a lawsuit.[10]

9.2.2 *School Policies and Practices that Encourage Active Transportation*

In contrast, some schools play a proactive role in identifying safe routes for children to get to school actively. In a study of 26 schools in Ottawa, Canada, we found that children were about 8 times more likely to engage in active transportation if school officials reported identifying safe routes and if traffic-calming features (e.g., speed hump, narrower intersections, traffic island, etc.) were observed around the school by study staff.[11] Fig. 9.1 illustrates this interaction between aspects of the school environment

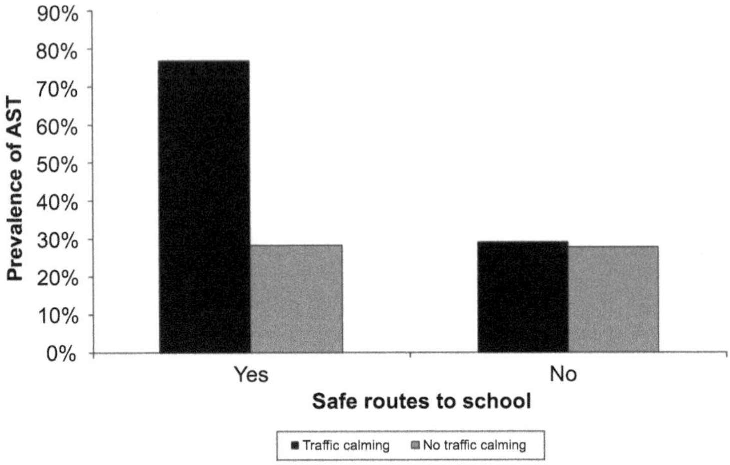

Figure 9.1 Joint association of safe routes to school and traffic calming measures with active school transport. Note: School administrators were asked whether their school identified safe routes for children to travel. The presence of traffic-calming measures around the school was observed as part of a standardized audit performed by study staff. *AST*, Active school transport. Reproduced from Larouche et al.[11]

and the built environment (here, traffic calming). Such an interaction supports the social–ecological model described in Chapter 6.

Interestingly, among the 397 schools that participated in the Canadian Health Behavior in School-aged Children survey, 28% reported that they identified safe routes for walking and/or cycling to school.[8] This can be done formally through the elaboration of a school travel plan as discussed in Chapter 14 and/or informally through road signage or newsletters sent to parents. In addition, 32% of schools surveyed organized "walk to school" days, 36% designated a "car-free zone," 87% provided bicycle racks and 71% allowed "small-wheeled vehicles" (e.g., skateboards, rollerblades and scooters) on school property.[8]

In the Czech Republic, researchers observed that 15-year-olds were about 3 times more likely to report walking or cycling to school if their school actively promoted active transportation.[12] The odds of active transportation were also greater if the school had a plan for implementing health promotion activities in general. Trapp et al.[13] also reported that school encouragement was associated with greater odds of walking to and from school in Australian girls, although such an association was not found in boys. Collectively, these findings emphasize the leadership role that schools can play.

9.3 Social Cohesion

Social cohesion has been described as "the glue that holds society together".[14] According to the United Nations Department of Economic and Social Affairs, a cohesive society is "*one where people are protected against life risks, trust their neighbors and the institutions of the state and can work towards a better future for themselves and their families. Fostering social cohesion is about striving for greater inclusiveness, more civic participation and creating opportunities for upward mobility.*"[14] In an era of growing economic inequities worldwide,[15] increasing social cohesion so that neighbours trust one another might help encourage active transportation. In neighbourhoods where social cohesion is perceived to be high, parents would presumably feel more confident that other adults in the neighbourhood will look after their children. They may therefore be more willing to allow their child to engage in active transportation. Indeed, research generally supports the idea that neighbourhood social cohesion can encourage children's active transportation[16–19] and physical activity in general.[20] Moreover, in a longitudinal study, Hume et al.[21] found that children whose parents reported that they knew many people in their neighbourhood had higher rates of active transportation.

Recently, many studies have examined the relationship between "collective efficacy" and active transportation. Collective efficacy is a concept that combines social cohesion and neighbours' willingness to intervene on behalf of the common good.[22] Kimbro et al.[23] reported that young children spent more time outdoors and travelled more frequently to parks and playground if their mother had a positive perception of her neighbourhood's collective efficacy. Collective efficacy was also associated with less TV viewing time. In an effort to shed light on the factors that may explain the decline in children' active transportation and outdoor play, Witten et al.[24] conducted interviews with parents in New Zealand. Parents notably discussed about issues such as the erosion of neighbourhood social connections, which was attributed to reduced time spent walking in the neighbourhood and increased residential mobility. Parents also invoked broader societal issues including the neoliberal policy context and increased distance between home and school.

However, the positive effect of social cohesion might be minimized in heavily trafficked neighbourhoods. In a classic study conducted in the 1970s, Donald Appleyard[25] asked adults living in 3 similar streets with different volumes of traffic (2000, 8000 and 16,000 vehicles/day) to indicate on a map where their friends and acquaintances lived and to trace the area that they considered their home territory. Participants living on the more trafficked street reported fewer friends and acquaintances and drew smaller home territories, suggesting that traffic undermines social cohesion. Furthermore, interviewed participants described how the heavily trafficked street had been friendly in the past but the activities that used to occur outside now took place inside the buildings. In other words, adults had retreated from the public realm. More recently, Bruce Appleyard[26] examined whether high volume and speed of traffic had similar effects in children. He asked 9- and 10-year-olds to draw a map of their neighbourhood and to participate in focus groups discussions. Without adequate walking and cycling facilities to provide shelter from traffic, children expressed negative feelings of dislike and danger and struggled to identify positive qualities of their neighbourhood environment. High traffic volume and speed was also associated with reduced spatial knowledge, suggesting that it may have adverse effects on children's cognitive development.

9.4 Bullying

In addition to heavy traffic and the associated risk of collision, fear of bullying may be another factor associated with motorized travel. Children interviewed in the city of Toronto expressed that they were actually more concerned about bullying on the school trip and about encountering dangerous dogs than about "stranger danger" per se.[1] In one of the few quantitative studies on the relationship between bullying and school travel mode, Cozma et al.[27] compared children in grades 6 to 10 who engaged in active transportation to those who travelled by car. They found that active travellers were 26% more likely to report that they were being bullied. A key limitation of that study is that the authors only included participants who were ineligible to travelling by school bus in their analyses.

Because bullying is more likely to happen in locations where there are lower levels of adult supervision,[28] one might expect that school buses would be conducive to bullying. Indeed, a study that used video cameras found that, on average, two incidents of bullying occurred per bus ride.[29] In another study, bus drivers reported that they frequently witnessed bullying in their bus and felt that they were being left out from their school district's bullying prevention efforts.[30] To my knowledge, only one study compared the likelihood of bullying between active transportation and school bus travel, using data from over 5000 participants in the 2013 Ontario Students Drug Use and Health Survey.[31] Boys who travelled by school bus were about 80% more likely to be victims of bullying than those who engaged in active transportation. Among girls, the use of public transit—an environment with greater adult supervision—was associated with 41% lower odds of bullying compared to active transportation. In contrast to the study by Cozma et al.,[27] active transportation was not associated with higher odds of bullying compared to car travel. The studies described herein suggest that bullying prevention efforts targeting the school trip may indirectly encourage active transportation. Future studies should also explore how and why the relationship between school travel mode and bullying might differ by gender.

9.5 Crime

The role of "tightly-knit" communities in preventing crime has been acknowledged for several decades. In her 1961 book *The Death and Life of Great American Cities*, Jane Jacobs[32] discussed the importance of "eyes on the street" as a crime prevention strategy. Specifically, she described how communities where people know each other well and look out for one another tend to deter crime. Because personal safety concerns are an important reason why parents restrict their children's independent mobility and often drive their children to school (Chapter 8), having more eyes on the street could favour active transportation by decreasing fear of crime.[33–35] For example, McMillan[35] reported that children were more likely to engage in active transportation when there were more windows facing the street. This implies that people could watch through the windows, and this would increase the likelihood that somebody might be able to intervene should a child be in danger. Foster et al.[33] also reported that parents were less concerned about strangers in neighbourhoods with natural surveillance generated by pedestrians. Moreover, parents' fears of strangers were lower in less trafficked neighbourhoods.

Although official statistics suggest that crime rates have declined over the last decades in many countries across the world,[36,37] parents often believe the opposite. This discrepancy between perception and reality is likely to be partly attributable to the increasingly ubiquitous media coverage of crime stories through multiple platforms such as TV, radio, internet and newspapers.[38] To test this hypothesis, Foster et al.[33] examined the factors associated with parental fears about strangers among parents of 10- to 12-year-olds in Australia. Parents who agreed with the statement "*I often see or hear news items about the danger of strangers to children walking or riding a bike without an adult present*" expressed greater concerns towards strangers. These findings were subsequently corroborated in a qualitative study.[34] For example, a parent mentioned: "*So many of my thoughts are influenced by things you hear in the media. You kind of go okay, well how much of it is just media hype, but when you hear stories like the little girl in Hyde Park that was abducted or killed in the toilet* (...) *whereas you might have previously let your kids go to the toilets, once that little girl was killed that changed it for everybody.*"[34] Such emotional experiences may be weighted more heavily than official crime statistics when parents consider the pros and cons of providing their children with opportunities to develop their independence.

This situation is akin to a self-fulfilling prophecy whereby media reports condition parents to fear strangers, which may encourage an overprotective parenting style, which restricts children's independence and physical activity.[39] In an attempt to minimize the perceived risk of "stranger danger," many parents drive their child to and from school, and doing so not only reduces the number of eyes on the street but also erodes social cohesion and increases the risk of road injuries for those children who still engage in active transportation, creating a vicious circle.[40]

Ironically, growing distrust towards strangers may make them less prone to help out in an emergency situation. For example, British author Tim Gill reported on the circumstances preceding the death of a toddler in the United Kingdom in an interview to *The Guardian*: "*Abigail Rae was a toddler who wandered out of her nursery, and drowned in a nearby pond. A male passerby told her inquest he had spotted her in the street, and been concerned. But he hadn't saved her life by stepping in for fear of looking like he was abducting her.*"[41] Although this is an extreme case, it suggests that a climate of suspicion may lead to the erosion of adult solidarity and social cohesion. These community-level factors may then influence parental decisions related to their children's travel behaviours and independent mobility.

It is worth noting that studies that have examined the relationship between crime-related indicators and measures of active transportation and overall physical activity have obtained mixed findings.[42] Some studies indicate, as one may intuitively expect, that concerns about crime are associated with lower odds of active transportation,[16,43–45] less independent mobility[17,46,47] and/or lower physical activity levels.[43,48,49] Yet, some other studies found no relationship between perceived crime safety and active transportation.[2,50,51] Although these latter findings are counterintuitive, they may be explained by at least three reasons. First, despite living in neighbourhoods with low crime-related concerns, some children may still be driven to school for other reasons. For instance, they may live too far from school or their parents may drive them on their way to work. Second, some children living in neighbourhoods with high crime-related concerns may have no choice but to engage in active transportation because they don't live far enough from school to be eligible to bussing and their parents don't have access to a vehicle. Such a situation may be associated with neighbourhood deprivation which is discussed in the neighbourhood deprivation section. Third, some studies used objective measures of crime whereas others investigated parent-perceived crime safety. Methodological differences may be partly responsible for inconsistent findings. That being said, there is no reason to believe that improving crime safety would have a negative impact on active transportation.

9.6 Neighbourhood Deprivation

Notwithstanding the multiple benefits of active transportation, some children living in deprived neighbourhoods and/or low-income countries may be obligated to walk or cycle to school due to the lack of alternatives, even though they might live in more "dangerous" areas.[52–54] For example, Rossen et al.[52] reported that neighbourhood incivilities (i.e., indicators of physical and social disorder, violence, alcohol and drug indicators) were associated with lower levels of perceived safety but with a much higher likelihood of active transportation. This situation raises issues of social inequities that should be addressed.

Social inequities were notably highlighted in studies reporting higher rates of active transportation in neighbourhoods perceived by parents as being unsafe[55] or not an "excellent" area for raising a child.[56] Cutumisu et al.[57] also reported that children living in neighbourhoods with higher material (i.e., low education, employment and income) and social (i.e., single-parent households) deprivation were much more likely to engage in active transportation to school.

Similarly, in a study conducted in Ottawa, Canada, we asked school officials (typically the principal, vice-principal or physical educator) to complete a survey for their school, and we linked this data with questionnaires completed by children. We observed that when school officials expressed greater concerns about crime safety in the school neighbourhood, children were *more* likely to engage in active transportation.[11] Although we could not rule out the possibility that school officials were more aware of crime safety issues *because* of the higher rates of active transportation at their school, these results are consistent with those discussed above and raise concerns about social justice.

It is of great concern that, of 30 intervention studies included in a recent systematic review, we found only one that explicitly emphasized attempting to reduce social inequities.[5] Similarly, a study conducted in New Zealand indicated that the majority of existing walking school buses were offered in the wealthiest neighbourhoods.[58] Interestingly, interviews with stakeholders involved in the implementation of active transportation interventions revealed that low-income communities struggled to access the resources needed.[59,60] For example, due to the lack of upfront funding, schools located in low-income communities of Texas could not afford to pay for infrastructure improvements to improve safety.[59] Additional efforts are clearly needed to ensure that children living in neighbourhoods where crime and road safety are major concerns can walk or cycle safely.

9.7 Social Norms

Previous chapters emphasized the importance of social norms as a potential enabler or deterrent to active transportation. Social norms are established at the community level, and they can vary substantially between communities. For example, it is common for children in Scandinavian countries to walk or bike several kilometres to and from school, whereas few North American children living beyond 1.6 km away from their school engage in active transportation.[61] It is important to stress that social norms are not set in stone. Indeed, 5 decades ago, it was fairly common for American children to walk more than 2 km to and from school.[62]

Empirical research supports the importance of social norms. For example, Timperio et al.[63] reported that children are more likely to engage in active transportation if their parents believe that other children in the neighbourhood do so. Similarly, McMillan[35] noted that parental perception that other family members approve their decision to let their child walk or bike to and from school was associated with higher odds of active transportation. However, unfavourable social norms and the fear of being judged negatively by other parents can be important barriers to active transportation. For example, a grandparent interviewed in a qualitative study argued: "*I think people are more worried that other parents would criticize you if something did happen, so it's not so much the actual danger, it's the culture that's changed… I don't let my granddaughter do as much as I let my kids do and it's got nothing to do with the danger. It's got to do with the fact that there's so much criticism around.*"[34] Parents often drive their children to school and other activities in part because they want to portray the image of a "good parent".[1,40]

Yet, the quote at the beginning of this chapter reminds us that by viewing children as incompetent to navigate their environment on their own, parents may plant the seed that will result in a long-lasting habit of driving. Parents' habit of driving children everywhere coupled with repeated exposure to the car industry's advertisement portraying the car as a symbol of freedom, prosperity and power,[64] likely lead children to internalize these messages, and then obtaining one's driver's license is viewed as a rite of passage into adulthood. In this context, it is not surprising that previous studies suggest that attitudes towards active transportation often evolve in a negative way as children get older.[65,66]

Changing social norms is a process that may take several years if not decades, but once such a change is achieved, it can have profound and lasting impacts on large populations. For example, comprehensive tobacco control efforts targeting multiple levels of the social–ecological model have been successful in changing the social norm (e.g., smoking is now seldom seen as "cool"), at least in high-income countries.[67] Chapter 17 provides some insights into how to make active transportation the norm rather than the exception.

9.8 Conclusion

This chapter illustrated the multiplicity of community factors that can encourage or discourage children from engaging in active transportation. On the positive side, children are generally more likely to walk or cycle to/from school if their school has programmes and policies in place to encourage active transportation and if they live in neighbourhoods with higher social cohesion and favourable social norms. On the other hand, crime, bullying, road safety concerns, an unfavourable social norm and unsupportive school policies and practices may deter active transportation. Of particular concern, children living in more deprived communities are more likely to engage in active transportation despite being exposed to a greater traffic volume, and these communities often struggle in accessing funding for interventions that support safe active transportation. These results emphasize a clear need for better programmes and policies and greater community engagement to improve walking and cycling conditions in low-income neighbourhoods.

9.9 Recommendations for Policy and Practice

1. School administrators should contribute to the implementation of programmes and policies to encourage more children to walk or bike to school. Such interventions may be particularly needed in low-income communities that often face environmental injustice associated with higher exposure to traffic and crime.[56]
2. Data demonstrating the frequency and outcomes of lawsuits against schools should be more widely disseminated. Such data may reassure school officials considering the possibility of implementing policies and practices to encourage active transportation.
3. The media should be less sensationalistic in its coverage of crime-related stories to avoid fuelling the fear of strangers and its detrimental effects on social cohesion, children's autonomy and the unsustainable use of cars for short trips.

9.10 Recommendations for Future Research

1. Because most of the research on community-level correlates of active transportation has focussed on the trip to and from school, there is a clear need for research examining active transportation to and from other places.
2. Researchers should investigate the factors associated with social cohesion in an effort to support the development of communities where parents might be more inclined to let their children engage in active transportation.
3. There remains a need for more research examining the relationship between specific school-level policies and practices and children's active transportation.

References

1. Buliung R, Larsen K, Hess P, Faulkner G, Fusco C, Rothman L. Driven to school: social fears and traffic environments. In: Walks A, editor. *The urban political economy and ecology of automobility: Driving cities, driving inequality, driving politics*. New York, NY: Routledge; 2015. p. 81–99.
2. Larouche R, Sarmiento OL, Broyles ST, Denstel KD, Katzmarzyk PT, Church TS, For the ISCOLE Research Group, et al. Are the correlates of active school transport context-specific? *Int J Obes Suppl* 2015;**5**:S89–99.
3. Rothman L, To T, Buliung R, Macarthur C, Howard A. Influence of social and built environment features on children walking to school: an observational study. *Prev Med* 2014;**60**:10–5. Available from: https://www.sciencedirect.com/science/article/pii/S0091743513004593.
4. Yang Y, Ivey SS, Levy MC, Royne MB, Klesges LM. Active travel to school: findings from the survey of US health behavior in school-aged children, 2009–2010. *J Sch Health* 2016;**86**:464–71.
5. Larouche R, Mammen G, Rowe DA, Faulkner G. Effectiveness of active school transport interventions: a systematic review and update. *BMC Publ Health* 2018;**18**:206.
6. National Highway Traffic Safety Administration. *Traffic safety facts: young drivers* Technical report no. DOT HS 811 622 Washington, DC: National Highway Traffic Safety Administration; 2012. Available from: https://crashstats.nhtsa.dot.gov/Api/Public/ViewPublication/811622.
7. Centers for Disease Control and Prevention. Barriers to children walking to or from school – United States. *Morb Mortal Wkly Rep* 2004;**54**(38):949–52. Available from: https://www.cdc.gov/mmwr/preview/mmwrhtml/mm5438a2.htm.
8. O'Loghlen S, Pickett W, Janssen I. Active transportation environments surrounding Canadian schools. *Can J Public Health* 2011;**102**(5):364–8.
9. Spengler JO, Carroll MS, Connaughton DP, Evenson KR. Policies to promote the community use of schools: a review of state recreational user statuses. *Am J Prev Med* 2010;**39**(1):81–8.
10. Zimmerman S, Kramer K, Trowbridge MJ. Overcoming legal liability concerns for school-based physical activity promotion. *Am J Public Health* 2013;**103**(11):1962–8.
11. Larouche R, Chaput JP, Leduc G, Boyer C, Bélanger P, LeBlanc AG, et al. A cross-sectional examination of socio-demographic and school-level correlates of children's school travel mode in Ottawa, Canada. *BMC Publ Health* 2014;**14**:497.
12. Hollein T, Vašíčová J, Bucksch J, Kalman M, Sigmundová D, van Dijk JP. School physical activity policies and active transport to school among pupils in the Czech Republic. *J Transp Health* 2017;**6**:306–12.
13. Trapp GSA, Giles-Corti B, Christian HE, Bulsara M, Timperio AF, McCormack GR, Villaneuva KP. Increasing children's physical activity: individual, social, and environmental factors associated with walking to and from school. *Health Educ Behav* 2012;**39**(2):172–82.
14. United Nations Department of Economic and Social Affairs. *Perspectives on social cohesion – the glue that holds society together*. New York, NY: United Nations Department of Economic and Social Affairs; 2012. Available from: http://www.un.org/en/development/desa/news/policy/perspectives-on-social-cohesion.html.
15. World Health Organization. *Closing the gap in a generation: health equity through action on the social determinants of health*. Geneva, Switzerland: World Health Organization; 2008. Available from: http://apps.who.int/iris/bitstream/10665/43943/1/9789241563703_eng.pdf.

16. Aarts M-J, Mathijssen JJP, van Oers JAM, Schuit AJ. Association between environmental characteristics and active commuting to school among children: a cross-sectional study. *Int J Behav Med* 2013;**20**(4):538–55.
17. Lin E-Y, Witten K, Oliver M, et al. Social and built-environment factors related to children's independent mobility: the importance of neighbourhood cohesion and connectedness. *Health Place* 2017;**46**:107–13.
18. McDonald NC. Travel and the social environment: evidence from Alameda county, California. *Transp Res Part D* 2007;**12**:53–63.
19. McDonald NC, Deakin E, Aalborg AE. Influence of the social environment on children's school travel. *Prev Med* 2010;**50**:S65–8.
20. Cradock AL, Kawachi I, Colditz GA, Gortmaker SL, Buka SL. Neighborhood social cohesion and youth participation in physical activity in Chicago. *Soc Sci Med* 2009;**68**(3):427–35.
21. Hume C, Timperio A, Salmon J, Carver A, Giles-Corti B, Crawford D. Walking and cycling to school: predictors of increases among children and adolescents. *Am J Prev Med* 2009;**36**(3):195–200.
22. Sampson RJ, Raudenbush SW, Earls F. Neighborhoods and violent crime: a multilevel study of collective efficacy. *Science* 1997;**277**:918–24.
23. Kimbro RT, Brooks-Gunn J, McLanahan S. Young children in urban areas: links among neighborhood characteristics, weight status, outdoor play, and television watching. *Soc Sci Med* 2011;**72**(5):668–76.
24. Witten K, Kearns R, Carroll P, Asiasiga L, Tava'e N. New Zealand parents' understandings of the intergenerational decline in children's independent outdoor play and active travel. *Child Geogr* 2013;**11**(2):215–29.
25. Appleyard D. *Livable streets*. Berkeley, CA: University of California Press; 1981.
26. Appleyard B. The meaning of livable streets to schoolchildren: an image mapping study of the effects of traffic on children's cognitive development of spatial knowledge. *J Transp Health* 2017;**5**:27–41.
27. Cozma I, Kukaswadia A, Janssen I, Craig W, Pickett W. Active transportation and bullying in Canadian schoolchildren: a cross-sectional study. *BMC Publ Health* 2015;**15**:99. Available from: https://bmcpublichealth.biomedcentral.com/articles/10.1186/s12889-015-1466-2.
28. Vaillancourt T, Brittain H, Bennett L, et al. Places to avoid: population-based study of student reports of unsafe and high bullying areas at school. *Can J Sch Psychol* 2010;**25**(1):40–54.
29. Raskauskas J. Bullying on the school bus: a video analysis. *J Sch Violence* 2005;**4**(3):93–107.
30. deLara EW. Bullying and aggression on the school bus: school bus drivers' observations and suggestions. *J Sch Violence* 2008;**7**(3):48–70.
31. Sampasa-Kanyinga H, Chaput JP, Hamilton HA, Larouche R. School bus travel is associated with bullying victimization among Canadian middle and high school male students. *Child Abuse & Neglect* 2016;**58**:141–8.
32. Jacobs J. *The death and life of great American cities*. New York, NY: Random House; 1961.
33. Foster S, Wood L, Francis J, Knuiman M, Villanueva K, Giles-Corti B. Suspicious minds: can features of the local neighbourhood ease parents' fears about stranger danger? *J Environ Psychol* 2015;**42**:48–56.
34. Francis J, Martin K, Wood L, Foster S. 'I'll be driving you to school for the rest of your life': a qualitative study of parents' fear of stranger danger. *J Environ Psychol* 2017;**53**:112–20.
35. McMillan TE. The relative influence of urban form on a child's travel mode to school. *Transp Res Part A* 2007;**41**:60–79.
36. Statista. Reported violent crime in the United States from 1990 to 2016. Available from: https://www.statista.com/statistics/191219/reported-violent-crime-rate-in-the-usa-since-1990/.
37. Tseloni A, Mailley J, Farrell G, Tilley N. Exploring the international decline in crime rates. *Eur J Criminol* 2010;**7**(5):375–94.

38. Stokes MA. Stranger danger: child protection and parental fears in the risk society. *Amsterdam Soc Sci* 2009;**1**(3):6–24.
39. Zubrick S, Wood L, Villanueva K, Wood G, Giles-Corti B, Christian H. *Nothing but fear itself: parental fear as a determinant of child physical activity and independent mobility*. Melbourne, Australia: Victorian Health Promotion Foundation (VicHealth); 2010.
40. Tranter P. Overcoming social traps: a key to child-friendly cities. In: Gleeson B, Sipe N, editors. *Creating child friendly cities: reinstating kids in the city*. New York, NY: Routledge; 2006. p. 121–35.
41. Aitkenhead D. *Why we need to set our kids free*. London, UK: The Guardian; November 3, 2007. Available from: https://www.theguardian.com/lifeandstyle/2007/nov/03/familyandrelationships.family5.
42. Giles-Corti B, Vernez-Moudon A, Reis R, Turrell G, Dannenberg AL, Badland H, et al. City planning and population health: a global challenge. *Lancet* 2016;**388**:2912–24.
43. Carver A, Timperio A, Crawford D. Playing it safe: the influence of neighbourhood safety on children's physical activity – a review. *Health Place* 2008;**14**(2):217–27.
44. Ghekiere A, Van Cauwenberg J, de Geus B, et al. Critical environmental factors for transportation cycling in children: a qualitative study using bike-along interviews. *PLoS One* 2014;**9**(9):e106696. Available from: http://journals.plos.org/plosone/article?id=10.1371/journal.pone.0106696.
45. Silva KS, Vasques DG, Martins CO, Williams LA, Lopes AS. Active commuting: prevalence, barriers, and associated variables. *J Phys Act Health* 2011;**8**:750–7.
46. Foster S, Villanueva K, Wood L, Christian H, Giles-Corti B. The impact of parents' fear of strangers and perceptions of informal social control on children's independent mobility. *Health Place* 2014;**26**:60–8.
47. Mitra R, Faulkner GEJ, Buliung RN, Stone MR. Do parental perceptions of the neighbourhood environment influence children's independent mobility? Evidence from Toronto, Canada. *Urban Stud* 2014;**51**(16):3401–19.
48. Janssen I. Crime and perceptions of safety in the home neighborhood are independently associated with physical activity among 11–15 year olds. *Prev Med* 2014;**66**:113–7.
49. Kneeshaw-Price SH, Saelens BE, Sallis JF, Frank LD, Grembowski DE, Hannon PA, et al. Neighborhood crime-related safety and its relation to children's physical activity. *J Urban Health* 2015;**92**(3):472–89.
50. DeWeese RS, Yedidia MJ, Tulloch DL, Ohri-Vachaspati P. Neighborhood perceptions and active school commuting in low-income cities. *Am J Prev Med* 2013;**45**(4):393–400.
51. Kerr J, Rosenberg D, Sallis JF, Saelens BE, Frank LD, Conway TL. Active commuting to school: associations with environment and parental concerns. *Med Sci Sports Exerc* 2006;**38**(4):787–94.
52. Rossen LM, Pollack KM, Curriero FC, et al. Neighborhood incivilities, perceived neighborhood safety, and walking to school among urban-dwelling children. *J Phys Act Health* 2011;**8**(2):262–71.
53. Salvo D, Reis RS, Sarmiento OL, Pratt M. Overcoming the challenges of conducting physical activity and built environment research in Latin America: IPEN Latin America. *Prev Med* 2014;**69**:S86–92.
54. Sarmiento OL, Lemoine P, Gonzalez SA, Broyles ST, Denstel KD, Larouche R, et al. Relationships between active school transport and adiposity indicators in school-age children from low-, middle- and high-income countries. *Int J Obes Suppl* 2015;**5**: S107–14.
55. Mendoza JA, Liu Y. Active commuting to elementary school and adiposity: an observational study. *Child Obes* 2014;**10**(1):1–8.

56. Pabayo RA, Gauvin L, Barnett TA, Morency P, Nikiéma B, Séguin L. Understanding the determinants of active transportation to school among children: evidence of environmental injustice from the Quebec longitudinal study of child development. *Health Place* 2012;**18**:163–71.
57. Cutumisu N, Bélanger-Gravel A, Laferté M, Lagarde F, Lemay J-F, Gauvin L. Influence of area deprivation and perceived neighbourhood safety on active transport to school among urban Quebec preadolescents. *Can J Public Health* 2014;**105**(5):e376–82.
58. Collins D, Kearns RA. Geographies of inequality: child pedestrian injury and walking school buses in Auckland, New Zealand. *Soc Sci Med* 2005;**60**:61–9.
59. Atteberry H, Dowdy D, Oluyomi A, Nichols D, Ory MG, Hoelscher DM. A contextual look at Safe Routes to School implementation in Texas. *Env Behav* 2016;**48**(1):192–209.
60. Mammen G, Stone MR, Buliung R, Faulkner G. "Putting school travel on the map": facilitators and barriers to implementing school travel planning in Canada. *J Transp Health* 2015;**2**(3):318–26.
61. Tremblay MS, Gray CE, Akinroye K, Harrington DM, Katzmarzyk PT, Lambert EV, et al. Physical activity of children: a global matrix of grades comparing 15 countries. *J Phys Act Health* 2014;**11**:113–25.
62. McDonald NC. Active transportation to school: trends among U.S. schoolchildren, 1969–2001. *Am J Prev Med* 2007;**32**(6):509–16.
63. Timperio A, Ball K, Salmon J, Roberts R, Giles-Corti B, Simmons D, et al. Personal, family, social, and environmental correlates of active commuting to school. *Am J Prev Med* 2006;**30**(1):45–51.
64. Parra DC, de Sá TH, Monteiro CA, Freudenberg N. Automobile, construction and entertainment business sector influences on sedentary lifestyles. *Health Promot Int* 2016;**1**:1–11.
65. Lorenc T, Brunton G, Oliver S, Oliver K, Oakley A. Attitudes to walking and cycling among children, young people and parents: a systematic review. *J Epidemiol Community Health* 2008;**62**:852–7.
66. Underwood SK, Handy SL, Paterniti DA, Lee AE. Why do teens abandon bicycling? A retrospective look at attitudes and behaviors. *J Transp Health* 2014;**1**(1):17–24.
67. Yach D, McKee M, Lopez AD, Novotny T. For Oxford Vision 2020. Improving diet and physical activity: 12 lessons from controlling tobacco smoking. *BMJ* 2005;**330**(7496):898–900.

Built and Physical Environment Correlates of Active Transportation

10

Anna Timperio, Jenny Veitch, Shannon Sahlqvist
Institute for Physical Activity and Nutrition (IPAN), School of Exercise and Nutrition Sciences, Deakin University, Geelong, Australia

Chapter Outline

10.1 Introduction

As outlined in Chapter 6, human behaviour is determined by multiple levels of influences, from the characteristics of the individual, to interpersonal influences within families and social networks, and to more distal influences in the community, built and physical environment, and policy contexts.[1] This chapter will explore links between the built and physical environments and active transportation among children.

Children's Active Transportation. https://doi.org/10.1016/B978-0-12-811931-0.00010-7

The term built environment refers to man-made or modified features (structures or places) in the environment.[2] It includes the way in which structures and places within neighbourhoods are laid out, different uses assigned to land (such as residential use, commercial use and education), the range of destinations or places available, public transport systems, the provision of roads, footpaths and cycle paths, and other design features and infrastructure that can make it easier to walk or cycle places, such as traffic calming, separation from traffic, road crossing infrastructure and lighting.[3] In contrast, the natural environment includes non-human-made features, such as the topography of an area (e.g., hilliness), natural features (e.g., beaches, rivers and forests) and climatic or weather conditions. Decisions that impact on the form and attributes of the built environment and how this interacts with the natural environment are made by a number of diverse professions at different levels of a government, including urban and town planners, landscape architects, land managers, transport planners and engineers. Private enterprises, such as land and property developers, can also play a role in shaping the built environment.

Over the past few decades, there has been a proliferation of research highlighting the role of the built and natural environment in encouraging physical activity among adults.[4] Research focused on children has also grown rapidly in recent years.[5,6] Among children, the built and natural environment can provide important opportunities and supportive infrastructure for active transportation. However, it may also present considerable barriers to walking and cycling that impact on the ease and acceptability of active transportation for children. Most notably, these barriers can contribute to parental perceptions about their neighbourhood, particularly safety-related concerns, that may impact decisions they make about whether or not their child is allowed to walk or cycle from place to place, and with whom, as discussed in Chapter 8.

In an increasingly urbanized world[7] with growing dependence on motorized travel, the need to understand how the design of neighbourhood environments can support and/or pose barriers to active forms of transport among children is critical, as new suburbs develop and existing urban centres, suburbs and townships evolve. As well as the health, environmental and economic gains that can be made from choosing active transportation over motorized travel outlined in Chapters 1–3, urban planning that supports walking and cycling as a mode of transport can have many other important 'co-benefits', including increased social connections, neighbourhood trust and safety, and reduced crime.[8]

10.2 Approaches to Measuring and Understanding the Built Environment

There are many ways in which the built environment can be measured. These can be grouped into subjective (perceived) versus objective measures. Recent evidence reviews have found no differences in the consistency of associations with transport-related physical activity between objective and perceived measures of the neighbourhood environment.[6,9]

10.2.1 Subjective Approaches

One of the most common methods of measuring the built environment with respect to active transporationt is to simply survey individuals (children and/or their parents) about the features of the neighbourhood in which they live, the environment surrounding their school, their route to school or barriers to walking or cycling that are environmental in nature. Several self-administered instruments have been developed for this purpose and perhaps the most commonly used instrument is the Neighbourhood Environment Walkability Scale,[10] which has been adapted to suit different countries[11,12] and to collect relevant data for different age groups.[13,14] Other approaches include qualitative interviews or focus groups with parents and/or children and asking individuals to draw maps of their neighbourhoods or routes to school and to use these to identify key attributes or barriers.[15,16] As these approaches are based on individual perceptions, they are highly subjective. Two neighbours, for example, could report different neighbourhood attributes based on the different levels of awareness of their neighbourhoods, their understanding of what the attribute is and their interpretation of terms such as ‘neighbourhood’ and the areas these cover. Indeed, parents of children living in very similar environments can have different perceptions of their neighbourhood,[17] and when researchers have compared people’s perceptions of attributes of neighbourhoods, such as physical activity facilities and walkability, to objective measures of the built environment, there has often been stark mismatch between the two, especially among those who are least active.[18,19]

10.2.2 Objective Approaches

Objective measures of features of the built and natural environment can be collected via physical auditing of specific neighbourhood features, streetscapes and routes.[20] This involves inspecting these areas in person or virtually via online imagery (e.g., Google Maps and Google Street View) and recording the existence and/or quality of specific destinations, facilities or design features. Another common way of measuring the built environment is to use spatial mapping techniques to ‘count’ or look at spatial relationships between neighbourhood attributes using Geographic Information Systems (GIS).[20,21] Using existing geographically referenced data on a range of attributes, these systems can ‘count’ features (e.g., the number of pedestrian crossings) within a user-specified area, compute distances between features (e.g., homes and schools or other destinations) using data about roads and/or pedestrian networks, compute amount of land allocated to specific uses and determine the topography of an area.

10.2.3 What About Scale?

As alluded to above, the size or extent of the area in which built and natural environment attributes are studied or measured (i.e., the spatial scale) can vary substantially.[22] For example, attributes can be measured within ‘perceived’ neighbourhoods defined as within ‘my local area’ or within a ‘15 min walk from home’, within administrative areas (e.g., census areas, suburbs or postal boundaries) and within radial (crow-fly) or road network distances that can vary widely from a few hundred metres to several kilometres around an individual's residential address or school.[22,23] Attributes can also be measured along the shortest or actual routes between a residential address and a destination of interest, such as a school.[24] However, it should be noted that the shortest route may not be the actual route taken, and thus attributes of the shortest possible and actual routes may differ.[25] Other routes may be taken for a variety of reasons, including to avoid attributes present in the shortest route.[25]

10.3 Built Environment Influences on Active Transportation

Most built environment attributes relevant to active transportation among children can be conceptualized as encompassing urban planning or design and street-level attributes. Overwhelmingly, most research examining links with active transportation among children has focused specifically on school travel.[9,26] Built environment correlates of active transportation to other destinations are less commonly studied.

10.3.1 Urban Planning and Design

The way in which land is developed and how urban areas, suburbs, towns and communities, and relevant amenities and infrastructure are laid out can be critical for determining travel patterns.[27] In particular, urban design can make an area more or less car-oriented, and likewise, more or less walking and cycling friendly. Among adults, active transportation has been strongly linked to the concept of 'walkability'.[28,29] Walkability refers to the extent to which an area encourages and supports walking, and is typically conceptualized as a composite measure of three core urban design elements: residential density, connectivity of streets and land use mix,[30,31] which work together to create conditions that make walking from place to place easier. At a conceptual level, areas with a diversity of different types of uses, such as residential, office, retail/commercial, industrial and public space that are well-integrated foster walking because destinations typically visited as part of daily life (e.g., homes, workplaces, shops and other services) are more likely to be situated close together.[27] Adequate residential density supports the need to provide services and amenities and the viability of different businesses and land uses. When these areas are serviced by a permeable, highly connected network of streets, travel to a range of places can be shorter and more direct, with a variety of route options available. Together, these three design elements (residential density, connectivity and land use mix) combine to create urban areas that are more compact and oriented to walking or cycling than other ways of designing urban environments where different land uses are not integrated (built apart), with long distances and indirect routes between residential areas and places where people need to go.[27] Among adults, living in an area with higher 'walkability' scores is associated with more walking in general,[32,33] as well as walking[28,29] and cycling[28] for transport. Consistent with this, on balance, studies with children show that walkability is associated with more active transportation to school.[9]

Among children, the vast majority of the research that has been undertaken to examine the role of the built environment on active transportation suggests that the most critical design decision that can determine walking or cycling to school is the siting of the school relative to residential areas. This is because 'distance' or 'proximity' to school has consistently been shown to be the strongest predictor of active transportation to school among youth, with children living shorter distances to school having much higher odds of using active forms of transport to school or doing so regularly.[6,26,34–36] Although studies examining how the built environment is related to active transportation more generally (i.e., walking or cycling to any destination as a form of transport) are relatively few compared to those looking specifically at school travel, there is some evidence that increasing levels of mixed land use[26] and greater access to recreation facilities[9] are positively associated with active transportation to other destinations. Population or residential density has also been shown to be a positive correlate of active transportation to school and other destinations among children.[9,26] This may in part be due to increased levels of surveillance resulting from having more people using streets or due to more compact development resulting in shorter distances on average.

However, some urban design elements that have been shown to contribute to an environment that fosters active transportation among adults may not have the same impact in children. For example, studies examining the association between street connectivity (measured in a variety of ways) and active transportation in children have produced mixed findings.[26] One reason that has been suggested for this is that connected street networks can expose children to more vehicular traffic than less connected networks with less through traffic, which may exacerbate traffic safety concerns. Indeed, in Perth, Western Australia, after adjusting for distance to school and other factors, Giles-Corti et al.[37] found that high street connectivity around schools was associated with lower odds of walking to school regularly, and low traffic volume was associated with higher odds. However, when they looked at this in more detail, they found that these variables 'interacted'. The odds of walking to school were more than three times higher among children with both high street connectivity and low traffic volume compared to those with low connectivity and high traffic volume. Thus, for children, the concept of 'walkability' may be more relevant with lower traffic volumes.[37]

10.3.2 Street-Level Attributes

Street-level design attributes such as sidewalks, walking and cycling paths, exposure to traffic and traffic speed, attributes that contribute to pedestrian safety such as crossings, lighting and separation from traffic, and aesthetics can be important influences on active transportation among children and youth.

10.3.2.1 Road Safety and Road Safety Infrastructure

The ability to safely move about neighbourhood environments and routes to school and other destinations by foot or bicycle is critical for active transportation. Parental concern about traffic or road safety is commonly cited as a barrier to walking and cycling for children.[38,39] Traffic conditions such as traffic speed, amount of traffic and lack of safe road crossings may influence perceptions of road safety and active transportation.

Several reviews have found that safety from traffic, including safe road crossing points and traffic calming, is positively associated with active transportation among children.[6,9,34,38] A review of studies conducted in the UK examining people's views on active transportation among young people aged up to 21 years found that parents cited risks from traffic as a reason to drive their children from place to place, particularly to school.[38] Longitudinal studies have also reported positive associations between road safety features and active transportation. In the UK, children whose parents reported it was inconvenient to use a car for school transport and higher route safety between home and school had higher odds of taking up and maintaining active transportation to school 12 months later.[40] In Belgium, a higher parent-reported neighbourhood safety score that included traffic, lighting, crosswalks, crime and strangers was associated with higher odds of maintaining active transportation in their leisure time over the transition to secondary school.[41] Similarly, in Australia, Veitch et al.[42] found that children whose mothers reported greater concerns over road safety (e.g., major barriers to walking or cycling, absence of lights, crossings or pedestrian overpasses, the need to cross busy or several roads) had lower odds of using active transportation to local destinations 2 years later.

The impact of road safety on active transportation may vary depending on the destination of interest (e.g., school vs. other neighbourhood destinations travelled to during leisure time) and country. In their recent review of mostly cross-sectional studies, D'Haese et al.[9] reported positive associations between traffic safety and all forms of active transportation to school, but limited evidence of associations between traffic safety and walking or cycling for transport during leisure time. D'Haese et al.[9] also found that traffic safety was associated with active transportation to school in North America and Australia but not in Europe. It has been suggested that in Europe, road safety and safety around schools is already relatively high and therefore active transportation is less dependent on safety in these contexts. Similarly, in their study comparing data from 12 country sites collected using the same survey items, Larouche et al.[35] found considerable variation in associations between perceived elements of road safety (traffic speed, drivers exceeding speed limits, traffic making it difficult or unpleasant for their child to walk, presence of crosswalks and signals on busy streets) with active transportation to school across the countries. For example, Brazilian children whose parents disagreed that most drivers go faster than the speed limit were about half as likely to engage in active school travel, but the opposite was found in India and Australia. Together, these findings highlight the importance of considering local context and suggest complex interactions with other aspects of the built environment. Furthermore, children in developing countries may have no choice but to walk, irrespective of the environment (see Chapter 12).

10.3.2.2 Walking and Cycling Infrastructure

Sidewalks and walking and cycling paths provide dedicated infrastructure to support walking and cycling that separate users from traffic, which may reduce parental concerns about traffic safety. If the network is connected, sidewalks and walking/cycling paths can provide routes between destinations and their presence could encourage walking and cycling. These infrastructures have been shown to be important correlates of active transportation in children and youth in some reviews.[5,6,26,36] However, D'Haese et al.[9] found that walking and cycling facilities were consistently positively associated with walking to school, most notably in North America, but not cycling to school or walking or cycling to other destinations during childrens' leisure time.

10.3.2.3 Aesthetics

Neighbourhood aesthetics is consistently associated with overall physical activity among adults.[43] While intuitively, pleasant and attractive surroundings would be expected to be associated with higher levels of active transportation among children, there is little evidence to support this. Most studies that have considered associations between aesthetics and active transportation in children have reported that aesthetics are not associated with active transportation in this age group.[6,9,26] While some studies have reported positive associations between parent perceptions that their neighbourhood is aesthetically pleasing[44] and the number of street trees within 5 m of each road edge[45] and active transportation to school, these findings are not common.

10.4 Natural Environment Influences on Active Transportation

Conceptually, elements of the natural environment such as topographical features and the weather could support or inhibit children's active transportation. However, natural environment elements such as these have not been frequently studied as correlates of active transportation in their own right.

10.4.1 Topographical Features

A study conducted in Melbourne, Australia, found that young children aged 5–6 years with an objectively measured steep incline of 10% on their shortest route to school had 70% lower odds of walking or cycling to school at least once/week compared with those without such an incline; however, there was no association among older children aged 10–12 years.[24] Another cross-sectional study conducted in Perth, Australia, among older children (10–13 years) also found no associations between parental perception of the presence of steep hills on the journey to school and walking[46] or cycling[47] to school at least once in the past week.

10.4.2 Weather

A small number of studies have examined the association between weather and active transportation to school. The findings from studies that used objective measures of weather collected by authorities are inconsistent. In Canadian school children (grades 6–10), lower average daily temperature was negatively associated, and the number of extreme hot days (>30°C or >80°F) positively associated, with walking and cycling to school among those living within 1 mile (1.6 km) from school.[48] In contrast, other studies in Canada[49,50] and studies in the United States[51,52] and New Zealand[53] found no associations between weather variables such as average temperature, rainfall or sunlight, and active transportation to school. Taking this further, a study of Dutch children (6–11 years) extracted data on weather conditions (including temperature and rainfall) at the time of the trip departure from home or school (determined using a Geographic Positioning System; GPS) and found no association with the mode of travel to school for these journeys.[54]

Studies comparing variations in active transportation according to season have also had mixed findings. While there is some evidence of seasonal variations in active transportation trips among children and youth in Norway[55] and the United States,[56] two studies in Canada found no seasonal variation.[49,50] In the Norwegian study, Borrestad et al.[55] found that fewer children aged 10–12 years reported cycling to or from school in winter (3%) compared with in fall (autumn) (52%) and spring (51%), while walking was far more common in winter (65%) than in fall (24%) or spring (25%).[55] The results suggest that conditions during Norwegian winters may make it difficult to cycle, but these conditions do not appear to inhibit walking.[55]

10.5 Conclusions

The built and natural environment can support or inhibit children's active transportation, particularly active transportation to or from school. Distance or 'proximity' to school, walkability, dedicated walking and cycling infrastructure and traffic safety attributes are consistently associated with active transportation among children. There is also some evidence that urban design features such as street connectivity may not support active transportation without also considering traffic exposure, suggesting that active transportation may be determined by complex interactions between different elements of the environment. Compared with the built environment, studies exploring attributes of the natural environment are less common. These studies provide equivocal evidence that aspects of the natural environment influence active transportation. Of note, most of the current evidence base focuses specifically on elementary school-aged children, urban environments and on journeys to and from school; comparatively, few studies have focused on adolescents, rural areas or on active transportation to other destinations during leisure time.

Guidance for incorporating healthy, active living considerations into design and the planning process exists in many countries (e.g., 57,58). This guidance must include a focus on children and design considerations (urban planning and street level) relevant to active transportation, specifically for this age group. Environments that support active transportation among children may also support active transportation among other vulnerable groups, such as older adults.[59] As cities become more urbanized, careful and appropriate planning to meet the needs of all residents, including children, is essential.

10.6 Recommendations for Policy and Practice

1. The likely impact of urban planning decisions, from master planning to neighbourhood renewal, should be assessed through the lens of child pedestrians and cyclists (as well as other vulnerable groups) prior to approval to ensure that they facilitate rather than inhibit walking and cycling to local destinations among all residents;
2. Well-connected dedicated walking and cycling infrastructure and measures to minimize exposure to traffic and help children safely cross roads should be prioritized in all neighbourhoods;
3. Careful consideration must be given to the siting of schools to maximize the proportion of students who can safely travel to and from school by walking, cycling or other active forms of transport, taking into account distance, route directness and exposure to traffic.

10.7 Recommendations for Future Research

Most research focused on the built environment and active transportation in children has adopted cross-sectional designs, focused predominantly on the school journey, collected data on 'home' neighbourhoods and focused on urban or suburban environments and children rather than adolescents. Future research should:

1. Adopt longitudinal designs with diverse populations. This is particularly important given that children gain independence and/or additional affordances with age;
2. Evaluate the impact of changes to the built environment on active transportation among children using natural experiment designs. Natural experiment designs can provide a higher level of evidence than cross-sectional designs, as they can assess changes in active transportation following a modification to the built environment, relative to a control group;[60]
3. Have a greater focus on built and natural environment influences on active transportation to a range of destinations during leisure time. There may be considerable opportunity for active transportation to replace short car trips after school and on weekends, and these types of journeys may be more amenable to change (see Chapter 17);
4. Ensure that behaviour-specific environmental attributes are studied. Built environment attributes examined should be conceptually related to active transportation;[22]
5. Increase the context-specificity of the areas under study.[22] For example, most studies have examined perceived or objective measures of the built and natural environment around homes or local neighbourhoods. However for some, the school and other journeys can extend beyond these spatial scales. Future research should examine the characteristics of routes and the environment immediately surrounding schools, in addition to home neighbourhoods. Focussing exclusively on the neighbourhood environment surrounding homes can ignore substantial segments of the journey to/from school.
6. Explore the complexity of built and natural environment influences on active transportation among children and youth using advanced statistical techniques. Moderation analyses, for example, can be used to examine whether the association between a particular attribute and active transportation depends on a second attribute. Cluster analysis techniques can also be used to generate different combinations or 'typologies' of route characteristics, and these combinations of attributes can be used to explore associations with active transportation;[61]

7. Ensure the use of a variety of technologies (e.g., GPS, GIS) that could be adopted to better understand built and natural environment influences on active transportation in children and youth (see Chapter 17);
8. Evaluate the feasibility and impact of 'Drop and Walk' points. As active transportation to or from school is highly dependent on distance, identifying appropriate and easily accessible locations for 'Drop and Walk' points could be a viable means of giving more students the opportunity to walk or cycle to school, at least part of the way;
9. Consider children's and young people's perspectives of their environment in addition to those of their parents.

Acknowledgments

Anna Timperio was supported by a Future Leader Fellowship from the National Heart Foundation of Australia (ID 100046). Jenny Veitch was supported by an Early Career Fellowship from the National Health and Medical Research Council (ID 1053426).

References

1. Stokols D. Translating social ecological theory into guidelines for community health promotion. *Am J Health Promot* 1996;**10**(4):282–98.
2. Australian Institute of Health and Welfare. *Health and the environment: a compilation of evidence. Cat. no. PHE 136.* Canberra: Australian Institute of Health and Welfare; 2011.
3. National Research Council. Committee on Physical Activity Land Use Institute of Medicine. *Does the built environment influence physical activity?: examining the evidence.* Transportation Research Board; 2005.
4. Harris JK, Lecy J, Hipp JA, Brownson RC, Parra DC. Mapping the development of research on physical activity and the built environment. *Prev Med* 2013;**57**(5):533–40.
5. Ding D, Sallis JF, Kerr J, Lee S, Rosenberg DE. Neighborhood environment and physical activity among youth a review. *Am J Prev Med* 2011;**41**(4):442–55.
6. Timperio A, Reid J, Veitch J. Playability: built and social environment features that promote physical activity within children. *Curr Obes Rep* 2015;**4**(4):460–76.
7. United Nations, Department of Economic and Social Affairs, Population Division. *World urbanization prospects: the 2014 revision, (ST/ESA/SER.A/366).* New York: United Nations; 2015.
8. Sallis JF, Spoon C, Cavill N, Engelberg JK, Gebel K, Parker M, Thornton CM, Lou D, Wilson AL, Cutter CL. Co-benefits of designing communities for active living: an exploration of literature. *Int J Behav Nutr Phys Act* 2015;**12**:30.
9. D'Haese S, Vanwolleghem G, Hinckson E, De Bourdeaudhuij I, Deforche B, Van Dyck D, Cardon G. Cross-continental comparison of the association between the physical environment and active transportation in children: a systematic review. *Int J Behav Nutr Phys Act* 2015;**12**:145.
10. Saelens BE, Sallis JF, Black JB, Chen D. Neighborhood-based differences in physical activity: an environment scale evaluation. *Am J Pub Health* 2003;**93**(9):1552–8.

11. Oyeyemi AL, Kasoma SS, Onywera VO, Assah F, Adedoyin RA, Conway TL, Moss SJ, Ocansey R, Kolbe-Alexander TL, Akinroye KK, Prista A, Larouche R, Gavand KA, Cain KL, Lambert EV, Aryeetey R, Bartels C, Tremblay MS, Sallis JF. NEWS for Africa: adaptation and reliability of a built environment questionnaire for physical activity in seven African countries. *Int J Behav Nutr Phys Act* 2016;**13**:33.
12. Adlakha D, Hipp JA, Brownson RC. Adaptation and evaluation of the neighborhood environment walkability scale in India (NEWS-India). *Int J Environ Res Pub Health* 2016;**13**(4):401.
13. Rosenberg D, Ding D, Sallis JF, Kerr J, Norman GJ, Durant N, Harris SK, Saelens BE. Neighborhood environment walkability scale for youth (NEWS-Y): reliability and relationship with physical activity. *Prev Med* 2009;**49**(2–3):213–8.
14. Cerin E, Sit CH, Cheung MC, Ho SY, Lee LC, Chan WM. Reliable and valid NEWS for Chinese seniors: measuring perceived neighborhood attributes related to walking. *Int J Behav Nutr Phys Act* 2010;**7**:84.
15. Loptson K, Muhajarine N, Ridalls T. Smart Cities HKRT. Walkable for whom? Examining the role of the built environment on the neighbourhood-based physical activity of children. *Can J Public Health* 2012;**103**(9 Suppl. 3):eS29–34.
16. Pearce A, Kirk C, Cummins S, Collins M, Elliman D, Connolly AM, Law C. Gaining children's perspectives: a multiple method approach to explore environmental influences on healthy eating and physical activity. *Health Place* 2009;**15**(2):614–21.
17. Lee C, Zhu X, Yoon J, Varni JW. Beyond distance: children's school travel mode choice. *Ann Behav Med* 2013;**45**(Suppl. 1):S55–67.
18. Ball K, Jeffery RW, Crawford DA, Roberts RJ, Salmon J, Timperio AF. Mismatch between perceived and objective measures of physical activity environments. *Prev Med* 2008;**47**(3):294–8.
19. Gebel K, Bauman A, Owen N. Correlates of non-concordance between perceived and objective measures of walkability. *Ann Behav Med* 2009;**37**(2):228–38.
20. Brownson RC, Hoehner CM, Day K, Forsyth A, Sallis JF. Measuring the built environment for physical activity: state of the science. *Prev Med* 2009;**36**(4 Suppl.):S99–123.
21. Sallis JF. Measuring physical activity environments: a brief history. *Am J Prev Med* 2009;**36**(4 Suppl.):S86–92.
22. Giles-Corti B, Timperio A, Bull F, Pikora T. Behavior and context specific ecological models of physical activity. *Exerc Sport Sci Rev* 2005;**33**(4):175–81.
23. Ball K, Timperio AF, Crawford DA. Understanding environmental influences on nutrition and physical activity behaviors: where should we look and what should we count? *Int J Behav Nutr Phys Act* 2006;**3**:33.
24. Timperio A, Ball K, Salmon J, Roberts R, Giles-Corti B, Simmons D, Baur LA, Crawford D. Personal, family, social, and environmental correlates of active commuting to school. *Am J Prev Med* 2006;**30**(1):45–51.
25. Buliung RN, Larsen K, Faulkner GEJ, Stone MR. The "path" not taken: exploring structural differences in mapped- versus shortest-network-path school travel routes. *Am J Pub Health* 2013;**103**(9):1589–96.
26. Pont K, Ziviani J, Wadley D, Bennett S, Abbott R. Environmental correlates of children's active transportation: a systematic literature review. *Health Place* 2009;**15**(3):827–40.
27. Saelens BE, Sallis JF, Frank LD. Environmental correlates of walking and cycling: findings from the transportation, urban design, and planning literature. *Ann Behav Med* 2003;**25**(2):80–91.

28. Van Holle V, Deforche B, Van Cauwenberg J, Goubert L, Maes L, Van de Weghe N, De Bourdeaudhuij I. Relationship between the physical environment and different domains of physical activity in European adults: a systematic review. *BMC Pub Health* 2012;**12**:807.
29. McCormack GR, Shiell A. In search of causality: a systematic review of the relationship between the built environment and physical activity among adults. *Int J Behav Nutr Phys Act* 2011;**8**:125.
30. Kent J, Thompson S, Jalaludin B. *Healthy built environments: a review of the literature*. Healthy Built Environments Program, City Futures Research Centre, The University of New South Wales; 2011.
31. Udell T, Daley M, Johnson B, Tolley R. *Does density matter? The role of density in creating walkable neighbourhoods*. Melbourne: National Heart Foundation of Australia; 2014.
32. Hajna S, Ross NA, Brazeau A-S, Bélisle P, Joseph L, Dasgupta K. Associations between neighbourhood walkability and daily steps in adults: a systematic review and meta-analysis. *BMC Pub Health* 2015;**15**:768.
33. Owen N, Humpel N, Leslie E, Bauman A, Sallis JF. Understanding environmental influences on walking; Review and research agenda. *Am J Prev Med* 2004;**27**(1):67–76.
34. Panter JR, Jones AP, van Sluijs EMF. Environmental determinants of active travel in youth: a review and framework for future research. *Int J Behav Nutr Phys Act* 2008;**5**:34.
35. Larouche R, Sarmiento OL, Broyles ST, Denstel KD, Church TS, Barreira TV, Chaput JP, Fogelholm M, Hu G, Kuriyan R, Kurpad A, Lambert EV, Maher C, Maia J, Matsudo V, Olds T, Onywera V, Standage M, Tremblay MS, Tudor-Locke C, Zhao P, Katzmarzyk PT. ISCOLE Research Group. Are the correlates of active school transport context-specific? *Int J Obes* 2015;**5**(Suppl. 2):S89–99.
36. Davison KK, Werder JL, Lawson CT. Children's active commuting to school: current knowledge and future directions. *Prev Chronic Dis* 2008;**5**(3):A100.
37. Giles-Corti B, Wood G, Pikora T, Learnihan V, Bulsara M, Van Niel K, Timperio A, McCormack G, Villanueva K. School site and the potential to walk to school: the impact of street connectivity and traffic exposure in school neighborhoods. *Health Place* 2011;**17**(2):545–50.
38. Lorenc T, Brunton G, Oliver S, Oliver K, Oakley A. Attitudes to walking and cycling among children, young people and parents: a systematic review. *J Epidemiol Comm Health* 2008;**62**(10):852–7.
39. Carver A, Timperio A, Crawford D. Playing it safe: the influence of neighborhood safety on children's physical activity – a review. *Health Place* 2008;**14**(2):217–27.
40. Panter J, Corder K, Griffin SJ, Jones AP, van Sluijs EM. Individual, socio-cultural and environmental predictors of uptake and maintenance of active commuting in children: longitudinal results from the SPEEDY study. *Int J Behav Nutr Phys Act* 2013;**10**:83.
41. Vanwolleghem G, Van Dyck D, De Meester F, De Bourdeaudhuij I, Cardon G, Gheysen F. Which socio-ecological factors associate with a switch to or maintenance of active and passive transport during the transition from primary to secondary school? *PLoS One* 2016;**11**:e0156531.
42. Veitch J, Carver A, Salmon J, Abbott G, Ball K, Crawford D, Cleland V, Timperio A. What predicts children's active transport and independent mobility in disadvantaged neighborhoods? *Health Place* 2017;**44**:103–9.
43. Choi J, Lee M, Lee JK, Kang D, Choi JY. Correlates associated with participation in physical activity among adults: a systematic review of reviews and update. *BMC Pub Health* 2017;**17**:356.
44. Kerr J, Rosenberg D, Sallis JF, Saelens BE, Frank LD, Conway TL. Active commuting to school: associations with environment and parental concerns. *Med Sci Sports Exerc* 2006;**38**(4):787–94.

45. Larsen K, Gilliland J, Hess P, Tucker P, Irwin J, He M. The influence of the physical environment and sociodemographic characteristics on children's mode of travel to and from school. *Am J Pub Health* 2009;**99**(3):520–6.
46. Trapp G, Giles-Corti B, Christian H, Bulsara M, Timperio A, McCormack GR, Villanueva K. Increasing children's physical activity: individual, social and environmental factors associated with walking to school. *Health Educ Behav* 2012;**39**(2):172–82.
47. Trapp GS, Giles-Corti B, Christian HE, Bulsara M, Timperio AF, McCormack GR, Villaneuva KP. On your bike! a cross-sectional study of the individual, social and environmental correlates of cycling to school. *Int J Behav Nutr Phys Act* 2011;**8**:123.
48. Gropp KM, Pickett W, Janssen I. Multi-level examination of correlates of active transportation to school among youth living within 1 mile of their school. *Int J Behav Nutr Phys Act* 2012;**9**:124.
49. Robertson-Wilson JE, Leatherdale ST, Wong SL. Social–ecological correlates of active commuting to school among high school students. *J Adolesc Health* 2008;**42**:486–95.
50. Mitra R, Faulkner G. There's no such thing as bad weather, just the wrong clothing: climate, weather and active school transportation in Toronto, Canada. *Can J Pub Health* 2012;**103**(Suppl. 3):S35–41.
51. Sirard J, Ainsworth BE, McIver KL, Pate RR. Prevalence of active travel at urban and suburban elementary schools in Columbia, SC. *Am J Pub Health* 2005;**95**(2):236–7.
52. Chillón P, Hales D, Vaughn A, Gizlice Z, Ni A, Ward DS. A cross-sectional study of demographic, environmental and parental barriers to active school travel among children in the United States. *Int J Behav Nutr Phys Act* 2014;**11**:61.
53. Oliver M, Badland H, Mavoa S, Witten K, Kearns R, Ellaway A, Hinckson E, Mackay L, Schluter PJ. Environmental and socio-demographic associates of children's active transport to school: a cross-sectional investigation from the URBAN Study. *Int J Behav Nutr Phys Act* 2014;**11**:70.
54. Helbich M, Zeylmans van Emmichoven MJ, Dijst MJ, Kwan M-P, Pierik FH, de Vries SI. Natural and built environmental exposures on children's active school travel: a Dutch global positioning system-based cross-sectional study. *Health Place* 2016;**39**:101–9.
55. Borrestad LA, Andersen LB, Bere E. Seasonal and socio-demographic determinants of school commuting. *Prev Med* 2011;**52**(2):133–5.
56. Yang Y, Diez Roux AV, Bingham CR. Variability and seasonality of active transportation in the USA: evidence from 2011 NHTS. *Int J Behav Nutr Phys Act* 2011;**8**:96.
57. Heart Foundation. *Healthy active by design*. http://www.healthyactivebydesign.com.au/.
58. Provincial Health Services Authority. *Healthy built environment linkages: a toolkit for design, planning, health, V1.1*. Canada: Provincial Health Services Authority; 2014.
59. Cerin E, Nathan A, van Cauwenberg J, Barnett DW, Barnett A, Council on E, Physical Activity – older Adults working g. The neighbourhood physical environment and active travel in older adults: a systematic review and meta-analysis. *Int J Behav Nutr Phys Act* 2017;**14**(1):15.
60. Craig P, Cooper C, Gunnell D, Haw S, Lawson K, Macintyre S, Ogilvie D, Petticrew M, Reeves B, Sutton M, Thompson S. Using natural experiments to evaluate population health interventions: new Medical Research Council guidance. *J Epidemiol Comm Health* 2012;**66**(12):1182–6.
61. Timperio A, Crawford D, Ball K, Salmon J. Typologies of neighbourhood environments and children's physical activity, sedentary time and television viewing. *Health Place* 2017;**43**:121–7.

Public Policy and Active Transportation

11

Richard Larouche[1], *Karl Saidla*[2]
[1]Faculty of Health Sciences, University of Lethbridge, Lethbridge, AB, Canada; [2]School of Human Kinetics, University of Ottawa, Ottawa, ON, Canada

Current urban transportation systems and travel behaviour are—for better or for worse—primarily the results of public policy

John Pucher[1]

Chapter Outline

11.1 Introduction

In this chapter, we shift our attention to policies implemented at broader levels by local, regional and national authorities. Many governmental, quasi-governmental and nongovernmental bodies recognize the need for large-scale interventions to promote active transportation. Public policies are important tools that governments can use to modify the built environment and implement programmes that promote active transportation. Policies that may affect active transportation can take many forms and may involve multiple sectors including (but not limited to) education, transportation, injury prevention, law enforcement, planning and public health. Prior to discussing specific policies and their effect on children's active transportation, we begin by introducing

Children's Active Transportation. https://doi.org/10.1016/B978-0-12-811931-0.00011-9

how policies can affect travel mode choice more generally and by reviewing calls to action for governments to implement policies to support active transportation. We do not discuss policies and practices that may be adopted by individual schools as these are discussed in Chapter 9.

It is broadly recognized that the likelihood of active transportation is considerably affected by the degree to which public policies support its choice relative to automobile use. Although research about the effectiveness of public policies for increasing children's active transportation remains limited, several studies have investigated the relationships between public policies and overall rates of active transportation.[1–5] Pointedly, Pucher[1] examined the links between public policy and travel mode choices in 12 major North American and Western European jurisdictions. Whereas automobile travel accounted for 74% and 82% of trips in Canada and the United States, respectively, it accounted for less than 50% in the selected Western European countries.

Pucher[1] attributed these disparities to transportation policies that were clearly more favourable to active transportation and public transport use in Western Europe than in North America. Examples of the more supportive policies of Western European countries included stronger subsidization of bicycle infrastructure construction, the provision of safer conditions for pedestrians and cyclists, and higher public transport service levels. He also noted the importance of policies that discouraged automobile use (e.g., high gas prices, high taxes on car ownership and high parking prices). Finally, he discussed the relatively weaker public subsidization of roadway building and the stronger involvement of governments in implementing land use and housing policies that were more conducive to sustainable travel in Western Europe. Overall, Pucher[1] concluded that 'current urban transportation systems and travel behaviour are—for better or for worse—primarily the results of public policy'.

It is thus not surprising that literature discussing recommended policies to encourage active transportation[6–8] points to investment in infrastructure and services such as dedicated facilities for walking and cycling, traffic calming, and public transport, as well as a variety of approaches to discourage automobile use. Furthermore, active transportation proponents typically favour the development of more compact, transit-oriented communities featuring mixed land uses that result in shorter distance between amenities.

11.2 Calls to Action for Policies to Support Active Transportation

Since the World Health Organization's[9] Ottawa Charter for Health Promotion, many prominent national and international organizations have issued calls to action for policies to support healthy active living, including physical activity and active transportation. We discuss some of the key documents and briefly list and summarize additional ones in Table 11.1. Without listing country-specific physical activity plans and guidelines, the scope and diversity of calls to action outlined in the table make it clear that the need to support physical activity and active transportation is strongly recognized at

Table 11.1 Calls to action for policies to support physical activity and active transportation

Organization (year)	Name	Sector and level of government	Details
Finnish Ministry of Social Affairs and Health (2006)[12]	Health in All Policies[a]	Multisectoral; targets national governments and lower levels of government	Health in All Policies requires that all government departments (e.g., transportation, agriculture, education, etc.) explicitly consider the health impacts of their policies.
International Society for Physical Activity and Health (2010)[13]	Toronto Charter for Physical Activity	PA; targets all levels of government, civil society, professional associations and the private sector	Calls for concerted intersectoral action across four key areas: (1) implement a national policy and action plan; (2) introduce policies that support physical activity; (3) reorient services and funding to prioritize physical activity; and (4) develop partnerships for action.
International Society for Physical Activity and Health (2016)[14]	Bangkok Declaration on Physical Activity for Global Health and Sustainable Development	PA; targets national governments and lower levels of government	Emphasizes the role that PA (including AT) can play in achieving the UN's Sustainable Development Goals while improving population health worldwide.
Swedish Road Administration (1997)[15,16]	Vision Zero[a]	Transportation; targets national and lower levels of government	Aims to eliminate all preventable road deaths. Because road safety concerns are a key reason for chauffeuring children, the Vision Zero initiative may help increase AT and PA.
UN (1989)[11]	Convention on the Rights of the Child	Multisectoral; targets UN member states	Human rights treaty that sets out the civil, political, economic, social, health and cultural rights of children. Recognizes, among others, children's right to play, which relates to PA and can be facilitated by AT.
UN (2011)[10]	High-level Meeting of the General Assembly on the Prevention and Control of Non-communicable Diseases	Multisectoral; targets UN member states	Political Declaration calls for a whole-of-government and a whole-of-society effort to prevent noncommunicable diseases worldwide, notably through action on leading risk factors: physical inactivity, unhealthy diets, smoking and alcohol use.
UN (2015)[17]	Sustainable Development Goals	Multisectoral; targets UN member states	Emphasizes the need for sustainable development in the context of climate change; recognizes AT as a way to curb greenhouse gas emissions from the transportation sector.

Continued

Table 11.1 Calls to action for policies to support physical activity and active transportation—cont'd

Organization (year)	Name	Sector and level of government	Details
United States Department of Health and Human Services (2015)[18]	Surgeon General's Call to Action to Promote Walking and Walkable Communities	Multisectoral; targets US government and lower levels of government	Includes five goals: (1) make walking a national priority; (2) design communities that make it safe and easy to walk for people of all ages and abilities; (3) promote programmes and policies to support walking where people live, learn, work and play; (4) provide information to encourage walking and improve walkability; and (5) fill surveillance, research and evaluation gaps related to walking and walkability.
WHO (1986)[9]	Ottawa Charter for Health Promotion	Multisectoral; targets WHO member states	First international conference on health promotion. Identified five key action areas extending beyond the health sector: building healthy public policy, creating supportive environments, strengthening community action, developing personal skills and reorienting health services.
WHO (2004)[19]	Global Strategy on Diet, Physical Activity and Health	Multisectoral; targets WHO member states	Emphasizes the need to increase PA levels. Addresses the role of prevention across sectors such as health services, food and agriculture policies, fiscal and regulatory policies, consumer education and communication, and school policies as they affect food and PA choices.
WHO (2010)[20]	Global Recommendations on Physical Activity for Health	PA; targets national governments and lower levels of government	Provides evidence-based PA recommendations for children, youth and adults. Individual countries have proposed similar recommendations.
WHO (2010)[21]	Decade of Action for Road Safety 2011–20	Multisectoral; targets WHO member states	Recognizes that road crashes cause about 1.25 million deaths per year, and that road safety is a prerequisite to ensuring healthy lives, promoting well-being and making cities inclusive, safe, resilient and sustainable.

AT, active transportation; *PA*, physical activity; *UN*, United Nations; *WHO*, World Health Organization.
[a] Similar initiatives exist in other jurisdictions.

the global level. At the highest level of international diplomacy, the General Assembly of the United Nations[10] issued a Political Declaration on the Prevention and Control of Non-communicable Diseases, which explicitly emphasized the need for governmental action on physical activity. With specific reference to children, the United Nations' Convention on the Rights of the Child[11] clearly emphasized children's right to play, obviously enhanced when children can get to parks and other play spaces on their own.

In addition, a broad approach called Health in All Policies emerged during Finland's presidency of the European Union in 2006. As the name implies, Health in All Policies suggests that all government departments (e.g., transportation, agriculture, education, etc.) explicitly consider the health impacts of their policies.[12,22,23] The key message of Health in All Policies is that decisions taken in 'non-health' sectors can have a profound influence on the health of individuals and populations. Accordingly, health outcomes should be an important consideration in a wide range of policy areas.

A particularly pertinent example is provided by Vision Zero[15,16] initiatives that aim to eliminate all preventable road deaths. This approach was first adopted in Sweden in the late 1990s, with many additional jurisdictions following suit. As discussed in Chapter 7, the risk of traffic crashes is one of the key reasons why many parents do not allow their children to walk or bike on their own. Although road fatalities have declined over the last few decades, in many Western countries they are still among the leading causes of death for young people. These deaths are often the result of human errors that should not normally result in fatalities. Claes Tingvall, the Director of Traffic Safety at the Swedish Road Administration, recognized that 'We know we won't reach zero, but we could probably reduce road accident fatalities by 80%–90% by adopting these fundamental principles'.[15] Indeed, when Vision Zero is implemented with genuine conviction, it can result in substantial declines in road casualties.[24] Ultimately, Vision Zero should help to encourage parents to allow their children to engage in active transportation as a result of safer traffic conditions. In this example, we observe that policymakers in the transportation sector are making a major and successful attempt to improve health.

More recently, the United Nations[17] has adopted the Sustainable Development Goals (SDGs) as a replacement for the previous Millennium Development Goals. As the name implies, the SDGs recognize the need for sustainable development in the context of climate change. Given its potential to improve individual health while reducing greenhouse gases emissions on a large scale (see Chapters 1 and 2), active transportation is recognized as a key strategy to achieve the SDGs. In particular, the International Society for Physical Activity and Health[14] released the Bangkok Declaration on Physical Activity for Global Health and Sustainable Development, which emphasizes the links between physical activity (notably active transportation) and achievement of the SDGs. Fig. 11.1 illustrates these relationships.

Common among these calls to action is the underlying objective of making healthy choices easy choices. In the context of active transportation, this implies using policies to help create supportive physical environments. However, research consistently suggests that by themselves, supportive physical environments are not enough to cause major changes in behaviour. For example, the perceived convenience of driving is one of the key reasons why parents drive their children to and from school.[25–27] Therefore,

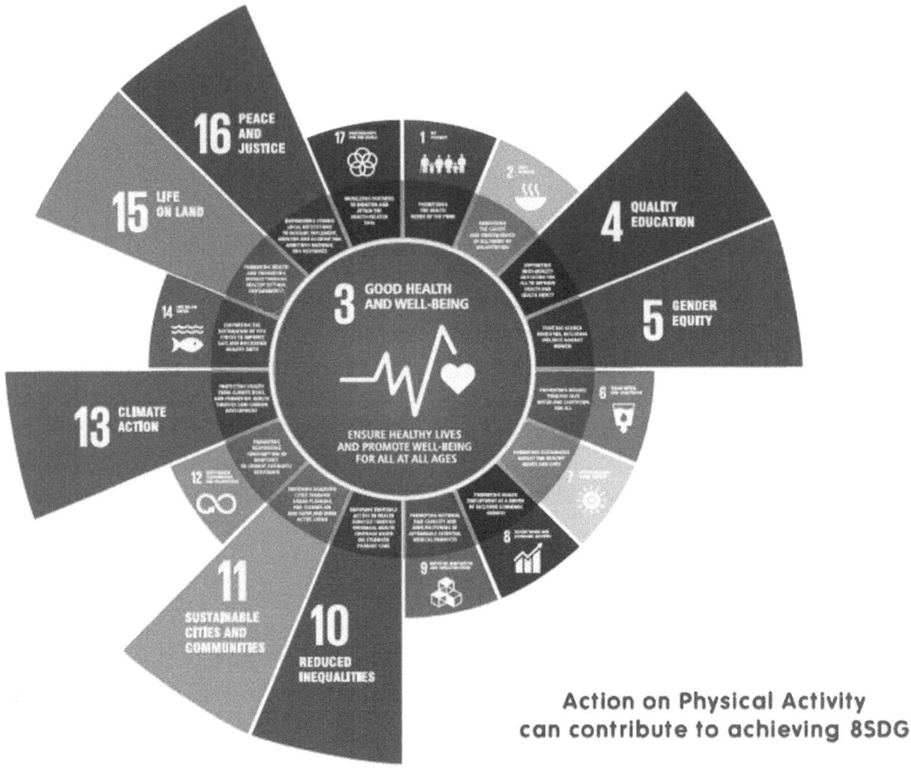

Figure 11.1 Sustainable Development Goals that physical activity can help achieve (For larger pdf version of the Bangkok Declaration: https://ispah-org-draft.squarespace.com/resources). Reproduced with permission from the International Society for Physical Activity and Health.[14]

in addition to creating walkable environments, policymakers should explicitly work to make driving *less* convenient for short walkable trips such as the journey to school (e.g., through parking restrictions, reduced speed limits and better traffic management around schools).

A further example illustrates the potential effectiveness of this type of approach. In a recent experiment in Australia, two adjoining healthcare facilities adopted diverging travel plans. One plan included only incentives for active transportation (the 'carrots only' approach), whereas the other included incentives for active transportation as well as parking management strategies to discourage workers from driving alone (the 'carrots and sticks' approach).[28] The 'carrots and sticks' approach proved to be much more effective, with the proportion of workers driving alone decreasing by 42%, while the 'carrots only' approach yielded only a 5% decrease. A transportation official interviewed by the authors pointedly mentioned that: 'the key thing is not to consider things in isolation. If you don't do parking management, you know, forget your behavior change, it's not going to work'.[29]

11.3 Policies Affecting Children's Active Transportation

11.3.1 National Policies and Programmes

Most of the policy initiatives and calls to action discussed so far do not specifically focus on children's active transportation. The United States' Safe Routes to School programme is perhaps the most well-known policy approach that deals explicitly with children's active transportation (see Chapter 13 for more details). Briefly, since 2005, this national programme has provided over US $1 billion to communities to construct new sidewalks, bicycle lanes, pathways and crosswalks, and to launch Safe Routes to School education, promotion and enforcement campaigns in elementary and middle schools. Interestingly, this programme was modelled after a Danish intervention.[30] In the 1970s, Denmark had one of the highest rates of child traffic accidents in Europe. To address this problem, the city of Odense required all of its 45 schools to identify and address specific road safety deficiencies. This programme led to an 80% reduction in road accidents and, following its success, was implemented widely across Denmark.[30] Then, similar programmes were established (generally at a smaller scale) in the United Kingdom and, later on, in many additional countries including Australia, Canada, New Zealand and the United States.[31] The level of government support provided, however, varies markedly across countries. For example, in Canada and New Zealand, school travel plans are generally implemented by nonprofit organizations with very limited support from provincial and national governments (see Chapter 14).

Fyhri et al.[32] conducted a comparative assessment of policies specifically related to children's active transportation in Denmark, Finland, Norway and the United Kingdom. In all of these countries, existing policies focussed almost exclusively on safety from traffic. For example, all four countries offered educational programmes to teach students how to behave in traffic and free public transport to the nearest school (based on varying distance thresholds). Interestingly, a systematic review of randomized controlled trials found no evidence that road safety education programmes actually improve safety outcomes.[33] According to Roberts and Edwards,[34] these 'feel-good' programmes are popular because they are relatively inexpensive and innocuous, and they do not challenge the prevailing automobility paradigm. They further argue that: '*The main function of road safety education is ideological. It tells children and their parents that traffic is here to stay and that unless they get out of the way they could die. The car makers worship road safety education, particularly for children in Africa and other rapidly motorizing regions. It tells the children to get out of the way*'.[34]

In the absence of a genuine commitment to a Vision Zero approach, these programmes often provide a convenient way to blame the victims when road crashes occur rather than the system that often fails to provide safe conditions for vulnerable road users (for example, by failing to properly separate pedestrians and cyclists from fast moving traffic). A detailed case study on the death of a 10-year-old pedestrian in New Zealand reported by Roberts and Coggan[35] demonstrated how easy and convenient it is to accuse road crash victims of 'jaywalking'—an offense actually invented by the car industry![34,36,37] The official record notes that the pedestrian ran across the street into the path of a van. The driver maintained that she was driving at 40 km/hour but did not have time to stop. It was *assumed* that the young girl did not look before crossing the street. Traffic analysis revealed, however, that although the road had a speed limit of 50 km/hour, approximately 86% of vehicles exceeded the limit and the likelihood of a vehicle travelling at 40 km/hour was below 1%. Ultimately, the evidence from the traffic analysis was disregarded.[35]

In an issue of the Smithsonian magazine, Thompson[37] reminds us of the carnage caused by cars in the days of Henry Ford and outlines the process by which society came to accept that road accidents involving pedestrians were typically the fault of pedestrians themselves. According to Thompson, '*By 1925, auto accidents accounted for two-thirds of the entire death toll in cities with populations over 25,000. An outcry arose, aimed squarely at drivers. The public regarded them as murderers*'. He then notes that car sales declined by 12% between 1923 and 1924 and that in response, the car industry worked to shift the blame for accidents to pedestrians by inventing the concept of 'jaywalking'. Effectively, this portrayed people who dared to venture in the streets on foot as careless and irresponsible. The car lobby quickly gained the support of newspapers, leading politicians to create the jaywalking offence through legislation.[37] Over time, this idea became so ingrained that we now frequently disregard the importance of the relationships between road design, exposure to traffic and road crashes involving (jaywalking) children.[35,38,39] This may explain the emphasis and popularity of today's innocuous road safety campaigns aimed at changing children's behaviour despite the lack of evidence of effectiveness.

Bearing this in mind, many scholars now argue in favour of a shift from the current automobility paradigm to one based on accessibility (see Chapter 17), combined with a more systematic approach to speed limits and traffic calming (see Chapter 16). Such a comprehensive approach holds promise for preventing road injuries and increasing active transportation and physical activity, particularly among children. Achieving such a paradigm shift, however, will require strong, long-term and coordinated effort from all levels of government.

Nevertheless, several examples of successful efforts by national governments are identifiable. For example, the policy comparison discussed earlier[32] highlighted an initiative of the British government that provides funding to schools to implement school travel plans and walking school buses (see Chapters 14 and 15 for more details on these initiatives). Similar programmes exist in Scandinavian countries, although financial support usually comes from local or regional authorities. In Denmark, the Road Traffic Act was amended in the 1970s to require police and road administrations to protect children from vehicles on their school journeys.[40] Furthermore, municipalities must provide free school travel for young children living more than 2.5 km away from their schools, as well as for teenagers living more than 6–7 km away. Finally, the Ministry of Justice also requires that children who have a hazardous route be granted free transportation. Given that local authorities pay for school travel, this creates an incentive for them to address road hazards in order to reduce expenses associated with bussing.[40] Similarly, Finnish law requires municipalities to provide free school transportation for students living over 5 km away from their school, although some municipalities such as Helsinki use smaller thresholds.[41]

Japan provides a compelling example of how a national government can set the agenda for promoting active transportation for children and youth. The School Education Act, which established compulsory education in 1947, requires that the distance to elementary and junior high schools be no more than 4 and 6 km, respectively.[42] In practice, most children travel much smaller distances, particularly in urban areas. This may result from the combination of dense school networks with a national policy that requires municipal boards of education to determine which schools children attend based on distance. In addition, it must be noted that Japan has a very strong public school system, a very low crime rate and a good safety record in general. Some sources report that up to 98% of Japanese children engage in active transportation to school.[42]

11.3.2 Regional Policies (e.g., Provincial, State, etc.)

To our knowledge, most of the literature examining the relationship between state policies and children's active transportation stems from the United States.[a] Chriqui et al.,[43] for example, explored the relationship between state laws that relate to active transportation and policies and practices among elementary schools in the United States. Overall, 81% of states had a policy requiring low-speed zones around schools. In contrast, policies that required the presence of crossing guards (9.8%), sidewalks (22.2%) or traffic control measures (38.6%) were much less common. Within states that required crossing guards or traffic control measures, surveyed school principals were substantially less likely to express concerns about these aspects.[43] In addition, Turner et al.[44] reported that schools in the United States were almost three times more likely to have a walking school bus programme if there was a state law requiring crossing guards around schools.

Overall, these examples suggest that when upper levels of government commit to policies favouring children's active transportation, the likelihood of supportive actions by lower-level institutions is increased. The existence of such a pattern is supported by a qualitative study involving stakeholders from multiple states designed to explore the factors associated with implementation of active transportation initiatives in schools.[45] Overall, participants emphasized that in order for school active transportation policies to be adopted and enforced, there is a need for: (1) strong collaboration between school personnel, public safety officials, parent and school district representatives; and (2) consideration of other state and local policies that might influence the effectiveness of new measures (e.g., bus time, school start time and choice policies). Participants also emphasized the importance of addressing issues related to personal safety and safety from traffic (e.g., low-speed zones, school drop-off policies and the promotion of safe routes). Finally, stakeholders highlighted the importance of considering the variety of facilitators and deterrents to active transportation such as existing infrastructure, provision of crossing guards and geographic factors.[45]

[a] It is worth noting that some countries do not have state or provincial governments. Finland is a good example as illustrated in Section 11.5.

In Canada, as part of a provincial active transportation strategy, the Ontario Ministry of Education recently announced that local stakeholders will be eligible to apply for up to CAD $100,000 for active school travel projects. This initiative strongly resembles the one from Great Britain described above but is being implemented at the provincial level. This appears promising given that a recent qualitative study examining stakeholders' perceptions of the Canadian Active & Safe Routes to School programme revealed that insufficient funding was a major barrier to implementation of key items from local school travel plans.[46]

11.3.3 Local Policies

In countries such as Denmark, Finland, Norway and the United Kingdom, the responsibility for school journeys rests primarily at the local or regional level.[32] In Denmark, most municipalities implement their own initiatives to promote safe active transportation,[32,40] with the example of the city of Odense having gained particularly strong international recognition.[30,40] As discussed above, as a result of incentive-based legislation, it is particularly advantageous for Danish municipalities to invest in active transportation to reduce costs associated with school buses.

More generally, Danish municipalities have considerable scope to encourage children's active transportation through interventions such as infrastructure changes, campaigns to encourage active transportation and to discourage car travel, changes in school hours and management of car traffic at schools.[40] Many municipalities carry out school route studies that include surveys conducted with children and parents concerning topics such as route choice, road safety, perceived risk and travel mode choice. Based on such surveys and analyses of additional information such as crash data, municipalities may develop action plans to improve school routes, or even broader plans to increase local road safety for people of all ages.[40] In Odense, the third largest city in Denmark with a population of around 200,000 inhabitants, 104 safe routes to school projects that included changes to road infrastructure were implemented between 1986 and 1999. Likely as a result of the program's comprehensiveness, child pedestrian and cyclist casualties fell by more than 80% during this period.[30] Importantly, the Odense interventions also reduced the burden of road injuries for adults, indicating that cost–benefit analyses should not focus exclusively on benefits observed among children![40]

11.3.4 School Board Policies

At least in the North American context, school boards are responsible for offering school bus service to children and youth living beyond a certain distance from school. The distance threshold is frequently set at 1 mile (1.6 km), although it is often larger for secondary school students. In many cases, children who live even closer are allowed to ride the school bus provided that there is a 'hazard' (often a highway or major arterial) on their route to school.[43] The low distance thresholds adopted by school transportation authorities may contribute to creating a social norm with a similarly low bar for what is considered an acceptable walking distance. In contrast to the situation in

North America, it is very common for children in countries such as Denmark and Finland to walk or cycle distances far longer than 1 mile.[47–49]

School transportation is an expensive business.[50–52] For example, the estimated costs of school bus services were CAD $800 million/year in the province of Ontario alone in 2008.[50] Similarly, the estimated costs of subsidizing bus transportation in England are £1 billion/year.[52] To the extent that the use of school buses for medium to long distances replaces car travel, a large proportion of these expenses may be worthwhile. At the same time, reallocating some of the expenses incurred from bussing children over short, walkable distances might be considered intelligent public policy.[51] A relevant example of such an approach is provided by the Ottawa School Transportation Authority, which started an innovative walking school bus programme. Contrary to most walking school bus schemes which rely on volunteers, this programme pays walking school bus coordinators in an effort to enhance sustainability. The programme was offered in 13 primary schools within the City of Ottawa in 2017–18. More information about this programme and walking school buses in general is provided in Chapter 15.

An additional potential avenue to increasing children's active transportation is related to school choice policies. Briefly, school choice policies that allow large numbers of parents to select particular schools for their children can have unintended negative impacts on the proportion of children engaging in active transportation to/from school[53–55] and the associated exhaust gas emissions.[56] For example, Mandic et al.[53] reported that 46.5% of adolescents who enrolled in the closest school engaged in active transportation compared to 8.8% of those who were enrolled at schools farther away. Importantly, one of the key identified reasons why children and youth do not enrol in the closest school is because they select a private school or a school that offers a special programme, whether arts, sport or language related.[53,57]

Scholars have argued for the promotion of neighbourhood schools (i.e., making sure that there are easily accessible schools in all neighbourhoods) as a strategy for maximizing the number of children who can reasonably be expected to engage in active transportation.[58,59] When schools are centrally located within a neighbourhood, the average distance between home and school is minimized, thereby increasing the likelihood of active transportation.[58] However, the promotion of neighbourhood schools would require substantial changes from current policies related to land use (e.g., those that have encouraged urban sprawl) and transportation planning in general.[59,60] For instance, new schools are typically built on the outskirts of cities were land is cheaper, and this trend has been exacerbated by policies requiring minimum acreage for schools.[61,62] Furthermore, in the last few decades, policies favouring the establishment of larger schools have led to the closure of many small neighbourhood schools. This has led to increases in average distances between homes and schools, a situation that evidently favours the choice of car and bus travel over active transportation. The neighbourhood schools model would, therefore, require especially strong collaboration between policymakers, school officials, urban planners and transportation engineers.

In contrast to the situation in North America, countries such as Denmark and Japan have maintained a decentralized network of small schools. As a result, most students live within a walkable distance of their school. Combined with a positive social norm and strong initiatives to improve road safety, this helps explain the high prevalence of active transportation among children.[40,42,63] Furthermore, the habit of walking and cycling may carry over into adulthood,[64] thus contributing to the reported differences between countries in overall rates of active transportation.[1,2,4,5]

11.4 Policy Case Study: Helsinki Versus Ottawa and the Importance of Political Context

In our experience, decision makers in North American cities often make statements such as 'we are not Amsterdam or Copenhagen' (e.g., our cities are too spread out, too cold, too hilly, etc. for active transportation to be popular) in an attempt to dismiss bolder proposals to invest in active transportation.[b] Research comparing the cities of Helsinki, Finland, and Ottawa, Canada, supports the position that the strength of political commitment is arguably more important in determining rates of active transportation.

Although Helsinki and Ottawa are very similar with respect to factors such as climate, topography, population density and car ownership, a recent case study indicated that Helsinki has managed to achieve a very high overall rate of noncar transportation (65%) relative to Ottawa (31%). Meanwhile, an international study of primary school children including both cities found that 79.2% of children in the Helsinki region walked or cycled to school compared to 34.9% in Ottawa.[65] Furthermore, 35 times more children cycled to school in the Finnish capital compared to Ottawa (24.4 vs. 0.7%)![66]

These disparities may logically be considered attributable to Helsinki's much stronger level of political commitment to active transportation as made evident by its much more extensive infrastructure for walking (87.5 km of pedestrianized streets vs. 1 km in Ottawa), cycling (3000 km of multiuse paths vs. 600 km in Ottawa) and public transit (271 km of rapid transit routes vs. 46 km in Ottawa).[c]

According to the case study research, Helsinki's stronger political commitment has been facilitated by factors related to land use, transportation planning and political systems.[65] With respect to land use, Helsinki has several advantages relative to Ottawa including city ownership of more than 60% of the land within its borders. In terms of transportation planning, Ottawa has embraced an automobile-focused approach (generally dominant within North America) to a much greater extent. Finally, Finland's generally more egalitarian political traditions, two-tiered system of government (featuring municipal and federal levels but no provincial level) and municipal electoral system (with representation according to political parties rather than geographically defined wards) appeared to facilitate the availability of much larger amounts of revenue and to result in less political conflict related to active transportation spending at the municipal level.

[b] For example, see the comments of the Mayor of Ottawa in the following article: http://ottawacitizen.com/news/local-news/no-car-culture-in-ottawa-mayor-says.

[c] More information about these elements are available in Ref. 55.

Taken together, these findings suggest that success in active transportation among children and adults may be more attributable to the strength of political commitment rather than to contextual characteristics (e.g., climate, topography and population density) often used to excuse poor active transportation performance.

11.5 Conclusion

This chapter summarized recent calls to action from various international organizations for the implementation of policies to encourage active transportation and discussed the influence of policies on children's travel behaviours. With some exceptions, few countries have strong national policies aiming to increase active transportation apart from pedestrian safety education schemes. However, many examples of proactive policies implemented by state and municipal authorities are evident. Bearing all of the reviewed evidence in mind, the policies that show the most promise are those that target the distance between home and school and those that aim to make the built environment safer for children to walk or cycle to school. The countries that have a higher prevalence of active transportation (e.g., Japan and Scandinavian countries) tend to have stronger policies supporting walking and cycling. Finally, it would appear that emphasizing only policies that encourage the choice of active transportation (i.e., 'making the healthy choice the easy choice') without explicitly working to discourage automobile travel appears unlikely to create major changes in children's travel behaviour. Ultimately, using a combination of carrots and sticks appears necessary.

11.6 Recommendations for Policy and Practice

1. Support the implementation of Health in All Policies approaches and assess their effectiveness in the context of children's active transportation. Most previous evaluations of health and economic benefits of sustainable transportation investments have focussed on adults.[22,67,68]
2. As emphasized in a recent position statement of the European Academy of Paediatrics, implement Vision Zero policies.[69]
3. When considering the potential benefits of implementing policies to promote children's active transportation, policymakers and economists should consider that adults can also benefit from such investments.[70]
4. Reduce economic inequalities in access to funding for active transportation interventions of the type highlighted in previous North American research.[46,71]

11.7 Recommendations for Research

1. Conduct more research examining the effectiveness of policies intended to increase children's active transportation. Evidence of effectiveness could then be used to support broader policy implementation.

2. Encourage collaboration between researchers and local stakeholders in order to evaluate the economic benefits of active transportation interventions and to disseminate the results to policymakers.
3. Conduct research to determine the most promising policies for increasing children's active transportation beyond school-related trips.

References

1. Pucher J. Urban travel behaviour as the outcome of public policy: the example of modal-split in Western Europe and North America. *J Am Plann Assoc* 1988;**54**(4):509–20.
2. Buehler R, Pucher J, Kunert U. *Making transportation sustainable: insights from Germany.* Washington, DC: The Brookings Institution, Metropolitan Policy Program; 2009.
3. Dill J. Bicycling for transportation and health: the role of infrastructure. *J Public Health Pol* 2009;**30**:S95–110.
4. Pucher J, Buehler R. Making cycling irresistible: lessons from The Netherlands, Denmark, and Germany. *Transp Rev* 2008;**28**(4):495–528.
5. Winters M, Buehler R, Götschi T. Policies to promote active travel: evidence from reviews of the literature. *Curr Envir Health Rep* 2017;**4**(3):278–85.
6. Banister D. *Unsustainable transport: city transport in the new century.* New York, NY: Routledge, Taylor and Francis Group; 2005.
7. Newman P, Kenworthy J. *Sustainability and cities: overcoming automobile dependence.* Washington, DC: Island Press; 1999.
8. Schiller PL, Bruun E, Kenworthy JR. *An introduction to sustainable transportation: policy, planning and implementation.* London, UK: Earthscan; 2010.
9. World Health Organization. *Ottawa charter for health promotion.* Geneva, Switzerland: World Health Organization; 1986. Available from: http://www.euro.who.int/__data/assets/pdf_file/0004/129532/Ottawa_Charter.pdf.
10. United Nations. *Political declaration of the high-level meeting of the general assembly on the prevention and control of non-communicable diseases.* New York, NY: United Nations; 2011. Available from: http://www.who.int/nmh/events/un_ncd_summit2011/political_declaration_en.pdf.
11. United Nations. *Convention on the rights of the child.* New York, NY: United Nations; 1989. Available from: http://www.ohchr.org/EN/ProfessionalInterest/Pages/CRC.aspx.
12. Ståhl T, Wismar M, Ollila E, Lahtinen E, Leppo K. *Health in all policies: prospects and potentials.* Helsinki, Finland: Ministry of Social Affairs and Health; 2006. Available from: http://medicine.englishcatania.com/10%20health_in_all_policies.pdf.
13. International Society for Physical Activity, Health. *The Toronto charter for physical activity: a global call for action.* Toronto, ON: International Society for Physical Activity and Health; 2010. Available from: http://www.interamericanheart.org/images/PHYSICALACTIVITY/TorontoCharterPhysicalActivityENG.pdf.
14. International Society for Physical Activity and Health. *The Bangkok declaration on physical activity for global health and sustainable development.* Bangkok, Thailand: International Society for Physical Activity and Health; 2016. Available from: https://static1.squarespace.com/static/559a3ff1e4b0b0193b9d9862/t/5843cdfbe3df28eae5f43c10/1480838663699/BKK_Declaration+FINAL+Dec2.pdf.
15. Tingvall C. The Swedish 'Vision Zero' and how parliamentary approval was obtained. Paper presented at the road safety research, policing, education conference. 16–17 November 1998, Wellington, New Zealand.

16. Tingvall C., Haworth N. Vision Zero - an ethical approach to safety and mobility. Paper presented to the 6th ITE International Conference Road Safety & Traffic Enforcement: Beyond 2000, Melbourne, 6–7 September 1999. Available from: http://avr.lu/wp-content/uploads/2015/12/Microsoft_Word___Vision_Zero_706.pdf.
17. United Nations. *Transforming our world: the 2030 agenda for sustainable development.* New York, NY: United Nations; 2015. Available from: https://sustainabledevelopment.un.org/content/documents/21252030%20Agenda%20for%20Sustainable%20Development%20web.pdf.
18. United States Department of Health and Human Services. *Step it up! The surgeon General's call to action to promote walking and walkable communities.* Washington, DC: United States Department of Health and Human Services, Office of the Surgeon General; 2015. Available from: https://www.surgeongeneral.gov/library/calls/walking-and-walkable-communities/call-to-action-walking-and-walkable-communites.pdf.
19. World Health Organization. *Global strategy on diet, physical activity and health.* Geneva, Switzerland: World Health Organization; 2004. Available from: http://www.who.int/dietphysicalactivity/strategy/eb11344/strategy_english_web.pdf.
20. World Health Organization. *Global recommendations on physical activity for health.* Geneva, Switzerland: World Health Organization; 2010. Available from: http://apps.who.int/iris/bitstream/handle/10665/44399/9789241599979_eng.pdf;jsessionid=726BA4FCA8131D7350735F26EBDFEA6F?sequence=1.
21. World Health Organization. *Decade of action for road safety 2011-2020.* Geneva, Switzerland: World Health Organization; 2010. Available from: http://www.who.int/violence_injury_prevention/publications/road_traffic/saving_millions_lives_en.pdf.
22. Kahlmeier S, Racioppi F, Cavill N, Rutter H, Oja P. "Health in all policies" in practice: guidance and tools to quantifying the health effects of cycling and walking. *J Phys Act Health* 2010;**7**(Suppl. 1):S120–5.
23. Puska P, Ståhl T. Health in all policies – the finnish initiative: background, principles, and current issues. *Annu Rev Public Health* 2010;**31**:315–28.
24. Johansson R. Vision Zero – implementing a policy for traffic safety. *Saf Sci* 2009;**47**(6): 826–31.
25. Faulkner GEJ, Richichi V, Buliung RN, Fusco C, Moola F. What's "quickest and easiest?": parental decision making about school travel mode. *Int J Behav Nutr Phys Act* 2010; **7**:62. Available from: http://ijbnpa.biomedcentral.com/articles/10.1186/1479-5868-7-62.
26. Lee C, Zhu X, Yoon J, Varni JW. Beyond distance: children's school travel mode choice. *Ann Behav Med* 2013;**45**(Suppl. 1):S55–67.
27. McDonald NC, Aalborg AE. Why parents drive children to school: implications for safe routes to school programs. *J Am Plann Assoc* 2009;**3**:331–42.
28. Petrunoff N, Rissel C, Wen LM, Martin J. Carrots and sticks vs carrots: comparing approaches to workplace travel plans using disincentives for driving and incentives for active travel. *J Transp Health* 2015;**2**(4):563–7.
29. Petrunoff N, Rissel C, Wen LM. If you don't do parking management... forget your behavior change, it's not going to work.": health and transport practitioner perspectives on workplace active travel promotion. *PLoS One* 2017;**12**(1):e0170064. Available from: http://journals.plos.org/plosone/article?id=10.1371/journal.pone.0170064.
30. Appleyard BS. Planning safe routes to school. *Planning* 2003;**69**(5):34–7.
31. Green Communities Canada. *Review of international school travel planning best practices.* Peterborough, ON: Green Communities Canada; 2007. Available from: http://smartcommute.ca/wp-content/uploads/2016/03/Review-of-International-School-Travel-Planning-Best-Practices.pdf.

32. Fyhri A, Hjorthol R, Mackett RL, Fotel TN, Kyttä M. Children's active travel and independent mobility in four countries: development, social contributing trends and measures. *Transp Pol* 2011;**18**(5):703–10.
33. Duperrex O, Bunn F, Roberts I. Safety education of pedestrians for injury prevention: a systematic review of randomised controlled trials. *BMJ* 2002;**324**:1129.
34. Roberts I, Edwards P. *The energy glut: the politics of fatness in an overheating world.* London, UK: Zed Books; 2010.
35. Roberts I, Coggan C. Blaming children for child pedestrian injuries. *Soc Sci Med* 1994;**38**:749–53.
36. Sallis JF. Are sidewalks for pedestrians? *America Walks* June 2017. Available from: http://americawalks.org/are-sidewalks-for-pedestrians/.
37. Thompson C. When pedestrians ruled the street. *Smithsonian Magazine* December 2014. Available from: https://www.smithsonianmag.com/innovation/when-pedestrians-ruled-streets-180953396/.
38. Hillman M, Adams J, Whitelegg J. *One false move... a study of children's independent mobility.* London, UK: Policy Studies Institute; 1990. Available from: http://john-adams.co.uk/wp-content/uploads/2007/11/one%20false%20move.pdf.
39. Parusel S, McLaren AT. Cars before kids: automobility and the illusion of school traffic safety. *Can Rev Sociol* 2010;**47**(2):129–47.
40. Jensen SU. How to obtain a healthy journey to school. *Transp Res Part A* 2008;**42**(3):475–86.
41. Broberg A, Sarjala S. School travel mode choice and the characteristics of the urban built environment: the case of Helsinki, Finland. *Transp Pol* 2015;**37**:1–10.
42. Mori N, Armada F, Willcox C. Walking to school in Japan and childhood obesity prevention: new lessons from an old policy. *Am J Public Health* 2012;**102**(11):2068–73.
43. Chriqui JF, Taber DR, Slater SJ, et al. The impact of state safe routes to school-related laws on active travel to school policies and practices in U.S. elementary schools. *Health Place* 2012;**18**:8–15.
44. Turner L, Chriqui JF, Chaloupka FJ. Walking school bus programs in U.S. public elementary schools. *J Phys Act Health* 2013;**10**(5):641–5.
45. Eyler AA, Brownson RC, Doescher MP, et al. Policies related to active transport to and from school: a multisite case study. *Health Educ Res* 2008;**23**:963–75.
46. Mammen G, Stone MR, Buliung N, Faulkner G. School travel planning in Canada: identifying child, family, and school-level characteristics associated with travel mode shift from driving to active school travel. *J Transp Health* 2014;**1**(4):288–94.
47. Christiansen LB, Toftager M, Schipperijn J, et al. School site walkability and active school transport – association, mediation and moderation. *J Transp Geogr* 2014;**34**:7–15.
48. Tammelin TH, Aira A, Hakamäki M, et al. Results from Finland's 2016 report card on physical activity for children and youth. *J Phys Act Health* 2016;**13**(Suppl. 2):S157–64. Available from: https://journals.humankinetics.com/doi/pdf/10.1123/jpah.2016-0297.
49. Tremblay MS, Barnes JD, González SA, et al. Global matrix 2.0: report card grades on the physical activity of children and youth comparing 38 countries. *J Phys Act Health* 2016;**13**(11 Suppl. 2):S343–66.
50. Green Communities Canada. *Saving money and tie with active school travel.* Peterborough, ON: Green Communities Canada; 2010. Available from: http://www.playbrucegrey.com/public_docs/documents/Saving_Money_and_Time_with_AT.pdf.
51. McDonald NC, Steiner RL, Palmer M, Bullock AN, Sisiopiku VP, Lytle BF. Costs of school transportation: quantifying the fiscal impacts of encouraging walking and bicycling for school travel. *Transportation* 2016;**43**(1):159–75.

52. Van Ristell JA, Quddus MA, Enoch MP, Wang C, Hardy P. Quantifying the impacts of subsidy policies on home-to-school pupil travel by bus in England. *Transportation* 2015;**42**(1):45–69.
53. Mandic S, Sandretto S, Bengoechea EG, et al. Enrolling in the closest school or not? Implications of school choice decisions for active transport to school. *J Transp Health* 2017;**6**:347–57.
54. Wilson EJ, Marshall J, Wilson R, Krizek KJ. By foot, bus or car: children's school travel and school choice policy. *Env Plann A* 2010;**42**(9):2168–85.
55. Yang Y, Abbott S, Schlossberg M. The influence of school choice policy on active school commuting: a case study of middle-sized school district in Oregon. *Env Plann A* 2012;**44**(8):1856–74.
56. Marshall JD, Wilson RD, Meyer KL, et al. Vehicle emissions during children's school commuting: impacts of education policy. *Env Sci Technol* 2010;**44**(5):1537–43.
57. Torres J, Lewis P. Proximité et transport actif. Le cas des déplacements entre l'école et la maison à Montréal et à Trois-Rivières. *Env Urbain* 2010;**4**:1–15. Available from: https://www.erudit.org/en/journals/eue/2010-v4-eue3952/044884ar/abstract/.
58. Kim HJ, Lee C. Does a more centrally located school promote walking to school? Spatial centrality in school-neighborhood settings. *J Phys Act Health* 2016;**13**(5):481–7.
59. McDonald NC. Children's mode choice for the school trip: the role of distance and school location in walking to school. *Transportation* 2008;**35**(1):23–35.
60. Ewing R, Schroeer W, Greene W. School location and student travel analysis of factors affecting mode choice. *Transp Res Rec* 2004;**1895**:55–63.
61. Council of Educational Facility Planners International. *Guide for planning educational facilities*. Scottsdale, AZ: Council of Educational Facility Planners International; 1991. Available from: http://eric.ed.gov/?id=ED344336.
62. Council of Educational Facility Planners, International & U.S. Environmental Protection Agency. *Schools for successful communities: an element of smart growth planning*. Scottsdale, AZ: Council of Education Facility Planners International; 2004. Available from: https://www.epa.gov/sites/production/files/2014-02/documents/smartgrowth_schools_pub.pdf.
63. Larsen LR, Troelsen J, Kirkegaard KL, et al. Results from Denmark's 2016 report card on physical activity for children and youth. *J Phys Act Health* 2016;**13**(Suppl.2):S137–42.
64. Yang X, Telama R, Hirvensalo M, Tammelin T, Viikari JSA, Raitakari OT. Active commuting from youth to adulthood and as a predictor of physical activity in early midlife: the young finns study. *Prev Med* 2014;**59**:5–11.
65. Saidla K. *Political challenges and active transportation: a comparison of Helsinki, Finland and Ottawa, Canada* [Doctoral dissertation] Ottawa, ON: University of Ottawa; 2017. Available from: https://ruor.uottawa.ca/bitstream/10393/37043/1/Saidla_Karl_2017_thesis.pdf.
66. Larouche R, Sarmiento OL, Broyles ST, Denstel KD, Katzmarzyk PT, Church TS, for the ISCOLE Research Group, et al. Are the correlates of active school transport context-specific? *Int J Obes Suppl* 2015;**5**:S89–99.
67. Andersen LB, Riiser A, Rutter H, Goenka S, Nordengen S, Solbraa AK. Trends in cycling and cycle related injuries and a calculation of prevented morbidity and mortality. *J Transp Health* 2018 (In Press, see: https://www.sciencedirect.com/science/article/pii/S2214140517306291?platform=hootsuite#!).
68. Mueller N, Rojas-Rueda D, Cole-Hunter T, et al. Health impact assessment of active transportation: a systematic review. *Prev Med* 2015;**76**:103–14.

69. Ludvigsson JF, Stiris T, del Torso S, Mercier J-C, Valiulis A, Hadjipanayis A. European Academy of Paediatrics Statement: Vision zero for child deaths in traffic accidents. *Eur J Pediatr* 2017;**176**:291–2.
70. Watson M, Dannenberg A. Investment in safe routes to school projects: public health benefits for the larger community. *Prev Chron Dis* 2008;**5**(3):A90.
71. Atteberry H, Dowdy D, Oluyomi A, Nichols D, Ory MG, Hoelscher DM. A contextual look at safe routes to school implementation in Texas. *Env Behav* 2016;**48**(1):192–209.

Prevalence and Correlates of Active Transportation in Developing Countries

12

Adewale L. Oyeyemi[1], *Richard Larouche*[2]
[1]College of Medical Sciences, University of Maiduguri, Maiduguri, Nigeria; [2]Faculty of Health Sciences, University of Lethbridge, Lethbridge, AB, Canada

An advanced city is not a place where the poor move about in cars, rather it's where even the rich use public transportation

Enrique Peñalosa (Mayor of Bogotá, Colombia)

Chapter Outline

12.1 Introduction

Previous chapters highlighted the prevalence and correlates of active transportation, but the focus was predominantly on high-income countries where most of the research on this topic has been conducted. Yet, the majority of children under the age of 15 years live in developing countries, and research suggests that about 80% of youths worldwide are insufficiently active.[1,2] Although the population of developing countries is relatively young, most deaths from communicable and noncommunicable diseases (NCDs) occur in developing countries.[3] This highlights the importance of targeting physical inactivity—one of the key risk factors for NCDs—in developing countries.[4]

For many children in developing countries, active transportation remains a necessity and not a choice as is mostly the case in high-income countries where a range

Children's Active Transportation. https://doi.org/10.1016/B978-0-12-811931-0.00012-0

of travel modes are accessible.[5–7] Comparatively, access to motorized transportation may be limited in developing countries, especially in rural areas, so children may have little choice than to travel by nonmotorized means. Also, the types of destinations and the purpose of travelling may be different for children in developing countries compared to high-income countries. For example, while school may be a ubiquitous destination for children to travel in high-income countries, many youth in developing countries may not attend school.[8] Further, many children in developing countries frequently walk long distances to other destinations including markets for trade, streams to fetch water and wash clothes, farms to work the field and forest to collect firewood.[9]

Since evidence from high-income countries may not apply to developing countries, understanding the prevalence and correlates of children's active transportation in developing countries could inform evidence-based strategies to improve current and future health of children in these countries. Also, understanding the correlates of children's active transportation that may be unique to developing countries may help inform culturally relevant interventions. This chapter introduces the physical activity transition model[10] and its application to travel behaviour and health in developing countries. It also summarizes recent research on the prevalence and correlates of active transportation in developing countries.

12.2 The Physical Activity Transition Model

Katzmarzyk and Mason[10] proposed the concept of the 'Physical Activity Transition' stemming from the epidemiological and nutrition transition to guide the understanding of changes in physical activity levels and their impacts on health in countries experiencing the most rapid economic development. The 'physical activity transition' model (Fig. 12.1) posits that as a country undergoes rapid economic growth and urbanization, there is a shift from a traditional lifestyle characterized by high energy expenditure to a modern Western lifestyle characterized by low energy expenditure. This shift is associated with deleterious health consequences including higher rates of obesity and NCDs. This shift is largely the result of lower occupational and domestic energy requirements, diminished use of active transportation and the dominance of sedentary behaviours during leisure-time.[10] According to the model, the shift is initially observed among the wealthier individuals within a country undergoing the physical activity transition,[11] but at a later stage of the transition, it affects entire populations.

In the current global context, the developing countries of sub-Saharan Africa and South Asia could be considered as experiencing the greatest shift in physical activity patterns because these are the regions of the world experiencing the greatest population growth, rapid economic transition and changes in urban environment.[1,12] In China, for example, increasing urbanization in the last 5 decades has led to a steady decline in the prevalence of physically demanding occupations like agriculture, fishing and forestry work, and a commensurate increase in the prevalence of less-demanding

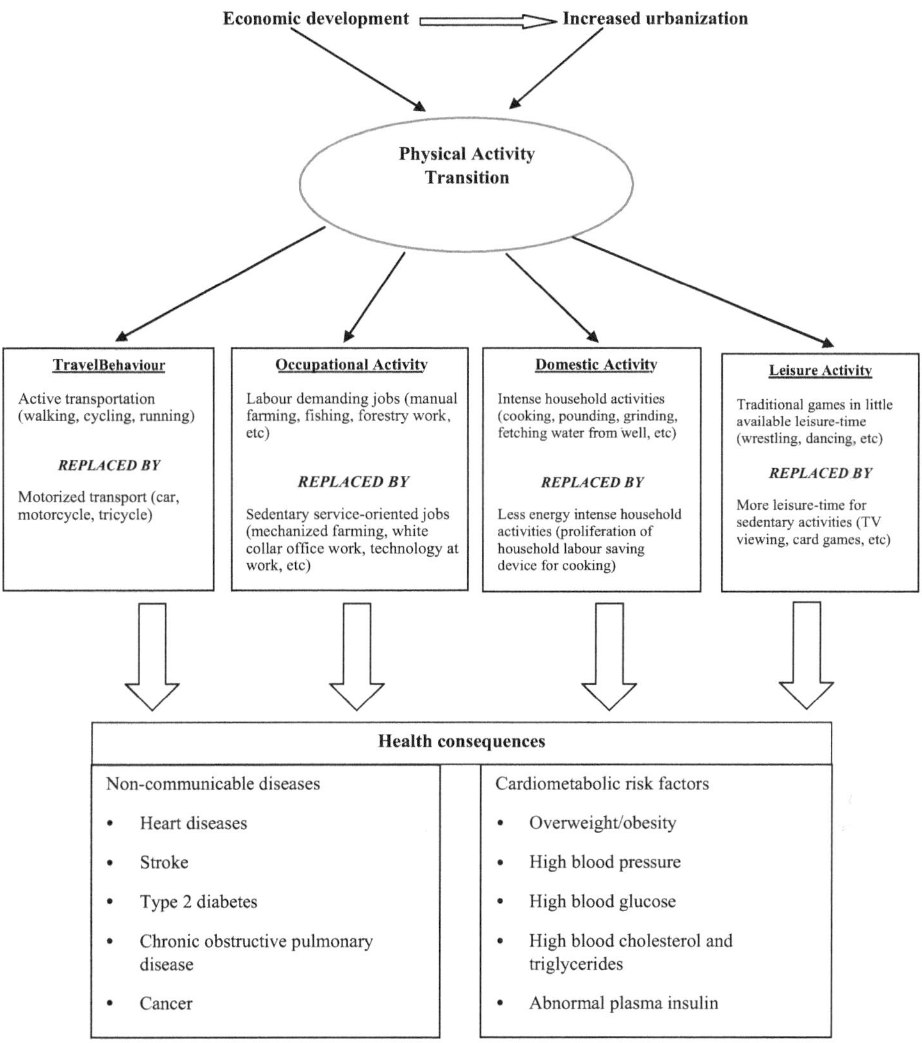

Figure 12.1 Physical activity transition model and health consequences in developing countries.

occupations like service-based jobs.[13] New technologies and labour-saving devices at the workplace and home have led to increasing sedentariness and are associated with large increases in the prevalence of obesity in the Chinese population.[12,14] In Western Africa, there is evidence that rapid urbanization and technological advancement have led to a change to high-calorie westernized diets and reduced physical activity levels with accompanying increases in the prevalence of childhood and adult overweight and obesity.[15]

12.3 Application of the Physical Activity Transition Model to Travel Behaviour in Developing Countries

Analyses of differences between urban and rural regions of developing countries suggest that the physical activity transition has a large impact on individuals' travel behaviour.[10] In Cameroon, for example, Sobnqwi et al.[16] observed that the disparity in total energy expenditure between urban- and rural-dwelling adults was due to the remarkably higher time spent in active transportation and to more physically demanding occupations among rural residents than their urban counterparts. Furthermore, the urban residents were 5 times more likely to be obese and 1.5 to 2 times more likely to be diabetic and hypertensive than the rural residents.[16] Similarly, a meta-analysis by Abubakari et al.[17] indicated that urban residents in West Africa were twice as likely as their rural counterparts to be physically inactive, and the prevalence of diabetes was significantly higher in urban adults (4.0%) than in rural adults (2.6%). Similar urban–rural differences in the prevalence of physical activity and NCDs risk factors have also been highlighted in the Indian population.[18] Rural Indian men and women, respectively, reported five times and seven times higher physical activity and active transportation levels compared with their urban and urban slum counterparts. The prevalence of obesity was the highest among urban (male=5.5%, female=12.6%) populations than their counterparts in urban slums (male=1.9%, female=7.2%) and rural areas (male=1.6%, female=3.8%).[18]

The physical activity transition model also has implications for the health behaviour of young people in developing countries. While the population prevalence of physical activity among youth is not improving in developing countries and globally,[4] there is evidence, for example in Africa, that the number of children who are overweight or obese has nearly doubled since 1990, increasing from 5.4 million to 10.3 million.[19] Furthermore, about 48% of the children under 5 years of age who are overweight now live in Asia and 25% in Africa.[20] The globalization of unhealthy diets and a decline in physical activity for transport and active play have been implicated as the major contributors to the rising rates of childhood obesity in urban areas of many developing countries of Asia and Africa.[21] This evidence supports the relevance of the 'physical activity transition' model for understanding the physical activity patterns, transport behaviours and health of children in developing countries.

12.4 Prevalence of Active Transportation of Children in Developing Countries

The Global School-based Student Health Survey. This survey developed by the World Health Organization examined health behaviours in 13- to 15-year-olds from predominantly low- and middle-income countries.[22] It included data on active transportation from a total sample of 72,845 adolescents from 34 countries that participated between 2003 and 2007. Adolescents were asked to report how often they walked or cycled to/from school during the past 7 days. They were classified as 'active travelers' if they reported at least one active trip, which as mentioned in Chapter 4, is a very liberal definition of active transportation.

There were large differences between countries in the prevalence of active transportation. Among girls, it ranged from 10.7% in the United Arab Emirates to 86.0% in China. Among boys, it ranged from 23.2% in the Cayman Islands to 83.2% in China. Across the 34 countries, the average prevalence of active transportation was significantly higher for boys (51.9%) than for girls (46.2). The key strength of this survey is that it used common methods across countries to assess active transportation; however, the data are somewhat dated. Motor vehicle ownership is increasing rapidly in many developing countries and this may, in turn, lead to a decrease in active transportation to/from school.

Because the prevalence of active transportation is likely to change rapidly as a result of the physical activity transition, we hereby review more recent studies. Similar to Chapter 4, we defined the prevalence of active transportation as the proportion of children reporting active transportation as their *usual travel mode* (mostly to and from school given the dearth of data on travel to other places). Consistent with data from the Global School-based Student Health Survey, we note that the prevalence of active transportation among children in the developing countries varies markedly between countries and World Health Organization regions. This variation may reflect differences in social norms, access to motorized vehicles, participants' age and the methods that were used to assess active transportation. Recent studies on the prevalence of active transportation in children at the country and regional level are summarized in Table 12.1.

In Africa, walking was the dominant mode of transportation to and from school. Its prevalence ranged from about 41% among Kenyan children aged 9–11 years in the Nairobi region[23] to about 81% among national samples of Zimbabwean and Ghanaian children.[24,25] Consistent with the physical activity transition model, prevalence estimates were generally lower in countries where data collection was only done in urban areas. There are few reports on the prevalence of bicycling among children in Africa. However, available studies suggest that the prevalence of bicycling to and from school ranged from 0.0% in Tanzania[26] to 7% in Ghana.[25] Interestingly, Onywera et al. reported that about 29% of rural Kenyan children ran to and from school,[27] a mode of transportation that is almost unheard of in other countries.

In Asia, there is large variation within and between countries in the prevalence of active transportation across studies. For example, the prevalence of active transportation to and from school among children aged 6–18 years in China varied from 32.3%[7]–69.3%.[28] The lowest prevalence was noted in a study that focussed on urban areas within the city of Tianjin, and the highest was observed in a national survey. In Thailand, the prevalence of active transportation to school among children aged 6–17 years was 51.2%[29]; however, 96.7% of children engaged in active transportation to/from community facilities.[30] Extremely large within-country variation in the prevalence of active transportation to and from school was noted in Indian children. While the prevalence was only 5.2% among 9- to 11-year-olds in the city of Bangalore,[7] it was 47.0% among 12- to 17-year-olds[31] in Hyderabad. Data from Malaysia indicate that 24.6% of children walked or cycled to/from school.[32] A study in Tehran (Iran) indicated that 43% of adolescents actively travelled to school and 49% actively travelled from school to home.[33] Similar to Africa, very few studies report on the rates of bicycling in Asian children. The available data suggest that 8.4%–10.1% of Chinese,[7,34] 6.4% of Malaysian[35] and 1.3%[7] of Indian children cycle to school.

Table 12.1 Prevalence of children's active transportation in developing countries

Country [reference]/Year data collected	Population/Age	Location	Prevalence (%)				Destination
			Walking	Running	Bicycling	Combined	
Africa							
Ghana [Ocansey et al.[25]]/2012	National/6–18 years	Urban + rural	74.0	–	7.0	81.0	To/from school
Kenya [Onywera et al.[27]]/2012	Subnational/5–17 years	Rural	58.0	29.0	–	87.0	To/from school
Kenya [Muthuri et al.[57]]/2012	Subnational/9–11 years	Urban	40.9	–	2.9	45.7	To/from school
Mozambique [Prista et al.[67]]/2015	National/9–13 years	Urban + rural	45.8	–	–	–	To/from school
Nigeria [Adeniyi et al.[68]]/2011	Subnational/5–18 years	Urban + rural	70.5	–	–	–	To/from school
South Africa [Uys et al.[45]]/2013	National/6–17 years	Urban + rural	63.0	–	–	–	To/from school
Tanzania [Malone and Rudner[51]]/2011	Subnational/7–15 years	Urban + sub-urban	62.5	–	–	–	To/from school
Tanzania [Bwire[26]]/2010	Subnational/7–15 years	Urban	48.0	–	0.0	48.0	To/from school
Zimbabwe [Manyanga et al.[24]]/2015	National/3–17 years	Urban + rural	80.8	–	–	–	To/from school
Asia							
China [Sarmiento et al.[7]]/2013	Subnational/9–11 years	Urban	22.2	–	10.1	32.3	To/from school
China [Liu et al.[34]]/2015	Subnational/6–18 years	Urban	32.7	–	8.4	41.0	To/from school
China [Yang et al.[28]]/2011	National/6–17 years	Urban + rural	-	–	–	69.3	To/from school
India [Sarmiento et al.[7]]/2013	Subnational/9–11 years	Urban	3.8		1.3	5.2	To/from school

India [Laxmaiah et al.[31]]/2007	Subnational/12–17 years	Urban	–	–	–	47.0	To/from school
Malaysia [Sharif et al.[32]]/2011	National/7–12 years	Urban + rural	18.2	6.4	–	24.6	To/from school
Thailand [Amornsriwatanakul et al.[30]]/2015	National/10–17 years	Urban + rural	–	–	–	96.7	To/from community facilities
Thailand [Amornsriwatanakul et al.[29]]/2015	National/6–17 years	Urban + rural	–	–	–	51.2	To/from school
Iran [Samimi and Ermagun][33]/2011	Subnational/12–17 years	Urban	–	–	–	46.0	To/from school
Americas							
Brazil [Nardo Jr et al.[37]]/2015	Subnational/7–12 years	Urban	–	–	–	64.0	To/from school
Brazil [Silva et al.[42]]/2011	Subnational/15–19 years	Urban + rural	–	–	–	51.8 61.6	To/from school To/from work
Brazil [Sarmiento et a[7]]/2013	Subnational/9–11 years	Urban	40.0	–	1.0	41.0	To/from school
Colombia [Gonzalez et al.[36]]/2015	National/11–18 years	Urban + rural	7.8	–	3.3	11.1	To/from school
Colombia [Sarmiento et al.[7]]/2013	Subnational/9–11 years	Urban	71.5	–	1.8	73.3	To/from school
Mexico [Galaviz et al.[39]]/2015	National/[3 years and older]	Urban + rural	54.8	–	1.6	56.4	To/from school
Mexico [Jáuregui et al.[40]]/2015	National/10–14 years	Urban + rural	68.8	–	2.0	70.8	To/from school
Venezuela [Herrera-Cuenca et al.[41]]/2009	Subnational/11–18 years	Urban	–	–	–	19.1	To/from school

Although most studies in the Americas (e.g., Central America, South America and Mexico) reported prevalence estimates between 40.0% and 70.0%, there are also some striking differences within and between countries. For example, while Sarmiento et al.[7] noted an active transportation prevalence of 73.3% among children aged 9–11 years in Bogotá (Colombia), a national study estimated that only 11.1% of 11- to 18-year-olds engage in active transportation.[36] In Brazil, the prevalence of active transportation varied between 41.0% and 68.0% across studies.[7,37,38] Similarly, national studies in Mexico indicated that 56.0% of children aged 3 years and above walked or bicycled to school,[39] whereas 71.0% of children aged 10–14 years did so.[40] These differences suggest that younger children are less likely to engage in active transportation. In contrast, a low prevalence of 19.1% was noted among Venezuelan children aged 11–18 years.[41] Compared to Asia and Africa, more studies reported on the prevalence of bicycling in the Americas (Table 12.1); although this may be an artefact of the relative paucity of research on bicycling conducted in Asia and Africa compared to the Americas. Indeed, the prevalence of bicycling in the Americas was low, ranging from 1.0% in Brazil[7] to 3.3% in Colombia.[36] These estimates are remarkably lower than those reported for children in the developed countries of Northern Europe (see Chapter 4 for details) despite the warmer weather.

Most studies in developing countries have focussed on school travel, reflecting the emphasis on this destination in most of the research on travel behaviour from developed countries. Larouche et al.[9] have highlighted the importance of advancing research on children's active travel in developing countries beyond trips to/from schools to other trips (i.e., to/from friends' and relatives' residence, shops, markets, water points [to collect household water], places of worship, parks and sport fields), which may represent important opportunities for physical activity and health. Data from Thailand notably suggest that active transportation to/from other destinations might be an important but largely overlooked source of physical activity.[30]

It is important to note that there is limited data on how travel behaviour of children in developing countries has changed over time. However, emerging evidence suggest that, in countries such as Brazil, China, South Africa and Vietnam, the prevalence of active transportation is declining and the use of motorized transportation is increasing, particularly in urban areas.[28,38,42–46] Of great concern, a national study by Yang et al. indicated a large decline in active transportation in China from 95.8% in 1997 to 69.3% in 2011.[28] Viewed another way, the proportion of children using motorized transportation has increased by over seven times in 14 years! In Ho Chi Minh City (Vietnam), the percentage of children who reported engaging in active transportation on at least 4 days per week declined remarkably from 27.8% in 2004 to 19.6% in 2009.[46] Data from the South Africa National Household Travel Survey show that the prevalence of active transportation declined from 76.0% to 63.0% between 2003 and 2013.[45] In Brazil, 10-year trends in school travel were examined in the states of São Paulo[38] and Santa Catarina[42] and changes were less dramatic than in China and Vietnam. In the state of São Paulo, the prevalence of active transportation declined from 70.0% to 61.0% in children and from 70.0% to 68.0% in adolescents.[38] In Santa Catarina, the prevalence declined from 56.3% to 51.3% among 15- to 19-year-olds. While this difference was not statistically significant, it is worth noting that the proportion of children travelling to school by car/motorcycle doubled within the same decade.[42] A small Kenyan study also illustrated that more parents used active transportation to and from school when they were young (rural = 99.0%; urban = 89.0%) compared to their children (rural = 87.0%; urban = 58.0%).[47] The authors point out that the dramatic change in active transportation across one generation, especially in urban areas, provide insight into the emerging physical activity transition in Kenya.[47] A similar pattern of decline in active transportation across generations has been reported in Nigeria.[48]

12.5 Correlates of Active Transportation in Developing Countries

While relatively few studies have examined the correlates of active transportation in developing countries, current evidence suggests that there is substantial urban–rural disparity in the prevalence of active transportation. As illustrated in Table 12.2, regardless of the country level of income, the prevalence of active transportation among children in developing countries was markedly higher in rural areas than in urban areas. For example, in Mexico, 82.7% of children who lived in rural areas engaged in active transportation compared with 65.5% of their urban counterparts.[40] Similarly, 78.6% of children whose family did not have access to a motor vehicle engaged in

Table 12.2 Urban–rural disparities in the prevalence of children's active transportation by country's income level in developing countries

	Prevalence (%)	
Income level [Reference]	**Urban areas**	**Rural areas**
Low-income countries		
Mozambique [Prista et al.[67]]	12.5	95.5
Zimbabwe [Manyanga et al.[24]]	78.0	88.0
Average	*45.3*	*91.8*
Lower middle-income countries		
Ghana [Ocansey et al.[25]]	64.0	85.0
India [Katapally et al.[69]]	47.0	75.0
Nigeria [Adeniyi et al.[68]]	61.0	80.0
Kenya [Onywera et al.[47]]	42.0	87.0
Average	*53.5*	*81.8*
Upper middle-income countries		
Brazil [Silva et al.[42]]	59.7	68.3
China [Cui et al.[44]]	77.6	89.2
Mexico [Jáuregui et al.[40]]	65.5	82.7
Average	*67.6*	*80.1*

active transportation compared with 58.5% of those who had access to a vehicle.[40] In South Africa, over 90% of adolescents in rural areas engaged in active transportation to and from school[49]; however, much lower rates of active transportation have been reported in urban regions.[50,51] In urban areas of Cape Town (South Africa) and Tianjin (China), children whose family had access to motorized vehicles were much less likely to report engaging in active transportation.[50] In urban areas of Nigeria, more than 70% of adolescents reported household ownership of one or more cars, and car ownership was associated with a lower rate of active transportation.[52] Generally, for urban children, rapid urbanization and economic prosperity seem to favour the use of motorized mode of transportation at the expense of active transportation to and from school.[40,42,52,53]

Based on available studies that compared urban and rural areas, on average, the prevalence of active transportation ranged from 45.3% in urban areas to 91.8% in rural areas in low-income countries. In lower middle-income countries, active transportation ranged from 53.5% in urban areas to 81.8% in rural areas. Similarly, the prevalence of active transportation ranged from 67.6% in urban areas to 80.1% in rural areas of upper middle-income countries. Although these averages should be interpreted with caution given that data was available for only a few countries and methods differed between studies, the aggregate data suggest that urban residence is an important negative correlate of children's active transportation in developing countries.

Fig. 12.2 provides a summary of active transportation by country levels of income. This figure was based on data from the 34 developing countries (low-income = 7, lower middle-income = 11, upper middle-income = 16) that participated in the Global

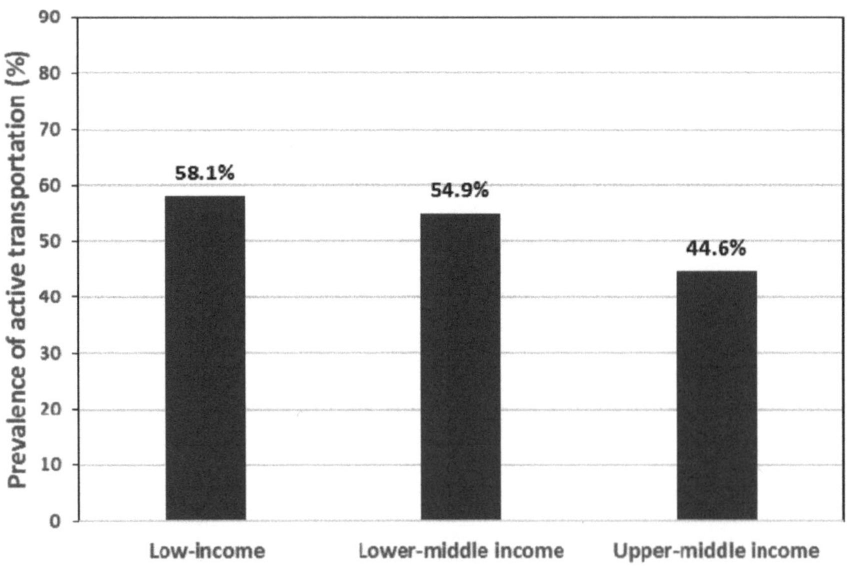

Figure 12.2 Prevalence of children's active transportation by World Bank country income status. Figure constructed from data presented by Guthold et al.[22]

School-based Student Health Survey.[22] The distribution of these data shows that prevalence of active transportation was highest in low-income countries (58.1%) and lowest in upper middle-income countries (44.6%). The data suggest that the prevalence of children's active transportation decreases as a country transitions from low-income (58.1%) to lower-middle income (54.9%), then seems to decline steeply as a country undergoes further economic development from lower middle income to upper middle income (44.6%). Although this difference should be interpreted cautiously given the small number of low-income countries, it appears that the transition from lower middle-income to upper middle-income levels is the most critical point for the decline in active transportation in developing countries. Increasing income at the country level is likely associated with concurrent changes in development and urbanization that lead to more motorized vehicle ownership and use with a corresponding decline in active transportation. These patterns provide important insights into the need for specific interventions to promote active transportation among children in countries experiencing the greatest shift in income levels.

In addition to country level income and urbanization, Table 12.3 shows that other correlates of children's travel behaviours in developing countries include demographic, biological, social, psychological and environmental factors. Cross-sectional studies have found that demographic factors such as higher age,[35,40] more siblings,[50] higher parental education[28,40,49] and higher family income and socioeconomic status[28,33,35,38,40,42,52] were associated with lower odds of children's active transportation in developing countries, although results are inconsistent for many of these potential correlates. While family income is expected to be associated with more access to motorized transportation, household motor vehicle ownership itself can favour motorized transportation in developing countries.[33,40,50,52] Attending a private school, which also reflects higher socioeconomic status, was associated with lower odds of active transportation in a Kenyan study.[23] In China, children in middle school were the most likely to engage in active transportation suggesting that the prevalence of active transportation might increase during childhood and then decrease during adolescence.[28] Higher body adiposity (overweight/obesity) was associated with reduced odds of active transportation among children in some studies,[7,40,52] while others found no associations.[54–56] Many studies indicate slightly higher rates of active transportation in boys,[22,46] although a study in Tehran (Iran) found the opposite.[33]

Regarding social and psychological factors, higher self-efficacy and social support have been identified in some studies as positive correlates of children's active transportation in developing countries.[4,50] For environmental factors, shorter distance or travel time,[28,33,40,46,50] absence of hills,[33] proximity of transit stops and pedestrian facilities,[57] access to destinations,[4,57,58] lower speed of traffic,[50] good lightning at night[57] and fewer cul-de-sac (dead end streets)[50,57] have been shown to be associated with active transportation in some studies. Of these factors, shorter distance or travel time has been consistently identified as an enabler of active transportation (Table 12.3). It should be noted that these correlates of active transportation may be country-specific, and there is no systematic review to confirm the

Table 12.3 Summary of studies on correlates of children's active transportation in developing countries

	Associated with active transportation			Not associated with active transportation		# Studies showing association	
	# Studies	References [# sample]	Association	# Studies	References [# sample]	+	–
Demographic, biological factors							
Age (older)	2	$35_{[1]}$, $40_{[1]}$	–	0			2/2
Gender (boy)	35	$22_{[34]}$, $46_{[1]}$	±	6	$50_{[6]}$	19/41[a]	6/41[a]
	1	$33_{[1]}$	–				
Siblings (more)	2	$50_{[2]}$	+	4	$50_{[4]}$	2/6	
Parent education (higher)	3	$28_{[1]}$, $40_{[1]}$, $49_{[1]}$	–	6	$50_{[6]}$		3/9
Family income and SES (higher)	7	$28_{[1]}$, $33_{[1]}$, $35_{[1]}$, $38_{[1]}$, $40_{[1]}$, $42_{[1]}$, $52_{[1]}$	–	0			7/7
Household motor vehicle (more)	5	$33_{[1]}$, $40_{[1]}$, $50_{[2]}$, $52_{[1]}$	–	4	$50_{[4]}$		5/9
Private school	1	$23_{[1]}$	+	0		1/1	
Higher adiposity (overweight/obesity	8	$7_{[6]}$, $40_{[1]}$, $52_{[1]}$	–	3	$54_{[1]}$, $55_{[1]}$, $56_{[1]}$		8/11
Social factors							
Social support (high)	3	$4_{[2]}$, $50_{[1]}$	+	5	$50_{[5]}$	3/8	
Psychological factors							
Self-efficacy (high)	2	$4_{[2]}$	+	5	$50_{[5]}$	2/8	1/8
	1	$50_{[1]}$	–				

Environmental factors							
Distance/travel time (shorter)	9	28[1], 33[1], 40[1], 46[1], 50[5]	+	1	50 [1]	9/10	
Hill (absence)	1	33 [1]	+	0		1/1	
Proximity of transit stop	1	57 [1]	+	6	50 [6], 58 [1]	1/8	
Pedestrian facilities	1	57 [1]	+	1	58 [1]	1/2	
Access to destinations	5	4 [3], 57 [1], 58 [1]	+	5	50 [5]	5/11	1/11
	1	50 [1]	−				
Good lightning at night	1	57 [1]	+	0		1/1	
Child safety concerns	1	57 [1]	+	0		1/1	
Lower speed of traffic	1	50 [1]	+	4	50 [1]	1/6	1/6
	1	50 [1]	−				
Cul-de-sac (fewer)	2	50 [1], 57 [1]	+	5	50 [5]	2/7	

SES, Socioeconomic status

Notes: [# sample] indicates number of sample in a cited study; + sign indicates positive associations (i.e., a variable is associated with higher odds of engaging in active transportation); – sign indicates negative associations (i.e., a variable is associated with lower odds of engaging in active transportation).

[a]For example, 19/41 studies showed that boys are more likely to engage in active transportation, 6/41 showed that girls are more likely to engage in active transportation and the remainder showed no association.

consistency of this evidence across developing countries. For example, Larouche et al.[50] in a multicountry study of low-, middle- and high-income countries found distinct country-specific patterns of correlates of children's active transportation. Nevertheless, the studies reviewed herein suggest that some correlates such as living in a rural area, lower household SES and car ownership, and shorter distance or travel time are rather consistently associated with active transportation in developing countries.

Independent mobility—children's freedom to move around in public space without adult supervision—is another important factor that influences active transportation among children in developing countries. Behrens and Muchaka[59] provide a detailed overview of how independent mobility varied considerably with age and between wealthy and poor households in South Africa. Children from poorer households were heavily reliant on walking (88.0% share of school trips) and were independently mobile at a relatively young age, for instance, 67.0% of 7-year-olds were allowed to travel from school alone. Conversely, South African children from wealthier households had much lower independent mobility (no 7-year-olds were allowed to travel from school alone) and were heavily reliant on cars (87.0% share of school trips).[59] Such patterns of high levels of independent mobility at an earlier age among children living in low-income urban environments have also been reported among participants from Tanzania, although independent mobility in Tanzanian children is higher than South African children.[51] Nevertheless, Bwire[26] reported that Tanzanian parents indicated that traffic danger, the perception that children are unreliable or too young, danger from adults, long distance to school and the opportunity for parents to spend time with their children and meet other people can lead them to escort their children to and from places. Also, the majority of parents indicated that they do not allow their children to go out after dark in order to keep them from 'evil things' and bad groups/thieves.[26]

12.6 Conclusions and Recommendations

This chapter shows that the prevalence and correlates of active transportation among children in developing countries varies widely. Consistent with the physical activity transition model, the prevalence of active transportation is generally much higher in rural areas than in urban areas. Additionally, there is consistent evidence that children from poorer families and those who live closer to their school are more likely to engage in active transportation. Although the evidence regarding correlates of active transportation remains limited, it seems that interventions targeting multiple levels of influence could help increase active transportation in developing countries, or at least prevent further declines in walking and cycling. As developing countries continue to urbanize, increasing physical activity through active transportation could prevent deleterious health consequences like obesity and NCDs, and achieve many co-benefits, including reducing transport-energy use and road traffic mortality, and associated air pollution.[60–62]

12.7 Recommendation for Policy and Practice

1. Given that many children in developing countries walk because they don't have access to any alternatives[5] and that developing countries face the lion's share of the burden of road traffic accidents,[63] there is an urgent need for implementing policies to make it safer for children to walk or cycle.[64]
2. Policymakers and practitioners should consider developing social-marketing campaigns to address the negative social norm associated with active transportation in developing countries. Active transportation and public transit should not be viewed as the way poor people get around.
3. Given the very high costs of building cities for cars,[62] policymakers in developing countries should sponsor research examining what could be done to prevent further declines in active transportation and develop relevant policies based on culturally relevant research findings.

12.8 Recommendations for Future Research

1. Most of the research on active transportation among children from developing countries has focussed on the trip to and from school, underscoring the need for examining active transportation to and from a broader range of destinations.
2. There is a clear need for more studies to examine the correlates of active transportation, especially factors from the broader levels of influence, including policies and the built and physical environment. Tools such as the Neighborhood Environment Walkability Scale for Africa have recently been developed to facilitate this research agenda.[65,66]
3. To provide stronger evidence on the correlates of active transportation, there is a need for longitudinal and intervention studies in developing countries.

References

1. United Nations, Department of Economic and Social Affairs, Population Division. World population prospects: the 2015 revision, key findings and advance Tables. Working Paper No. ESA/P/WP.241.
2. Hallal P, Andersen LB, Bull FC, Guthold R, Haskell W, Ekelund U, for the Lancet Physical Activity Series Working Group. Global physical activity levels: surveillance progress, pitfalls and prospects. *Lancet* 2012;**380**(9838):247–57. Available from: https://doi.org/10.1016/S0140-6736(12)60646-1.
3. World Health Organization. *Global status report on noncommunicable diseases 2014*. Geneva 2015. Available from: http://www.who.int/nmh/publications/ncd-status-report-2014/en/.
4. Sallis JF, Bull FC, Guthold R, Heath GW, Inoue S, Kelly P, et al. Progress in physical activity over the Olympic quadrennium. *Lancet* 2016;**388**(10051):1325–36.
5. Salvo D, Reis RS, Sarmiento OL, Pratt M. Overcoming the challenges of conducting physical activity and built environment research in Latin America: IPEN Latin America. *Prev Med* 2014;**69**:S86–92.
6. Tremblay MS, Barnes JD, González SA, Katzmarzyk PT, Onywera VO, Reilly JJ, et al. Global matrix 2.0: report card grades on the physical activity of children and youth comparing 38 countries. *J Phys Act Health* 2016;**13**(Suppl. 2):S343–66. Available from: https://doi.org/10.1123/jpah.2016-0594.

7. Sarmiento OL, Lemoine P, Gonzalez SA, Broyles ST, Denstel KD, Larouche R, et al. Relationships between active school transport and adiposity indicators in school-age children from low-, middle- and high-income countries. *Int J Obes Suppl* 2015;**5**:S107–14.
8. Population Reference Bureau. The world's youth 2013 data sheet. Available from: http://www.prb.org/Publications/Datasheets/2013/youth-datasheet-2013.aspx/.
9. Larouche R, Oyeyemi AL, Prista A, Onywera VO, Akinroye KK, Tremblay MS. A systematic review of active transportation research in Africa and the psychometric properties of measurement tools in children and youth. *Int J Behav Nutr Phys Act* 2014;**11**(129). Available from: http://ijbnpa.biomedcentral.com/articles/10.1186/s12966-014-0129-5.
10. Katzmarzyk PT, Mason C. The physical activity transition. *J Phys Act Health* 2009;**6**:269–80.
11. Broyles ST, Denstel KD, Church TS, Chaput J-P, Fogelholm M, Hu G, for the ISCOLE Research Group, et al. The epidemiological transition and the global childhood obesity epidemic. *Int J Obes Suppl* 2015;**5**(Suppl. 2):S3–8.
12. Popkin BM, Adair LS, Ng SW. NOW AND THEN: the global nutrition transition: the pandemic of obesity in developing countries. *Nutr Rev* 2012;**70**(1):3–21.
13. Monda KL, Gordon-Larsen P, Stevens J, Popkin BM. China's transition: the effect of rapid urbanization on adult occupational physical activity. *Soc Sci Med* 2007;**64**:858–70.
14. Wang H, Du S, Zhai F, Popkin BM. Trends in the distribution of body mass index among Chinese adults, aged 20–45 years (1989–2000). *Int J Obes* 2007;**31**:272–8.
15. Bosu WK. An overview of the nutrition transition in West Africa: implications for non-communicable diseases. *Proc Nutr Soc* 2015;**74**:466–77.
16. Sobnqwi E, Mbanya JCN, Urwin NC, Kengne AP, Fezeu L, Minkoulou EM, et al. Physical activity and its relationship with obesity, hypertension and diabetes in urban and rural Cameroon. *Int J Obes Relat Metab Disord* 2002;**26**:1009–16.
17. Abubakari AR, Lauder W, Jones MC, Kirk A, Agyemang C, Bhopal RS. Prevalence and time trends in diabetes and physical inactivity among adult West African populations: the epidemic has arrived. *Publ Health* 2009;**123**(9):602–14. https://doi.org/10.1016/j.puhe.2009.07.009.
18. Yadav K, Krishnan A. Changing patterns of diet, physical activity and obesity among urban, rural and slum populations in north India. *Obes Rev* 2008;**9**(5):400–8. https://doi.org/10.1111/j.1467-789X.2008.00505.x. Epub 2008 July 9.
19. World Health Organization. *Report of the commission on ending childhood obesity*. Geneva: World Health Organization; 2016.
20. UNICEF, WHO, World Bank. *Levels and trends in child malnutrition: UNICEF-WHO-World Bank joint child malnutrition estimates*. 2015. UNICEF, New York; WHO, Geneva; World Bank, Washington DC.
21. Ng M, Fleming T, Robinson M, Thomson B, Graetz N, Margono C, et al. Global, regional, and national prevalence of overweight and obesity in children and adults during 1980–2013: a systematic analysis for the Global Burden of Disease Study 2013. *Lancet* 2014;**384**:766–81.
22. Guthold R, Cowan MJ, Autenrieth CS, Kann L, Riley LM. Physical activity and sedentary behavior among school children: a 34-country comparison. *J Pediatrics* 2010;**157**(1):43–9.
23. Muthuri SK, Wachira LJM, Onywera VO, Tremblay MS. Correlates of objectively measured overweight/obesity and physical activity in Kenyan school children: results from ISCOLE-Kenya. *BMC Publ Health* 2014;**14**:436. Available from: http://www.biomedcentral.com/1471-2458/14/436.
24. Manyanga T, Makaza D, Mahachi C, Mlalazi TF, Masocha V, Makoni P, et al. Results from Zimbabwe's 2016 report card on physical activity for children and youth. *J Phys Act Health* 2016;**13**(Suppl. 2):S337–42. Available from: https://doi.org/10.1123/jpah.2016-0304.

25. Ocansey R, Aryeetey R, Sofo S, Nazzar A, Delali M, Pambo P, et al. Results from Ghana's 2016 report card on physical activity for children and youth. *J Phys Act Health* 2016;**13**(Suppl. 2):S165–8. Available from: https://doi.org/10.1123/jpah.2016-0272.
26. Bwire H. Children's independent mobility and perceptions of outdoor environments in Dar es Salaam City, Tanzania. *Global Studies of Childhood* 2011;**1**(3):185–206. Available from: https://doi.org/10.2304/gsch.2011.1.3.185.
27. Onywera VO, Muthuri SK, Hayker S, Wachira LJM, Kyallo F, Mang'eni RO, et al. Results from Kenya's 2016 report card on physical activity for children and youth. *J Phys Act Health* 2016;**13**(Suppl. 2):S195–200. Available from: https://doi.org/10.1123/jpah.2016-0359.
28. Yang Y, Hong X, Gurney JG, Wang Y. Active travel to and from school among school age children during 1997–2011 and associated factors in China. *J Phys Act Health* 2017;**0**(0):1–25. Ahead of Print. Available from: https://doi.org/10.1123/jpah.2016-0590.
29. Amornsriwatanakul A, Lester L, Bull FC, Rosenberg M. Are Thai children and youth sufficiently active? Prevalence and correlates of physical activity from a nationally representative cross-sectional study. *Int J Behav Nutr Phys Act* 2017;**14**(1):72.
30. Amornsriwatanakul A, Nakornkhet K, Katewongsa P, Choosakul C, Kaewmanee T, Konharn K, et al. Results from Thailand's 2016 report card on physical activity for children and youth. *J Phys Act Health* 2016;**13**(Suppl. 2):S291–8. Available from: https://doi.org/10.1123/jpah.2016-0316.
31. Laxmaiah A, Nagalla B, Vijayaraghavan K, Nair M. Factors affecting prevalence of overweight among 12- to 17-year-old urban adolescents in Hyderabad, India. *Obesity* 2007;**15**(6):1384–90.
32. Sharif R, Chong KH, Zakaria NH, Ong ML, Reilly JJ, Wong JE, et al. Results from Malaysia's 2016 report card on physical activity for children and adolescents. *J Phys Act Health* 2016;**13**(Suppl. 2):S201–5. Available from: https://doi.org/10.1123/jpah.2016-0404.
33. Samimi A, Ermagun A. Students' tendency to walk to school: case study of Tehran. *J Urban Plann Dev* 2013;**139**(2):144–52.
34. Liu Y, Tang Y, Cao ZB, Chen PJ, Zhang JL, Zhu Z, et al. Results from Shanghai's (China) 2016 report card on physical activity for children and youth. *J Phys Act Health* 2016;**13**(Suppl. 2):S124–8. Available from: https://doi.org/10.1123/jpah.2016-0362.
35. Wong JE, Parikh P, Poh BK, Deurenberg P. Physical activity of Malaysian primary school children: comparison by sociodemographic variables and activity domains. *Asia Pac J Public Health* 2016;**28**(5 Suppl.):35S–46S.
36. González SA, Castiblanco MA, Arias-Gómez LF, Martinez-Ospina A, Cohen DD, Holguin GA, et al. Results from Colombia's 2016 report card on physical activity for children and youth. *J Phys Act Health* 2016;**13**(Suppl. 2):S129–36. Available from: https://doi.org/10.1123/jpah.2016-0369.
37. Nardo Jr N, Silva DAS, Ferrari GL, Petroski EL, Pacheco RL, Martins PC, et al. Results from Brazil's 2016 report card on physical activity for children and youth. *J Phys Act Health* 2016;**13**(Suppl. 2):S104–9. Available from: https://doi.org/10.1123/jpah.2016-0398.
38. de Sá TH, Garcia LMT, Mielke GI, Rabacow FM, de Rezende LFM. Changes in travel to school patterns among children and adolescents in the São Paulo Metropolitan Area, Brazil, 1997–2007. *J Transp Health* 2015;**2**(2):143–50. Available from: https://doi.org/10.1016/j.jth.2015.02.008.
39. Galaviz KL, Arroyo MA, González-Casanova I, Villalobos MFG, Jáuregui A, Ulloa EJ, et al. Results from Mexico's 2016 report card on physical activity for children and youth. *J Phys Act Health* 2016;**13**(Suppl. 2):S206–12. Available from: https://doi.org/10.1123/jpah.2016-0363.

40. Jáuregui A, Medina C, Salvo D, Barquera S, Rivera-Dommarco JA. Active commuting to school in Mexican adolescents: evidence from the Mexican national nutrition and health survey. *J Phys Act Health* 2015;**12**(8):1088–95.
41. Herrera-Cuenca M, Méndez-Perez B, Morales VC, Martín-Rojo J, Tristan B, Bandy AT, et al. Results from Venezuela's 2016 report card on physical activity for children and youth. *J Phys Act Health* 2016;**13**(Suppl. 2):S314–29. Available from: https://doi.org/10.1123/jpah.2016-0610.
42. Silva KS, Lopes AD, Hardman CM, Cabral LGA, da Silva SG, Nahas MV. Commuting to school and to work among high school students in Santa Catarina state, Brazil: a comparative analysis between 2001 and 2011. *J Phys Act Health* 2014;**11**:1458–67. Available from: https://doi.org/10.1123/jpah.2012-0410.
43. Costa FF, Silva KS, Schmoelz CP, Campos VC, de Assis MAA. Longitudinal and cross-sectional changes in active commuting to school among Brazilian schoolchildren. *Prev Med* 2012;**55**(3):212–4.
44. Cui Z, Bauman A, Dibley MJ. Temporal trends and correlates of passive commuting to and from school in children from 9 provinces in China. *Prev Med* 2011;**52**(6):423–7.
45. Uys M, Bassett S, Draper CE, Micklesfield L, Monyeki A, de Villiers A, et al. Results from South Africa's 2016 report card on physical activity for children and youth. *J Phys Act Health* 2016;**13**(Suppl. 2):S265–73. Available from: https://doi.org/10.1123/jpah.2016-0409.
46. Trang NH, Hong TK, Dibley MJ. Active commuting to school among adolescents in Ho Chi Minh City, Vietnam: change and predictors in a longitudinal study, 2004 to 2009. *Am J Prev Med* 2012;**42**(2):120–8. Available from: https://doi.org/10.1016/j.amepre.2011.10.006.
47. Onywera VO, Adamo KB, Sheel AW, Waudo JN, Boit MK, Tremblay M. Emerging evidence of the physical activity transition in Kenya. *J Phys Act Health* 2012;**9**:554–62.
48. Ekpenyong CE, Akpan EE. Urbanisation drift and obesity epidemic in sub-Saharan Africa: a review of the situation in Nigeria. *Eur J Sustain Dev* 2013;**2**:141–64.
49. Micklesfield LK, Pedro TM, Kahn K, Kinsman J, Pettifor JM, Tollman S, et al. Physical activity and sedentary behavior among adolescents in rural South Africa: levels, patterns and correlates. *BMC Publ Health* 2014;**14**(1):40.
50. Larouche R, Sarmiento OL, Broyles ST, Denstel KD, Katzmarzyk PT, Church TS, for the ISCOLE Research Group, et al. Are the correlates of active school transport context-specific? *Int J Obes Suppl* 2015;**5**:S89–99.
51. Malone K, Rudner J. Global Perspectives on Children's Independent Mobility: a socio-cultural comparison and theoretical discussion of children's lives in four countries in Asia and Africa. *Global Studies of Childhood* 2011;**1**(3):243–59. Available from: https://doi.org/10.2304/gsch.2011.1.3.243.
52. Oyeyemi AL, Ishaku CM, Oyekola J, Wakawa HD, Lawan A, Yakubu S, et al. Patterns and associated factors of physical activity among adolescents in Nigeria. *PLoS One* 2016;**11**(2):e0150142. https://doi.org/10.1371/journal.pone.0150142.
53. Ojiambo RM, Easton C, Casajus JA, Konstabel K, Reilly JJ, Pitsiladis Y. Effect of urbanization on objectively measures physical activity levels, sedentary time, and indices of adiposity in Kenyan adolescents. *J Phys Act Health* 2012;**9**:115–23.
54. Bovet P, Chiolero A, Madeleine G, Paccaud F. Prevalence of overweight and underweight in public and private school in the Seychelles. *Int J Pediatr Obes* 2010;**5**:274–8.
55. Taleb S, Agli AN. Obésité de l'enfant: rôle des facteurs socioéconomiques, obésité parentale, comportement alimentaire et activité physique, chez des enfants scolarisés dans une ville de l'Est Algérien. *Cah Nutr Diététique* 2009;**44**:198–206.
56. Walker ARP, Walker BF, Mngomezulu QN. Serum high density lipoprotein cholesterol levels in African schoolchildren living near or very far from school. *Atherosclerosis* 1982;**41**:35–40.

57. Muthuri SK, Wachira LJ, Onywera VO, Tremblay MS. Associations between parental perceptions of the neighborhood environment and childhood physical activity: results from ISCOLE-Kenya. *J Phys Act Health* 2016;**13**(3):333–43.
58. Oyeyemi AL, Ishaku CM, Deforche B, Oyeyemi AY, De Bourdeaudhuij I, Van Dyck D. Perception of built environmental factors and physical activity among adolescents in Nigeria. *Int J Behav Nutr Phys Act* 2014;**11**:56.
59. Behrens R, Muchaka P. Child independent mobility in South Africa: the case of Cape Town and its hinterland. *Global Studies of Childhood* 2011;**1**(3):167–84. Available from: https://doi.org/10.2304/gsch.2011.1.3.167.
60. Giles-Corti B, Vernez-Moudon A, Reis R, Turrel G, Dannenberg AL, Badland H, et al. City planning and population health: a global challenge. *Lancet* 2016;**388**(10062):2912–24.
61. Sallis JF, Bull F, Burdett R, Frank LD, Griffiths P, Giles-Corti B, et al. Use of science to guide city planning policy and practice: how to achieve healthy and sustainable future cities. *Lancet* 2016;**388**(10062):2936–47.
62. Whitelegg J. Mobility: a new urban design and transport planning philosophy for a sustainable future. *Createspace Independent Publishing Platform* 2016.
63. World Health Organization. *Global status report on road safety 2015*. Geneva, Switzerland: World Health Organization; 2015. Available from: http://www.who.int/violence_injury_prevention/road_safety_status/2015/en/.
64. Onywera VO, Blanchard C. Road accidents: a third burden of 'disease' in sub-Saharan Africa. *Global Health Promotion* 2013;**20**(4):52–5.
65. Oyeyemi AL, Kasoma SS, Onywera VO, Assah F, Adedoyin RA, Conway TL, et al. NEWS for Africa: adaptation and reliability of a built environment questionnaire for physical activity in seven African countries. *Int J Behav Nutr Phys Act* 2016;**13**:33.
66. Oyeyemi AL, Conway TL, Adedoyin RA, Akinroye KK, Aryeetey R, Assah F, et al. Construct validity of the neighbourhood environment walkability scale for Africa. *Med Sci Sports Exerc* 2017;**49**(3):482–91.
67. Prista A, Daca T, Tchonga F, Machava E, Macucule C, Ribeiro E. Results from the Mozambique 2016 report card on physical activity for children and adolescents. *J Phys Act Health* 2016;**13**(Suppl. 2):S213–7. Available from: https://doi.org/10.1123/jpah.2016-0526.
68. Adeniyi AF, Odukoya OO, Oyeyemi AL, Adedoyin RA, Ojo OS, Metseagharun E, et al. Results from Nigeria's 2016 report card on physical activity for children and youth. *J Phys Act Health* 2016;**13**(Suppl. 2):S231–6. Available from: https://doi.org/10.1123/jpah.2016-0305.
69. Katapally TR, Goenka S, Bhawra J, Mani S, Krishnaveni GV, Kehoe SH, et al. Results from India's 2016 report card on physical activity for children and youth. *J Phys Act Health* 2016;**13**(Suppl. 2):S176–82. Available from: https://doi.org/10.1123/jpah.2016-0393.

Safe Routes to School (SRTS) 13

Orion T. Stewart
Institute for Population Health Improvement, University of California Davis Health, Sacramento, CA, United States

Chapter Outline

13.1 Introduction

Safe Routes to School (SRTS) is a movement to make walking, cycling and other forms of active travel to and from school safer while simultaneously encouraging these school commute modes. In the United States, bicycling and walking are relatively safe school travel modes, with an occurrence of 9.6 and 4.6 child fatalities for every 100 million student trips, respectively.[1] Yet, these active travel modes are still 6 and 3 times, respectively, more dangerous than riding to school in a parent's car. Due in part to the real and perceived threat of safety, as well as to long distances between homes and schools, and the perceived convenience of driving, only 12.3% of children in the kindergarten through 8th grade in the United States walked or biked to school in 2009, while 45.3% were driven by car.[2] This represents a near complete reversal from 1969, when 47.7% of children walked or biked and 12.2% were driven. The benefits of increasing the proportion of children safely walking and biking to and from school are many: fewer deaths and injuries among vulnerable road users, more physically active and potentially fewer overweight or obese children, decreased traffic congestion, less pollution and greater childhood independence, among others. SRTS programmes aim to realize these benefits through localized interventions tailored to individual school-based communities.

Children's Active Transportation. https://doi.org/10.1016/B978-0-12-811931-0.00013-2

13.2 The 6 Es

The term 'Safe Routes to School' encompasses any effort to promote safe walking and cycling to school. A *comprehensive* SRTS programme, however, involves a suite of coordinated efforts designed to 'create safe, convenient and fun opportunities for children to bicycle and walk to and from their schools.'[3] It attempts to achieve this goal through activities that fall under the 6 Es: evaluation, engineering, education, encouragement, enforcement and equity.[4]

Evaluation involves collecting information on current travel conditions at a school, including mode split (i.e., percentage of children engaging in active transportation) and barriers/facilitators to walking to school. These data are often collected through interviews with key informants such as the school principal or teachers, parent surveys, student travel tallies, community meetings, and walk or bicycle audits. The information gathered during the evaluation helps identify specific activities that should be taken to help leverage facilitators and eliminate barriers to safely walk and bike to school. Evaluation activities are also critical for establishing baseline conditions so that any effects of the SRTS intervention can be documented.

Engineering is the construction of pedestrian and bicycle infrastructure improvements, such as sidewalks, multiuse paths, traffic-calming devices, traffic signals, and pedestrian and bicycle crossing improvements. These improvements may require substantial planning and funding to execute. Quicker, lower cost solutions include landscaping maintenance, altering the timing of traffic lights, painting crosswalks or installing stop signs.

Education teaches children and parents about pedestrian and bicyclist safety. In the United States, lessons for children aged 6–8 years focus on safe walking skills; and at ages 8–10 years, children are taught the basics of bicycling. To address personal safety, SRTS programmes often enlist police officers to teach children what to do when approached by a stranger. Some educational programmes are also directed at parents, encouraging them to practice walking and bicycling with their children and to follow the rules of the road when they themselves are driving, walking or bicycling. Educational safety campaigns sometimes extend to the entire community, helping to make drivers aware that they need to share the road with school children who are walking and biking in the area.

Encouragement involves special events, contests and other methods of inspiring students to walk or bike to school. Walk to School Day and Bike to School Day are annual, international events designed to get students to try a new way of getting to school and perhaps catalyze a long-term habit. In the 2016–17 school year, nearly 5000 walk-to-school events and 3000 bike-to-school events were registered across the United States.[5] Encouragement efforts also include contests between individual students or classrooms, which can help encourage maintenance of new behaviours and provide positive role models. Other encouragement programmes aim to provide fun ways to safely walk or bike to school on a daily basis. 'Walking school buses' and 'bike trains' are such programmes where parents or other adults supervise groups of children who live in the same neighbourhood as they travel to school on foot or by bike and pick up friends along the way (see Chapter 15). Walking school buses and bike trains incorporate both encouragement and education activities, as they provide a fun and adventurous way to get to school while an adult provides instruction on pedestrian or bicycle safety and children get an opportunity to practice what they have learnt.

Enforcement efforts focus on changing driver behaviour to increase pedestrian safety through police or crossing guard presence or automated devices, such as signs that show drivers how fast they are going. Enforcement often involves partnerships with local law enforcement agencies. But efforts can also be community-based, such as neighbourhood watch programmes directed at addressing safety from crime.

Equity cuts across the other Es and represents an effort to direct SRTS activities into communities where the dangers of walking and bicycling to school are greater and travel choices are fewer. Often these are low-income communities with greater proportion of racial minorities who have been historically marginalized.[6,7] Not only do these communities often face greater dangers during the school trip but also face greater challenges in securing resources to address these dangers.[8] SRTS funding can be strategically allocated to help eliminate the disparities in opportunities for children's safe, active and healthy travel to and from school.[9]

13.3 History

The comprehensive SRTS programme originated from a Danish pilot programme in the 1970s.[10] At this time, Denmark had the highest rate of child traffic fatalities in Western Europe. In response, the city of Odense implemented a pilot programme to identify and address specific traffic dangers through infrastructure improvements, including traffic islands, narrowed roads and a network of bicycle and pedestrian paths. By the early 1980s, this demonstration project was credited with helping to reduce child pedestrian and bicycle collisions during the school journey by 82%. Following Odense's success, Denmark established a national SRTS programme.[11,12] During the 1980s and 1990s, the Danish concept began to spread to the UK, Canada, Australia and New Zealand, where it developed into the school travel planning system (see Chapter 14).

SRTS reached the United States in 1997 when the first programmes appeared in the state of Florida[13] and the New York City borough of the Bronx.[10] In 1999, California launched the first statewide SRTS programme.[14] The California programme was similar to the original Danish model that focused on safety via infrastructure improvements. In 2000, two comprehensive SRTS demonstration projects were funded by the National Highway Traffic Administration and completed in Marin County, California, and Arlington, Massachusetts. These projects included classroom education, walk and bike days, mapping of routes, walking school buses and bike trains, newsletters and infrastructure improvements and demonstrated an increase in rates of walking, biking and carpooling.[15] SRTS momentum built on these successes: grassroots SRTS programmes sprouted throughout the United States and advocacy organizations began lobbying for federal SRTS funding. These efforts helped establish a national SRTS programme under the Federal Highway Administration in 2005, when the Congress passed the federal surface transportation bill, SAFETEA-LU (Safe, Accountable, Flexible, Efficient Transportation Equity Act: A Legacy for Users).[16]

From 2005 to 2012, the US Congress appropriated $1.2 billion for the SRTS programme. These funds were distributed to state departments of transportation (DOTs), who then made grants to state, local and regional agencies, including nonprofit organizations, to implement SRTS programmes. To ensure that schools in poorer areas were not underfunded, SAFETEA-LU established a 100% federal share for the SRTS projects—no matching state or local funds were required. Each state DOT received funding proportionate to the statewide elementary and middle school enrolment. State DOTs were required to split funds between infrastructure (i.e., engineering) and noninfrastructure activities (i.e., evaluation, education, encouragement and enforcement). No less than 10% and no more than 30% of funds were to be spent on noninfrastructure activities. Infrastructure improvements were also to be located within bicycling and walking distance of school, defined as 2 miles. SAFETEA-LU also established the National Center for Safe Routes to School, a clearinghouse of resources and technical assistance for state and local SRTS programmes. By the end of 2012, the federal SRTS programme reached almost 14,000 elementary and middle schools, many of which served low-income and minority communities.[17] The programme was largely considered a success, although some communities expressed difficulties in navigating the regulatory process and financing projects when funds were not available upfront.[18] In addition, SRTS applications in many states far exceeded the available funding, suggesting that the programme was insufficient to address the needs of all the communities that the programme was intended to help.[9]

Dedicated federal SRTS funding in the United States terminated in June 2012 when Congress passed a new transportation bill, MAP-21 (Moving Ahead for Progress in the 21st Century). Under the new bill, SRTS was combined with other bicycle and pedestrian funding streams into a new programme called 'Transportation Alternatives.' Several smaller changes were also made to the SRTS programme itself, for example, projects could no longer fund 100% of the project's costs with federal money—local communities were now required to contribute 20% in matching funds. The new bill also cut total bicycle and pedestrian funding by 30% compared to the prior fiscal year. Under MAP-21, SRTS projects must now compete against other bicycling and walking projects for a smaller pot of money. The extent to which SRTS programmes are supported are now largely up to state DOTs.[16]

13.4 Safe Routes to School in the Developing World

SRTS efforts are neither unique to developed countries nor government-funded programmes. The nonprofit Safe Kids Worldwide and FedEx initiated a 'Walk This Way' programme in 1999 to help address child pedestrian safety. The programme includes awareness and advocacy events, school zone improvements and culturally sensitive educational programmes. It now exists in 11 countries: Brazil, Canada, China, India, Mexico, the Philippines, South Africa, South Korea, Thailand, the United States and Vietnam. In 2012 alone, the programme reached more than 2 million children in nearly 4000 schools with 5411 hours of volunteer support from FedEx employees.[19]

Implementation of SRTS programmes in developing countries often face challenges of lack of reliable data, lack of coordination between government agencies and small budgets.[20] These challenges are not insurmountable. In Dar es Salaam, Tanzania, for example, Amend, a road safety nongovernmental organization, surveyed primary schools on traffic-related injury incidence. It used these data to identify high-risk schools where at least 1% of children suffered a traffic-related injury annually. These high-risk schools received an intervention similar to a comprehensive SRTS programme: a systematic assessment of areas around schools, identification of measures that will improve road safety and the implementation of those measures through action by Amend and delivery from the local authority. Like most school travel plans, countermeasures are designed through a review of the behaviour of children, of drivers and other road users, and household surveys of injury rates and patterns. Countermeasures often take the form of relatively low-cost infrastructure improvements, such as speed bumps, bollards, sidewalks, signage and new school gates, as well as noninfrastructure activities such as community-based crossing patrols and road safety education. Amend estimates that the programme costs an average of US $25,000 per school area[21] in contrast to the nearly $110,000 cost per school for similar SRTS programmes in the United States.[22]

Developing countries also face greater challenges to address traffic safety for children who walk or bike to or from school than developed countries. Gradual increases in motorization since the 1970s in developed countries have kept pace with investment in road safety measures, including drunk driving enforcement, driver training and licensing systems, speed management near schools, improved road design and uncorrupt traffic law enforcement. In countries with fast-developing economies and rapid motorization, the same gradual road safety systems and generational learning has not yet taken place. Roads and streets around schools often lack pedestrian facilities, making it difficult for large numbers of children on foot and bike and fast moving traffic to safely coexist. This combined with inadequate traffic speed laws and enforcement creates particularly hazardous conditions. SRTS programmes in these conditions often prioritize efforts to reduce the speed of vehicles through targeted engineering interventions, since reducing traffic speed is the most effective means to prevent the most serious injuries. Modified engineering improvements are commonly used to achieve this goal—when zebra crossings are added, for example, they will often be flanked with speed bumps or other traffic-calming measures.[20]

SRTS programmes are targeted, community-based efforts to improve safety for specific trips. However, SRTS activities can also be complimentary to broader efforts to achieve ‘Vision Zero’ goals of eliminating traffic fatalities.[23] In South Korea, for example, road traffic fatalities for children under the age of 14 years were reduced by 95% from 1988 to 2012 as part of a holistic effort to create a safe transportation system. In addition, to engineering safer school zones, broader efforts included supporting civil society organizations in advocating for road safety, mandatory prosecution of drivers involved in crashes within school zones, a doubling of fines for traffic violations occurring within school zones and compulsory road safety education.[24] In countries that have yet to make such impressive strides in traffic safety, SRTS are seen as a starting point for efforts to build sustained government support for safer school zone infrastructure and stronger speed legislation and enforcement.[20]

13.5 Safe Routes to School Evaluation

Numerous case studies have highlighted SRTS success stories at individual schools or communities (see Sidebar). Large-scale evaluations of SRTS programmes are less common, in part because impact evaluations are generally not required as part of SRTS funding mechanisms. But some larger-scale studies do exist. The first multistate evaluation of the federally funded US SRTS programme included 55 schools that received SRTS interventions in the US states of Florida, Mississippi, Washington and Wisconsin. These schools experienced an average increase in the walk-to-school rate from 9.8% to 14.2% after implementation of SRTS.[25] Rates of biking to school increased on average from 2.5% to 3%. This evaluation's main limitation is that it lacked control schools for comparison—the increases observed may have just reflected broader temporal trends occurring across all schools. This limitation was addressed in a later study of 801 schools in the District of Columbia, Florida, Oregon and Texas.[26] This study compared federally funded SRTS schools to non-SRTS schools while also adjusting for school location, demographics and other factors that could have accounted for changes in school commute mode split. SRTS engineering improvements were associated with a 3.3 percentage-point per year increase in walking or biking rates. Education and encouragement programmes were also associated with a 1 percentage-point per year increase in rates of walking and biking. These infrastructure and noninfrastructure effects were independent of one another, suggesting that an SRTS programme that combines engineering improvements with education and encouragement could realize additive benefits, especially if noninfrastructure activities are continued over multiple years.

Not all SRTS evaluations have delivered positive results. A study of fourth grade students in Texas schools that received either infrastructure or noninfrastructure funding found that few outcomes changed in these schools compared to control schools over time.[27] However, perceived walkability and afternoon active school travel increased in all schools over time, suggesting that broader efforts to address childhood obesity and promote sustainable travel could be delivering results even in schools without SRTS funding. Additionally, nuances in the delivery of the SRTS programme could impact its effectiveness. In Texas, infrastructure and noninfrastructure activities were funded separately, and many grants went directly to municipalities with little school involvement, perhaps resulting in interventions that lacked community buy-in and perceived relevance.

Because perceived safety is such a strong barrier to parents and caregivers in allowing their children to walk or bike to school,[28–30] evidence that SRTS results in increases in active transportation may suggest that SRTS programmes increase perceived safety. Yet evidence also exists that SRTS programmes impact objectively measured safety. A New York City study analyzed child pedestrian injuries during school travel hours from 2001 to 2010 and found a 44% reduction in injury rates in census tracts with schools that received SRTS interventions, compared with no change in similar census tracts with schools that did not have SRTS interventions.[31] The estimated net savings of New York City's SRTS programme due to injury reduction were $230 million over 50 years.[32] The total economic benefit of the SRTS programme would likely be greater if the health and environmental benefits of increased active and reduced motorized travel were also quantified in this cost-effectiveness analysis.

13.5.1 Limitations

The primary limitation of SRTS evaluation efforts thus far are their reliance on natural experiments and quasi-experimental study designs, which are susceptible to self-selection bias—schools and communities that successfully implemented SRTS may differ systematically from those that did not implement an SRTS, and it may be this difference that drives changes to rates of walking and biking to school. Experts frequently claim that successful SRTS programmes depend on local champions taking ownership of the project and engaging in positive relationships with a variety of stakeholders.[20,33] The comprehensive nature of SRTS programmes means that parents and children may help identify unsafe segments of walk and bicycle routes, city engineers may help design countermeasures, teachers may deliver curriculum, advocacy groups may organize events and police may help enforce traffic laws. It is possible that this sort of collaboration cannot simply be prescribed anywhere. A randomized trial of the SRTS programme could help answer this question and determine if SRTS programmes would be effective at any school, or just among schools that proactively select to implement an SRTS programme.

Most SRTS research has been conducted in the United States where both active travel to school and severe pedestrian injuries are relatively rare. This body of research may not be generalizable to contexts where active travel is already the norm. For example, a study of a Danish programme involving infrastructure changes and promotional efforts to encourage safe cycling to school observed neither increases in cycling nor decreases of cycling injuries between the 13 intervention schools and the 12 control schools after 1 year.[34] These findings may be attributed to the fact that most children already cycled to school at baseline and that the Danish environment was already safe.[12]

The US body of research is also probably not generalizable to developing countries where children and their families have fewer transportation choices and face greater risks of traffic injury. Evidence from East Africa shows that SRTS efforts can result in increased school attendance[20] and that for every 286 children affected by an SRTS intervention, 1 road traffic injury per year is prevented.[21] Such improvements could have a substantial effect throughout a child's community and across their lifespan. Long-term studies—in any part of the globe—would be valuable in capturing the lifelong benefits that SRTS programmes potentially deliver.

13.6 Conclusion

SRTS programmes have been shown to be effective tools in increasing the numbers and safety of children walking and cycling to school. The targeted, community-based nature of SRTS programmes is likely responsible for much of their success. But the SRTS programme is not a panacea for supporting children's active travel. Land use planning and school policies (e.g., neighbourhood school attendance) are needed to ensure that schools and families are located within reasonable walking and cycling distance from one another so that active travel is a reasonable choice for the school trip. Complete street policies and other funding mechanisms are necessary to ensure that bicycle and pedestrian facilities exist for other destinations that children travel to, such as the local park, grocery store or friend's house. In many cases, even with appropriate traffic facilities, community events and programming that breaks down distrust of neighbours and build social cohesion will also be needed to overcome parental fears of abduction and other crimes. In spite of these challenges, SRTS may be a first step towards safe routes to everywhere.

13.7 Recommendations for Policy and Practice

1. Continue to develop SRTS programmes that are tailored to the communities where they are to be implemented;
2. Make SRTS funding easily accessible to communities that have organized themselves around the need for safer, healthier and more sustainable school travel;
3. Coordinate SRTS activities with broader efforts to achieve Vision Zero safety goals and a larger shift from motorized to active transportation;
4. Fund SRTS evaluations to advance the knowledge on how the programme can optimally achieve its goals.

13.8 Recommendations for Future Research

1. Conduct randomized trials of SRTS programmes to help understand if the programme is effective even if communities do not proactively choose to implement one;
2. Design and execute studies to identify specific SRTS activities or combinations of activities that are most effective at increasing rates and/or safety of active travel;
3. Conduct comparative research to understand how SRTS programmes' effectiveness differs among communities with differing norms and risk surrounding active school travel modes;
4. Conduct cost-effectiveness analyses that more completely capture the multifaceted benefits of active school travel;
5. Conduct studies with long-term follow-up to understand how early childhood participation in an SRTS programme impacts later-life behavioural and health outcomes.

Sidebar Example Safe Routes to School Programme

Oak Grove Elementary, Metropolitan Atlanta, Georgia[35]

In 2008, Oak Grove parent volunteers formed an SRTS Task Force that included the school principal, school nurse, physical education (PE) teacher, county police, public works staff, board of health and a county commissioner. The Task Force identified goals of increasing walking to/from school, decreasing car travel to/from school and traffic congestion, and improving air quality around the school.

Evaluation prior to the start of the programme identified the most commonly cited barriers to walking or biking to school among parents: safety of intersections and crossings (68%), the amount of traffic along the route (64%), and the speed of traffic (55%). Community capacity building enabled the SRTS Task Force to submit a petition to the director of public works demanding changes to the neighbouring street environment. **Engineering** improvements were subsequently implemented: 5 crosswalks were striped at high-volume intersections and 2 new intersection lights were installed along with disability ramps and pedestrian countdown signals.

The **education** component of the SRTS programme targeted students, parents, faculty and staff. The PE teacher delivered pedestrian safety curriculum to staff and students. Parentme–teacher association meetings and the weekly school e-newsletter were used to educate parents on the benefits of walking and biking to school, as well as to provide maps of specific safe pathways to school.

To **encourage** walking, Wednesday was chosen as the designated Walk to School Day. A nearby church provided space for families who lived beyond walking distance to park and then walk to school. In addition, the SRTS task force published names and contact information of walking school bus volunteer leaders. Small incentives such as pencils and stickers were given for participation, reminder notices were posted on the school marquis and t-shirts were designed and worn by parents and students on International Walk to School Day.

To **enforce** posted speed limits, the local police department set up a speed monitoring unit on the main road outside the school and participated in escorting the walking school bus.

Based on **evaluation** of parental survey responses, walking to school in the morning on most days increased from 18% in the fall of 2008 to 42% in the fall of 2010. Parental perceptions about the health benefits, enjoyment and school support of walking/biking to school also increased during the 2-year intervention.

References

1. Committee on School Transportation Safety. *The relative risks of school travel: a national perspective and guidance for local community risk assessment. Special Report 269*. Washington, DC: Transportation Research Board of the National Academies; 2002. Available from: http://onlinepubs.trb.org/onlinepubs/sr/sr269.pdf.
2. McDonald NC, Brown AL, Marchetti LM, Pedroso MS. U.S. school travel, 2009 an assessment of trends. *Am J Prev Med* 2011;**41**(2):146–51.
3. Safe Routes to School National Partnership. *Safe routes to school: 2007 state of the states report*. 2007. Available from: http://www.saferoutespartnership.org/sites/default/files/pdf/rpt_SRTSstates2007.pdf.
4. Safe Routes to School National Partnership. *Safe routes 101: the 6 E's*. Available from: http://www.saferoutespartnership.org/healthy-communities/101/6Es.
5. National Center for Safe Routes to School. *Walk to school day*. 2017. Available from: http://www.walkbiketoschool.org.
6. Macpherson A, Roberts I, Pless IB. Children's exposure to traffic and pedestrian injuries. *Am J Public Health* 1998;**88**(12):1840–3.
7. Zhu X, Lee C. Walkability and safety around elementary schools economic and ethnic disparities. *Am J Prev Med* 2008;**34**(4):282–90.
8. McDonald NC. Critical factors for active transportation to school among low-income and minority students. Evidence from the 2001 National Household Travel Survey. *Am J Prev Med* 2008;**34**(4):341–4.
9. Moudon AV, Stewart OT, Lin L. *So many choices, so many ways to choose: how five state departments of transportation select safe routes to school programs for funding. WA-RD 743.2*. Washington State Department of Transportation; 2011. Available from: https://www.wsdot.wa.gov/research/reports/fullreports/743.2.pdf.
10. National Center for Safe Routes to School. *SRTS guide*. 2015. Available from: http://guide.saferoutesinfo.org.

11. Hubsmith DA. Safe routes to school in the United States. *Child Youth Environ* 2006;**16**(1):168–90.
12. Appleyard BS. Planning safe routes to school. *Planning* 2003;**69**(5):34.
13. Steiner RL, Crider LB. SafeWays to school: combining resources at the state, county and local level to improve safety to schools. In: *Annual Conference of the TRB. Washington D.C.* 1999.
14. Mennesson M. *Safe routes to school: the story begins*. 2015. Available from: http://www.saferoutespartnership.org/blog/safe-routes-school-story-begins.
15. Staunton CE, Hubsmith D, Kallins W. Promoting safe walking and biking to school: the Marin County success story. *Am J Public Health* 2003;**93**(9):1431–4.
16. Safe Routes to School National Partnership. *Safe routes 101: funding history of safe routes to school*. 2017. Available from: http://www.saferoutespartnership.org/healthy-communities/101/history.
17. McDonald NC. *Impact of safe routes to school programs on walking and biking*. San Diego, CA: Active Living Research; 2015. Available from: http://activelivingresearch.org/sites/default/files/ALR_Review_SRTS_May2015.pdf.
18. Atteberry H, Dowdy D, Oluyomi A, Nichols D, Ory MG, Hoelscher DM. A contextual look at safe routes to school implementation in Texas. *Environ Behav* 2016;**48**(1):192–209.
19. Safe Kids Worldwide. *Walk this way*. 2016. Available from: https://www.safekids.org/walk-way.
20. Silverman A, Billingsley S. *Safe to learn. UNICEF and the FIA foundation*. 2015. Available from: https://www.unicef.org/education/files/Safe_to_Learn_report.pdf.
21. Billingsley S, Bishop T, Poswayo A, Silverman A, Witte J. Step change: an action agenda on safe walking for Africa's children. Amend and the FIA Foundation. Available from: https://www.childhealthinitiative.org/media/402416/step-change-spreads.pdf.
22. Moudon AV, Stewart OT. *Moving forward: safe routes to school progress in five states. WA-RD 743.3*. Washington State Transportation Center; 2012. Available from: https://www.wsdot.wa.gov/research/reports/fullreports/743.3.pdf.
23. National Center for Safe Routes to School. Focusing on the safety of children can propel vision zero initiatives. Available from: http://152.2.173.188/saferoutesinfo/wp-content/uploads/2017/03/SRTS_brief_VisionZero_web.pdf.
24. Jaehoon S, Jun L, Su KD, et al. Korea's 95% reduction in child traffic fatalities: policies and achievements. In: *Korea's best practices in the transport sector*. The Korea Transport Institute; 2014. Available from: https://www.koti.re.kr/component/file/ND_fileDownload.do?q_fileSn=4948&q_fileId=20140423_0004948_00150840.
25. Stewart O, Moudon AV, Claybrooke C. Multistate evaluation of safe routes to school programs. *Am J Health Promot* 2014;**28**(3 Suppl.):S89–96.
26. McDonald NC, Steiner RL, Lee C, Rhoulac Smith T, Zhu X, Yang Y. Impact of the safe routes to school program on walking and bicycling. *J Am Plann Assoc* 2014;**80**:153–67.
27. Hoelscher D, Ory M, Dowdy D, et al. Effects of funding allocation for safe routes to school programs on active commuting to school and related behavioural, knowledge, and psychosocial outcomes. *Environ Behav* 2016;**48**(1):210–29.
28. Ahlport KN, Linnan L, Vaughn A, Evenson KR, Ward DS. Barriers to and facilitators of walking and bicycling to school: formative results from the non-motorized travel study. *Health Educ Behav* 2008;**35**(2):221–44.
29. Chaufan C, Yeh J, Fox P. The safe routes to school program in California: an update. *Am J Public Health* 2012;**102**(6):e8–11.
30. Timperio A, Ball K, Salmon J, et al. Personal, family, social, and environmental correlates of active commuting to school. *Am J Prev Med* 2006;**30**(1):45–51.

31. Dimaggio C, Li G. Effectiveness of a safe routes to school program in preventing school-aged pedestrian injury. *Pediatrics* 2013;**131**(2):290–6.
32. Muennig PA, Epstein M, Li G, DiMaggio C. The cost-effectiveness of New York City's safe routes to school program. *Am J Public Health* 2014;**104**(7):1294–9.
33. Mackie H. *Improving school travel systems*. NZ Transport Agency; 2010. Available from: https://www.nzta.govt.nz/assets/resources/research/reports/420/docs/420.pdf.
34. Ostergaard L, Stockel JT, Andersen LB. Effectiveness and implementation of interventions to increase commuter cycling to school: a quasi-experimental study. *BMC Publ Health* 2015;**15**:1199. Available from: https://www.ncbi.nlm.nih.gov/pmc/articles/PMC4665862/.
35. Henderson S, Tanner R, Klanderman N, Mattera A, Webb LM, Steward J. Safe routes to school: a public health practice success story—Atlanta, 2008–2010. *J Phys Activ Health* 2013;**10**(2):141–2.

School Travel Plans

14

Erica Hinckson[1], *Guy Faulkner*[2]
[1]Faculty of Health and Environmental Sciences, Centre for Child Health Research, Human Potential Centre, Auckland University of Technology, Auckland, New Zealand; [2]School of Kinesiology, University of British Columbia, Vancouver, BC, Canada

> *...the results from that have been significant in terms of traffic movement and I'm talking both pedestrian and vehicle traffic around the school, congestion at the school gate has changed significantly.*
>
> ***School Principal, NZ***

> *School travel planning was successful in terms of putting school travel on the map at least, just to even get the words out there and start a bit of dialogue, because before that I don't think people even realized what AST (active school travel) was, or that there were even any other [travel mode] options.*
>
> ***Ontario School Travel Plan Facilitator***

Chapter Outline

14.1 Introduction

As discussed in Chapters 6–12, the factors that shape school travel behaviour are complex and span across socioecological levels of influence.[1] At the intrapersonal (i.e., child) and interpersonal (i.e., parent, family and peers) levels, children's age, gender and ethnicity and their parents' work schedule, socioeconomic status and perceptions regarding safety can all influence school travel behaviour.[2–5] At the organizational level (i.e., school), the school location, socioeconomic status (SES) and ethnic composition, and the openness of the school staff to promoting physical activity may have an influence.[6–10] At the physical 'built environment' level, the distance between the home

Children's Active Transportation. https://doi.org/10.1016/B978-0-12-811931-0.00014-4

and school environments, street density and connectivity, the presence and quality of pedestrian infrastructure and environmental aesthetics have been shown to facilitate or hinder levels of active school travel.[11–16] Policies relating to school siting decisions, catchment areas and transportation services have also been identified as influencing active school travel.[4,9,17,18]

Given such complexity, it is likely that interventions designed to increase active travel may be more effective when addressing a range of these levels of influence. A systematic review of 14 active school travel interventions[19] stressed the lack of interventions addressing these multilayered influences. The authors attribute the small effect sizes (Cohen's d=0.1–0.4) across most studies to the implementation of 'one-off' educational or encouragement initiatives that do not consider broader environmental factors that may be impeding active school travel. The review further emphasized the value of addressing all ecological levels of influence by involving multidisciplinary stakeholders and implementing a combination of noninfrastructure (e.g., education initiatives and enforcement rules) and infrastructure (e.g., sidewalk or bike-rack implementation) strategies. One such comprehensive intervention addressing the multifaceted factors via stakeholder engagement is School Travel Planning.

14.2 School Travel Planning

School Travel Plan (STP) is a collaborative process involving multidisciplinary stakeholders who assess and intervene in schools by means of a documented 'school travel plan'. These stakeholders compose an STP committee with representation from various disciplines including safety (e.g., police officer), transportation (e.g., traffic engineer), municipal planning (e.g., member of city council), health (e.g., public health nurse) and education (school administration/teachers, and student and parent representatives). Based on their perspectives, the stakeholders play a role in identifying strategies to alleviate school-specific barriers. A key component of the STP model is the designation of an individual as the STP 'facilitator'. Led by this STP facilitator, participating schools, assisted by community stakeholders, are typically guided through the following reflective and iterative five-stage STP process:

1. Programme setup: development of STP committee, including school staff, parents, interested community members and students. A project timeline is determined.
2. Data collection and problem identification: classroom-based hands-up student and family surveys are conducted. School site visits and walkabouts are coordinated with key stakeholders. The walkabout involves an environmental audit by the STP committee to identify potential built environment barriers to active school travel.
3. Action plan development: a written STP developed by the STP facilitator with the school's STP committee that summarizes background data and outlines detailed action plan that includes intervention details.
4. Implementation: action items are carried out.
5. Ongoing monitoring: post-plan/follow-up data collection to evaluate progress towards goals.

Analyses of STPs typically outline four types of strategies emerging from the action plans[20]: educational strategies (e.g., hosting educational workshops to promote the awareness and benefits of active school travel), activities and events (e.g., organizing active school travel supervision via walking school bus schemes [see Chapter 15), capital improvement projects (e.g., installing a sidewalk or bike rack) and enforcement initiatives (e.g., increased police presence or crossing guards).

The concept of STP was developed in the United Kingdom in 1997 and led by the Department of Transport and Education. With the assistance of significant capital and revenue funding, 81% of schools in England (primary and secondary) had a STP in place by March 2009.[21] Rowland et al.[22] first evaluated STP in 21 of these schools using a randomized control trial and parent surveys (n = 1386) to measure children's active school travel levels (i.e., walk, bike or public transport). Results revealed no changes in active school travel following the intervention, possibly because walking rates were already very high across intervention and control schools at baseline (70.0%/71.0%). In this chapter, we will describe the implementation and evaluation of STP in Canada and New Zealand and identify key lessons learned from the experience. Recommendations for future practice and research will also be presented.

14.3 New Zealand

The STP programme (part of the wider Travelwise programme) was funded by New Zealand Transport and facilitated by partnerships between the Auckland Transport and the Auckland Council. STP has been implemented in primary, intermediate and secondary schools across the Auckland region since 2004 with the primary objectives of encouraging active travel and use of public transport, reducing school-related traffic congestion and improving neighbourhood traffic safety. The first pilot STPs were developed in 2002 in the North Shore region of Auckland City. Auckland Transport, with the support of the Prime Minister in March 2005, significantly expanded this activity as part of the Sustainable Cities Programme with funding ($1.5 million New Zealand dollars) from the government through the Ministry for the Environment.

STP was primarily introduced in 20 North Auckland schools and then expanded to the rest of the Auckland region. The first evaluation was conducted in 2006, and data from these schools[23] indicated an overall decline in car use of 3.8%. A decrease in family car use over the STP period (3 years) was reported by 15 of the 18 schools. Walking had increased by 3.6%. Fourteen of the 18 schools reported an increase in walking over the STP period. The percentage change ranged from −5% to +21%. All 18 schools reported an increase in car sharing over the STP period. The percentage change for vehicle sharing ranged from 1% to 5%.[23] By 2006, the STP intervention had engaged 46 of the 397 primary schools (student aged 5–10 years) and 22,707 of the 116,707 students. Hinckson and Badland[24] analysed data from 33 schools (72%) that implemented actions from the STP and found a 6% (±7%) increase in active transportation compared to baseline travel modes.

The unique aspect of the New Zealand STP programme was the joint effort in the planning process which included input from an Auckland Transport travel planner, and school staff, council, the local community and other stakeholders working together to develop a plan tailored to the needs of each school. During the phases (as mentioned above), the Auckland Transport travel planner and students, senior leadership team, board of trustees and community members assess the existing situation; decide on an overall timeframe, key aims and actions; and develop an engineering action plan and an evaluation framework. The engineering plan is formed by information gathered about the school and the community, collated and analysed data from the baseline travel survey and conversations with the community. Once the relevant issues are identified, the travel planner facilitates the development of an action plan that combines engineering, education, enforcement, encouragement and policy strategies. Activities include road safety and active transportation education programmes embedded within a curriculum framework, cycle/scooter safety training; promotion of Road Safety Week, Back to School, Slow Down Around Schools, Wheels Day; appropriate facilities for bikes, staff patrolling the crossing facilities and parents helping in drop off zones. The travel planner assists the school and its community with the implementation of the programme and data collection.

Six evaluations[23,25–28] were conducted for the STP programme. The first five evaluations collated annual data from the student, parent and staff travel surveys, principal/lead travel teacher interviews, student focus groups and school environmental audit (2006 evaluation only). A sixth evaluation combined all the survey data and compared travel modes before and after implementation of the STP programme.[29] The results showed that there was an overall increase in active commuting by the third year of STP implementation when compared with baseline levels (40.5%–42.2%). Students of high socioeconomic background showed greater improvements in active commuting than those from mid- and low-decile schools (38.9%–39.1%). STP appealed more to senior than junior primary school students (43.6%–44.3%). The STP was equally effective in schools with small- to medium-size student rolls as it was in large schools (34.1%–36.5%), and schools in Auckland Central showed significant improvements when compared with schools in North Auckland (47.2%–48.1%).

To complement the quantitative assessment, several focus groups were established to provide a qualitative component to the STP evaluation. In 2008, the evaluation focused on secondary school students[30] and parents of primary school students. Overall, parents of primary school children perceived an increase in people walking to school since STP implementation. Similarly, in intermediate schools and secondary schools, staff and students commented that more students walked independently. Parents whose children were part of the walking school bus commented that walking was beneficial to their health and provided children with the opportunity to get to know their neighbours and environment. Primary schools considered the walking school bus a major success of the STP programme because it brought the community together, provided an opportunity to interact with neighbours and the local environment, and brought health benefits. However, parents commented that there were still many cars on the road during drop off and pick up times, and this made them reluctant to allow children to walk. Weather seemed to be a major barrier to walking. Participants perceived that more children walked to school in the summer, either on their own or in walking school buses, than in the winter. Children sitting in classrooms in wet clothes was the main reason parents did not allow children to walk to school in the rain. For secondary school students, walking was seen as a good way to exercise, enjoy the fresh air and an opportunity to talk to peers.[30] It was observed that since the implementation of the STP programme, more students walked during breaks, more sport teams were available and, generally, more people were playing sport. Secondary school students who travelled to school by car said that convenience, laziness, injury and bad weather were the main reasons for their choice.[28]

Auckland Council representatives from the different areas of Auckland involved with the STP programme and travel planners were also interviewed. Overwhelmingly, Council staff enjoyed opportunities to interact with schools and their students, especially during life skills training, promotion of walking school buses and involvement in family fun evenings. Seeing schools succeed in developing an active transportation profile, making the roads safer and schools realising the bigger picture had been worthwhile outcomes. As the number of schools on the programme increased, so too did the workload for travel planners and the Council. It was commented that more staff would be needed to reach targets and at the same time ensure sustainability of the programme in the existing schools. The programme was constantly evolving and becoming more complex. The need of schools with 'completed' travel plans is at risk of being overlooked because of the challenge of keeping up with new schools joining the programme. Travel coordinators agreed that resourcing was a challenge. However, they clarified that their role was not to implement the programme but to engage, inspire and empower schools to execute the programme independently. When schools did not engage from the beginning, expectations of outside help were high and resourcing became an issue. Although a good range of educational material and ideas for implementing travel plan initiatives in primary schools is available, similar resourcing for high schools and colleges is lacking, especially for schools in rural areas. High school students needed to be engaged differently, and student ownership of the travel plan was an essential element for the programme to be successful in these schools. Success of the programme was judged against changes in modal shifts and did not include safety. Many schools already enjoyed a high proportion of students using active transportation. Dramatic changes in the modal profile of these schools were consequently not possible. Instead, councils suggested that the success of the STP should be measured on both modal shift and improved safety for child pedestrians and cyclists. Travel planners also commented that shifting parents' perceptions about safety was essential to achieve the target reductions in car use.[28]

On the basis of the results from the six evaluations (2006–11), Auckland Transport responded to the challenges reported. This is evidenced by the expansion and availability of resources held centrally for easy access, using a different approach to engage secondary school students through empowerment and leadership, and road safety engineers working closely with the school and local community to find ways to improve road safety and promote alternative transport options around schools. Since its inception in 2004, the Travelwise programme has involved over 250,000 students in the Auckland programme to date. Seventy five percent of all Auckland school-aged students attend a Travelwise School, and there has been a 58% reduction in crashes around schools that involve pedestrians and cyclists aged 5–13 years (https://at.govt.nz/cycling-walking/school-travel/travelwise-schools/).

14.4 Canada

Green Communities Canada (GCC), a nongovernment organization advocating for sustainable transportation, has led the delivery of STP interventions across Canada. Informed by detailed reviews of best practices (GCC, 2007), GCC received a grant in 2007 from the Public Health Agency of Canada to pilot an STP framework across Canada. STP was pilot tested in 12 schools across four provinces. Using data from these schools, Buliung et al.[20] found a 2% increase (student reported) in active school travel and a 13% reduction in driving (parent reported) at 1-year follow-up. In 2009, the Canadian Partnership Against Cancer organization and the Public Health Agency of Canada gave GCC a Coalitions Linking Action and Science for Prevention (CLASP; www.partnershipagainstcancer.ca) grant worth 1.6 million Canadian dollars to build upon the pilot study and deliver STP in schools across Canada. The STP intervention engaged 106 public schools (kindergarten to Grade 8; ages from 6 to 14 years) in a 1-year period. The Canadian STP model had a four-tier structure with GCC at the national level followed by provincial or territorial organizations, local school facilitators and school stakeholder committees. The CLASP project consisted of four steps. In Step 1 (January 2010), the provincial or territorial organizations and facilitators recruited stakeholders and schools. Each STP committee selected their schools based on prior relationships with municipalities and school boards. An honorarium of $1000 Canadian dollars at completion of baseline and follow-up surveys was received by the schools which could be used to support active school travel initiatives at the school level. In Step 2, three sources of baseline data (September 2010) were collected: take-home family survey, hands-up classroom survey over 5 days, an environmental scan (i.e., walkabout) to identify intersections or features that may pose barriers to active school travel and possible solutions. The information derived from Step 2 informed Step 3 (action planning), whereby stakeholder committees developed a written plan of action for dealing with school-specific issues and challenges for active school travel (AST). In the final step, strategies were implemented and follow-up data were requested to be collected 1 year after baseline (September 2011).

Three evaluations of this national project were conducted. Using student-reported data, Mammen et al.[31] found some evidence of localized success (1%–23% active school travel increase) in nearly half of the schools, but overall, there was no change in AST 1 year following implementation. There may have been individual successes identifiable at a more local scale. Nearly half of the schools saw an increase in AST in the morning period. Schools with larger enrolment (>368) showed greater AST changes at follow-up compared to schools with fewer students. In particular, the largest schools demonstrated the greatest increase in AST in the morning by 3.2%. An examination of school locations revealed that these larger schools were mostly located in urban centres and neighbourhoods with high street connectivity and potentially higher levels of walkability which have been found to be correlated with AST.[8,32]

To provide an additional indication of STP effectiveness on a national scale, Mammen et al.[33] subsequently used follow-up parent-reported data. This study showed more promise, there was a 17% mode shift from driving to AST 1 year following STP implementation. Furthermore, out of the approximately 1200 students who changed travel modes, the majority (~82%) changed to active modes such as walking and biking. Overall, 14% of the sample surveyed, representing 4% of the total number of students enrolled at all schools (i.e., 24,893) changed to AST at follow-up. These results are promising given the short time-frame and are in line with findings from New Zealand (3% increase in AST[29]). A novel objective of this study was to identify those students, families and schools that are more or less likely to respond behaviourally to STP. There is spatiotemporal complexity (e.g., AST is more common in some neighbourhoods compared to others; AST is typically more common in the afternoon) in school travel mode share[34] across Canada and likely most developed countries. The STP process remains best suited to addressing this complexity. However, this study demonstrated that it may not be suitable for every school. STP appeared more suitable for children in higher grades and for suburban- and urban-based schools, where a high proportion of households are within 'walkable' distance but many children are driven.

A final qualitative study assessed facilitators and barriers to effective STP implementation among 34 Canadian STP facilitators. The notable finding from this study was the broader impact that STP was considered to have had on school communities beyond changes in mode share. STP was considered primarily successful because it had started a conversation about school travel among community and school-level stakeholders that had lead to multidisciplinary consideration of potential solutions to promote AST. Such broader benefits are likely crucial to the sustainability of any STP impact.

The long-term goal of the CLASP initiative was to motivate changes to municipal and school-board policies and practices, so that active transportation to and from school is commonplace, providing a foundation for future local sustainability. Stimulating cultural change requires continued efforts; thus, by design, STP contained elements that built in long-term sustainability of the intervention. In particular, STP did not rely on a single organization or sector and instead involved a range of stakeholder groups and a diverse funding base for the local facilitator who engaged with schools. Intervention materials (e.g., intervention guidebook and posters) were made available online for free download, so that schools and communities could continue to use STP resources beyond the end of the funding period (http://www.saferoutestoschool.ca/school-travel-planning/). A lack of funding has prevented an evaluation of the sustainability of the initial STP intervention or of whether such planning is still happening.

14.5 Lessons Learnt

Overall, evidence from Canada and New Zealand has demonstrated a positive impact of school travel planning, that the intervention is well received by stakeholders and that it may have a broader impact than changes in mode share alone. An important lesson is that changes in mode share will likely take some time to be seen. For example, the STP analysis in Auckland, New Zealand,[29] demonstrated that AST rates were similar after 1 year, and modest behaviour change from passive to active modes of school travel only surfaced 3 years following implementation. A longer period of time may be required for action plans to be implemented and ingrained in the school community culture before a significant difference in AST rates is observed.[35]

An important lesson from the Canadian work was the likelihood that school travel planning may be better suited for particular types of schools located in built environments conducive to AST. A greater change in mode share was seen in larger schools which were mostly located in urban centres and neighbourhoods with high street connectivity.[35] More comparative studies are needed between varying contexts such as urban versus rural and high-enrolment versus low-enrolment schools to determine appropriate school-selection criterion for STP implementation.

A vital ingredient for successful school travel planning was the need for multisectoral collaboration, which was a successful outcome in both New Zealand and Canada. Multidisciplinary teams are advantageous in tackling complex issues by using the team's collective wisdom, expansive perspective and a holistic, integrated approach.[36] The process of school travel planning started a conversation about school travel among community and school-level stakeholders that called for multidisciplinary consideration of potential solutions to promote AST.[37] The involvement of school champions (e.g., principals, parents and students) in the STP process was also considered critical to effective implementation. Such champions are integral in building an AST culture within a school by increasing the awareness of AST and assisting with the various promotional strategies. Engaging and supporting ongoing buy-in of stakeholders remains a critical component of STP intervention.

While STP embraces a broad, multicomponent approach to school travel which can include education, enforcement or infrastructure improvements, the latter has been noted as being particularly critical in New Zealand. Some schools were located in challenging environments near major arterial routes. Previous work was not able to determine whether infrastructural changes or shifting parental/child travel perceptions had the greatest influence in changing travel behaviours. New Zealand parents, however, perceived an increase in traffic safety when physical changes around schools were realized. Similarly, in Canada, infrastructure improvements were reported as the most important component of the STP by parents.[35]

14.6 Conclusion

The case for school travel planning as an intervention approach makes strong intuitive sense given the spatiotemporal complexity in school travel mode share[34] across Canada and New Zealand and likely most developed countries. The STP process remains best suited to addressing this complexity in allowing schools to identify school-specific solutions to increasing active school travel. Evidence from Canada and New Zealand demonstrate modest effects at a national or regional scale, but such effects may take at least 2–3 years to manifest. At the same time, some evaluations demonstrate that perhaps it is not suited for every school and further consideration is needed in how best to match STP to schools that will most likely benefit. Longitudinal research and evaluations may be needed to support continued adoption and maintenance of school travel planning.

14.7 Recommendations for Policy and Practice

1. In the case of New Zealand, the programme needs to continue to be implemented in more cities and also evaluated. The development of resourcing mechanisms which provides ongoing support to schools with completed Travel Plans is also needed to ensure sustainability.
2. Practitioners and policymakers in other jurisdictions should consider implementing STP interventions.
3. In Canada, school travel planning has been largely supported by nongovernmental organizations reliant on inconsistent funding. There likely needs to be a shift to centralized, sustainable funding at the federal, provincial/territorial or municipal levels. From a critical perspective, STP could be considered more of a 'band-aid' solution to the pervasive barriers to AST that stem from the broader environmental and political climate.[37]
4. In terms of practice, two issues are worthy of closer future consideration. The majority of school travel intervention work worldwide has focused on the elementary or primary school level. There may be an important missed opportunity in not attempting to intervene at the secondary school context. Although school travel planning has been piloted in 7 secondary schools in Ottawa, Canada, change in mode share was not reported.[38] Given the typically greater distances between home and school for secondary students, it is likely that such plans will need to incorporate transit-related activity and strategies to encourage safe cycling.[39]
5. The focus of STP work in New Zealand has been on walking rather than cycling due to several barriers observed. Appropriate and more school cycle paths, cycle trains led by an adult, the presence of secure storage facilities at schools, cycle safety training and lower speed limit around schools and more safe places provided to cross the roads are recommended. Lessons for promoting cycling may be derived from the Danish Safe Routes to School intervention (see Chapter 13).

14.8 Recommendations for Future Research

In Canada at least, STP has largely been a grassroots initiative.[31] This has meant limited resources to support STP implementation and even less for evaluation. Lack of control schools, convenience sampling, reliance on self-report data and inconsistent timing of data collection are limitations in the Canadian context. Additionally, the degree of STP implementation was not assessed. Schools had approximately 1 year to form STP committees, collect baseline data, create action plans, implement action items and administer follow-up data. More rigorously designed longitudinal STP interventions (e.g., 2–4 years) are needed to provide stronger evidence in determining STP's long-term effectiveness and sustainability. Similar to the case of New Zealand, future research should adopt a detailed case study approach in examining how the STP intervention may work in different settings.

In determining the importance of infrastructural change versus changing perceptions, a research study involving a sample of schools undergoing infrastructural changes only compared to a sample of schools undergoing a shift in travel perceptions only may be necessary to determine the magnitude of the impact in travel behaviour change. In addition, case study schools should be followed longitudinally to better understand behaviour change motivators.

References

1. Sallis JF, Cervero RB, Ascher W, Henderson KA, Kraft MK, Kerr J. An ecological approach to creating active living communities. *Annu Rev Public Health* 2006;**27**:297–322.
2. Ahlport KN, Linnan L, Vaughn A, Evenson KR, Ward DS. Barriers to and facilitators of walking and bicycling to school: formative results from the non-motorized travel study. *Health Educ Behav* 2008;**35**(2):221–44.
3. Carver A, Timperio A, Hesketh K, Crawford D. Are children and adolescents less active if parents restrict their physical activity and active transport due to perceived risk? *Soc Sci Med* 2010;**70**(11):1799–805.
4. Loitz CC, Spencer-Cavaliere N. Exploring the barriers and facilitators to children's active transportation to and from school from the perspectives of practitioners. *J Phys Act Health* 2013;**10**(8):1128–35.
5. Panter J, Corder K, Griffin SJ, Jones AP, van Sluijs EM. Individual, socio-cultural and environmental predictors of uptake and maintenance of active commuting in children: longitudinal results from the SPEEDY study. *Int J Behav Nutr Phys Act* 2013;**10**(1):83. Available from: https://ijbnpa.biomedcentral.com/articles/10.1186/1479-5868-10-83.
6. Crawford S, Garrard J. A combined impact-process evaluation of a program promoting active transport to school: understanding the factors that shaped program effectiveness. *J Environ Public Health* 2013;**2013**.
7. McDonald NC. Children's mode choice for the school trip: the role of distance and school location in walking to school. *Transportation* 2008;**35**(1):23–35.
8. Mitra R, Buliung RN. The influence of neighborhood environment and household travel interactions on school travel behavior: an exploration using geographically-weighted models. *J Transp Geogr* 2014;**36**:69–78.
9. Yang Y, Abbott S, Schlossberg M. The influence of school choice policy on active school commuting: a case study of a middle-sized school district in Oregon. *Environ Plan A* 2012;**44**(8):1856–74.
10. Zhu X, Lee C. Walkability and safety around elementary schools: economic and ethnic disparities. *Am J Prev Med* 2008;**34**(4):282–90.
11. Gropp KM, Pickett W, Janssen I. Multi-level examination of correlates of active transportation to school among youth living within 1 mile of their school. *Int J Behav Nutr Phys Act* 2012;**9**(1):124. Available from: https://ijbnpa.biomedcentral.com/articles/10.1186/1479-5868-9-124.
12. Handy SL, Boarnet MG, Ewing R, Killingsworth R. How the built environment affects physical activity: views from urban planning. *Am J Prev Med* 2002;**23**(2S):64–73.
13. Larsen K, Gilliland J, Hess P, Tucker P, Irwin J, He M. The influence of the physical environment and sociodemographic characteristics on children's mode of travel to and from school. *Am J Public Health* 2009;**99**(3):520.
14. McMillan TE. The relative influence of urban form on a child's travel mode to school. *Transp Res Pol Pract* 2007;**41**(1):69–79.
15. Panter JR, Jones AP, Van Sluijs EMF, Griffin SJ. Neighborhood, route, and school environments and children's active commuting. *Am J Prev Med* 2010;**38**(3):268–78.
16. Schlossberg M, Greene J, Phillips PP, Johnson B, Parker B. School trips: effects of urban form and distance on travel mode. *J Am Plann Assoc* 2006;**72**(3):337–46.
17. Chriqui JF, Taber DR, Slater SJ, Turner L, Lowrey KM, Chaloupka FJ. The impact of state safe routes to school-related laws on active travel to school policies and practices in US elementary schools. *Health Place* 2012;**18**(1):8–15.

18. Eyler AA, Brownson RC, Doescher MP, Evenson KR, Fesperman CE, Litt JS, et al. Policies related to active transport to and from school: a multisite case study. *Health Educ Res* 2008;**23**(6):963–75.
19. Chillón P, Evenson KR, Vaughn A, Ward DS. A systematic review of interventions for promoting active transportation to school. *Int J Behav Nutr Phys Act* 2011;**8**(1):10. Available from: https://ijbnpa.biomedcentral.com/articles/10.1186/1479-5868-8-10.
20. Buliung R, Faulkner G, Beesley T, Kennedy J. School travel planning: mobilizing school and community resources to encourage active school transportation. *J Sch Health* 2011;**81**(11):704–12.
21. Atkins Limited. *An evaluation of the 'travelling to school initiative' programme: final report*. Birmingham, UK: Atkins Ltd; 2010.
22. Rowland D, DiGuiseppi C, Gross M, Afolabi E, Roberts I. Randomised controlled trial of site specific advice on school travel patterns. *Arch Dis Child* 2003;**88**:8–11.
23. Hinckson EA, Badland HM. *Auckland regional transport authority school travel plan evaluation 2006*. Auckland, New Zealand: Centre for Physical Activity and Nutrition Research, Auckland University of Technology; 2006. Report No.: 0890–1171.
24. Hinckson EA, Badland HM. School travel plans: preliminary evidence for changing school-related travel patterns in elementary school children. *Am J Health Promot* 2011;**25**(6):368–71.
25. Hinckson EA, Snowling N, Batts P, Badland H, Schofield G. *Evaluation of the school travel plan programme*. Auckland: Auckland Regional Transport Authority; 2007.
26. Hinckson EA, Duncan J, Kearns R, Badland H. *Auckland Regional Transport Authority: school travel plan evaluation-2007 school year*. Auckland: Auckland Regional Transport Authority; 2008.
27. Hinckson EA. *A school travel plan evaluation 2008: supplement*. Auckland: Auckland Regional Transport Authority; 2009.
28. Hinckson EA. *A school travel plan evaluation 2009: supplement*. Auckland: Auckland Regional Transport Authority; 2010.
29. Hinckson EA, Garrett N, Duncan JS. Active commuting to school in New Zealand Children (2004–2008): a quantitative analysis. *Prev Med* 2011;**52**:332–6.
30. Hinckson E. Perceived challenges and facilitators of active travel following implementation of the School Travel-Plan programme in New Zealand children and adolescents. *J Transp Health* 2016;**3**(3):321–5.
31. Mammen G, Stone MR, Faulkner G, Ramanathan S, Buliung R, O'Brien C, et al. Active school travel: an evaluation of the Canadian school travel planning intervention. *Prev Med* 2013.
32. Wong BY-M, Faulkner G, Buliung R, Irving H. Mode shifting in school travel mode: examining the prevalence and correlates of active school transport in Ontario, Canada. *BMC Publ Health* 2011;**11**(1):618. Available from: https://bmcpublichealth.biomedcentral.com/articles/10.1186/1471-2458-11-618.
33. Mammen G, Stone MR, Buliung R, Faulkner G. School travel planning in Canada: identifying child, family, and school-level characteristics associated with travel mode shift from driving to active school travel. *J Transp Health* 2014;**1**(4):288–94.
34. Mitra R, Buliung R, Roorda M. Built environment and school travel mode choice in Toronto, Canada. *Transport Res Rec* 2010;**2156**:150–9.
35. Mammen G, Stone MR, Faulkner G, Ramanathan S, Buliung R, O'Brien C, et al. Active school travel: an evaluation of the Canadian school travel planning intervention. *Prev Med* 2014;**60**:55–9.

36. Haggis C, Sims-Gould J, Winters M, Gutteridge K, McKay HA. Sustained impact of community-based physical activity interventions: key elements for success. *BMC Publ Health* 2013;**13**(1):892. Available from: https://bmcpublichealth.biomedcentral.com/articles/10.1186/1471-2458-13-892.
37. Mammen G, Stone MR, Buliung R, Faulkner G. "Putting school travel on the map": facilitators and barriers to implementing school travel planning in Canada. *J Transp Health* 2015;**2**(3):318–26.
38. Green Communities Canada. *Review of international school travel planning best practices.* 2007. http://www.saferoutestoschool.ca/downloads /STP-Best-Practice-Final.pdf.
39. Yang CC, Hsu YL. A review of accelerometry-based wearable motion detectors for physical activity monitoring. *Sensors* 2010;**10**(8):7772–88.

Walking School Buses and Bicycle Trains

15

Richard Larouche[1], *Jason A. Mendoza*[2,3,4]
[1]Faculty of Health Sciences, University of Lethbridge, Lethbridge, AB, Canada; [2]Department of Pediatrics, University of Washington School of Medicine, Seattle, WA, United States; [3]Center for Child Health, Behavior and Development, Seattle Children's Research Institute, Seattle, WA, United States; [4]Health Disparities Research Center, Fred Hutch/ UW Cancer Consortium, Seattle, WA, United States

> *I used the walking bus for nine months but now I'm walking to school on my own. I liked walking to school with all my friends and because I walked with lots of people, it didn't seem to take very long to get to school at all. I was taught how to cross roads safely and now I walk to school with two friends who used to be part of the walking bus. I give the walking bus 10 out of 10 because it helped me walk to school on my own.*
>
> ***10-year-old child interviewed about the walking school bus.***[a]

Chapter Outline

15.1 Introduction

Walking school buses (WSBs) are groups of children walking together on a set route under the supervision of at least one adult who typically volunteers as 'drivers' (or coordinators). Children are 'picked up' at different stops along the route, just like they would if they were using a regular school bus. The concept was initially proposed by an Australian activist, David Engwicht,[1] as a strategy to increase children's

[a] Source: Friends of the Earth (2000) https://www.foe.co.uk/sites/default/files/downloads/walking_bus.pdf.

Children's Active Transportation. https://doi.org/10.1016/B978-0-12-811931-0.00015-6

independent mobility and active transportation. The rationale is that by providing supervision, parental safety concerns can be alleviated while still allowing children to reap the benefits of active transportation. In this regard, Engwicht argued that WSBs should be viewed as the first step on a child's road to independence. He added that once children have developed their road safety skills and confidence, they should be allowed to walk without adult supervision and enjoy true independent mobility.

An attractive feature of WSBs is that they have the potential to make walking more convenient for parents. Indeed, parents can save time by not escorting their child to and from school every day.[2] Instead, they can take turns in leading a group of children participating in a WSB, similar to carpools in which parents take turns transporting their children to and from school. This is important because previous research has shown that parents tend to select the mode of transportation that they perceive as the quickest and easiest,[3,4] and adults have been conditioned to associate cars with speed, even though this reasoning may be flawed.[2]

According to Kearns et al.,[5] the first WSB was implemented in St. Albans, England, in 1998, and it resulted in a 30% decrease in driving to and from school. Following the success of this pilot study, the concept rapidly spread across the United Kingdom and to other countries such as Australia, Canada, New Zealand and the United States. In one of the first WSB studies from North America, Staunton et al.[6] reported on a Safe Routes to School programme in Marin County, California, that included WSBs and bicycle trains. This report showed increases in children's walking (64%), cycling (114%) and carpooling (91%), with 39% fewer trips carrying only one student in private vehicles. This intervention included many additional components including infrastructure improvements, classroom education, walk and bike to school days, newsletters, etc. Therefore, we can't tell the percent changes in school travel modes that are due specifically to the WSBs and bicycle trains. Anecdotal reports show that WSBs also exist in many continental European countries such as Belgium, France, Germany, Italy and Switzerland. In the 2009/2010 school year, a national survey of public elementary schools in the United States indicated that WSBs were offered in 6.2% of schools.[7]

WSBs may be included as part of a larger intervention such as Safe Routes to School (see Chapter 13) or school travel planning (see Chapter 14), but they are often implemented as a standalone intervention. More recently, bicycle trains[b] have been developed as a natural extension of the WSBs concept. Yet, very few studies have examined bicycle trains.[8]

In this chapter, we first review previous research about the effectiveness of WSBs for increasing active transportation and physical activity. We then discuss how WSBs are perceived by key stakeholders such as children, parents and school officials. Next, we highlight the limitations of WSBs and discuss about previous research that has examined whether these interventions can be maintained over time in the absence of dedicated funding. We conclude by providing recommendations for future interventions.

[b] More resources about bicycle trains can be found here: http://www.saferoutespartnership.org/sites/default/files/pdf/OrganizingBikeTrains-TipSheet_Final.pdf.

15.2 Effectiveness of Walking School Buses

Over the last 10–15 years, a number of studies have examined the effectiveness of WSBs (or bicycle trains) in increasing active transportation and physical activity.[8–16] These studies, summarized in Table 15.1, have predominantly been conducted in the United States among small samples of participants. Nevertheless, most of these interventions resulted in substantial increases in active transportation and decreases in driving. Given that school travel may account for 10%–14% of the number of private vehicles on the road during rush hour,[17] it is likely that broader implementation of WSBs could help reduce traffic and its associated greenhouse gas emissions.

Table 15.1 Effectiveness of walking school buses and bicycle trains interventions

Lead author (year)	Setting and participants	Study design[a]	Effect on travel behaviours	Effect on physical activity
Heelan (2009)	324 grades 1–5 students in 3 schools in Nebraska (USA)	Quasi-experimental with control group	School-wide level of walking to school at least 50% of the time was 27% higher in the 2 WSB schools than in the control school	MVPA increased by 17.4 min/day in the intervention group
Kong (2010)	28 students in kindergarten to grade 5 in New Mexico (USA)	Quasi-experimental	Not reported	Frequency of physical activity increased from 4.3 days/week to 5.3 days/week
Mackett (2005)	WSBs in Hertfordshire (UK); 3- to 11-year-olds	Retrospective survey[a]	62% of WSB users previously travelled by car	Switching from car travel to a WSB was associated with walking an additional 22 min/day
Mendoza (2009)	653 students in kindergarten to grade 5 from 3 schools in Seattle (USA)	Quasi-experimental with control group	At 12-month follow-up, 25% of students in the school that offered WSBs walked to school versus 7% in the control schools	Physical activity was not assessed

Continued

Table 15.1 Effectiveness of walking school buses and bicycle trains interventions—cont'd

Lead author (year)	Setting and participants	Study design[a]	Effect on travel behaviours	Effect on physical activity
Mendoza (2011)	149 grade 4 students in 8 low-SES schools in Houston (USA)	Randomized controlled trial	The WSB intervention led to a 38% increase in walking to school	MVPA increased by 7 min/day in the intervention group
Mendoza (2017)	54 grades 4–5 students in 4 low-SES schools in Seattle (USA)	Randomized controlled trial	The bicycle train intervention led to a 44.9% increase in the frequency of cycling to/from school	MVPA increased by 21.6 min/day in the intervention group
O'Fallon (2002)	112 primary school students in Christchurch, New Zealand	Quasi-experimental	62% of parents of WSB users reported that they previously drove their children to school	31% of parents reported that their child's physical activity increased as a result of the WSB
Sayers (2012)	77 8- to 9-year-olds in 3 schools in Columbia (USA)	Case–control analysis between participants and nonparticipants in a WSB	Effects on travel behaviours were not reported	There were no differences in the percentage of time spent in MVPA between participants and nonparticipants
Sirard (2008)	12 grades 3–5 students in one school in Menlo Park (USA)	Randomized controlled trial	All participants from the experimental group switched from car travel to walking	MVPA increased by 14 min/day in the intervention group

MVPA, moderate-to-vigorous physical activity; *SES*, socioeconomic status.
[a]Study designs are explained in more details in Chapter 6.

In the United Kingdom, Mackett et al.[11] reported that 62% of children who used WSBs were previously driven to school by car. In turn, switching from car travel to the WSBs was associated with 22 additional minutes of walking per school day. Similarly, Mendoza et al.[8] observed that participation in a bicycle train programme was associated with an extra 21.6 min of daily moderate-to-vigorous physical activity. Such a difference represents about one-third of the quantity of daily physical activity recommended by the World Health Organization.[18] Only one study that examined the effects of WSBs on physical activity did not observe positive effects[15] and that study was limited by a weaker study design and a small sample size.

To provide the reader with more concrete examples of the effectiveness of these interventions, we have summarized in more details two cluster randomized controlled trials that have assessed WSBs[13] (Panel 15.1) and bicycle trains[8] (Panel 15.2).

Panel 15.1 Randomized controlled trial of walking school buses in Houston, Texas

In a first-of-its-kind study, Mendoza et al.[13] tested the impact of a walking school bus programme on children's rates of walking to school and physical activity in Houston, USA. Eight public schools, which primarily served low-income families and racial/ethnic minorities, and 149 students in fourth grade participated. Schools were randomly chosen to receive the walking school bus programme or to receive no intervention (control schools). Over 4–5 weeks, students from the intervention schools significantly increased their walking to school by 38% compared to controls. Likewise, students from the intervention schools significantly increased their minutes of moderate-to-vigorous physical activity by 7 minutes/day compared to controls. This study provides proof of concept for the walking school bus programme and has implications for decreasing health inequities related to children's school transportation and physical activity.

Panel 15.2 Randomized controlled trial of bicycle trains in Seattle, Washington

In another first-of-its-kind study, Mendoza et al.[13] conducted a cluster randomized controlled trial to test the impact of the bicycle train programme on rates of cycling to school and physical activity in Seattle, USA. Four public schools that primarily served low-income families and racial/ethnic minorities, and 54 students in fourth and fifth grades participated. Participants at all schools received bicycles, helmets, lights, locks and a bicycle safety course. Schools were randomly chosen to receive the bicycle trains or no intervention (control schools). Compared to controls, students from the intervention schools significantly increased their cycling to school by 44.9% and their moderate-to-vigorous physical activity by 21.6 minutes/day over 4–6 weeks. This pilot study provides preliminary evidence that bicycle trains are very promising for increasing children's cycling to school and physical activity, as well as for reducing inequities in physical activity among children from racial/ethnic minorities and low-income families.

The schools that volunteered for these studies were randomly assigned to either an intervention group that received WSBs or bicycle trains, or to a control group that did not receive an intervention. This is the most robust study design to test the effectiveness of an intervention (see Chapter 6). In both studies, Mendoza et al.[8,13] observed significant increases in the proportion of children engaging in active transportation and in the time spent engaging in health-enhancing moderate-to-vigorous physical activity.

Another aim of WSBs is to teach children road safety skills in an attempt to prevent road injuries. To our knowledge, only Mendoza et al.[19] have assessed whether WSBs improve pedestrian behaviour. They found that following the implementation of WSBs, children were 5 times more likely to cross the street at the crosswalk; however, they were 5 times less likely to stop at the curb. These preliminary results should be interpreted with caution because pedestrian behaviour was observed for all primary school children, whereas the WSBs were only offered to fourth-grade students. Moreover, it can be impractical for a group of children to have each child stop at the curb rather than allow the group leader to determine the best time for the entire group to cross the street. In the broader injury literature, there is some evidence that pedestrian safety education targeting children can change observed road crossing behaviour, but it remains unclear if this actually translates into a reduced risk of injury.[20]

Cost-effectiveness of WSBs has only been assessed in one simulation study,[21] which suggested that the WSBs programme in Victoria (Australia) is not a cost-effective intervention to reduce obesity. Yet, the very narrow focus on obesity is likely the reason why the authors made that conclusion. Reducing obesity is only one of the many potential benefits of physical activity, and the authors omitted other potential benefits of WSBs such as the many other health benefits, reduced traffic congestion and greenhouse gas emissions. Clearly, there is a need for more robust research on the cost-effectiveness of WSB interventions using real world data.

15.3 Stakeholders' Perception of Walking School Buses

Many researchers have interviewed stakeholders (e.g., children, parents, schools and community members) about the perceived benefits of WSBs (Table 15.2). These benefits should also apply to bicycle trains. Many stakeholders have emphasized the role of WSBs in providing opportunities for physical activity. For example, a parent made a link between physical activity and classroom behaviour: '*The children let off steam walking to school; they are more settled upon arrival to school*'.[22] When asked what she liked about WSBs, a participant mentioned '*The fresh air. Exercise is good for you. And sometimes we even beat the cars. That's why I like going on the bus.*'[5] An older man who volunteered as a WSB coordinator also stressed the importance of physical activity: '*I'm nearly 70 years old. I've seen men my age fading away and dying because they don't do anything. I'm not going to be like them!*'[5]

In an Australian study, participation in a WSB was described as one of the only opportunities for children to engage with their community outside of the school

Table 15.2 Perceived benefits of walking school buses for different stakeholders

Children	Parents	Schools	Communities
Enjoyment of walking with friends	Can save time and stress involved in escorting children to/from school	Can help reduce traffic around the school	Can help reduce traffic and vehicle emissions
Opportunity for physical activity and spending time outside	Opportunity for physical activity	Can increase safety for pedestrians	Enhances community spirit
Physical activity may increase concentration and academic achievement	Allows parents to spend quality time with their child	Can assist schools in promoting physical activity	Can improve social cohesion
May minimize risk of accidents	Experience a sense of community		
Experience a sense of community			

context.[23] Rooney[23] also asked children to draw pictures of how they got to school and what they saw during their journey. She observed that, whereas children who were driven to school drew distant and generic images, those who used the WSB drew images that portrayed relationships with others, evoked happiness and illustrated a richer knowledge of the built and physical environment.

Parents have reported that WSBs can help reduce the stress associated with getting ready and escorting children to school.[16] It can also help them save time as this parent explains: '*I was sick and tired of the struggle and fight with getting the kids in the car and the seatbelts, the traffic and stress of driving, compared with the few mornings where I had walked with the children.*'[24]

Furthermore, benefits of WSBs may extend to the broader community. In the words of a respondent to the study by Collins and Kearns[22]: '[It's] *a focal point in the community* [that] *gives neighbours a reason to communicate*'. Another parent explained how participating in a WSB was a good way for her to get to know her neighbours: '*There's um a boy further up the street... they've been here for eight or nine years and I didn't even know they existed* [before the WSB].'[23] A city councilor interviewed by the Canadian Cancer Society (which has received substantial funding to implement WSBs in Canada) also mentioned '*What a nice unifying project! City Council is proud to support [*walking school buses*] (...) The WSB help boost sense of community, make school trips safer and promote active transportation and healthy active living among kids and grown-ups. All of this at a lower cost.*'[25]

15.4 Limitations of Walking School Buses

Collins and Kearns[22] argued that while WSBs challenge some practices associated with car dependence in Auckland (New Zealand), they also reinforce the perception that children are unpredictable pedestrians who are incapable of safely navigating streets independently. This perception has been identified as a key reason why, over the last few decades, children have retreated from public space in many Western cities.[26–28] In this regard, WSBs do not change the power relationship between children and adults. As pointed out by Kearns et al.[5]: '*Although WSBs offer children some agency as vulnerable road users, they are highly structured initiatives that ultimately seek to control children as opposed to traffic, and have only a limited ability to address congestion and automobile dependence (restricted, as they are, to primary schools).*' Along the same lines, Hillman[29] argued that while WSBs can increase physical activity, children remain under constant adult supervision and do not enjoy the benefits of independent mobility. He added that, while well intentioned, such programmes fail to address the root cause of the problem, which is the increase in traffic and the speed of vehicles. He also believed that WSBs reinforce the perception that the outdoor environment is hostile and, therefore, children need to be closely supervised.

Contrary to this negative perception of WSBs, research conducted in New Zealand suggests that an increase in children's independent mobility was a perceived benefit of WSBs.[30–32] For example, a WSB coordinator mentioned that '*It gives the kids some security on their way to school, but also gives them some independence because they aren't being taken to school every day by their parents*'.[32] The quote at the beginning of this chapter also conveys the idea of 'graduating' from WSBs to independent walking. Interestingly, one of the key reasons given by coordinators to explain why WSBs were discontinued was that the children had gotten older and more competent, and they wanted to walk on their own.[30] These qualitative findings support the view of WSBs as a stepping stone for children's independent mobility as initially proposed by Engwicht.[1]

Of greater concern, WSBs are much more frequent in high-income neighbourhoods, which raises issues of equity. For example, Collins and Kearns[24] found almost half of the WSB routes were located in neighbourhoods that were among the wealthiest 10%. Almost none existed in the poorer neighbourhoods. This situation is likely attributable to the possibility for wealthier parents to enjoy more flexible work conditions. Regardless, it is concerning because children living in more deprived neighbourhoods are usually exposed to greater traffic volume and are more likely to be victims of road accidents.[24,33,34] Nevertheless, it is particularly encouraging that randomized controlled trials show that WSBs and bicycle trains can be efficacious in low-income schools.[8,12,13] Further investigation is needed to examine whether the success of these interventions led by Mendoza can be replicated in less tightly controlled research conditions.

Finally, WSBs may not be necessary for developing children's independent mobility in some settings. For example in Japan, where school location policies, safety measures, boards of education, school walking curricula and parental expectations result in very high rates of children walking to school.[35] With such high numbers of children walking to school, often in groups, even many first graders in Japan walk to school unaccompanied by parents. Clearly, there are lessons to be learned from countries and settings where walking to school is a cultural cornerstone of childhood.

15.5 Sustainability of Walking School Buses

To date, limited research has examined whether WSB interventions can persist over time. This is a legitimate concern because WSBs typically rely on parent volunteers. After the enthusiasm associated with the establishment of a new WSB wanes, some volunteers may lose interest, and, in turn, this may lead to the collapse of a particular route.[30] Recruiting new volunteers to replace those who quit may be a challenge. In addition, volunteers may be less likely than paid employees to show up on cold, rainy or snowy days.

An investigation of WSB routes in Auckland (New Zealand) from 2002 to 2006 provides some reassurance in this regard.[22] According to this survey, the number of routes increased from 39 to 158 while the number of registered children rose from 575 to 2873. In 27 of 53 schools that were surveyed in 2003, at least one route had been in operation for at least 1 year. Some coordinators interviewed also emphasized that the implementation of WSBs was helpful in advocating for safer walking infrastructure, such as the implementation of traffic islands.[5,22]

However, a study in Christchurch (New Zealand) indicated that out of 56 WSBs that had been introduced since 2000, only 30 were still operational in 2003; thus 46% of routes were discontinued.[30] Kingham and Ussher[30] interviewed 16 former WSB coordinators to shed light on the reasons explaining discontinuation. All parent coordinators mentioned that when they quit, their children were old enough to walk or bike alone. Other reasons included lack of other volunteers, changes in family circumstances, such as moving out of the neighbourhood, and returning to work (and dropping children at school on the way). These reasons imply that there was nobody to take over the role of the coordinator after they left. Coordinators also mentioned that they were satisfied with the support that they received from City Council and from the school for setting up the WSBs; however, following implementation, they received limited support and recognition for their efforts. Based on the conflicting findings, there remains a need for further investigation on the sustainability of WSBs.

In an effort to make WSBs more sustainable, Green Communities Canada[36] (a nonprofit organization that implements school travel plans in Canada), has partnered with other organizations in the City of Ottawa to develop a pilot project that included trained, insured and paid WSB coordinators. The project initially took place from late September to December in 8 schools. Routes were designed to require less than 30 minutes to complete and to arrive at school no later than 5 minutes before the bell. Fifty-four parents registered their children of whom 21 previously traveled by bus or car only. The WSB leaders recorded the number of children participating each day, and these numbers were averaged for each week. Ridership remained relatively stable with a range from 23 to 32 students per day. School administrators and parents interviewed were highly satisfied and expressed positive views about the paid model.

Following this evaluation, additional funding has been provided by the Ottawa Student Transportation Authority (an organization responsible for bus transportation) to offer the programme throughout the school year.[c] The programme is now offered in 13 primary schools within the city of Ottawa. Future research is warranted to compare the effectiveness of such a programme to traditional WSBs with volunteer coordinators. If conclusive, such programmes could help address the difficulty of maintaining WSBs in low-income neighbourhoods.

15.6 Conclusion

Our review of the literature suggests that WSBs may be an effective intervention in primary school settings to increase children's active transportation and physical activity and reduce car travel. However, much of the research so far has been conducted in small samples of children in the United States. Children, parents and other stakeholders pointed out many benefits of WSBs such as physical activity, spending time outdoors, saving time, helping children develop road safety skills and reducing stress, traffic congestion and pollution. Nevertheless, important limitations of WSBs include the reliance on volunteers who may lose their enthusiasm over time and the limited provision of WSBs in low-income neighbourhoods where children are exposed to a greater amount of traffic. Furthermore, there remains a lack of research examining the sustainability of WSBs over time.

15.7 Recommendations for Policy and Practice

1. As a strategy to increase the sustainability of WSBs, policymakers should consider paying WSB coordinators, just like school bus drivers and crossing guards are paid for their work.
2. From an equity perspective, practitioners should strive to implement more WSBs in low-income neighbourhoods where children are exposed to greater traffic volume and where the risk of collisions with motor vehicles is greater.
3. Policymakers and practitioners should provide resources and support for parents interested in setting up a WSB.

15.8 Recommendation for Future Research

1. There remains a clear need for long-term studies on the effectiveness of WSBs.
2. Given that only one study has assessed the effectiveness of bicycle trains,[8] there is a need for further investigation.
3. Studies examining the feasibility and effectiveness of WSBs in low- and middle-income countries are warranted.

[c] More details about this programme (including videos) can be found at this website: http://www.saferoutestoschool.ca/walking-school-bus.

References

1. Engwicht D. *Towards an eco-city: calming the traffic*. Sydney (Australia): Envirobook; 1992.
2. Tranter P. How to save time and money: using the walking school bus to increase your 'effective speed'. *World Transp Pol Pract* 2008;**14**(1):56–63.
3. Faulkner GEJ, Richichi V, Buliung RN, Fusco C, Moola F. What's 'quickest and easiest?': parental decision making about school travel mode. *Int J Behav Nutr Phys Act* 2010;**7**:62. Available from: http://ijbnpa.biomedcentral.com/articles/10.1186/1479-5868-7-62.
4. McDonald NC, Aalborg AE. Why parents drive children to school: implications for safe routes to school programs. *J Am Plann Assoc* 2009;**3**:331–42.
5. Kearns RA, Collins DCA, Neuwelt PM. The walking school bus: extending children's geographies? *Area* 2003;**35**(3):285–92.
6. Staunton CE, Hubsmith D, Kallins W. Promoting safe walking and biking to school: the Marin County success story. *Am J Public Health* 2003;**93**(9):1431–4.
7. Turner L, Chriqui JF, Chaloupka FJ. Walking school bus programs in U.S. public elementary schools. *J Phys Act Health* 2013;**10**(5):641–5.
8. Mendoza JA, Haaland W, Jacobs M, et al. Bicycle trains, cycling, and physical activity: a pilot cluster RCT. *Am J Prev Med Epub* June 2017;**28**.
9. Heelan KA, Abbey BM, Donnelly JE, Mayo MS, Welk GJ. Evaluation of a walking school bus for promoting physical activity in youth. *J Phys Act Health* 2009;**6**:560–7.
10. Kong AS, Burks N, Conklin C, Roldan C, Skipper B, Scott S, et al. A pilot walking school bus program to prevent obesity in Hispanic elementary school children: role of physician involvement with the school community. *Clin Pediatr* 2010;**49**(10):989–91.
11. Mackett R, Lucas L, Paskins J, Turbin J. *Walking buses in Hertfordshire: impacts and lessons*. London (UK): University College London; 2005. Available from: http://www.eltis.org/sites/eltis/files/case-studies/documents/walking_bus_report_-_ucl_3.pdf.
12. Mendoza JA, Levinger DD, Johnston BD. Pilot evaluation of a walking school bus program in a low-income, urban community. *BMC Publ Health* 2009;**9**:122.
13. Mendoza JA, Watson K, Baranowski T, Nicklas TA, Uscanga DK, Hanfling MJ. The walking school bus and Children's physical activity: a pilot cluster randomized controlled trial. *Pediatrics* 2011;**128**(3):e537–44.
14. O'Fallon C, Sullivan C, Cottam P. Walking school bus networks: a 'flaxroots' approach to cleaner air. In: *Paper presented to the 16th International Clean Air & Environment Conference, Christchurch, New Zealand*. 2002. Available from: http://www.pinnacleresearch.co.nz/research/WSB/O%27Fallon2002WSB.pdf.
15. Sayers SP, LeMaster JW, Thomas IM, Petroski GF, Ge B. A walking school bus program: impact on physical activity in elementary school children in Columbia, Missouri. *Am J Prev Med* 2012;**43**(5S4):S384–9.
16. Sirard JR, Alhassan S, Spencer TR, Robinson TN. Changes in physical activity from walking to school. *J Nutr Educ Behav* 2008;**40**(5):324–6.
17. McDonald NC, Brown AL, Marchetti LM, Pedroso MS. U.S. school travel, 2009: an assessment of trends. *Am J Prev Med* 2011;**41**(2):146–51.
18. World Health Organization. *Global recommendations on physical activity for health*. Geneva (Switzerland): World Health Organization; 2010. Available from: http://apps.who.int/iris/bitstream/10665/44399/1/9789241599979_eng.pdf.
19. Mendoza JA, Watson K, Chen T-A, Baranowski T, Nicklas TA, Uscanga DK, Hanfling MJ. Impact of a pilot walking school bus intervention on children's pedestrian safety behaviors: a pilot study. *Health Place* 2012;**18**(1):24–30.

20. Duperrex O, Bunn F, Roberts I. Safety education of pedestrians for injury prevention: a systematic review of randomised controlled trials. *BMJ* 2002;**324**:1129.
21. Moodie M, Haby M, Galvin L, Swinburn B, Carter R. Cost-effectiveness of active transport for primary school children - walking School Bus program. *Int J Behav Nutr Phys Act* 2009;**6**:63. Available from: https://ijbnpa.biomedcentral.com/articles/10.1186/1479-5868-6-63.
22. Collins D, Kearns RA. Walking school buses in the Auckland region: a longitudinal assessment. *Transp Policy* 2010;**17**:1–8.
23. Rooney M. 'Oh, you're just up the street!' the role of walking school bus in generating local community for children and adults. *World Transp Pol Pract* 2008;**14**(1):39–47.
24. Collins D, Kearns RA. Geographies of inequality: child pedestrian injury and walking school buses in Auckland, New Zealand. *Soc Sci Med* 2005;**60**:61–9.
25. Société canadienne du cancer. *Trottibus en bref* 2018. Available from: http://www.trottibus.ca/trottibus-en-bref/.
26. Gleeson B, Sipe N. *Creating child friendly cities: reinstating kids in the city*. London: Routledge; 2006.
27. Roberts I. Why have child pedestrian death rates fallen? *BMJ* 1993;**306**:1737–9.
28. Roberts I, Edwards P. *The energy glut: the politics of fatness in an overheating world*. London (UK): Zed Books; 2010.
29. Hillman M. The impact of transport policy on children's development. In: *Canterbury Safe routes to schools project seminar*. Canterbury (UK): Canterbury Christ College University; 1999. Available from: http://old.spokeseastkent.org.uk/mayer.php.
30. Kingham S, Ussher S. Ticket to a sustainable future: an evaluation of the long-term durability of the Walking School Bus programme in Christchurch, New Zealand. *Transp Policy* 2005;**12**(4):314–23.
31. Kingham S, Ussher S. An assessment of the benefits of the walking school bus in Christchurch, New Zealand. *Transp Res Part A* 2007;**41**:502–10.
32. Kingham S, Ussher S. Walking School Buses in Christchurch – do they encourage or discourage independent mobility? *World Transp Pol Pract* 2008;**14**(1):27–38.
33. Morency P, Gauvin L, Plante C, Fournier M, Morency C. Neighborhood social inequalities in road traffic injuries: the influence of traffic volume and road design. *Am J Public Health* 2012;**102**(6):1112–9.
34. Roberts I, Norton R, Taua B. Child pedestrian injury rate: the importance of 'exposure to risk' relating to socioeconomic and ethnic differences, in Auckland, New Zealand. *J Epidemiol Community Health* 1996;**50**:162–5.
35. Mori N, Armada F, Willcox DC. Walking to school in Japan and childhood obesity prevention: new lessons from an old policy. *Am J Public Health* 2012;**102**(11):2068–73.
36. Green Communities Canada. *Case study: the Ottawa walking school bus pilot project*. Ottawa (ON): Green Communities Canada; 2015. Available from: http://saferoutestoschool.ca/sites/default/files/Ottawa%20WSB%20Pilot%20case%20study%2C%20final%20May%202015_0.pdf.

Taming Traffic to Encourage Children's Active Transportation

16

Paul Tranter
School of Physical, Environmental and Mathematical Sciences, University of New South Wales Canberra, Canberra, Australia

Children today walk less than ever before in the history of humanity.[1]

Chapter Outline

16.1 Introduction

One reason children in many nations walk and cycle less than in previous generations is that parents are concerned about traffic danger and stranger danger (children getting abducted or molested).[2] A common response to these concerns is an individualistic response—to drive or accompany children, or restrict their mobility. This chapter explains how an alternative response, involving collective action to tame traffic in areas where children move, can effectively overcome these concerns.

This collective action has been identified as an urgent and highly cost-effective public health intervention; a proven area-wide 'vaccine' against serious injury.[3]

Children's Active Transportation. https://doi.org/10.1016/B978-0-12-811931-0.00016-8

Recognizing that 'low speeds save lives', the Global Initiative for Child Health and Mobility calls for the reduction and enforcement of 'traffic speeds to a level safe for children everywhere, prioritising low speed zones in residential areas and near schools'.[3] This chapter describes strategies to tame traffic that help improve road safety and achieve higher levels of children's active travel (as well as more livable environments for all citizens). These strategies include lowering posted speed limits (PSLs), re-designing residential streets and implementing play streets at specific times of the day/week. Evidence for the success of these strategies is outlined.

16.2 Why Lower Speeds Make Sense for Children's Active Transportation

There is a growing realization that speeds above 30 km/h (or 20 mph) are not compatible with a child-friendly (and walking- and cycling-friendly) environment. To understand why this is the case requires understanding the laws of physics, the limitations of human bodies to withstand sudden impacts, the psychology of the use of streets and feedback effects arising from reducing speeds.

The laws of physics help to explain why lower speeds are safer. Kinetic energy is directly proportional to the mass of the object and to the square of its velocity. This means that a slight increase in speed can have devastating impacts on pedestrian injury.[7] In addition, avoiding a collision is significantly easier at lower speeds due to greatly reduced stopping distances.

Few motorists appreciate the substantial increase in risk accompanying even minor increases in speed. Svenson et al. (2012, p. 488)[7a] explain how 30 km/h, compared with 50 km/h driving speed, results in a child not being hit by a car (30 km/h) and being killed or seriously injured (50 km/h):

> *'We assume a reaction time of 1 s and at a speed of 30 km/h a car will travel 8.33 m during that time before the brakes start to apply. If the speed is 50 km/h the corresponding distance is 13.89 m. This is a little longer than the total stopping distance from 30 km/h (12.75 m). This means that a driver who could stop from 30 km/h in front of an obstacle would hit that obstacle at a speed of 50 km/h if she drove at 50 km/h under the same conditions'.*

Setting speed limits of 30 km/h recognizes the ability of the human body to withstand impact. Humans have evolved to withstand the impact of colliding with an object at maximum running speeds.[8, p. 44] As Hamilton-Baillie explains, there is a kink in graphs showing the relationship between impact speed and severity of pedestrian injury. There is a sharp increase in severity above 30 km/h; the chances of a pedestrian surviving, after being hit by a car, decrease rapidly above this speed.[9]

Some local government areas, in Australia and elsewhere, have introduced 40 km/h speed limits in residential neighbourhoods. While this is likely to improve pedestrian safety compared with 50 km/h limits, the differences in stopping distances and risk of death between 40 and 30 km/h are substantial. Researchers at the Monash University

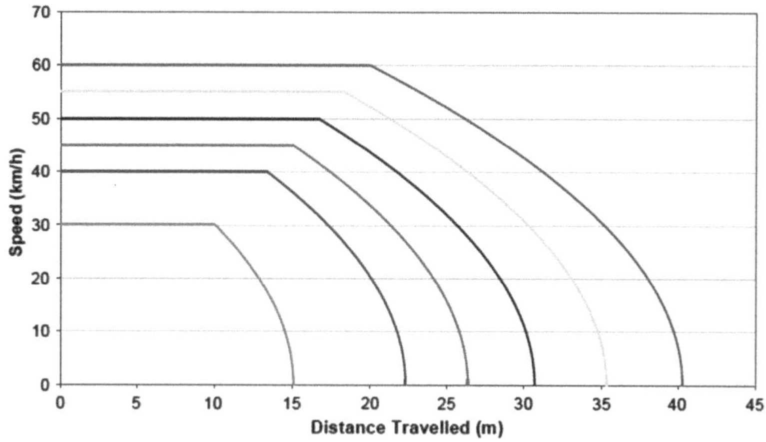

Figure 16.1 Stopping distance profiles for a range of initial travel speeds. Reproduced with thanks to Corben, D'Elia and Healy (2006).[10]

Accident Research Centre explain; if driving at 30 km/h, a motorist would stop within 15 m, assuming a driver's perception-reaction time of 1.2 s. The same motorist travelling at 40 km/h would hit a pedestrian at about 36 km/h at the 15-m mark (Fig. 16.1). Choosing a travel speed of 30 km/h compared with 40 km/h is estimated to reduce the risk of death to a pedestrian by almost 80%.[10]

Another value of lower vehicle speeds is the psychology of low-speed streets. Despite the seemingly irrefutable logic of the above reasoning in support of 30 km/h speed limits, travel behaviour change experts understand that such arguments may be 'unlikely to engender a massive mode shift to walking and cycling'.[11, p. 13] Yet, when motorized vehicles travel at 30 km/h (instead of 40 or 50 km/h), this changes the psychological feel of the streets; the streets 'feel' safer. Retaining eye contact with other people becomes much more difficult when we move faster than a fast running speed; eye contact between motorists and other road users decreases rapidly as speeds increase above 30 km/h.[8] As we move faster, our field of vision also narrows. Verbal and nonverbal communication between road users is an important aspect of an effectively functioning urban public space. 'Thus it appears that speed may be a factor in urban quality in a wider context than simple safety and accident reduction'.[8, p. 45]

As a result of increased feelings of safety in low-speed streets, more people of all ages use the streets as pedestrians and cyclists, thus creating a 'safety in numbers' effect.[12] Parents are more confident allowing children to play in (or beside) the street because of reduced traffic danger and reduced stranger danger associated with increased surveillance in communities with more frequent face-to-face interactions.[11]

Other feedback impacts may promote children's active transportation. When lower speeds encourage more walking and cycling, this can lead to more local shopping and more viable local shops (especially if shops are near local schools). This in turn creates a positive cycle; more people use local facilities as they become more attractive, which strengthens local communities, which reduces concerns about strangers.

16.3 Strategies to Tame Traffic and Their Impact on Road Safety

Lower speeds unarguably make streets safer for vulnerable road users and create environments where children's active transportation can be more safely increased. Several strategies have been employed to achieve lower motorized traffic speeds. The simplest approach is to lower the PSL. While this has limited effectiveness in reducing speeds in any particular street, it can be cost-effective over large areas. Another approach is physical traffic calming, sometimes in combination with lower PSLs. In Britain, this is referred to as 'low speed zones'. This can be done with either 30 km/h speed limits or with very low speeds (20 km/h or less), as in the Dutch woonerven or British Home Zones. Another strategy is 'psychological traffic calming', relying on changing the perception of streets to reduce speeds.[13] The final example outlined here is the 'play street', involving temporary closing of a residential street to motorized vehicles and using the street as play space.[11]

16.3.1 Lower Posted Speed Limits

Some road safety researchers argue 'the most direct and cost-effective way of managing speed has been to reduce the posted speed limit (PSL)'.[14, p. 483] However, it is also recognized that speed limits may not automatically reduce speeding, and if road conditions suggest that the PSL is too low, drivers may simply ignore it.[15] To maximize the effect of any new speed limit, streets ideally should be designed to match the designated speed.

Despite these limitations, speed limit reduction is now the standard recommendation of road safety researchers and practitioners, and jurisdictions throughout the world are introducing lower speed limits.[14] Speeds of 50 or 60 km/h are regarded as inappropriate in residential streets, considering the high likelihood of human interaction with motor vehicles, including children playing and people walking, cycling or crossing the street.[14]

'Studies consistently show that crash incidence or crash severity decline whenever speed limits have been reduced'.[16, p. 57] In Victoria, Australia, lowering speed limits from 60 to 50 km/h in residential streets produced a 12%–13% reduction in all casualty crashes, 19%–22% reduction in pedestrian casualty crashes and a 40%–46% reduction in pedestrian fatal and serious injury crashes. The reduced speed limits increased travel times, but only by 9 s per trip.[16, p. 58]

In a growing number of cities, particularly in Germany, the Netherlands, Denmark and Britain, speed limits of 30 km/h have been introduced across large areas. However, lowering speed limits to 30 km/h can trigger opposition from community groups, at least when first proposed.

The first city to introduce lower speed limits across an entire urban area was Graz, Austria. In 1992, 30 km/h speed limits were introduced across the city, on all streets except a few priority roads, with a 50 km/h limit. When first proposed, the majority of citizens opposed the lower limits. Using the argument that people could not effectively judge a situation that they had not experienced, the government introduced the lower speed limits despite low public approval. Within 2 years, there was majority support for the new limits, even from motorists; they appreciated the increased livability of the city and showed greater consideration to one another on 30 km/h streets.[17,18] In July 1994, the scheme was made permanent.[19] Lower speed limits in Graz led to a 12% reduction of accidents with injury, 24% reduction in serious injury, 17% reduction in pedestrian injury and a 14% reduction in injury to car users. There was also a marked increase in cycling.

When speed limits alone are introduced, this may lead to only minor reductions in average speeds.[20] Typically, reductions of around 2 mph or less can be expected when 20 mph limits replace 30 mph limits.[14,21] Reductions in speed after the introduction of 'low speed zones' (lower speed limits accompanied by physical changes to streets such as speed humps and chicanes) could be as high as 10 mph.[20]

This does not mean that 30 km/h speed limits by themselves are not useful. Lower speed limits are much cheaper to implement at an area-wide level. Even if less effective than low-speed zones in particular streets, they can be cost-effective. As King and Semlyen[22] argue, unless implementation cost is considered, comparing the value of low-speed zones versus speed limits alone is futile. The cost of physical traffic calming is about £60,000 per km compared to £1100 per km for speed limits alone. For the cost of 1 km of physical calming, 50 km of roads could have 20 mph limits, or about 250 people compared to 12,500 people being influenced.[22] King and Semlyen estimate that each 1 mph reduction in average speed leads to 5%–6% fewer casualties. A reduction of 1–2 mph over a whole network leads to 'much more benefit to more residents than a large reduction on a few streets in a zone'.[22, p. 66] These arguments are supported by other researchers: 'it is a fundamental principle of epidemiology that small reductions in risk in the entire population save more lives than do big reductions in risk in the small number of high-risk individuals'.[23, p. 140]

If speed limits are consistently applied over large areas, this 'conveys the message that 20 mph is a suitable, normal speed in residential areas'.[21] Isolated physically calmed zones convey a message 'speed up' as drivers exit the zones.[22] If lower speed limits are to be effectively employed, it is important that 20 mph limits are seen 'as the new norm for urban areas'.[24, p. 165]

A sensible strategy for lowering speeds across a city would be to start with 30 km/h speed limits and progressively introduce physical traffic-calming measures. This should be accompanied by education campaigns explaining the value of lower speeds, along with ongoing consultation with local communities. Enforcement of the speed limits is also important.[9,14] Speed cameras, for example, have been shown to have an immediate and significant impact on both deaths and case fatality rates (the proportion of casualties who die, which is independent of distance travelled).[23] However, enforcement alone may lead to community backlash.

16.3.2 Physical Traffic Calming

Physical traffic calming has been successfully implemented in cities throughout the world, with the primary aims of reducing environmental and safety problems, altering driver behaviour and improving conditions for pedestrians and vulnerable road users. PSLs, changes to street alignments, street narrowing, vehicular obstacles and other design tactics act to lower travel speeds. Area-wide traffic-calming schemes are commonly implemented in residential neighbourhoods, sometimes in combination with a clear road hierarchy to direct through traffic away from residential streets. In some cases, streets are closed to through traffic.[2]

A meta-analysis of studies on road safety impacts of area-wide traffic calming showed that they effectively reduce injury accidents (by around 25% in residential streets).[25] Traffic calming is remarkably successful in reducing child road deaths. For example, in the 1970s, Denmark had the highest rate of child road deaths in Western Europe. In 1976, the Danish government introduced legislation requiring local governments to reduce speeds to a norm of 30 km/h and to invest in infrastructure to encourage walking and cycling. Denmark now has much lower casualty rates than the UK.[2, p. 108]

In Britain, traffic-calming strategies in the '20-mph zones', where PSLs are combined with traffic calming, led to speed limits becoming self-enforcing. Studies of the impacts of these zones in Britain found some zones achieved dramatic decreases in casualties.[26] An earlier study of the impact of 20-mph zones in London found similar results.[27] Relative to other roads, and controlling for background reductions in road injuries, 20-mph zones reduced traffic speed and volume and led to a 40% reduction in casualties and collisions from 1986 to 2006.[27] There was no increase in casualties in adjacent areas. The reduction in casualties was the greatest for younger children (48.5%).[27] These findings are also reflected in other studies[28] that provide clear evidence that '20 mph zones and limits are effective means of improving public health via reduced accidents and injuries'.[29]

16.3.3 Shared Streets: Woonerven and Home Zones

Home zones and woonerven represent a specific type of physical traffic calming. In the 1970s, a new residential street layout was introduced in the Dutch city of Delft. Instead of segregating pedestrians and cars, they were integrated—sharing street space.[30] This approach, known as 'woonerf' meaning 'living yard' (woonerven plural) was given a legal status by the Dutch government. Similar models emerged in many Western nations, including Denmark, Britain, Japan, Australia, New Zealand and Israel. These streets, where cars are expected to proceed very slowly, removed the distinction between pavements for pedestrians and carriageways for cars, allowing pedestrians and children to reclaim street space.[31] Studies of shared streets in several nations have found considerable reductions in traffic accidents.[30]

In Denmark, the importance of such streets for children's play is indicated in their name: 'Rest and Play' streets, with 15 km/h speed limits.[32] In Britain, similar streets are referred to as 'Home Zones'. Like woonerven, Home Zones have a surface shared by people and cars, without grade separation between the roadway and pedestrian pavement. There is also often tree planting, better lighting, textured surfaces and symbolic gateway entrances.[2, p. 108] New residential developments designed with Home Zone concepts in mind have advantages over traditional estates; shared streets reduce costs, as less space is allocated to streets and density can increase without affecting privacy.[30]

Despite these advantages, Home Zones and Woonerven have limitations. While they challenge the conventional view of streets being primarily for cars, they have little impact on the child-friendliness of cities as a whole. When distinctively designed Home Zone streets appear, 'this can imply that drivers must drive carefully in these zones, but it is acceptable to drive less carefully in other parts of the city'.[11,20]

16.3.4 Psychological Traffic Calming

Physical traffic calming effectively reduces speed and accidents but can be unpopular and expensive. Alternative calming techniques make use of psychological (non-physical) measures, which can significantly reduce driving speeds. One proponent of psychological traffic calming identified three broad themes: uncertainty, intrigue and humour.[13] In *Mental Speed Bumps*, Engwicht argued that motorists drive slowly when there is uncertainty about whether people will be on the street, and when they are intrigued; if streetscapes inspire curiosity, drivers slow down to observe the environment. In terms of humour, drivers rarely hurry when amused.

Psychological design principles generate lower speeds by more complex street environments, limiting distant views, disturbing linearity, creating uncertainty, increasing roadside activity or changes to perception that make the streets seem less safe.[33] While making streets seem less safe may appear counterintuitive, it has been remarkably effective in civilizing streets.

Hans Monderman, the head of road safety for Friesland in the Netherlands in the 1980s, discovered that safety improved when streets were designed to encourage drivers to think for themselves. He made roads safer by making them seem more dangerous. Removing safety barriers and signs made streets more like a village, and even he was surprised when speeds, where familiar safety treatments had been removed, dropped dramatically, much more than with traditional traffic calming.[34] Monderman's innovations were the first steps towards what is now known as 'psychological traffic calming'.[35]

Psychological traffic calming does not need to be instigated by a planning or government authority. Residents can enact subtle changes in their behaviour that can influence the way streets are used. When parents start a walking school bus (see Chapter 15), this can generate psychological traffic calming; drivers are more careful when driving past groups of children walking with adults, especially if the drivers know the people who are walking.[36] Tim Gill, a longstanding advocate for child-friendly urban planning and design in Britain, argues that children's mosaics and other public art may increase symbolic control of streets. As Engwicht explained: The speed on most streets is determined to a large extent by the degree to which the residents have psychologically retreated from their street.[11,13] Even something as simple as sitting on the front steps of houses can help to change the psychological feel of streets.[11,37]

16.3.5 Temporary Changes to Tame Traffic: Play Streets

Play streets involve temporary closing of streets to motorized traffic to allow children to use the street for play (Fig. 16.2). The practice of closing streets for children's play has a long history. As early as the 1920s, 60 streets in New York were closed to allow children to play during certain times.[38, p. 41] In the 1950s, 700 play streets operated across England and Wales.[39] They almost disappeared in Britain by the 1980s, then

Figure 16.2 Fairbridge Road Play Street, Islington, London, in Year 2 of operation, October 2015. Photo courtesy of London Play.

re-appeared in 2009, when the model promoted by 'Playing Out' began in a Bristol street. By 2017, more than 500 streets across Britain were play streets at certain times. Similar schemes exist in other nations. Belgium's Speelstraat programme operates in a similar way to British play streets: 'residents formally request the city government to temporarily close off a residential street to enable children to play'.[11,19]

Closing streets for a few hours is easily implemented without built environment changes. Play streets have the potential to be introduced in a large number of streets quickly and cheaply. Many street closures occur at least once a month. Procedures for operating play streets successfully have been developed by the UK organisation 'Playing Out', which believes 20-mph zones complement street play initiatives.

A limitation of play streets is that play on streets may be regarded as something that can only be allowed under rare and regimented conditions. The 'Playing Out' organization acknowledges this limitation, arguing: 'We are aware that the current model is not the long-term answer... but until a real culture of playing out is restored it is good to feel that there is a way to realize some of the benefits of street play right now'.[40]

16.4 Evidence of the Impact of Taming Traffic on Children's Active Transportation

Research on the impact of taming traffic on active transportation is methodologically challenging. Many transport interventions are introduced to improve road safety, rather than to increase physical activity: 'information on wider health impacts is not... routinely considered in the transport decision-making process'.[41] 'Studies of children's physical activity for journeys other than the trip to school are still relatively rare',[5] and traffic calming is rarely examined in children's travel research.[42] Thus while it seems logical that taming traffic will increase children's active transportation, the understanding of the effect of road safety-related interventions on active travel is limited. Nevertheless, existing evidence indicates that strategies for taming traffic outlined above have a positive impact on active transportation. However, while taming traffic has an immediate positive effect on road safety, the impact on children's active transportation may take time. 'Increases in active travel would follow once people felt that roads were safer'.[26, p. 705]

What is clear, from several studies, is that both traffic speed and volume have an impact on how streets are used. A famous study in three San Francisco streets showed how the volume of traffic markedly affected residents' use of streets.[43] Those living on a light-trafficked street knew more of their neighbours, had a greater sense of belonging and were more familiar with its physical features. When the study was replicated in Bristol, similar patterns emerged.[44] The speed of traffic significantly affects the social function of the street.[45] Biddulph's research in British Home Zones found that streets with the highest traffic speeds had the lowest levels of children's play; the combination of low traffic speed and low volume produced the most street play.[46]

16.4.1 Lower Posted Speed Limits

Most research on the impact of lower speed limits has been on road safety. Other possible benefits include improved air quality, narrowing of inequalities, greater social inclusion, reduced noise pollution, greater community cohesion and increased active travel.[26] A British study of low speed areas (20 mph signs only) in Bristol, found increased general walking, cycling and independent mobility for children. Increases in general walking ranged from 1% to 21% (depending on area surveyed and weekday versus weekend) and increases in cycling ranged from 4% to 22%.[9]

16.4.2 Traffic Calming

Whilst the main aim of traffic calming is usually to decrease the frequency and severity of road crashes there may be an increase in active transportation due to improvements in both actual and perceived safety.[22] A review of 71 studies examining traffic calming and active transportation found that several studies 'reported significant associations between safety or perceptions of safety and walking and cycling for transport'.[9] Traffic-calming measures in Denmark were not only successful in reducing child road deaths but also led to much higher levels of walking and cycling than in the UK.[2, p. 108]

A large-scale US study concluded that traffic calming was significantly associated with higher levels of children's active travel to elementary (primary) school.[47] Here, 'traffic calming' was defined as devices such as speed bumps, rumble strips, curb extensions and roundabouts. A review of 50 walking studies also identified traffic calming being associated with both more walking and less child pedestrian injury.[48]

An Australian study examined the extent to which road safety measures such as traffic calming (e.g., speed humps) had influenced the level of active travel amongst children and young people and identified positive relationships, especially for girls.[49]

Research in the United Kingdom quantified increases in active travel associated with traffic-calmed 20-mph zones. One study reported increases in active travel of between 12% and 25% (Bristol) and a three-fold increase in cycling to school (Edinburgh).[26]

A street design that creates a type of traffic calming is the cul-de-sac. Children are more likely to use culs-de-sac for play and movement,[50] as they have less traffic, meaning lower parental concerns about traffic.[14]

16.4.3 Woonerven and Home Zones

Possible benefits of woonerven and Home Zones, apart from reducing road traffic accidents, include engendering greater social interaction and a sense of ownership, reducing the fear of crime and providing places for children's informal recreation close to home.[2] Research on woonerven identified increased levels of social interaction and play, as well as high levels of resident satisfaction.[30] Home Zones also encourage children's use of the streets and independent mobility.[51] The relative success of traffic-calmed streets versus Home Zone streets has also been examined; there is more social interaction by people of all ages in the Home Zones, as well as more time spent playing by children.[52]

16.4.4 Play Streets

Recent research indicates that play streets promote children's physical activity.[53] An evaluation of the Street Play project run by Play England found that the time children spent outdoors and active during the period that streets were closed was more likely to take the place of sedentary behaviour indoors, rather than active behaviour after school.[54] Children were three to five times more active during the street play sessions than they were on a typical day after school.[55] Residents and organizers of temporary street closures in Britain reported that children learned or improved physical and social skills, including bike riding and interacting with other children.[55] Street closures also increased social interaction between children and adults, as well as perceived street safety. This increased safety was 'an important precursor to promoting increased independent mobility in children'.[6,54] When social interaction increases, this promotes children's freedom by improving the likelihood that residents know their neighbour's children and can look out for them.

Play streets may have impacts on dominant cultural norms about the use of streets. Clusters of street closures may help 'challenge the current dominant social norm that streets are largely for motorised transport only'.[6,54]

16.5 Conclusion

There is a growing international trend towards reducing the speed of motorized traffic. City-wide approaches, emerging in European cities, help develop a culture where entire cities are seen as spaces where 'children and active transportation users have priority over cars, and streets once again become places where walking, cycling, social interaction and playing become legitimate uses'.[11] As well as substantial progress in European cities, signs of change are now appearing in developing nations.[3,19] Support for speed reduction now comes from organizations as diverse as United Nations International Children's Emergency Fund (UNICEF), United Nations Environment Programme (UNEP), the World Resources Institute, Institute for Transport and Development Policy and the Fédération Internationale de l'Automobile (FiA) Foundation, all of which support the Global Initiative for Child Health and Mobility, which argues:

> *To ensure a 'Safe System' in which serious injury to children is prevented, urban traffic speeds on residential streets and on school routes where traffic and children come into direct contact must be kept below 30 km/h. If this can't be enforced the road must be designed to physically prevent higher speed.*[3]

16.6 Recommendations for Policy and Practice

Several strategies can be employed, either by individuals or by policymakers, to encourage taming traffic in a city or local neighbourhood. These include:

1. starting a discussion about lower speed limits in your city/neighbourhood,
2. trials of low speed limits can help build public support prior to reducing speed limits permanently,
3. appeals to the economic bottom line, outlining savings in health costs, stronger local economies and increased housing values,
4. explaining how lower speeds will not necessarily mean a loss of time.[56,57]

16.7 Recommendations for Further Research

While evidence exists about the value of taming traffic for enhancing children's active travel, there are significant gaps in research. More research is needed on:

1. changes in children's active transportation that occur with traffic-calming measures. This should include active travel for journeys to and from school and to other locations, as well as children's use of the streets for play
2. the most effective ways to convince sceptical citizens of the value of taming traffic in residential streets.

References

1. Roberts I, Edwards P. The energy glut: the politics of fatness in an overheating world. London: Zed Books; 2010.
2. Whitzman C, Romero V, Duncan M, Curtis C, Tranter P, Burke M. Links between children's independent mobility, active transport, physical activity and obesity. In: Waters E, Swinburn B, Seidell J, Uauy R, editors. *Preventing childhood obesity: evidence policy and practice*. Sydney: Wiley-Blackwell; 2010.

3. Global Initiative for Child Health & Mobility. *Speed kills children, use the vaccine # slowdown, Global Health Initiative for Child Health and Mobility*. 2016. https://www.Fiafoundation.Org/media/429590/speed-vaccine-booklet-lr.Pdf.
4. Deleted in review.
5. Lin E-Y, Witten K, Smith M, Carroll P, Asiasiga L, Badland H, et al. Social and built-environment factors related to children's independent mobility: the importance of neighbourhood cohesion and connectedness. *Health & Place* 2017;**46**:107–13.
6. Fyhri A, Hjorthol R, Mackett RL, Fotel TN, Kyttä M. Children's active travel and independent mobility in four countries: Development, social contributing trends and measures. *Transp Policy* 2011;**18**:703–10.
7. Rosén E, Sander U. Pedestrian fatality risk as a function of car impact speed. *Accid Anal Prev* 2009;**41**:536–42.
7a. Svenson O, Eriksson G, Gonzalez N. Braking from different speeds: Judgments of collision speed if a car does not stop in time. *Accid Anal Preven* 2012;**45**:487–92.
8. Hamilton-Baillie B. Improving traffic behaviour and safety through urban design. *Civ Eng Proc ICE* 2005;**158**:39–47.
9. Brown V, Moodie M, Carter R. Evidence for associations between traffic calming and safety and active transport or obesity: a scoping review. *J Transp Health* 2017;**7**(Part A):23–37.
10. Corben BF, D'Elia A, Healy D. Estimating pedestrian fatal crash risk. In: *Proceedings from the Australasian road safety research, policing and education conference*, vol. 10. Monash University; 2006.
11. Tranter P. Children's play in their local neighborhoods: rediscovering the value of residential streets. In: Evans B, Horton J, Skelton T, editors. *Play, recreation, health and well being, geographies of children and young people*. Singapore: Springer; 2016. p. 211–36.
12. Jacobsen P. Safety in numbers: more walkers and bicyclists, safer walking and bicycling. *Br Med J* 2003;**9**:205.
13. Engwicht D. *Mental speed bumps: the smarter way to tame traffic*. Sydney: Envirobook; 2005.
14. Islam MT, El-Basyouny K, Ibrahim SE. The impact of lowered residential speed limits on vehicle speed behavior. *Saf Sci* 2014;**62**:483–94.
15. Morrison DS, Petticrew M, Thomson H. What are the most effective ways of improving population health through transport interventions? Evidence from systematic reviews. *J Epidemiol Community Health* 2003;**57**:327–33.
16. Oxley J, Corben B, Fildes B, O'Hare M, Rothengatter T. Older vulnerable road users- measures to reduce crash and injury risk. *Monash Univ Accid Res Centre Rep* 2004:162.
17. Sammer G. General 30 kph speed limit in the city: the results of a model project in the city of Graz. In: *Proceedings of the third international conference on safety and the environment in the 21st century: lessons from the past, shaping the future, November 7–10, 1994, Tel Aviv, Israel*. 1995.
18. Hoenig M. *The Graz traffic calming model and its consequences for cyclists*. 2000. Available at: www.velomondial.net/velomondiall2000/pdf/honig.pdf.
19. Woolsgrove C. *The power of 30k speed limit. 30k Analysis*. 2013. Available at: http://www.ecf.com/?post_type=news&p=20043&preview=true.
20. Mackie A. *Urban speed management methods, TRL report 363*. Crowthorne: Transport Research Laboratory; 1998.
21. Calvert T. *Evidence measure review no. 6: environmental zones*. 2015. Available from: http://evidence-project.Eu/.

22. King R, Semlyen A. Some comments on measure review number 6 specifically relating to 20mph/30 kph policies and interventions. *World Transp Policy Pract* 2016;**22**:66–8.
23. Richter ED, Berman T, Friedman L, Ben-David G. Speed, road injury, and public health. *Annu Rev Public Health* 2006;**27**:125–52.
24. Toy S, Tapp A, Musselwhite C, Davis A. Can social marketing make 20mph the new norm? *J Transp Health* 2014;**1**:165–73.
25. Elvik R. Area-wide urban traffic calming schemes: a meta-analysis of safety effects. *Accid Anal Prev* 2001;**33**:327–36.
26. Jones SJ, Brunt H. Twenty miles per hour speed limits: a sustainable solution to public health problems in Wales. *J Epidemiol Commun Health* 2017; **71**(201):699–706.
27. Grundy C, Steinbach R, Edwards P, Green J, Armstrong B, Wilkinson P. Effect of 20 mph traffic speed zones on road injuries in London, 1986-2006: Controlled interrupted time series analysis. *BMJ Br Med J* 2009;**339**:b4469.
28. Ameratunga S. Traffic speed zones and road injuries. *BMJ* 2009;**339**. b4743.
29. Cairns J, Warren J, Garthwaite K, Greig G, Bambra C. Go slow: an umbrella review of the effects of 20 mph zones and limits on health and health inequalities. *J Public Health* 2014;**37**:515–20.
30. Ben-Joseph E. Changing the residential street scene: adapting the shared street (woonerf) concept to the suburban environment. *J Am Plan Assoc* 1995;**61**:504–15.
31. Hass-Klau C. The pedestrian and city traffic. London: Belhaven Press; 1990.
32. Karndacharuk A, Wilson DJ, Dunn R. A review of the evolution of shared (street) space concepts in urban environments. *Transp Rev* 2014;**34**:190–220.
33. Kennedy JV, Gorell R, Crinson L, Wheeler A, Elliot M. *Psychological traffic calming.* TRL Report 641, Transport Research Laboratory; 2005. http://www.20splentyforus.org.uk/UsefulReports/TRLREports/Psychological_traffic calming_TRL_2005.pdf.
34. Hamilton-Baillie B. Shared space: reconciling people, places and traffic. *Built Environ* 2008;**34**:161–81.
35. Engwicht D. Street reclaiming; creating livable streets and vibrant communities. Sydney: Pluto Press; 1999.
36. May M, Tranter PJ, Warn JR. Progressing road safety through deep change and transformational leadership. *J Transp Geogr* 2011;**19**:1423–30.
37. *Playing Out. It's the little things.... Community, Neighbourliness, Playing Out, Practical suggestions.* 2014. Available at: http://playingout.net/little-things/.
38. Gaster S. Historical changes in children's access to us cities: a critical review. *Children's Environ* 1992:23–36.
39. *London Play. The history of play streets.* 2014. Available at: http://www.londonplay.org.uk/content/29934/our_work/recent_work/play_streets/the_history_of_play_streets.
40. *Playing Out. Why play out? Ten good reasons for street play.* 2014. Available at: http://playingout.net/play-ten-good-reasons-street-play/.
41. Brown V, Moodie M, Carter R. Congestion pricing and active transport–evidence from five opportunities for natural experiment. *J Transp Health* 2015;**2**:568–79.
42. Buliung RN. *Children's independent mobility across the city of Toronto.* 2015. Toronto http://smartcommuteca/wp-content/uploads/2016/03/Phase-2-Childrens-Independent-Mobility-in-Toronto-ENpdf.
43. Appleyard D, Gerson MS, Lintell M. Livable streets, protected neighborhoods. University of California Press; 1981.
44. Hart J, Parkhurst G. Driven to excess: impacts of motor vehicles on the quality of life of residents of three streets in Bristol UK. *World Transp Policy & Pract* 2011;**17**:12–30.

45. Forman H. *Residential street design and play: a literature review of policy, guidance and research on residential street design and its influence on children's independent outdoor activity*. Bristol: Playing Out; 2017. www.playingout.net/wp_content/uploads/2017/02/helen_forman_street_design_and_play.pdf.
46. Biddulph M. *The impact of innovative designs on activity in residential streets*. School of City and Regional Planning, Cardiff University, Cardiff (Wales); 2011. http://orca.cf.ac.uk/11251/1/Final%20Report%20draft%20smaller.pdf.
47. Nicholson LM, Turner L, Slater SJ, Abuzayd H, Chriqui JF, Chaloupka F. Developing a measure of traffic calming associated with elementary school students' active transport. *Transp Res part D Transp Environ* 2014;**33**:17–25.
48. Rothman L, Buliung R, Macarthur C, To T, Howard A. Walking and child pedestrian injury: a systematic review of built environment correlates of safe walking. *Inj Prev* 2014;**20**:41–9.
49. Carver A, Timperio A, Hesketh K, Crawford D. Are safety-related features of the road environment associated with smaller declines in physical activity among youth? *J Urban Health* 2010;**87**:29–43.
50. Sharmin S, Kamruzzaman M. Association between the built environment and children's independent mobility: a meta-analytic review. *J Transp Geogr* 2017;**61**:104–17.
51. Gill T. *Can I play out?-lessons from london play's home zones project*. London: London Play; 2007.
52. Biddulph M. Street design and street use: comparing traffic calmed and home zone streets. *J Urban Des* 2012;**17**:213–32.
53. Ferguson A, Page A. Supporting healthy street play on a budget: a winner from every perspective. *Int J Play* 2015;**4**:266–9.
54. Page A. *Why temporary street closures for play make sense for public health*. Play England; 2016. http://www.playengland.org.uk/wp-content/uploads/2017/07/StreetPlayReport1web-4.pdf.
55. Ferguson A. *New evidence shows impact of street play*. 2017. Available at: http://playingout.Net/street-play-is-good-for-health-and-communities/.
56. America Walks. *Why we are stuck at high speed, and what we are going to do about it*. 2012. https://www.Scribd.Com/document/88754974/why-we-are-stuck-at-high-speed-and-what-we-are-going-to-do-about-it.
57. Tranter P. Active travel: a cure for the hurry virus. *J Occup Sci* 2014;**21**:65–76.

Active Transportation—Is the School Hiding the Forest?

17

Richard Larouche[1], Olga L. Sarmiento[2], Tom Stewart[3]
[1]Faculty of Health Sciences, University of Lethbridge, Lethbridge, AB, Canada; [2]Facultad de Medicina, Universidad de los Andes, Bogota, Colombia; [3]Human Potential Centre, Auckland University of Technology, Auckland, New Zealand

> *If you create a great city for an 8 year old and an 80 year old, you will create a successful city for all people.*
>
> ***Gil Peñalosa***

Chapter Outline

17.1 Introduction

So far, most of this book's content has focussed on the trip to and from school. This focus is in line with the overwhelming majority of the research on children's active transportation. It is understandable given that school attendance is mandatory in many countries, and children are typically required to travel to and from school on roughly 180–200 days per year. Engaging in active transportation to school is therefore an opportunity to increase physical activity and decrease vehicle emissions, and this can result in substantial economic benefits (see Chapters 1–3). As discussed in Chapter 4, the distance between home and school is the strongest environmental barrier to active transportation,[1,2] yet current interventions (e.g., Safe Routes to School, school travel planning, walking school buses, etc.) are not designed to address distance.[3] Research suggests that the average distance between home and school has increased substantially in the last few decades, and this has contributed to the observed decline in the percentage of children engaging in active transportation to and from school.[4]

Children's Active Transportation. https://doi.org/10.1016/B978-0-12-811931-0.00017-X

Beyond distance, an important reason why parents drive their children to and from school is because they believe it is more convenient for them. Parents may drop their children to school on the way to work in an effort to save time.[5,6] In a survey of American parents, 75% of those who drove their children to school for less than 2 miles (3.2 km) did so for convenience.[6] Similarly, parents who drove their children to school in Toronto did so because they viewed driving as the quickest and easiest way to get around.[5] With the possible exception of walking school buses, current active transportation interventions are designed to change neither the perceived convenience of driving versus walking or cycling nor the distance between locations. By not addressing these 'elephants in the room', most interventions tend to fiddle around the edges. Therefore, different interventions are needed to address the issues of distance and convenience, especially given that some children may really live too far from school for walking or cycling to be feasible options for the school trip.

17.2 Other Destinations

Interestingly, other destinations such as parks, shops, sport venues, and friends' and relatives' houses may be located closer than a child's school, thereby providing alternative opportunities for active transportation.[7] Even though the school trip is among the most frequently travelled, other destinations may *cumulatively* amount to more walking opportunities. Focusing exclusively on the school trip and disregarding other destinations may lead one to underestimate the public health significance of active transportation. In this sense, the school may be like the proverbial tree that hides the forest! In addition to the physical activity that can be obtained by walking or cycling to other destinations, some may provide additional opportunities for physical activity beyond the transportation domain (e.g., playing in a park or playground).

From an urban planning perspective, trips to other destinations may be less likely to occur during peak travel periods, and thus may contribute less to traffic congestion and vehicle emissions. Nevertheless, we believe that these trips should not be overlooked, because by demonstrating competence in going to nearby destinations on their own, children may extend their independent mobility incrementally (see Chapter 5). They may then develop a habit of independent active transportation that can persist over time.

One possible reason why limited research has focussed on active transportation to a broader range of destinations is the complexity involved in measuring trips that are less mandatory and regular compared to the school trip. These behaviours are often measured by questionnaires or travel diaries which may be completed by children and/or their parents. We have recently developed and validated surveys that can measure the number of trips that a child takes to and from a broad range of destinations.[8] This method has the advantages of being inexpensive and not requiring much time from study participants, allowing the collection of data in large populations. Despite being a relatively easy way to capture trip frequency, it is more difficult to survey other characteristics of these trips, notably the distance between locations. Moreover, trip chains (e.g., when one goes to multiple places without going back home in-between) are particularly difficult to measure using questionnaires or diaries.[9]

Many of these problems can be overcome by using Global Positioning Systems (GPS) to capture travel patterns. As GPS data points are timestamped, travel times, distances and precise routes can be derived. When these data are time-matched to physical activity data collected by accelerometers (see Chapter 1 for more details on accelerometers), detailed activity patterns can be investigated. These methods have been used to show that active transportation is the most important source of physical activity among youth living in urban and suburban areas in Halifax, Canada.[10] Similarly, these techniques have also been used to show that adolescents who do not use active transportation to school still accumulate most of their physical activity in the transportation domain, highlighting the importance of other destinations for active transportation and physical activity.[11] These types of data could also be used to evaluate if active transportation enables children to be more active in other contexts, such as accessing parks and sport fields.

The disadvantage of these techniques is that extensive expertise and time are required to process the data. However, these issues are becoming less problematic as automated data-processing tools are developed.[12] The practical limitations of collecting GPS data are well documented (e.g., short battery life and associated burden of recharging), which means data collection is usually limited to short timeframes (e.g., 1 week) and may not reflect true travel patterns over a longer period. These issues may become less pertinent in future research using smartphones (which are already routinely carried by individuals) to collect GPS data.[13] Smartphone applications could also be used to send a short survey to children when they visit a 'new' destination. More recently, interactive online mapping surveys have started to gain traction, as they allow individuals to locate frequently visited destinations and travel routes on a map and to report other information such as travel companions and their likes and dislikes.[14] This has created new possibilities for exploring children's mobility from their own perspective.

17.3 Changing the Social Norm

In addition to the overlooked opportunity to promote active transportation to and from 'non-school' destinations, there is a clear need to change the social norm, so that active transportation can be seen as the default option. Social norms are customary rules that govern behaviour and specify what is acceptable and what is not in groups and societies.[15] As explained in Chapter 4, many parents see driving children to school and organized activities as a sign of 'good' parenting, and there are large cultural differences in the distance that children are willing to walk (or that parents are willing to let their child walk). For example, while it is not uncommon that Finnish and Danish children living 3–5 km away from their school engage in active transportation, this is extremely rare in North America.[16] In high-income countries where many people engage in active transportation by choice rather than necessity, the quality of walking and cycling infrastructure can also explain the high cycling rates in Northern European countries. In other settings, like Kenya, Colombia and South Africa, many children walk more than 30 minutes to and from school.[17,18] In these countries, where car ownership is low, children are likely to walk for transportation due to a lack of alternatives (see Chapter 12). In low- and middle-income countries, we need to develop interventions to maintain social norms that are likely to change when motorized vehicles ownership increases. This suggests that cultural and socioeconomic factors may influence the willingness to walk or cycle for a given distance. Addressing these issues will take more than school travel plans and walking school buses alone.

In parallel, while large decreases in children's independent mobility have been reported over the last few decades (as discussed in Chapter 5), a recent survey in 16 countries has also illustrated large differences between countries.[19] Of particular interest, around 80% of 7-year-old Japanese children were granted permission to travel home from school alone.[19] Children from other Northern European countries such as Denmark, Finland, Germany, Norway and Sweden were also granted substantially more independent mobility compared to children from other regions of the world. Conversely, less than 20% of 7- and 8-year-olds in Australia, England, France, Ireland, Italy and Portugal were allowed to travel home from school alone. The rates of active transportation are generally much higher in countries were younger children are granted more independent mobility (see Chapter 4). This situation supports Roberts'[20] view that *'With only a handbrake and a handful of birthdays between the passenger's seat and the driver's seat, it may be unrealistic to expect the chauffeured children of today to become the ambulant adults of tomorrow'*. Given that children tend to have much more favourable attitudes towards active transportation than adolescents and adults do,[21] it is critical to allow them to develop a habit of walking and/or cycling early in life.

Malone and Rudner[22] offer interesting insights into the large differences in independent mobility between Australian and Japanese children. They explain how in the Australian culture, it is widely believed that as children get older, they develop their competence to negotiate the environment in a linear and sequential fashion. This view is explicit in policies and government advice that rigidly promote the idea that children are incompetent until a certain age. To protect children from their assumed incompetency, the social norm is that parents should constantly monitor their children and restrict their independent mobility. Following this norm, risk aversion is perceived as 'good' parenting.[22] This results in a feedback loop, whereby an increase in the number of parents chauffeuring their children begets further increases in driving, creating what Tranter[23] referred to as 'social traps'. Similar phenomena have been described in many other countries including Canada, the United Kingdom and the United States,[24,25] and even in South Africa.[22]

The practice of promoting an arbitrary age threshold for children's competency may be based on some research illustrating a relationship between age and a child's ability to estimate the speed of motor vehicles accurately in deciding when to cross the road.[26,27] However, there are good reasons to believe that the apparent effect of age on a child's competence is actually attributable to experience, rather than age. Put another way, how can we expect a child who has never walked alone to be as competent as a child who has been walking alone for years in deciding when it is appropriate to cross a road? Yet, such studies emphasizing children's 'incompetence' are used to discourage parents from granting their child independent mobility, even though there are major negative consequences from a broader children's rights perspective. If, based on results such as O'Neal et al.,[26] governmental agencies pretended that children are incompetent at crossing streets until 14 years of age, then this would encourage parents to escort their child, likely by car due to the perceived convenience of driving, thereby putting other children at risk, notably, the poor whose parents can't afford a car. Such an approach to risk mitigation would deprive many children of their agency and their right to play, contrary to the United Nations' Convention on the Rights of the Child.[28] It would also indirectly reward the 'endangerers' who are protected by their multi-ton vehicles, at the expense of the more vulnerable pedestrians and cyclists.

Although Japanese parents are also concerned about their children's safety, they tend to value independence to a greater extent and believe that it is essential that children develop their risk management skills.[22] Summarizing the results of a study examining perceptions of safety, Provi Drianda[29] concluded that *'Instead of restricting children, it is better for adults to educate children about how to deal with various stranger-danger situations, introduce them to more people on whom they can rely when they are in trouble, and provide them with opportunities to contribute to local community action projects which seek to enhance the safety of their neighbourhood'*. Japanese children commonly walk to school in large groups, sometimes with older children who may play a similar role to that of a walking school bus coordinator.[30] Moreover, children are viewed as active agents who help maintain the social norm, encouraging children to enjoy the benefits of independent mobility. By demonstrating their competence, they can help adults overcome their safety concerns. A previous report mentioned that as much as 98.3% of Japanese children engaged in active transportation to school.[30] Interestingly, a large survey has shown that independent mobility does not vary substantially between the ages of 7 and 15 years in Japan,[19] which challenges the common assumption that independent mobility should incrementally increase with age.

Changing the social norm will likely be a long and arduous process, but history is replete with evidence of changing social norms.[31] The abolition of slavery, women's right to vote, the legalization of gay marriages and the success of tobacco control efforts in high-income countries are all clear examples of social norm changes! In recent years, researchers and practitioners have increasingly recognized the benefits of so-called 'risky play'[a], which includes the concept of independent mobility.[32–34] In Canada, after ball games during school recess had been banned in many schools and after the quintessential Canadian game of road hockey had been forbidden in several jurisdictions, some people started to realize that the pendulum had gone too far in the direction of eliminating all risks, no matter how small they might be.

[a] Sandseter[34] defined risky play as thrilling and exciting play that can include the possibility of physical injury. Types of risky play include playing at height, speed, near dangerous elements (e.g., water, fire), with dangerous tools, rough and tumble play (e.g., play fighting), where there is the potential for disappearing or getting lost. Independent mobility is implicit in the latter.

In 2015, a group of researchers and practitioners representing various disciplines (education, public health, parks and recreation, injury prevention, etc.) released a Position Statement on Active Outdoor Play which states that: *'Access to active play in nature and outdoors—with its risks— is essential for healthy child development. We recommend increasing children's opportunities for self-directed play outdoors in all settings—at home, at school, in child care, the community and nature'*.[25] The position statement has sparked interest in outdoor and risky play among many stakeholders in Canada and elsewhere (e.g., see Ref. 35 for a report from New Zealand). Providing more opportunities for children to engage in active transportation is likely an important piece of the puzzle, but an even broader paradigm shift may be needed to address the perceived convenience of driving and to overcome the barrier of distance between locations.

17.4 Embracing an Accessibility Paradigm

A paradigm is defined as *'a set of assumptions, concepts, values, and practices that constitutes a way of viewing reality for the community that shares them, especially in an intellectual discipline'*.[b] Recently, many authors have emphasized that in order to achieve crucial objectives such as minimizing greenhouse gases emissions from the transport sector, reducing traffic congestion and increasing the percentage of trips using sustainable travel modes, we will need to shift from the current 'mobility paradigm' to an 'accessibility paradigm'.[31,36,37]

The mobility paradigm implies that increasing speed is desirable, hence the large investments in expansive infrastructure such as major roads and highways over the last century. To accommodate growing vehicular fleets, an enormous amount of public space has been dedicated to parking and roads, and billions have been invested to widen roads despite clear evidence that this only induces more traffic.[31,37] This has resulted in millions of individuals driving longer distances to reach ever more distant schools, workplaces and other destinations. This paradigm is linked with many of the leading causes of global morbidity and mortality, notably physical inactivity, air pollution and road crashes.

To add insult to injury, the mobility paradigm has even been unsuccessful at reducing average daily travel time which has remained constant at around 1 hour/day in many areas of the world.[31,38] Even worse, the proliferation of motor vehicles in Beijing has reduced the average speed of cars from 45 to 12 km/h between 1994 and 2003 as bicycles were rapidly replaced by motor vehicles![31] Yet, the construction of new roads or the enlargement of existing ones is often justified by the myth that this will save time. In traditional cost–benefit analysis, the hypothetical value of time savings is often used as a key element to justify such projects![37] The time needed for drivers to earn the money to pay for all expenses associated with car ownership is also omitted from such analyses.[39]

In contrast, the accessibility paradigm emphasizes that *'transportation plans should aim for ease of access to activities rather than ease of movement'*.[36] This entails that

[b]As defined in the American Heritage Dictionary. https://www.ahdictionary.com/word/search.html?q=paradigm.

the pursuit of speed would become futile because a wide range of destinations would be accessible by foot, bike or transit. This has profound implications in terms of equity because under the current mobility paradigm, children, older adults and those who cannot afford a car are left behind, especially those who live in more deprived neighbourhoods.[31,40] People living in such neighbourhoods are much more likely to be victims of road crashes compared to their wealthier counterparts.[41,42] They are also more likely to live on or close to major roads with the traffic, pollution and loud noise that it entails and thus have an increased risk of chronic diseases and mortality.[43,44] In contrast, greater accessibility is associated with higher social capital, which essentially refers to a more closely knit community where individuals have productive relationships.[45]

Many cities, particularly in Northern Europe and Japan, have embraced this paradigm to varying degrees. For example, London and Stockholm have successfully implemented congestion charges that have decreased congestion and greenhouse gases emissions, combined with modest increases in active transportation.[31,46] While the impact of these schemes has been relatively modest, it could be increased markedly by broadening the congestion charge zone. The Netherlands are famous for their *woonerven* (singular: *woonerf*), which literally means 'living street', where traffic is restricted to pedestrian speed and where people are explicitly granted priority over cars.[47] Such streets are also very common in Germany. Further up North, 77% of trips in Helsinki were made using active transportation and public transit in 2013—despite the climate and relatively low density by European standards—and the city has recently vowed to make car ownership pointless by 2025.[48]

Examples of policies embracing an accessibility paradigm also exist in developing countries. Of particular interest, Ciclovía Recreativa programmes provide an innovative nonschool destination to promote active travel. The Ciclovía-Recreativa of Bogotá is a multisectoral community programme in which main streets are temporarily closed to motor vehicle traffic, allowing children and adults to enjoy a safe, free space in the city for walking, cycling, skating or other cultural activities.[49] The first Ciclovía-Recreativa in Bogotá took place in 1974, and in 1982, it became a weekly event when the mayor established a strategy to give public space back to the citizens. From 1995 to 2003, a succession of mayors promoted new cultural practices, improved infrastructure and strengthened the Ciclovía-Recreativa programme. Specifically, Enrique Peñalosa created infrastructure and public space that intended to give priority to children and older adults. Reflecting on transportation planning, he said *'We really have to admit that over the past 100 years we have been building cities much more for mobility than for people's well-being'*. Instead of investing in new highways, he invested in sidewalks, pedestrian streets, parks, bicycle paths and a high-quality bus rapid transit system. His brother, Gil Peñalosa, was the Commissioner of Parks and Recreation in Bogotá at the time, and he is now the Director of 8 80 Cities, a nonprofit organization that applies similar ideas in consulting with policymakers and communities across the world. Ciclovía-Recreativa programmes (also referred to as Open Streets in English-speaking countries) are expanding rapidly worldwide: 485 were implemented in the Americas, two in Europe, five in Asia, one in Africa and one in Oceania.[50]

Another example from Bogotá is the programme Al Colegio en bici[51] (bike to school programme) which promotes cycling among young people as a strategy to create a more inclusive, sustainable, protective and safe city. The programme began in 2013 and has provided improved and safer access to education to low-income populations living more than 2 km away from school. It provides bicycles to the schools, and children are taught how to use a bike, from riding it to fixing it. Students ride their bicycles to a meeting point before school starts, and then cycle as a group guided by four guardians, just like the bicycle trains described in Chapter 15. In 2015, 3194 students were part of the first cycle of training and 2031 bicycles were given to schools. Al Colegio en Bici may help increase access to education, sustainable transportation and associated health benefits.

17.5 Towards More Comprehensive Interventions ...

Now that we have emphasized the need for a paradigm shift and identified some jurisdictions that have embraced the new paradigm to varying degrees, it is important to discuss what this paradigm might look like when the rubber hits the road. We will first discuss Complete Streets, an attractive and flexible policy that has some important caveats. We will then summarize recent literature that has tried to get to the root of what makes a successful active transportation city.

In an effort to make pedestrians and cyclists feel more 'welcomed' on the streets, a number of jurisdictions have recently adopted Complete Streets policies.[52] Such policies are popular in North America, and they intend to better accommodate the different users of the roads (e.g., pedestrians, cyclists, transit users and motorists) and create more livable communities.[53] Their purported benefits include improved accessibility via active transportation, cost savings and reduced vehicle emissions.[53] Implementing a Complete Streets policy is not a 'cookie-cutter' process—Complete Streets may look very different in Auckland, Bogotá, Cape Town, Delhi or Edinburgh! This flexibility can be advantageous by allowing policymakers to tailor the policy to the local context. At the same time, the vague definition of Complete Streets can afford loopholes through which one could justify half measures that do not really address the needs of vulnerable road users. For example, research shows that sharrows (painted signs on roadways featuring a chevron and a bicycle symbol) may create a false sense of safety and actually increase crash risk among cyclists in Chicago.[54]

In many cities, Complete Streets are implemented in an incomplete way! A survey of 385 metropolitan planning organizations indicated that only 3% of relevant local, regional and state entities formally implemented Complete Streets policies.[55] Furthermore, it is common place that streets that need to undergo major renovations (e.g., sewer repairs) are repaved with some 'Complete Streets' features designed for pedestrians and cyclists such as better sidewalks and bike lanes. However, In North American cities, these 'complete streets' are often poorly linked, and as a result, pedestrians and cyclists may still have to use unsafe streets to get from point A to point B. Such a piecemeal approach is unlikely to achieve a marked increase in children's active transportation.

Instead, a comprehensive package of complementary sustainable transportation policies should be implemented that would make active transportation safer and more attractive and driving less convenient.[47,56,57] Such policies should simultaneously target multiple levels of influence. Table 17.1 illustrates examples of policies that have been shown to encourage active transportation in adults or children according to a

Table 17.1 Policies that can promote active transportation

Policies	Rationale
Reduced speed limit for motor vehicles	Makes active transportation safer. Increases the relative speed of cycling compared to driving
Higher cost of car ownership and use	Makes car use less attractive compared with other travel modes
Limited provision of parking spaces	Makes car travel less convenient than other modes
Reduce the cost of public transport	One must do some active transportation to get to and from transit stops. Lower cost may encourage a shift from car travel to public transport
Zoning regulations requiring a greater mix of land uses and/or greater housing density	May increase access to a wide range of destinations by walking and cycling; however, greater density may be associated with increased traffic, thereby deterring children's active transportation[2]
Transit-oriented development (including light rail trains and bus rapid transit)	Makes transit use more convenient
Car-free city centres	Makes car travel less convenient and makes walking and cycling safer
More opportunities to cross roadways	Reduce the distance of walking and cycling routes. This can also slow down cars
Invest in a well-connected network of high-quality walking and cycling infrastructure	Makes walking and cycling safer (and likely more enjoyable too)
Offer end-of-trip facilities (e.g., secure bike parking, showers and the possibility to carry bikes on transit)	Makes cycling more convenient
Implement programmes targeting individuals (e.g., workplace travel plans, fiscal incentives, social-marketing campaigns, etc.)	May encourage walking and cycling, but evidence suggests that such programmes are not very effective when implemented as standalone interventions without disincentives for car travel
Hire crossing guards	Can help reduce parental road safety concerns, as they relate to crossing busy intersections
Promote broader adoption of UNICEF's Child Friendly Cities approach[58]	Helps ensure that children's rights and views are taken into account in policies, laws, programmes and budgets. This can help ensure that streets are conducive to active transportation

While some of these policies may have more direct impact on adults' travel behaviour, we believe that a 'package' including many of these policies could also lead to a substantial increase in children's active transportation.

recent review of the literature by Winters et al.[57] It also includes other policies that may be particularly relevant for children. Of particular interest, there is consistent evidence that a dense and well-connected network of high-quality infrastructure, as exists notably in many European cities, is associated with higher rates of walking and cycling.[31,47,56,57,59–61]

It is worth noting that some of these policies may be perceived as more politically acceptable than others. However, the main point is that a clever combination of policies that reinforce each other is needed to achieve large changes in travel behaviour at the population level. To this end, lessons can be drawn from the public health successes of tobacco control in high-income countries.[62] Some of the lessons that can be particularly important for the promotion of active transportation are shown in Table 17.2.

Such a network can be complemented by adopting a Vision Zero policy[c], which states that *'eventually no one will be killed or seriously injured within the road transport system'*.[66] Vision Zero was first introduced in Sweden in 1997 and, following its success in decreasing road deaths, it has been adopted in many other jurisdictions. It is based on the simple fact that humans make mistakes, but such mistakes should not carry the death penalty.[66] While zero deaths might be seen as an idealistic target in big cities like New York and Paris, adopting such a policy is a commitment to do everything than can reasonably be done to prevent road crashes, and its implementation should make active transportation much safer.

A great example of a comprehensive intervention specifically targeting children is the 'safe routes to school' project, as it was implemented in Danish cities such as Odense. In the mid-1970s, Denmark had the highest child pedestrian accident rate in Western Europe.[67] To address this issue, the city of Odense invested in the creation of an extensive network of pedestrian and bicycle paths, narrowed roads, added traffic islands and mandated all of its 45 schools to identify specific road-safety issues to be addressed. After 10 years, child pedestrian and cyclist casualties had decreased by 80%, and this programme was implemented in other Danish cities.[67] Such an approach makes active transportation safer for people of all ages! In comparison, the US Safe Routes to School programme and the school travel planning interventions in countries such as Canada, New Zealand and the United Kingdom are much less comprehensive, and this reduces their reach and effectiveness.

The Netherlands' road guidelines are another great example of a comprehensive approach. Specifically, the Dutch Design Manual for Bicycle Traffic requires different types of infrastructure based on the street type and speed limit, the amount of traffic and the number of road lanes.[68] For example, cycle tracks physically separated from traffic are expected on any street with more than two lanes, any urban street with a speed limit exceeding 50 km/h and any rural roads with a speed limit exceeding 60 km/h. Research has shown that Dutch cyclists are about 6 times less likely to be killed and 25 times less likely to be injured in a crash than their American

[c] More details about Vision Zero can be found here: http://www.visionzeroinitiative.com/.

Table 17.2 Lessons from tobacco control that could help promote active transportation

Lessons	Rationale
'Address the issue of individual responsibility versus collective or environmental action early and often'	Rather than putting the onus on individuals to change their travel behaviours, policymakers and practitioners should make active transportation the easy choice.
'Decisions to act need not wait for evidence of the effectiveness of interventions'	Early tobacco control interventions were based on sound judgement rather than evidence of effectiveness. In the absence of hard evidence, potentially scalable active transportation interventions can be tested at a smaller scale. Then, based on positive evidence, they can be implemented more broadly. Notably, this was the reasoning behind the well-known pop-up projects launched by Janette Sadik-Khan in New York City.[63]
'Fully implement interventions known to be effective'	Evidence of jurisdictions that have been successful in increasing cycling is available,[47,56,60] although other jurisdictions often implement only small parts from a successful package of interventions.
'Real and perceived needs and concerns of developing countries need to be addressed even if they involve going beyond the initial scope of the risk being addressed'	In developing countries, people often engage in active transportation by necessity rather than by choice[64] (see Chapter 12). As these countries have the lion's share of the burden of road traffic injuries,[65] interventions must be put in place to make the environment safer for vulnerable road users, to reduce traffic congestion and improve access for emergency vehicles.
'The more comprehensive the package of measures considered, the greater the impact'	This issue is elaborated upon throughout this chapter as well as in many other publications.[31,47,56,57,59–61]
'Broad based, well networked, vertical and horizontal coalitions are key'	Achieving a large increase in active transportation requires both vertical (e.g., between municipal, regional and national governments) and horizontal (between policymakers, researchers, practitioners and nongovernment organizations) collaborations.
'Change in support for tobacco control took decades of effort led by media savvy and politically astute leaders'	Replacing the mobility paradigm by an accessibility paradigm will require strong leaders too. Interestingly, leaders in countries such as the Netherlands, Denmark and Germany have implemented bold sustainable transportation policies since the 1970s.[47]
'Modest, well spent funds can have a massive impact, but without clear goals funding may not be sustainable'	Having a clear plan is needed to harmonize measures taken to promote active transportation, design safe and convenient walking and cycling infrastructures and build support for such measures. The plan should be used as an accountability mechanism to monitor progress towards key objectives.

counterparts.[47] Furthermore, between 1990 and 2014, there has been less progress in reducing cycling fatalities in the United States compared to other high-income countries.[69] A previous international study of child cycling injuries had also indicated that there are fewer fatalities in countries with higher rates of cycling.[70] These data support the Safety in Numbers hypothesis which posits that a given mode of transportation is relatively safer when more people use it.[71]

17.6 Conclusion

There is a clear need to extend our focus on active transportation beyond the trip to/from school, and interventions should target the distance barrier more directly. To achieve a large increase in children's active transportation, we will need to change social norms and to shift from a mobility to an accessibility paradigm. This should translate in the development of more compact cities and the implementation of policies and practices to make walking and cycling safer and more attractive and car use less convenient.

17.7 Recommendations for Practice

1. Active transportation interventions should focus on a broader range of destinations.
2. Policies that increase accessibility to various destinations are needed to overcome the distance barrier and increase the likelihood that children and youth will engage in active transportation.
3. Practitioners and policymakers should draw inspiration from countries such as Denmark, the Netherlands and Germany, where sustainable transportation infrastructure and traffic calming are implemented in a more comprehensive fashion.
4. Emerging programmes in low- to middle-income countries should be evaluated and then implemented more broadly, as these countries are undergoing rapid urbanization and infrastructure development (see Chapter 12).

17.8 Recommendations for Research

1. As focus shifts towards the full gamut of local destinations, researchers should examine the relative importance of different destination types for children's active transportation and physical activity.
2. As more cities and communities move towards creating accessible environments, effort should be made to evaluate the effectiveness of new policies for improving children's active transportation and independent mobility to a range of destinations.
3. Researchers should utilize emerging measurement technologies (e.g., GPS and smartphones) to collect more robust data on travel behaviours over longer periods of time.
4. Research investigating active transportation to/from a broader range of destinations in low- and middle-income countries is urgently needed.

References

1. Stewart O. Findings from research on active transportation to school and implications for safe routes to school programs. *J Plann Lit* 2011;**26**(2):127–50.
2. Wong BYM, Faulkner G, Buliung R. GIS measured environmental correlates of active school transport: a systematic review of 14 studies. *Int J Behav Nutr Phys Act* 2011;**8**:39. Available from: https://ijbnpa.biomedcentral.com/articles/10.1186/1479-5868-8-39.
3. McDonald NC. Active transportation to school: trends among U.S. schoolchildren, 1969-2001. *Am J Prev Med* 2007;**32**(6):509–16.
4. McDonald NC. Children's mode choice for the school trip: the role of distance and school location in walking to school. *Transportation* 2008;**35**(1):23–35.
5. Faulkner GEJ, Richichi V, Buliung RN, Fusco C, Moola F. What's 'quickest and easiest?': parental decision making about school travel mode. *Int J Behav Nutr Phys Act* 2010;**7**:62. Available from: http://ijbnpa.biomedcentral.com/articles/10.1186/1479-5868-7-62.
6. McDonald NC, Aalborg AE. Why parents drive children to school: implications for safe routes to school programs. *J Am Plann Assoc* 2009;**3**:331–42.
7. Larouche R, Barnes J, Tremblay MS. Too far to walk or bike? *Can J Public Health* 2013;**104**(7):e487–9.
8. Larouche R, Eryuzlu S, Livock H, Leduc G, Faulkner G, Trudeau F, Tremblay MS. Test-retest reliability and convergent validity of measures of children's travel behaviours and independent mobility. *J Transp Health* 2017;**6**:105–18.
9. Oliver M, Mavoa S, Badland HM, Carroll PA, Asiasiga L, Tavae N, et al. What constitutes a 'trip'? Examining child journey attributes using GPS and self-report. *Child Geogr* 2014;**12**(2):249–56.
10. Rainham DG, Bates CJ, Blanchard CM, Dummer TJ, Kirk SF, Shearer CL. Spatial classification of youth physical activity patterns. *Am J Prev Med* 2012;**42**(5):e87–96.
11. Stewart T, Duncan S, Schipperijn J. Adolescents who engage in active school transport are also more active in other contexts: a space-time investigation. *Health Place* 2017;**43**:25–32.
12. Klinker CD, Schipperijn J, Toftager M, Kerr J, Troelsen J. When cities move children: development of a new methodology to assess context-specific physical activity behaviour among children and adolescents using accelerometers and GPS. *Health Place* 2015;**31**:90–9.
13. Birenboim A, Shoval N. Mobility research in the age of the smartphone. *Ann Am Assoc Geogr* 2016;**106**(2):283–91.
14. Kyttä M, Broberg A, Kahila M. Urban environment and Children's active lifestyle: SoftGIS revealing Children's behavioral patterns and meaningful places. *Am J Health Promot* 2012;**26**(5):e137–48.
15. Bicchieri C, Muldoon R. Social norms. In: *Stanford encyclopedia of philosophy, Stanford, CA*. 2011. Available from: https://plato.stanford.edu/entries/social-norms/.
16. Tremblay MS, Barnes JD, González SA, Katzmarzyk PT, Onywera VO, Reilly JJ, et al. Global matrix 2.0: report card grades on the physical activity of children and youth comparing 38 countries. *J Phys Act Health* 2016;**13**(11 Suppl. 2):S343–66.
17. Larouche R, Sarmiento OL, Broyles ST, Denstel KD, Katzmarzyk PT, Church TS, for the ISCOLE Research Group, et al. Are the correlates of active school transport context-specific? *Int J Obes Suppl* 2015;**5**:S89–99.
18. Sarmiento OL, Lemoine P, Gonzalez SA, Broyles ST, Denstel KD, Larouche R, for the ISCOLE Research Group, et al. Relationships between active school transport and adiposity indicators in school age children from low-, middle- and high-income countries. *Int J Obe Suppl* 2015;**5**:S107–14.

19. Shaw B, Bicket M, Elliot B, Fagan-Watson B, Mocca E, Hillman M. *Children's independent mobility: an international comparison and recommendations for action*. London: Policy Studies Institute; 2015. Available from: http://westminsterresearch.wmin.ac.uk/15650/.
20. Roberts I. Walking to school has future benefits. *BMJ* 1995;**312**:1229.
21. Lorenc T, Brunton G, Oliver S, Oliver K, Oakley A. Attitudes to walking and cycling among children, young people and parents: a systematic review. *J Epidemiol Community Health* 2008;**62**:852–7.
22. Malone K, Rudner J. Global perspectives on children's independent mobility: a socio-cultural comparison and theoretical discussion of Children's lives in four countries in Asia and Africa. *Global Studies of Childhood* 2011;**1**(3):243–59.
23. Tranter P. Overcoming social traps: a key to child-friendly cities. In: Gleeson B, Sipe N, editors. *Creating child friendly cities: reinstating kids in the city*. New York: Routledge; 2006. p. 121–35.
24. Roberts I, Edwards P. *The energy glut: the politics of fatness in an overheating world*. London: Zed Books; 2010.
25. Tremblay M, Gray C, Babcock S, Barnes J, Bradstreet CC, Carr D, et al. Position statement on active outdoor play. *Int J Environ Res Public Health* 2015;**12**:6475–505. Available from: http://www.mdpi.com/1660-4601/12/6/6475?utm_source=health.mazavr.tk&utm_medium=link&utm_compaign=article.
26. O'Neal EE, Jiang Y, Franzen LJ, Rahimian P, Yon JP, Kearney JK, Plumert JD. Changes in perception–action tuning over long time scales: how children and adults perceive and act on dynamic affordances when crossing roads. *J Exp Psychol Hum Percept Perform* 2018;**44**. Epub April 20, 2017.
27. Wann JP, Poulter DR, Purcell C. Reduced sensitivity to visual looming inflates the risk posed by speeding vehicles when children try to cross the road. *Psychol Sci* 2011;**22**(4):429–34.
28. United Nations. *Convention on the rights of the child*. New York (NY): United Nations; 1989.
29. Provi Drianda R. The 'Stranger Danger' Issue in Japanese Neighbourhoods: children's perceptions, experiences and drawings. *Childhoods Today* 2010;**4**(1):1–26.
30. Mori N, Armada F, Willcox DC. Walking to school in Japan and childhood obesity prevention: new lessons from an old policy. *Am J Public Health* 2012;**102**(11):2068–73.
31. Whitelegg J. Mobility: a new urban design and transport planning philosophy for a sustainable future. *Createspace Independent Publishing Platform* 2016.
32. Brussoni M, Gibbons R, Gray C, Ishikawa T, Sandseter EBH, Bienenstock A, et al. What is the relationship between risky outdoor play and health in children? A systematic review. *Int J Environ Res Public Health* 2015;**12**:6423–54. Available from: http://www.mdpi.com/1660-4601/12/6/6423?utm_source=health.mazavr.tk&utm_medium=link&utm_compaign=article.
33. Brussoni M, Brunelle S, Pike I, Sandseter EBH, Herrington S, Turner H, et al. Can child injury prevention include healthy risk promotion?. *Inj Prev* 2015;**21**:344–7. Available from: http://injuryprevention.bmj.com/content/injuryprev/21/5/344.full.pdf.
34. Sandseter EBH. Categorising risky play—how can we identify risk-taking in children's play? *Eur Early Child Educ Res J* 2007;**15**:237–52.
35. Duncan S, McPhee J. *State of play: executive report*. Auckland (NZ): Auckland University of Technology; 2015. Available from: https://www.persil.co.nz/wp-content/uploads/sites/10/2015/11/AUT_State_Of_Play-141015.pdf.
36. Handy S. Roundabouts of a figurative kind. *Transp Rev.* 2017;**37**(4):407–11.
37. Litman T. Transportation and public health. *Annu Rev Public Health* 2013;**34**:217–33.

38. Marchetti C. Anthropological invariants in travel behavior. *Technol Forecast Soc Change* 1994;**47**:75–88.
39. Tranter P. Effective speed: cycling because it's faster. In: Pucher J, Buehler R, editors. *City cycling*. Cambridge (MA): Massachusetts Institute of Technology Press; 2012.
40. Engwicht D. *Towards an eco-city: calming the traffic*. Sydney (Australia): Envirobook; 1992.
41. Morency P, Gauvin L, Plante C, Fournier M, Morency C. Neighborhood social inequalities in road traffic injuries: the influence of traffic volume and road design. *Am J Public Health* 2012;**102**(6):1112–9.
42. Roberts I, Norton R, Taua B. Child pedestrian injury rate: the importance of 'exposure to risk' relating to socioeconomic and ethnic differences, in Auckland, New Zealand. *J Epidemiol Community Health* 1996;**50**:162–5.
43. Brook RD, Rajagopalan S, Pope A, et al. Particulate matter air pollution and cardiovascular disease: an update to the scientific statement from the American Heart Association. *Circulation* 2010;**121**:2331–78. Available from: http://circ.ahajournals.org/content/121/21/2331.short.
44. Brugge D, Durant JL, Rioux C. Near-highway pollutants in motor vehicle exhaust: a review of epidemiologic evidence of cardiac and pulmonary health risks. *Environ Health* 2007;**6**:23. Available from: https://ehjournal.biomedcentral.com/articles/10.1186/1476-069X-6-23.
45. Rogers SH, Gardner KH, Carlson CH. Social capital and walkability as social aspects of sustainability. *Sustainability* 2013;**5**(8):3473–83. Available from: http://www.mdpi.com/2071-1050/5/8/3473.
46. Larouche R. The environmental and population health benefits of active transport: a review. In: Liu G, editor. *Greenhouse gases – emissions, measurement and management*. Rijeka (Croatia): InTech; 2012. p. 413–40.
47. Pucher J, Buehler R. Making cycling irresistible: lessons from The Netherlands, Denmark and Germany. *Transp Rev* 2008;**28**(4):495–528.
48. Saidla K. Health promotion by stealth: active transportation success in Helsinki, Finland. *Health Promot Int* 2018. Available from: https://academic.oup.com/heapro/advance-article/doi/10.1093/heapro/daw110/2967373.
49. Sarmiento OL, del Castillo AD, Triana CA, Acevedo MJ, Gonzalez SA, Pratt M. Reclaiming the streets for people: insights from Ciclovías recreativas in Latin America. *Prev Med* 2017. Epub Aug 3, 2016.
50. Díaz del Castillo A, Sarmiento OL, Reis RS, Brownson RC. Translating evidence to policy: urban interventions and physical activity promotion in Bogotá, Colombia and Curitiba, Brazil. *Transl Behav Med* 2011;**1**(2):350–60.
51. Hidalgo D, Miranda L, Lleras N, Ríos J. Al Colegio en Bici. Bike-to-School Program in Bogotá, Colombia. *Transp Res Rec* 2016;**2581**:66–70.
52. Moreland-Russell S, Eyler A, Barbero C, Hipp JA, Walsh H. Diffusion of complete streets policies across US communities. *J Public Health Manag Prac* 2013;**19**(3):S89–96.
53. Litman T. *Evaluating Complete Streets: the value of designing roads for diverse modes, users and activities*. Victoria (BC): Victoria Transport Policy Institute; 2012. Available from: http://www.vtpi.org/compstr.pdf.
54. Ferenchak NN, Marshall WE. The relative (in)effectiveness of bicycle sharrows on ridership and safety outcomes. In: *Paper presented at the transportation research Boards's 95th annual meeting: Washington, DC*. 2016. Available from: https://websites.godaddy.com/blob/751507ec-eff4-4501-85ea-633fe2283804/downloads/1bhdb1mk5_776676.pdf?214c4e59.

55. Tolford T, Fields B, Longoria T. *Evaluation of complete streets policy implementation by metropolitan planning organizations.* New Orleans (LA): Southwest Region University Transportation Center; 2015. Available from: https://static.tti.tamu.edu/swutc.tamu.edu/publications/technicalreports/600451-00119-1.pdf.
56. Pucher J, Dill J, Handy S. Infrastructure, programs, and policies to increase bicycling: an international review. *Prev Med* 2010;**50**(Suppl.):S106–25.
57. Winters M, Buehler R, Götschi T. Policies to promote active travel: evidence from reviews of the literature. *Curr Envir Health Rep* 2017. Epub Jul 10, 2017.
58. Malone K. United Nations: a key player in a global movement for child friendly cities. In: Gleeson B, Sipe N, editors. *Creating child friendly cities: Reinstating kids in the city.* London: Routledge; 2006.
59. Giles-Corti B, Vernez-Moudon A, Reis R, Turrell G, Dannenberg AL, Badland H, et al. City planning and population health: a global challenge. *Lancet* 2016;**388**(10062):2912–24.
60. Pucher J, Buehler R. *City cycling.* Cambridge (MA): Massachusetts Institute of Technology Press; 2012.
61. Stevenson M, Thompson J, de Sá TH, Ewing R, Mohan D, McClure R, et al. Land use, transport, and population health: estimating the health benefits of compact cities. *Lancet* 2016;**388**(10062):2925–35.
62. Yach D, McKee M, Lopez AD, Novotny T, for Oxford Vision 2020. Improving diet and physical activity: 12 lessons from controlling tobacco smoking. *BMJ* 2005;**330**(7496):898–900.
63. Sadik-Khan J, Solomonow S. *Streetfight: handbook for an urban revolution.* New York (NY): Penguin Random House; 2016.
64. Salvo D, Reis RS, Srmiento OL, Pratt M. Overcoming the challenges of conducting physical activity and built environment research in Latin America: IPEN Latin America. *Prev Med* 2014;**69**(Suppl.):S86–92.
65. World Health Organization. *Global status report on road safety 2015.* Geneva (Switzerland): World Health Organization; 2015. Available from: http://www.who.int/violence_injury_prevention/road_safety_status/2015/en/.
66. Johansson R. Vision Zero – Implementing a policy for traffic safety. *Safety Sci.* 2009;**47**:826–31.
67. Appleyard B. Planning safe routes to school. *Planning* 2003;**69**(5):34–7.
68. Furth P. Bicycle infrastructure for mass cycling: a transatlantic comparison. In: Pucher J, Buehler R, editors. *City cycling.* Cambridge (MA): Massachusetts Institute of Technology Press; 2012. p. 105–40.
69. Buehler R, Pucher J. Trends in walking and cycling safety: recent evidence from high-income countries, with a focus on the United States and Germany. *Am J Public Health* 2017;**107**(2):281–7.
70. Christie N, Towner E, Cairns S. *Road safety research report no. 47. Children's road traffic safety: an international survey of policy and practice.* London (UK): Department for Transport; 2004. Available from: https://pdfs.semanticscholar.org/0eae/2eaea4955df347c30ac3eae78905de898355.pdf.
71. Jacobsen PL. Safety in numbers: more walkers and bicyclists, safer walking and bicycling. *Inj Prev* 2003;**9**(3):205–9.

Conclusion

18

Richard Larouche[1], Paul Tranter[2]
[1]Faculty of Health Sciences, University of Lethbridge, Lethbridge, AB, Canada; [2]School of Physical, Environmental and Mathematical Sciences, University of New South Wales Canberra, Canberra, Australia

> *To achieve more child-friendly cities, and hence to achieve more sustainable cities, will require much more than changes to speed limits, or widespread traffic calming, or even increases in the density of provision of services. It will require a fundamental change in social values, a cultural revolution, towards greater collective responsibility and away from individualism[1]*

Chapter Outline

18.1 Benefits of Active Transportation

The first section of the book emphasized the consistent evidence that children who engage in active transportation are more physically active. It demonstrated that active transportation is particularly important for young people who are at greater risk of physical inactivity, specifically girls and adolescents. Chapter 1 also reviewed studies indicating that adolescents who cycle for transportation have greater cardiovascular fitness and reduced cardiovascular disease risk factors. Interestingly, a large proportion of children would prefer to cycle to and from school if they had the choice.[2–4] However, with the exception of Northern and Central European countries, a very low proportion of children actually cycle for transportation (Chapter 4). Addressing this discrepancy between children's preference and their actual behaviour should be a public health priority.

The benefits of increasing the prevalence of active transportation extend far beyond public health. For example, in many cities, school travel represents a sizable percentage of car trips during the morning and afternoon peak hours, underscoring the potential to reduce congestion and vehicle emissions.[5] Importantly, previous research on the environmental benefits of active transportation is limited by the lack of studies using a life-course perspective. Children who develop the habit of engaging in active transportation are presumably more likely to keep this habit later in life, which may result

Children's Active Transportation. https://doi.org/10.1016/B978-0-12-811931-0.00018-1

in less driving and greenhouse gas emissions. This hypothesis is supported by longitudinal results from the Young Finns Study in which individuals were followed up from youth (9–18 years) to adulthood (30–45 years).[6] Specifically, Yang et al.[6] observed that youth who consistently engaged in active transportation were more active from young adulthood to midlife. Continued use of active transportation has likely contributed to these findings about physical activity. Moreover, a recent article in the *Journal of the American Medical Association* concluded that, compared to other climate change mitigation strategies, active transportation may "*offer the most direct benefits by reducing health-damaging pollution emissions and enhancing personal fitness simultaneously*."[7] Thus, policy-makers and urban planners interested in co-benefits—reducing vehicle emissions, road congestion and fuel and maintenance costs, as well as enhancing human health—should not overlook children's active transportation.[8]

The economic benefits of active transportation provide a key area where more robust studies are needed to convince policy-makers of the financial value of interventions. As emphasized in Chapter 3, such studies should not focus on a single outcome such as childhood obesity. Instead, researchers should model the effects of active transportation on multiple issues, including outcomes such as physical activity and health, injuries, traffic congestion, vehicle emissions, etc. Nevertheless, it is encouraging that even an incomplete evaluation of the Safe Routes to School programme that focussed solely on road safety impacts found that the intervention was highly cost-effective in New York City.[9]

18.2 Correlates of Active Transportation

The second section of the book highlighted the multiplicity of factors associated with active transportation based on the social–ecological model, which encompasses individual, interpersonal, community, built environment and policy factors. Current theoretical models posit that parents make decisions about their child's travel mode based on a number of factors, including the perceived convenience of different travel modes, concerns about "stranger danger" and road safety, social norms, distance/travel time and environmental characteristics of the route.[10,11] With age, children gain more input into the decision-making process, and their independent mobility expands, which could provide new opportunities for promoting active transportation.[10,11]

Distance between home and school is clearly the strongest and most consistent correlate of active transportation (Chapter 10). Notwithstanding the differences between countries in the distance that children are willing to walk or bike, the likelihood of active transportation decreases as distance increases. Furthermore, the average distance between home and school has increased over recent decades, and this increased distance is likely one of the key factors that explain the decrease in active transportation observed in many countries (Chapter 4). Secondary schools generally have much larger catchment areas than primary schools, and this results in increased distance, thus decreasing the likelihood of active transportation.

Arguably, distance has increased as decision-makers have designed cities for cars rather than for people. To accommodate growing fleets of vehicles while attempting to minimize traffic congestion, the amount of land allocated to roads continues to increase, resulting in urban sprawl and greater distance between destinations.[12] The new roads quickly become clogged, then are widened until they get clogged once again. This predictable vicious circle increases urban heat island effects, decreases rainwater drainage and makes it harder for pedestrians to cross roads, especially for young children and older adults. This mobility paradigm, combined with short-sighted closure of small schools and the construction of large schools in the outskirts of cities, has made it more difficult for children to engage in active transportation.

18.3 Active Transportation Interventions

The third section of the book discussed the effectiveness of active transportation interventions such as Safe Routes to School, school travel planning and walking school buses (Chapters 13–15). It is encouraging to note that most interventions included in a recent systematic review have been successful in increasing active transportation to and from school.[13] However, the magnitude of the observed increases was small, suggesting that additional efforts are needed. Furthermore, insufficient funding has plagued many interventions and, as a result, some components of the interventions—especially infrastructure changes—have not been implemented as planned.[13] This has likely limited the effectiveness of these interventions. However, a key limitation of most interventions to date is that they have failed to address two of the strongest barriers, namely distance and the perceived convenience of driving. Indeed previous research shows that parents select the mode of transportation that is quickest and easiest.[14,15]

Therefore, Chapter 17 made the case for active transportation interventions to extend their focus beyond the trip to and from school, and to more directly address the issue of distance by shifting from a mobility paradigm towards an accessibility paradigm where reaching destinations by walking and cycling would be much more convenient. The prevailing mobility paradigm emphasizes travel speed, creates inequities for those who cannot afford a vehicle (e.g., children, the poor and the elderly) and is linked with heavy car use and its associated greenhouse and exhaust gas emissions. We believe that a paradigm shift is essential to change the social norm, reversing the decline in children's independent mobility and making active transportation the default option.

18.4 Changing Social Values: Addressing Individualism and Speed

As the opening quote for this chapter indicates, in addition to the strategies discussed in the third section of the book, fundamental cultural changes may be necessary before significant improvement is evident in levels of children's active transportation. As well as changes in city transport systems, we believe that some values in modern Western society need to change. In many nations, a culture of individualism has affected children's mobility.[16] Parents have accepted that it is their responsibility to keep their children "safe," and this typically involves responses such as driving their children to school and to other activities. Collectively, these responses make neighbourhoods less safe for children, both in terms of traffic danger and stranger danger.[17] A cultural change is needed towards more collective, community-based responses to create neighbourhoods in which allowing children to walk and cycle feels safe to parents and is supported by a community that values their presence.

As well as this cultural change towards more collective responsibility, the current societal obsession with speed should also be addressed. A culture of the glorification of speed dominates societies in most parts of the world.[12] To change this culture will involve the celebration of slowness, as is powerfully described in Carl Honoré's book *In Praise of Slow*.[17] There is a growing international interest in various "slow" movements. Starting with slow food, there are now slow cities, slow travel and slow living.

Some authors talk about the need to cure our "addiction" to speed: "*We are addicted to speed. In a world where the gods seem to have deserted, speed has become the opiate of the people. It's the fix we can't do without... rushing to keep up, we lose ourselves and lose touch with the natural world that sustains us*."[18] To help cure this addiction, we could consider such strategies as changing the legislation surrounding the advertising of cars and the practices of the car industry. Since the days of Henry Ford, mass advertising has emphasized cars as a key ingredient of one's freedom, mobility and status.[19] Using strategies such as lobbying, donations to political parties, public relations and the creation of "think tanks," the car industry has campaigned against regulations aiming to make cars safer and less polluting and/or to encourage other travel modes.[19]

We could also rethink the common practice of turning city streets into motor racing spectacles. There is powerful symbolism in allowing significant public spaces to be used for motor racing events.[20] If policy-makers are genuinely committed to make cities safer by making them slower, motor racing spectacles could be replaced with *ciclovias*, slow living or slow food events, which would help instil a culture of slowness that allows people to enjoy life at a more relaxed pace.[21] Children's active transportation fits perfectly into the culture of slow cities.

The preoccupation with speed in modern societies has strongly influenced our current way of urban life. What is needed is a major cultural change in attitudes towards lower traffic speeds so that citizens view streets as places where people can walk, cycle, socialize and play, rather than simply as movement corridors for cars. Without this cultural change, including "*changes in the mentality of both drivers and residents*,"[22] the success of any scheme aimed at increasing levels of active transportation may be limited. This cultural change can be instigated by individuals reclaiming their streets through psychological traffic calming[23] or local governments implementing low-speed zones, home zones or play streets. However, in the long term, national planning policy as well as local development frameworks should make children's active transportation and traffic taming a major focus for urban planning.

In their analysis of the impacts of speed on road safety, Richter et al.[24] note that there are major barriers in accepting the role of speed in road fatalities. Many of these barriers also impede progress towards taming traffic to enhance children's active transportation. They suggest that "*pseudo conservative opposition is based on libertarian opposition to regulation, and fears of loss of privacy, and is similar to objections to gun control laws ... [claiming] an infringement of civil rights.*"[24] Their response is that "*life and safety are the most basic of all human rights, and governments have a responsibility to protect these rights.*" Governments also have responsibility to protect the rights of children to play and to provide environments that allow free and safe movements for children. Taming traffic and reducing motorized vehicle speeds is a necessary step in protecting these rights.

The United Nations' Convention on the Rights of the Child,[25] Article 31, recognizes children's right to play: the right of every child to rest, leisure, play, recreational activities and free and full participation in cultural and artistic life. However, the United Nations Committee on the Rights of the Child has expressed concerns about the lack of recognition of these rights by governments. In 2013, the United Nations issued a General Comment calling on governments to elaborate their plans for legislating, planning and funding to provide for the Rights of the Child.[26]

An important part of creating the context for the realization of Article 31 is the creation of environments that are "*sufficiently free from pollution, traffic and other hazards that impede free and safe movement.*"[26] Such environments require the introduction of measures in consultation with children. One important measure is municipal planning that prioritizes environments that promote the well-being of children, including "*zones with priority for pedestrians, players and bikers over motorized traffic.*"[26] Such zones can create more child-friendly environments that encourage children's active transportation.

18.5 Towards Sustainable Happiness ...

Collectively, the recommendations provided in this book can help make our streets more vibrant, inclusive and safer in a variety of ways. For example, as discussed in Chapter 9, low-traffic streets are associated with enhanced social cohesion, which can help increase parental confidence in letting their children walk or bike on their own. Because parents are influenced by the behaviour of other parents, this could help change the social norm in favour of active transportation. More broadly, increasing social cohesion would also contribute to better relationships between neighbours and a stronger sense of belonging to the community, which could also help prevent crime. It is particularly telling that adults and children interviewed about 35 years apart both clearly recognized the adverse effects of traffic on social cohesion, knowledge and enjoyment of the community, and even happiness.[27,28] In short, slower and safer streets would arguably benefit people of all ages—not only children. It may even contribute to sustainable happiness—"*the pursuit of happiness that does not exploit other people, the environment or future generations.*"[29] O'Brien[29] also argues that "*Children's view of transportation (when walking to school) reminds us that transportation is not only about 'moving people and goods'. It is about wonder, discovery, joy and happiness.*"

In 2015, the Surgeon General of the United States issued a call to action to promote walking and walkability.[30] This message is addressed to a broad range of sectors, including transportation, land use, community design, parks and recreation, schools, colleges, universities, worksites, nonprofit organizations, healthcare, the media and public health. It targets the five following goals:

1. make walking a national priority;
2. design communities that make it safe and easy to walk for people of all ages and abilities;
3. promote programmes and policies to support walking where people live, learn, work and play;
4. provide information to encourage walking and improve walkability; and
5. fill surveillance, research and evaluations gaps related to walking and walkability.

We reiterate these goals and argue that they should:

1. be extended to all jurisdictions;
2. specifically target accessibility; and
3. be applied to all sustainable travel modes.

In summary, promoting children's active transportation is a valuable and achievable goal. Given the large co-benefits resulting from improving children's active transportation, all citizens, both now and in the future, will likely reap benefits if the ideas presented here can be implemented. It is our hope that this book will be a modest contribution to make our streets great again!

References

1. Tranter P, Pawson E. Children's access to local environments: a case-study of Christchurch, New Zealand. *Local Environ* 2001;**6**(1):27–48.
2. Larouche R, Stone M, Buliung RN, Faulkner G. "I'd rather bike to school!": profiling children who would prefer to cycle to school. *J Transp Health* 2016;**3**(3):377–85.
3. Lorenc T, Brunton G, Oliver S, Oliver K, Oakley A. Attitudes to walking and cycling among children, young people and parents: a systematic review. *J Epidemiol Community Health* 2008;**62**:852–7.
4. Shaw B, Bicket M, Elliot B, Fagan-Watson B, Mocca E, Hillman M. *Children's independent mobility: an international comparison and recommendations for action*. London, UK: Policy Studies Institute; 2015. Available from: http://www.psi.org.uk/docs/7350_PSI_Report_CIM_final.pdf.
5. McDonald NC, Brown AL, Marchetti LM, Pedroso MS. U.S. school travel, 2009: an assessment of trends. *Am J Prev Med* 2011;**41**(2):146–51.
6. Yang Y, Telama R, Hirvensalo M, et al. Active commuting from youth to adulthood and as a predictor of physical activity in early midlife: the Young Finns Study. *Prev Med* 2014;**59**:5–11.
7. Patz JA, Frumkin H, Holloway T, et al. Climate change: challenges and opportunities for global health. *JAMA* 2014;**312**(15):1565–80.
8. Rissel CE. Active travel: a climate change mitigation strategy with co-benefits for health. *NSW Public Health Bull* 2009;**20**(2):10–3.

9. Muennig PA, Epstein M, Li G, DiMaggio C. The cost-effectiveness of New York City's safe routes to school program. *Am J Public Health* 2014;**104**(7):1294–9.
10. Mitra R. Independent mobility and mode choice for school transportation: a review and framework for future research. *Transp Rev* 2013;**33**(1):21–43.
11. Panter JR, Jones AP, van Sluijs EMF. Environmental determinants of active travel in youth: a review and framework for future research. *Int J Behav Nutr Phys Act* 2008;**5**:34. Available from: https://ijbnpa.biomedcentral.com/articles/10.1186/1479-5868-5-34.
12. Whitelegg J. *Mobility: a new urban design and transport planning philosophy for a sustainable future*. Createspace Independent Publishing Platform; 2016.
13. Larouche R, Mammen G, Rowe DA, Faulkner G. Effectiveness of active school transport interventions: a systematic review and update. *BMC Publ Health* 2018;**18**(1):206. Available from: https://bmcpublichealth.biomedcentral.com/articles/10.1186/s12889-017-5005-1.
14. Faulkner GEJ, Richichi V, Buliung RN, Fusco C, Moola F. What's "quickest and easiest?": parental decision making about school travel mode. *Int J Behav Nutr Phys Act* 2010;**7**:62. Available from: http://ijbnpa.biomedcentral.com/articles/10.1186/1479-5868-7-62.
15. McDonald NC, Aalborg AE. Why parents drive children to school: implications for safe routes to school programs. *J Am Plann Assoc* 2009;**3**:331–42.
16. Tranter P. Overcoming social traps: a key to child-friendly cities. In: Gleeson B, Sipe N, editors. *Creating child friendly cities: reinstating kids in the city*. New York, NY: Routledge; 2006. p. 121–35.
17. Honoré C. *In praise of slow: how a worldwide movement is challenging the cult of speed*. London: Orion; 2004.
18. Taylor MC. *Speed limits: where time went and why we have so little left*. New Haven, CT: Yale University Press; 2014.
19. Parra DC, de Sá TH, Monteiro CA, Freudenberg N. Automobile, construction and entertainment business sector influences on sedentary lifestyles. *Health Promot Int* 2016;**1**:1–11.
20. Tranter P, Lowes M. The crucial 'where' of motorsport marketing: is motorsport now "a race out of place"? *Int J Sports Mark Spons* 2009;**11**:60–79.
21. May M, Tranter P, Warn J. Towards a holistic framework for road safety in Australia. *J Transp Geogr* 2008;**16**:395–405.
22. Cairns J, Warren J, Garthwaite K, Greig G, Bambra C. Go slow: an umbrella review of the effects of 20 mph zones and limits on health and health inequalities. *J Public Health* 2014;**37**:515–20.
23. Engwicht D. *Towards an eco-city: calming the traffic*. Sydney, Australia: Envirobook; 1992.
24. Richter ED, Berman T, Friedman L, Ben-David G. Speed, road injury, and public health. *Annu Rev Public Health* 2006;**27**:125–52.
25. United Nations. *Convention on the rights of the child*. New York, NY: United Nations; 1989. Available from: http://www.ohchr.org/EN/ProfessionalInterest/Pages/CRC.aspx.
26. International Play Association. *Summary United Nations General Comment no. 17 on the right of the child to rest, leisure, play, recreational activities, cultural life and the arts (article 31)*. 2013. Available from: http://ipaworld.org/wp-content/uploads/2013/11/IPA-Summary-of-UN-GC-article-31_FINAL1.pdf.
27. Appleyard D. *Livable streets*. Berkeley, CA: University of California Press; 1981.
28. Appleyard B. The meaning of livable streets to schoolchildren: an image mapping study of the effects of traffic on children's cognitive development of spatial knowledge. *J Transp Health* 2017;**5**:27–41.
29. O'Brien C. Sustainable happiness and the trip to school. *World Transp Pol Pract* 2008;**14**(1):15–26.

30. United States Department of Health, Human Services. *Step it up! the surgeon general's call to action to promote walking and walkable communities*. Washington, DC: United States Department of Health and Human Services, Office of the Surgeon General; 2015. Available from: https://www.surgeongeneral.gov/library/calls/walking-and-walkable-communities/call-to-action-walking-and-walkable-communites.pdf.

Glossary

Accelerometer Accelerometers are movement monitors that have the ability to measure accelerations of the trunk and/or limbs. "Acceleration is directly proportional to the muscular forces and therefore is related to energy expenditure."[1]

Active transportation Active transportation refers to "any form of human-powered transportation—walking, cycling, using a wheelchair, in-line skating or skateboarding."[2]

Built environment "Includes land use patterns, the transportation system, and design features that together provide opportunities for travel and physical activity. Land use patterns refer to the spatial distribution of human activities. The transportation system refers to the physical infrastructure and services that provide the spatial links or connectivity among activities. Design refers to the aesthetic, physical, and functional qualities of the built environment, such as the design of buildings and streetscapes, and relates to both land use patterns and the transportation system."[3]

Ciclovía A Ciclovía is a "free, community-based program in which streets are closed temporarily to motorized transport, allowing access to walkers, runners, rollerbladers, and cyclists only."[4] In English-speaking countries, they are often referred to as "Open Streets" events.[5]

Collective efficacy Refers to "social cohesion among neighbors combined with their willingness to intervene on behalf of the common good."[6]

Complete Streets "Complete Streets are streets that are designed to be safe for everyone: people who walk, bicycle, take transit, or drive, and people of all ages and abilities."[7]

Confounder A confounder is a "third variable" that is associated with the two variables that a researcher is truly interested in. For example, age may be related to both whether a child participates in an active transportation intervention and to a child's travel behaviour. The presence of a confounder may lead the researcher to draw misguided conclusions about the effect of an intervention. Yet, the effect of a confounder can be controlled for using appropriate statistical analyses.[8]

Connectivity "Connectivity relates to the availability and directness of travel routes used to move through a network from an origin to a destination."[9]

Correlate A correlate is a variable that is associated with our variable of interest (i.e., active transportation in this book). The term correlate is preferred for cross-sectional studies wherein the researchers cannot determine the direction of the relationships observed between different variables.[8]

Cost–benefit analysis "Cost–benefit analysis is a weighing-scale approach to making business decisions: all the pluses (the benefits) are put on one side of the balance and all the minuses (the costs) are put on the other. Whichever weighs the heavier wins."[10]

Cost-effectiveness analysis Cost-effectiveness is broadly defined as a method for assessing the comparative costs and benefits of different interventions.[11]

Cross-sectional study Study wherein all data are collected at a single point in time.[12]

Determinant A determinant is a variable whose fluctuation causes change in our variable of interest. For example, a researcher may find that an increase in distance decreases the likelihood of active transportation. The term determinant is often used interchangeably with correlate. However, this is a mistake because determinant is a much stronger term.[8]

Geographic information systems (GIS) GIS are electronic platforms that "offer the opportunity to integrate spatial information from a range of disparate sources into a single framework, and to use these data to develop precise measures of the built environment."[9]

Global positioning system (GPS) A GPS is a "device that uses a satellite system to pinpoint a stationary location on the earth to a latitude and longitude coordinate."[9]

Health "Health is a state of complete physical, mental and social well-being and not merely the absence of disease or infirmity."[13]

Home zone "Home zones are residential streets in which the road space is shared between drivers of motor vehicles and other road users, with the wider needs of residents (including people who walk and cycle, and children) in mind. The aim is to change the way that streets are used and to improve quality of life, by making them places for people, not just for traffic."[14]

Independent mobility Defined as children's freedom to move around in public space without adult supervision.[15]

Intervention study Study design in which the effect of an intervention (e.g., school travel plans) on a variable of interest (e.g., active transportation) is measured by the researchers.

Land use mix "Broad categories of typical land uses include (but are not limited to) residential, office, commercial, industrial, and recreational and there are multiple existing measures of land use mix" (i.e., the heterogeneity of land uses within a given area).[9]

Life cycle analysis A systematic set of procedures for compiling and examining the inputs and outputs of materials and energy and the associated environmental impacts directly attributable to the functioning of a product or service system throughout its life cycle.

Longitudinal study Study design in which repeated measures are taken from the same individuals over prolonged periods of time.

Mediator A mediator is an intermediate variable that is necessary to explain the relationship between two variables. In other words, it can be described as a mechanism through which a variable influences another. For example, an intervention may lead to an increase in active transportation by decreasing parental concerns about road safety. In this case, parental concerns would be a mediator.[8]

Meta-analysis "Quantitative procedure for summarizing the effects of a number of research studies on a common topic."[12]

Moderator A moderator is a variable that affects the direction and/or the strength of the relationship between two variables. For example, researchers may observe that an intervention may result in larger changes in active transportation in boys compared to girls. In this case, gender would be a moderator.[8]

Natural experiment Intervention study in which the intervention is implemented by a third party (often a government or other legislative body) rather than by the researchers.[16]

Physical activity Defined as "any bodily movement produced by skeletal muscles that requires energy expenditure."[17]

Physical environment Defined as "the part of the human environment that includes purely physical factors (as soil, climate, water supply)." [Merriam-Webster dictionary].

Prevalence Refers to the proportion of the population who have a specific condition (or engage in a specific behavior such as active transportation) at a specific time or during a specific period.[18]

Population-based studies Studies that use representative samples.

Qualitative research "A method of inquiry widely used in the social sciences that encompasses a diverse range of methodological tools and strategies (e.g., case study, discourse analysis, ethnography, narrative analysis); concerned with generating an understanding of how the social world is interpreted, understood, experienced, produced or constituted."[18]

Quantitative research "A method of inquiry where data collection includes measurements, and different groups are compared making possible statistical testing of hypotheses."[18]

Quasi-experimental study Intervention study in which the researchers are unable to randomly assign participants (or groups of participants) to an experimental or a control group.

Randomized controlled trial Intervention study wherein participants (or groups of participants such as schools) are randomly assigned to an experimental group that gets the intervention and a control group that does not get the intervention.

Representative sample (or probabilistic sample) A sample in which individuals are randomly selected from the population and every individual in the population has a known probability of being included. Observations from a representative sample can be generalized to the population.[18]

Safe Routes to School An intervention that "aims to create safe, convenient, and fun opportunities for children to bicycle and walk to and from school. (...) The most successful Safe Routes to School programs incorporate the Six E's: evaluation, education, encouragement, engineering, enforcement, and equity."[19]

School travel planning A collaborative process involving diverse stakeholders (e.g., school officials, parents, city planners, public health nurses, students, etc.) aiming to assess and intervene on barriers to active school transportation through a documented school travel plan tailored to a school.

Statistically significant A difference is commonly said to be statistically significant if the likelihood that it is due to chance is less than 5% (although some researchers may use a different threshold).

Smart growth An approach to urban planning that "covers a range of development and conservation strategies that help protect our health and natural environment and make our communities more attractive, economically stronger, and more socially diverse."[20]

Social cohesion a cohesive society is "one where people are protected against life risks, trust their neighbors and the institutions of the state and can work towards a better future for themselves and their families. Fostering social cohesion is about striving for greater inclusiveness, more civic participation and creating opportunities for upward mobility."[21]

Social environment "The immediate physical or social setting in which people live or in which something happens or develops. It includes the culture that the individual was educated or lives in, and the people and institutions with whom they interact."[22]

Social norm Social norms are "customary rules that govern behavior and specify what is acceptable and what is not in groups and societies."[23]

Social traps Refers to a social dilemma wherein an individual chooses to satisfy their own goals over those of the community or society as a whole.[24] For example, parents may choose to drive their children to school to protect them from traffic, thus exposing other children to more traffic.

Stranger danger Popular expression referring to the fear that strangers may be harmful, which is one of the key perceived barriers to active transportation reported by parents.

Systematic review "A systematic review attempts to collate all empirical evidence that fits pre-specified eligibility criteria in order to answer a specific research question. It uses explicit, systematic methods that are selected with a view to minimizing bias, thus providing more reliable findings from which conclusions can be drawn and decisions made."[25]

Traffic calming "The combination of mainly physical measures that reduce the negative effects of motor vehicle use, alter driver behavior and improve conditions for non-motorized street users."[26] Traffic calming includes speed bumps and other obstacles for vehicles, street narrowing, etc.

Vision Zero Policy initiative that aims to eliminate all preventable road deaths.

Walkability Refers to the extent to which a neighbourhood is "walking friendly." In practice, it is often measured as an aggregate of street connectivity, land use mix and residential density.[27]

Walking school bus A group of children walking together on a set route under the supervision of at least one adult who typically volunteer as "driver" (i.e., coordinator). Children are "picked up" at different stops along the route, just like they would if they were using a regular school bus.[28]

Woonerf Dutch word that means "living yard." Refers to streets where cars are expected to proceed very slowly (less than 15 km/h) and where the distinction between sidewalks for pedestrians and carriageways for cars is removed, allowing pedestrians and children to reclaim street space.

References

1. Freedson PS, Miller K. Objective monitoring of physical activity using motion sensors and heart rate. *Res Q Exerc Sport* 2000;**71**(Suppl. 2):21–9.
2. Public Health Agency of Canada. *What is active transportation?*. Ottawa, ON: Public Health Agency of Canada; 2017. Available from: https://www.canada.ca/en/public-health/services/health-promotion/healthy-living/physical-activity/what-active-transportation.html.
3. Transportation Research Board & Institute of Medicine. *Does the built environment influence physical activity? Examining the evidence*. Washington, DC: Transportation Research Board; 2005. Available from: http://onlinepubs.trb.org/onlinepubs/sr/sr282.pdf.
4. Sarmiento O, Torres A, Jacoby E, Pratt M, Schmid TL, Stierling G. The Ciclovía-Recreativa: a mass-recreational program with public health potential. *J Phys Act Health* 2010;**7**(Suppl. 2): S163–80.
5. Kuhlberg JA, Hipp JA, Chang G. Open streets initiatives in the United States: closed to traffic, open to physical activity. *J Phys Act Health* 2014;**11**(8):1468–74.
6. Sampson RJ, Raudenbush SW, Earls F. Neighborhoods and violent crime: a multilevel study of collective efficacy. *Science* 1997;**277**:918–24.
7. Complete Streets for Canada. *What are complete streets?*. Toronto, ON: Complete Streets for Canada; 2017. Available from: http://completestreetsforcanada.ca/what-are-complete-streets.
8. Bauman AE, Sallis JF, Dzewaltowski DA, Owen N. Toward a better understanding of the influences on physical activity: the role of determinants, correlates, causal variables, mediators, moderators, and confounders. *Am J Prev Med* 2002;**23**(2 Suppl. 1):5–14.
9. Thornton LE, Pearce JR, Kavanagh AM. Using Geographic Information Systems (GIS) to assess the role of the built environment in influencing obesity: a glossary. *Int J Behav Nutr Phys Act* 2011;**8**:71. Available from: https://ijbnpa.biomedcentral.com/articles/10.1186/1479-5868-8-71.
10. The Economist. *Cost-benefit analysis*. [Internet] 2009. Available from: https://www.economist.com/node/14298838.
11. Weinstein MC, Stason WB. Foundations of cost-effectiveness analysis for health and medical practices. *N Engl J Med* 1977;**296**:716–21.
12. Dishman RK, Heath GW, Lee I-M. *Physical activity epidemiology*. 2nd ed. Champaign, IL: Human Kinetics; 2013.

13. World Health Organization. *Constitution of the World Health Organization*. Geneva, Switzerland: World Health Organization; 1946. Available from: http://www.who.int/about/mission/en/.
14. Department for Transport. *Home zones: challenging the future of our streets*. London, UK: Department for Transport; 2005. Available from: https://nacto.org/docs/usdg/home_zones_department_transpot.pdf.
15. Hillman M, Adams J, Whitelegg J. *One false move... A study of children's independent mobility*. London, UK: Policy Studies Institute; 1990.
16. Ramanathan S, Allison KR, Faulkner G, Dwyer JJM. Challenges in assessing the implementation and effectiveness of physical activity and nutrition policy interventions as natural experiments. *Health Promot Int* 2008;**23**(3):290–7.
17. World Health Organization. Physical activity [Internet]. Available from: http://www.who.int/topics/physical_activity/en/.
18. Bassil K, Zabkiewicz D. *Health research methods: a Canadian perspective*. Don Mills, ON: Oxford University Press; 2014.
19. Safe Routes to School National Partnership. Safe routes to school 101 [Internet]. Available from: https://www.saferoutespartnership.org/healthy-communities/101/about.
20. Environmental Protection Agency. About smart growth [Internet]. Available from: https://www.epa.gov/smartgrowth/about-smart-growth.
21. United Nations Department of Economic and Social Affairs. *Perspectives on social cohesion – the glue that holds society together*. New York, NY: United Nations Department of Economic and Social Affairs; 2012. Available from: http://www.un.org/en/development/desa/news/policy/perspectives-on-social-cohesion.html.
22. Barnett E, Casper M. A definition of "social environment". *Am J Public Health* 2001;**91**(3):465.
23. Bicchieri C, Muldoon R. *Social norms*. Stanford, CA: Stanford Encyclopedia of Philosophy; 2011. Available from: https://plato.stanford.edu/entries/social-norms/.
24. Platt J. Social traps. *Am Psychol* 1973;**28**(8):641–51.
25. Cochrane Collaboration. *What is a systematic review?*. [Internet] 2017. Available from: http://community.cochrane.org/handbook-sri/chapter-1-introduction/11-cochrane/12-systematic-reviews/122-what-systematic-review.
26. Lockwood I. ITE traffic calming definition. *ITE J* 1997;**67**:22–4.
27. Frank LD, Schmid TL, Sallis JF, Chapman J, Saelens BE. Linking objectively measured physical activity with objectively measured urban form: findings from SMARTRAQ. *Am J Prev Med* 2005;**28**(2 Suppl. 2):117–25.
28. Engwicht D. *Towards an eco-city: calming the traffic*. Sydney, Australia: Envirobook; 1992.

Index

'*Note*: Page numbers followed by "f" indicate figures, "t" indicate tables and "b" indicate boxes.'

FSC
www.fsc.org
MIX
Papier | Fördert gute Waldnutzung
FSC® C083411

Kolibri 360 GmbH
Ferdinand-Jühlke-Straße 7
99095 Erfurt, Deutschland
produktsicherheit@kolibri360.de